The National...

In this comparative an ...iele Caramani studies
the macrohistor
of newly collect
European count
ticipation and su
mid-nineteenth
elections towaro
empirical analys
The inclusion o
state–church, rι
sess the nationa
the National ar
cultural and cen
institutional, an
centered explan
ences among na

Daniele Carama
pean Social Res
European Univ
Geneva, Floren
Comparative Pc
is the author of
(2000).

Cambridge Studies in Comparative Politics

General Editor

Margaret Levi   *University of Washington, Seattle*

Assistant General Editor

Stephen Hanson   *University of Washington, Seattle*

Associate Editors

Robert H. Bates   *Harvard University*
Peter Hall   *Harvard University*
Peter Lange   *Duke University*
Helen Milner   *Columbia University*
Frances Rosenbluth   *Yale University*
Susan Stokes   *University of Chicago*
Sidney Tarrow   *Cornell University*

Other Books in the Series

Stefano Bartolini, *The Political Mobilization of the European Left, 1860–1980: The Class Cleavage*
Mark Beissinger, *Nationalist Mobilization and the Collapse of the Soviet State*
Carles Boix, *Democracy and Redistribution*
Carles Boix, *Political Parties, Growth and Equality: Conservative and Social Democratic Economic Strategies in the World Economy*
Catherine Boone, *Merchant Capital and the Roots of State Power in Senegal, 1930–1985*
Catherine Boone, *Political Topographies of the African State: Territorial Authority and Institutional Choice*
Michael Bratton and Nicolas van de Walle, *Democratic Experiments in Africa: Regime Transitions in Comparative Perspective*
Valerie Bunce, *Leaving Socialism and Leaving the State: The End of Yugoslavia, the Soviet Union and Czechoslovakia*
Ruth Berins Collier, *Paths Toward Democracy: The Working Class and Elites in Western Europe and South America*
Nancy Bermeo, ed., *Unemployment in the New Europe*
Donatella della Porta, *Social Movements, Political Violence, and the State*
Gerald Easter, *Reconstructing the State: Personal Networks and Elite Identity*

Continued on page following the Index.

Our concern is not only with a process in time *but also with a process in* space.

Stein Rokkan, *Citizens, Elections, Parties*, 1970

The Nationalization of Politics

THE FORMATION OF NATIONAL ELECTORATES AND PARTY SYSTEMS IN WESTERN EUROPE

DANIELE CARAMANI

University of Mannheim

CAMBRIDGE
UNIVERSITY PRESS

PUBLISHED BY THE PRESS SYNDICATE OF THE UNIVERSITY OF CAMBRIDGE
The Pitt Building, Trumpington Street, Cambridge, United Kingdom

CAMBRIDGE UNIVERSITY PRESS
The Edinburgh Building, Cambridge CB2 2RU, UK
40 West 20th Street, New York, NY 10011-4211, USA
477 Williamstown Road, Port Melbourne, VIC 3207, Australia
Ruiz de Alarcón 13, 28014 Madrid, Spain
Dock House, The Waterfront, Cape Town 8001, South Africa

http://www.cambridge.org

First published 2004

Printed in the United States of America

Typeface Janson Text 10/13 pt.　　*System* LATEX 2$_\varepsilon$　[TB]

A catalog record for this book is available from the British Library.

Library of Congress Cataloging in Publication Data

Caramani, Daniele.
The nationalization of politics : the formation of national electorates and party systems in
Western Europe / Daniele Caramani.
　p.　cm. – (Cambridge studies in comparative politics)
Includes bibliographical references and index.
ISBN 0-521-82799-X – ISBN 0-521-53520-4 (pbk.)
1. Elections – Europe, Western.　2. Political parties – Europe, Western.
I. Title.　II. Series.
JN94.A95C368　2004
324′.094 – dc21　　　　　　　　　　　　　　　　　　　　　2003053201

ISBN 0 521 82799 X hardback
ISBN 0 521 53520 4 paperback

Contents

Tables

Figures

List of Figures

Abbreviations and Symbols

Abbreviations

CRII	Cumulative regional inequality index (Rose and Urwin)
CV	Variability coefficient
d'H	D'Hondt formula
HB	Hagenbach-Bischoff formula
IPR	Index adjusted for party size and number of regions
LEE	Lee index
LR-Hare	Largest remainders (Hare or simple quota) formula
MAD	Mean absolute deviation
MSD	Mean squared deviation
N.a.	Not available
PR	Proportional representation
STV	Single transferable vote
Unc.	Uncontested constituency/unopposed seat

Symbols

–	Not applicable
...	Data not available (missing)

Country Abbreviations and Numbering

When required by reasons of space limitations, countries have been abbreviated as follows in tables and figures: Austria (AU), Belgium (BE), Denmark (DK), Finland (FI), France (FR), Germany (GE), Greece (GR), Iceland (IC),

Ireland (IR), Italy (IT), the Netherlands (NL), Norway (NO), Portugal (PT), Spain (SP), Sweden (SW), Switzerland (SZ), United Kingdom (UK). For Britain (when Ireland 1832–1918 or Northern Ireland 1922–present are not included) GB has been used.

The numbering of countries runs from 1 to 18 as for *EWE-1815* (this abbreviation is used throughout this volume for the handbook supplemented with a CD-ROM *Elections in Western Europe since 1815: Electoral Results by Constituencies*; see Caramani 2000), with Luxembourg no. 11 excluded from the analysis.

Preface and Acknowledgments

The goal of this book is to describe and explain the formation over a century and a half of nationwide electoral alignments, party systems, and cleavage constellations in Western Europe. The progressive transformation of politics from local into national is often referred to as the "nationalization of politics" – or "electoral politics" – that is, the formation of national parties and party systems that parallels (but is not simply a reflection of) the creation of a national community through the expansion of state administration, the building and integration of national identities, and the process of social and geographical mobilization triggered by the Industrial Revolution. This macrophenomenon of "democratic integration" is analyzed over time and across countries and is broken down for all cleavages – state–church, center–periphery, rural–urban, and the class cleavage – as well as for the major party families that emerged from them.

When I began working on this project, it soon became clear that the necessary data would not be easily available. The comparative and historical analysis of the territorial structures of electorates, party systems, and voting behavior in Europe requires electoral data at the constituency level, and very soon in the course of the analysis, it also became clear that a long-term historical perspective would be necessary to analyze earlier periods of modern elections – that is, the periods of *formation of national party systems and electoral competition*. I therefore started a systematic collection of election results at the University of Geneva and, later, at the European University Institute, which I thought possible to complete in "a couple of years." Things obviously turned out differently, and the original project bifurcated in two different directions. The collection of data paralleled by a thorough documentation eventually developed into an independent project, which was completed in 1999 at the Mannheim Centre for European Social Research (MZES) and transformed into a book supplemented with a CD-ROM (*Elections in Western Europe since 1815: Electoral Results by Constituencies* [London and New York: Macmillan, 2000]). That work aimed to present and thoroughly document the wealth of historical and institutional material collected on elections, parties, and representation systems in Europe, with a CD-ROM making electoral results by constituencies available to the wider scientific community in several machine-readable formats for the first time.

The present volume – based on those unexplored electoral data – addresses more directly analytical macrohistorical and comparative questions. Long delayed by the burden of data collection, however, the original theoretical framework looked unsatisfactory to me (a first essay on the nationalization of electoral politics had appeared in the *Rivista Italiana di Scienza Politica* in 1994 and was then translated into a shorter article in *West European Politics* in 1996). I have therefore modified and simplified it. In this book, furthermore, most technicalities have been omitted (some of which have been relegated to the appendixes) and are limited to the indispensable data description. For more details on data and sources, readers can refer to *Elections in Western Europe since 1815* (henceforth I shall use the abbreviated form *EWE-1815* since I often refer to that work myself).

This book has been written in several steps, from the early work at the European University Institute to the completion of data collection at the MZES from 1996 to 1998 and again from 2000 to 2002 at the Robert Schuman Centre for Advanced Studies (EUI). I am deeply grateful to these institutions and their former directors, Peter Flora and Yves Mény, for their generosity and substantive support. I have also greatly profited from a Jemolo Fellowship at Nuffield College, the University of Oxford, in the summer of 2001. I wish to express grateful thanks to Stefano Bartolini for his constant advice and support since the early days of the project. This book owes much to his approach to empirical comparative and historical research. My regret is that too many of his suggestions remain unrealized. Among the many other persons who over the years read earlier versions of the work, I am particularly indebted to Hanspeter Kriesi, Peter Mair, and Charles Tilly for their valuable comments. The suggestions of Margaret Levi and the anonymous reviewers of Cambridge University Press also proved extremely helpful. I wish to thank them for their attentive reading of the manuscript. For all shortcomings and errors in the final product, I obviously remain the only one to blame.

Introduction

HOMOGENEITY AND DIVERSITY IN EUROPE

The nationalization of politics is a major long-term political phenomenon over almost two centuries. Nationalization processes represent a broad historical evolution toward the formation of national electorates and party systems, party organizations and campaigns, as well as issues and party programs. Through nationalization processes, the highly localized and territorialized politics that characterized the early phases of electoral competition in the nineteenth century is replaced by national electoral alignments and oppositions. Peripheral and regional specificities disappear, and sectional cleavages progressively transform into nationwide functional alignments. Through the development of central party organizations, local candidates are absorbed into nationwide structures and ideologies. Programs and policies become national in scope and cancel out – or at least reduce – the scope of local problems, with the most relevant issues being transferred from the local to the national level. These processes of political integration translate in the *territorial homogenization of electoral behavior*, both electoral participation and the support for the main party families.

Nationalization processes therefore represent a crucial step in the *structuring of party politics*. The nineteenth century witnessed the most striking changes in political life with the transition from absolutist to parliamentary regimes and with the progressive entry of the masses on the political stage through the extension of voting rights. Parliaments, that in many cases had not been convened since the end of the Middle Ages, were reintroduced (Bendix 1961; Hintze 1970). Although in some cases they were still based on estate or curial representation, in all countries these bodies soon transformed into modern parliaments based on general representation. Yet, in spite of the general democratization of West European political systems, national electoral alignments and party organizations did not appear

1

suddenly in the aftermath of democratic reforms. The systems that developed in the nineteenth century long remained unstructured and highly territorialized and, in the absence of national party organizations and nationwide oppositions, politics remained dominated by local issues and candidates, which prolonged the control by elites of the past on political life.

This means that the formation of national electorates and party systems is not only a crucial aspect of the construction of national political spaces and of the structuring of party systems, but also of the development of a *political democratic citizenship*. The nationalization of electoral alignments and political parties has meant the transition from a fragmented and clientelistic type of politics dominated by local political personalities to *national representation*. National party organizations structured along nationwide cleavages replaced an atomized type of political representation. Candidates in the various constituencies became increasingly "party candidates" who no longer merely represented local interests but instead nationwide functional interests and values, giving the masses the possibility to influence directly national decision-making processes (Rokkan 1970a: 227–34).

In spite of its central position within West European electoral developments, the territorial dimension of the construction of national political spaces in Europe has received little attention. The necessary comparable electoral data disaggregated at the constituency level for several countries might have been one of the causes for this neglect. The analysis of the territorial dimension of elections in Europe requires cross-country electoral results by parties for single constituencies. Furthermore – as will become clear in the course of the analysis – such data are needed from the early stages of electoral development after the major transitions toward representative parliamentary systems in the nineteenth century. The formation of national parties and party systems must be analyzed from the beginning of competitive elections, that is, during the phases of formation of party alternatives and cleavage constellations.

The great variety of party systems and electoral formulas in Europe has also helped to discourage systematic and comprehensive macroanalyses of the territorial dimension of voting patterns in a cross-country perspective.[1] Not only do formulas vary a great deal between countries, but over time too

[1] The last major attempts to analyze territorial politics in Europe are represented in particular by two books by Stein Rokkan and Derek Urwin, *The Politics of Territorial Identity* (1982) and *Economy, Territory, Identity* (1983). *Center–Periphery Structures in Europe* by Rokkan et al. (1987) – addressed more specifically to students in the form of a handbook – is a text of the same period of work.

electoral systems have undergone major changes with the almost general transition from majoritarian to proportional representation (PR) formulas around World War I. In particular, the difference in the size and number of territorial units between formulas creates several difficulties for the analysis of longitudinal data. Furthermore, whereas single-member plurality systems magnify the geographical dimension of voting patterns and allow the analysis to focus on voting patterns at very localized levels (this has been possible notably in North America and the United Kingdom), PR electoral systems have been predominant in continental Europe since World War I.

Lacking empirical foundations, the macrophenomenon of a progressive national integration of electorates and party systems in Europe has been taken for granted. The thesis of the nationalization of politics – both in the explicit and more implicit formulations – seemed not to need to rely upon empirical evidence and has never been submitted to a thorough work of empirical verification. As J. Agnew notes, the "[a]cceptance of the nationalization thesis is based largely upon intellectual foundations *independent* of empirical demonstration" (1988: 301). Apart from country-specific case studies whose conclusions can rarely be raised to the level of analytical generalization, broad encompassing comparative work has often remained at the level of mere theoretical typologies. Empirical investigations have mostly focused on single countries or have been limited to short time periods. Only one major research is comparative but limited to the 1945–75 period (Rose and Urwin 1975). In most other cases, studies in this area have taken the form of case studies of single countries with a myopic focus on recent periods, not directly comparable, and therefore not leading to an overall picture of Europe. In opposition to these many short-term and case-oriented analyses, this book adopts a broader perspective presenting a general and concise picture of the *political-territorial structures in Europe over the nineteenth and twentieth centuries*, allowing to highlight the effects of key evolutionary steps – state formation, democratization, industrialization – on the territorial structures of the vote.

Long-term comparative electoral analysis has so far focused almost exclusively on the "functional dimension" of the political space – mainly the left–right dimension.[2] Both theories of state formation and nation-building, and the hegemony in political thought of the class cleavage and left–right

---

[2] These works deal with the well-known "freezing hypothesis" formulated by Lipset and Rokkan in 1967. On the one hand, electoral change has been associated with the aggregate changing distribution of electoral support among political parties representing the organizational expression of social groups. This interpretation has given rise to measures

alignments, have turned the attention of political studies away from the spatial-territorial dimension. Much of the literature has considered the progressive formation of national electorates and party systems in the course of the nineteenth and twentieth centuries to be closely associated with processes of political modernization as well as with more general socioeconomic processes of modernization of Western societies. Work on political development has emphasized the integration of peripheral cultural identities and economic areas within broader national contexts.[3] As noted by Derek Urwin, because of both fashion trends and the supremacy of the socio-economic dimension, "[t]raditionally, political science has displayed little sympathy for groups that were thought to have lost in the historical game" (Urwin 1983: 222).[4]

This work is therefore also an attempt to "bring territory back in" and to reintroduce the basic spatial concepts devised by the pioneers of electoral analysis. Studies like those of M. Hansen (*Norsk Folkepsikologi* of 1898) and A. Siegfried (*Tableau Politique de la France de l'Ouest* of 1913) belong to the "golden age" of an electoral geographical tradition that had not yet been challenged by other techniques of social inquiry (in particular surveys and individual data). The analysis carried out in this book is broken down at the level of single constituencies: European territories are much too diverse and their variety much too large to limit our data to the level of nation-states. All political cleavages and social divisions – cultural and center–periphery, as well as the left–right dimension – are analyzed as they are configured on the territorial space. The territorial structures of electoral behavior in

of stability/instability based on aggregated data (Rose and Urwin 1970; Pedersen 1983; Bartolini and Mair 1990). On the other hand, change meant the weakening of the individual relation between voters and parties. Research attempted to establish the extent to which the same social groups continued to support parties and the extent to which the social base of partisan support – independently from their size – had undergone a change. This has been carried out mainly through survey techniques and has led to indices of class voting (see, e.g., Franklin et al. 1992). The theoretical debate on cleavages too has largely neglected the territorial dimension (Rae and Taylor 1970; Zuckerman 1975).

[3] For an analysis of demographic integration in Western Europe, see Watkins (1991). Following the sociological tradition from Marx to Durkheim and Parsons, who described the transition from traditional (primordial) communities to modern societies, modernization breaks down territory, ethnicity, and religiosity as central elements of the political process. For a representative sample of work on political integration, see Almond and Coleman (1960), Almond and Powell (1966), Apter (1965), Black (1967), Deutsch (1953), and Kautsky (1972). Against the mainstream "integrationist literature" of the 1960s, see Connor (1967). For a further critique see Connor (1972), and for a recent discussion see Fox (1997).

[4] "A territorial approach to politics . . . seemed to disappear from the academic lexicon after 1945" (Rokkan and Urwin 1983: 1).

Europe reflect multiple cultural, political, and socioeconomic factors. They have created over centuries complex territorial assessments and overlapping sedimentations, and historical conflicts have projected their lines of division on European territories, creating an intricate web of sociopolitical cleavages. Territories – so to speak – contain the "fossils," the crystallized memory of European conflicts.

Results presented in this work attest to a general process of national political integration, that is, an evolution toward the *nationalization or homogenization* of politics. The transformation of territorial structures of electoral behavior in most European countries is characterized by the progressive reduction of territorial diversity in the course of the nineteenth and twentieth centuries. This has led to the increasing integration of peripheral electorates into national political life and the transformation of local electorates and segmented party systems into national electoral constellations. Albeit to different degrees, nationwide functional alignments progressively replaced territorial cleavages in all countries.

This process of nationalization of electorates and party systems has to a large extent been the result of the *hegemony of the left–right cleavage* over ethnolinguistic, religious, center–periphery, and urban-rural cleavages – that is, the main preindustrial cleavages. Industrialization and the simultaneous extension of voting rights in the second half of the nineteenth century have imposed the supremacy of the class dimension in West European party systems.[5] The regionally disaggregated approach of this book shows in the first place that the left–right cleavage is a source of territorial homogeneity *within* European nations. Furthermore, the European-wide comparison supports the view that this cleavage is at the same time a source of similarity *between* countries. Not only is the territorial distribution of the left–right dimension the most uniform – compared to cultural and center–periphery dimensions – but this is the case in most European countries. The long-term historical perspective since the mid-nineteenth century indicates that the electoral support for the parties of the left–right cleavage spread and homogenized rapidly after the Industrial Revolution and remained stable with the "freezing" of party systems in the 1920s.

However, the perspective of this work is not only that the increasingly homogeneous territorial distributions of party support reflect the general integration of societies or that parties merely adapt to changing social structures that eroded territorial oppositions. This book tries to demonstrate

---

[5] For the historical and comparative analysis of the left–right cleavage see Bartolini (2000b).

that national electoral behavior and party systems are also the result of parties' *competitive strategies* aimed at expanding through territory in search of electoral support. This work thus tries to combine a "bottom-up" sociological perspective with a "top down" actor-centered approach.[6] Evidence shows that the erosion of territorial cleavages is not deterministically a consequence of the general integration of societies, but also the product of the action of parties and of their inherently competitive strategies. Parties increasingly tend to challenge other parties in their former strongholds and to spread through constituencies that were hitherto in adversaries' hands. At the territorial level – as later at the ideological level – they tend to cover as much "space" as possible.

These processes will be analyzed in relation to the main historical institutional changes – the extension of franchise and the introduction of PR. However, this perspective, more centered on the behavior of agents, suggests that the competitive mechanisms working in the functional-ideological dimension (described and analyzed since the time of Downs 1957) worked at an earlier stage of electoral development in the territorial dimension independently of the main institutional changes. Evidence presented here indicates that competition in the territorial space preceded competition in the functional-ideological space, especially during phases of restricted electorates. Parties were "catchallover parties" before turning into "catchall parties."[7] Beside macroprocesses of political and socioeconomic integration, therefore, competitive factors contribute to generate nationalized party systems in which the most important parties are present in the entire national territory.

Yet, in spite of this general process, regional diversity and territorial cleavages in Europe have not disappeared. To different degrees, territorial politics survives in a number of countries. This book wishes to contribute to research on political cleavages by including in the analysis the sources of *diversity, variation,* and *discontinuity* among European party systems. Besides factors of homogeneity and similarity, a number of cultural cleavages have maintained their strength in European party systems in spite of the general process toward the homogenization of electoral behavior. To give a

---

[6] For such a "top-down" perspective, see Lipset and Rokkan (1967a: 50) and Sartori (1968: 22).

[7] As a matter of fact, models in which competition takes place in the "ideological space" were inspired by work on spatial competition carried out by economists (Hotteling 1929; Smithies 1941). These models are therefore ideological analogies. For the concept of "catchall party" see Kirchheimer (1966).

complete picture of the European cleavage constellation, this work therefore opposes two sets of cleavages:

- *homogenizing* socioeconomic cleavages at the origin of *countries' similarities*: left–right cleavage and nationwide oppositions in regard to secularization and democratization (between liberals and conservatives in particular);
- preindustrial, mainly cultural, cleavages at the origin of the *fragmentation* of European territories and *country differences*: religious, ethnolinguistic, and urban–rural cleavages, as well as peripheral oppositions to national administrative centralization and cultural standardization.

These cleavages are analyzed through the *comparison of the different party families*: those of the first phases of state formation and parliamentary life (conservatives and liberals), those of the industrial age (socialists, agrarians, and later communists), and those that, more than others, account for territorial diversity and cross-country variations: religious parties (Catholics, Protestants, interconfessional people's parties) and ethnolinguistic or regionalist parties stemming from peripheral resistance to national integration.

Whereas, on the one hand, macro-sociopolitical processes led to an increasing integration of political life on a national scale, on the other hand the diversity of patterns of state formation and nation-building, the imperfect correspondence between state and ethnocultural borders, differences in center–periphery relations, and religious fragmentation account for the persistence of a marked territorial fragmentation of the vote and, consequently, for country differences. By including other cleavages besides the left–right one, this book examines the extent to which territorial diversity has survived in spite of the homogenizing forces leading to increasingly nationalized electorates and party systems in the course of the nineteenth and twentieth centuries. The combined analysis of all cleavages shows that processes of state formation and nation-building, industrialization, and urbanization were unable to compress fully territorial diversity. In particular, the book aims to estimate the weight of *cultural factors* – religious and ethnolinguistic cleavages – on regional diversity in Europe today.

The persistence of diversity in European territories implies that processes of nationalization were strongly at work but not inevitable. Because of the survival of territorial politics in a number of cases, it is legitimate to question whether processes of nationalization of electorates and party systems can actually be reduced to a unidirectional and deterministic

7

view. In other words, it is legitimate to ask whether macroprocesses of modernization of Western societies necessarily imply a process of nationalization of politics. Patterns toward more integrated national electorates and party systems varied to a large extent among countries according to their religious and ethnic structures, trajectories of state formation and nation-building, timing of democratization, and formation of stable party alignments. An analysis of European nationalization processes can therefore not avoid being a comparative analysis.

Recent events of regionalization and reterritorialization of politics within European nations have drawn the attention of scholars back to the spatial dimension of political conflicts and have led them to question the unidirectionality of nationalization processes (Keating 1988). On the one hand, transformations at the ideological level – with the decline of the left–right ideological hegemony after 1989 – liberated room in several political systems for feelings of ethnic and territorial identity. On the other hand, the process of European integration and of supranational construction of a European political system led to a significant loss in the normative role of nation-states. These transformations have encouraged several authors to predict the "end" of the traditional nation-state and the birth of a European regionalized and decentralized institutional framework (Harvie 1994). These developments are associated with the idea of a "crisis" of unitarian, centralized, and homogeneous political systems. The breakup of several East European countries, as well as the devolutionary tendencies in many West European ones, seem to attest to the advance of a postnational phase. A transformation toward regionalization can therefore not be excluded a priori at the present time, and the territoriality of political phenomena remains an important dimension of analysis.

To give a complete picture of this macrophenomenon, the analysis presented in this book encompasses more than 150 years of electoral history in 17 West European countries, providing dynamic longitudinal analyses of so far unexplored disaggregated data. Within the broad field of works on nationalization processes, this work focuses on the more specific electoral aspects – *electorates and party systems*. Electoral data represent a helpful tool for the empirical analysis of diverse and complex territorial configurations. The use of such data for the investigation of the complexity of European territories allows in the first place for a systematic analysis. The measurement of nationalization processes through electoral data constitutes a thread to follow in the complex labyrinth of cleavage lines, dimensions of conflict, and territorial divisions. First, this indicator is able to "boil down" the extreme diversity of territorial configurations in Europe. Second, it allows for the cross-country comparison and, above all, allows us to go back in history through a numerical and standard measure. Third, electoral behavior is a major indicator of mass political attitudes. Electoral alignments reflect socioeconomic and cultural divisions, and political cleavages translate into party organizations. This indicator will not, of course, tell the entire story, but it constitutes a "skeleton" allowing for the reconstruction of the history of European territorial structures.

Electorates and party systems are analyzed through *electoral participation* and *electoral support for political parties*. Regional variations of turnout and party strength in national general elections measure distinct aspects of the nationalization of politics. The former indicates the persistence of peripheral regions in terms of socioeconomic development: economic structure (the persistence of traditional society), literacy, and forms of political culture (local clientelism). The latter is an indicator of the strength of the territoriality of political cleavages: socioeconomic (wage earners/ employers-owners, rural/urban), cultural (ethnic, linguistic, religious), and center–periphery.

The disaggregated election results collected for *EWE-1815* (Caramani 2000) provide the empirical basis of a series of systematic comparative analyses. The description and explanation of the three following variations constitute the basic structure of the empirical investigation:

- The analysis of the *general trend* through time of the territorial structures of voting behavior in Europe (turnout and party support).
- The *cross-country comparison* of the territorial structures of voting behavior (and their temporal evolution).
- The comparison of the territorial structures of support between *cleavages and party families* (and their temporal evolution).

The West European countries included in this research are those of Table I.1.[8] Central and East European countries have been excluded given the problematic access to sources and the diverse political experience of these countries since 1945. This leaves the analysis with a homogeneous "universe" of 17 West European countries (Rokkan 1970a: 110). For these countries, national general legislative elections to the lower houses are considered. No by-elections or elections to upper houses or regional

---

[8] Several countries have been excluded because of their small territorial size. Luxembourg is the main one for which data are available in *EWE-1815*.

Table I.1. *Countries, Periods Covered, and Number of Parties and Elections*

Country	Period Covered	Number of Elections (Turnout Cases)	Number of Parties (Election Averages)	Number of Party Cases
Austria	1919–95	21	4.0	84
Belgium	1847–1995	32	6.6	211
Denmark	1849–1998	65	5.1	330
Finland	1907–95	32	6.7	213
France	1910–97	17	9.0	132
Germany	1871–1998	36	8.4	297
Greece	1926–96	21	5.9	123
Iceland	1874–1995	42	3.5	150
Ireland	1922–97	26	5.2	133
Italy	1861–1996	33	6.5	213
Netherlands	1888–1998	30	7.5	226
Norway	1882–1997	33	5.2	156
Portugal	1975–95	9	4.5	41
Spain	1977–96	7	12.3	86
Sweden	1866–1998	44	5.2	157
Switzerland	1848–1995	45	7.3	329
United Kingdom	1832–1997	42	5.6	162
TOTAL	1832–1998	535	6.1	3,043

Notes: The analysis considers all parties that received at least 5 percent of the vote within at least one constituency. Other parties, dispersed and unknown votes, and independent candidates are not included. The overall number of cases consists of all parties at each election for every country. Ireland 1832–1918 (the last all-Ireland election) and Northern Ireland 1922–97 included under the United Kingdom.

parliaments are included. The periods of time covered for each country are also presented in Table I.1. Periods of time end with the most recent elections published by 1999. The number of constituencies – in some cases even more disaggregated units such as the provinces in Italy – varies from a minimum of 8 in Iceland (1959–95) to a maximum of 641 in Britain (1997).[9]

Differences in the number of elections between countries are determined by historical factors (state formation, democratization, and structuring of party systems), as well as by the availability of data – depending on the "archivistic revolution" states carried out in recording information during

[9] Only metropolitan territories are included (namely, for France, the Netherlands, and Portugal), and overseas possessions have always been excluded. The detail on the levels of aggregation is given in Chapter 2 and Appendix 2.

the nineteenth century (Caramani 2000: 1005–15). The number of elections considered depends therefore upon the length of the time period (and the frequency with which elections are held) and varies from a maximum of 65 elections for Denmark to a minimum of 7 elections for Spain. Overall, the number of elections considered is 535. For earlier periods, the number of countries is smaller than the number today. Progressively, because of the availability of data and patterns of democratization, more countries are included (more recently Portugal and Spain since the 1970s).

As far as party support is concerned, the basic cases of the analysis are *political parties at single elections*. All parties receiving at least 5 percent of the vote within at least one constituency have been considered (meaning that they may receive less than 5 percent nationwide). The number of parties considered in each country varies according to the degree of fragmentation of the party system. Overall, the number of parties for all countries and all elections is 3,043.[10] For each of these parties (at each national election), a number of indicators of nationalization have been computed on the basis of the support received in each constituency. Measures of nationalization are therefore in the first place *party measures* that can be aggregated into European *party families* (across countries) and *national values*.[11]

Hence, this research can be defined as a *Europeanwide comparison – across time, countries, and party families – of within-nation territorial variations of electoral behavior (turnout and party support)*. Because of the large amount of new data, this work represents in the first place a broad *exploratory* analysis, preliminary in nature, mapping the territorial patterns of electoral behavior in Europe. Insofar as the amount of quantitative material hinders case-specific and in-depth analyses, this work has been designed as a macro-analysis of the overall figures and processes devoted in the first place to a concise and structured description of the data. In addition, the analysis

---

[10] Other parties, dispersed and unknown votes, and independent candidates have not been included. No second ballots are included in this count, or distinctions between *Erststimmen* (candidates' vote) and *Zweitstimmen* (lists' vote) in Germany, plurality and PR votes in Italy since 1994, partial and general elections in Belgium until World War I, and multiple votes and 1:1 estimates in multiple voting systems. Independent candidates are also excluded from the count, as are indirect elections. In cases of a large number of constituencies for which information is missing, parties have been excluded (see Appendix 3). Results for single candidates of the same party have been aggregated to form party results. Details are given in Chapter 2 and in the appendixes.

[11] The fact that the basic cases are parties and not party *systems* complicates the scheme of comparison. The comparative analysis can be carried out not only through space (countries) and time (elections), but also between political parties (within a single country or across countries), as well as between party families across countries.

11

introduces a series of hypotheses to test the *temporal variations* of the nationalization electorates and party systems, and it identifies the factors determining the *cross-country variations* in the levels of homogeneity of electorates. Accordingly, the book is divided into three parts. Part I (Framework) is theoretical and methodological. Part II (Evidence) describes data along three dimensions of variations: time (development), space (cross-country comparison), and cleavages (party families). Part III (Toward an Explanation) accounts for temporal and cross-country variations in the levels of nationalization of party systems.

PART I

Framework

1

The Structuring of Political Space

Territoriality versus Functionality

The task of this chapter is to identify the elements of the structuring of the space of political systems, with specific reference to the territorial dimension. Throughout this volume these elements – in particular the dualism between "territoriality" and "functionality" – will be used to interpret empirical evidence. The best-known expression of the two-dimensionality of the space of a political system as composed of a territorial and a functional dimension is Max Weber's definition of a *politischer Verband*: "We say of a group of domination that it is a *political group* [*politischer Verband*] insofar as its existence and the validity of the norms are assured in a permanent way within a *territory* [*Gebiet*]. What characterises the political group . . . is the fact that it claims the domination of its administrative leadership and of its norms upon a territory" (Weber 1978: part I, Chapter 1, 17.1).[1]

For Weber, territorial and functional aspects are at the basis of fundamental principles of social organization and reflect the image societies have of themselves. Political domination can follow either territorial criteria (laws in the modern nation-states are spatially bounded) or functional ones (the feudal hierarchical relationship). However, the distinction between territoriality and functionality can be fruitfully applied to many other aspects to understand the structuring of the space of political systems: Membership can be defined with respect to both social and territorial boundaries; representation channels can be organized in relation to

[1] E. Wilson too defines a territory by means of the concept of group: "Territory: an area occupied more or less exclusively by an animal or group of animals by means of repulsion through overt defence or advertisement" (Wilson 1975, quoted in Rokkan et al. 1987: 17). On the meaning of territory and the spatial aspects in politics see Gottmann (1973, 1980).

15

territorial or functional criteria (estates, corporations); cleavages can be ordered in a two-dimensional space composed of functional and territorial dimensions.

After Weber, "[f]ew sociologists have gone as far as Rokkan in making the *territoriality* of political systems one of the pillars of his comparative analyses" (Flora 1999: 63). Indeed, processes of formation of national electorates and party systems can be best interpreted starting from Rokkan's concepts of the *structuring of the space of political systems* – as complemented by Albert O. Hirschman's concepts of "exit" and "voice"[2] – and adapting them more specifically to the *territorial-geographical dimension of space*, as opposed to the membership or functional dimension.

However, within the large amount of work on the formation of national electorates and party systems, a number of writings also exist on the nationalization of politics that developed mainly in the United States in the wake of Elmer E. Schattschneider's seminal book on American politics, *The Semisovereign People: A Realist's View of Democracy in America* (1960).[3] Second, almost as a terminological coincidence, the concept of nationalization was employed in works making no direct reference to the American tradition of analysis. Third, the same concept has been used implicitly in other important studies – notably works on electoral geography – making reference neither to the American literature nor to the term nationalization itself. This chapter attempts to present a unified picture of these works.[4]

---

[2] See Hirschman (1970) and the works collected in the special issue of *Social Science Information*, Hirschman (1974), Finer (1974), and Rokkan (1974a, 1974b).

[3] See in particular Chapter 5, "The Nationalization of Politics. A Case Study in the Changing Dimensions of Politics," (pp. 78–96). See also Sundquist (1973) for a similar use of the nationalization concept in the American context. Of particular relevance are Stokes's articles on the variance components model (1965, 1967), which constitute the starting point of the debate on the problems of nationalization. For a theoretical and methodological critique of Stokes's work, see in the same issue of the *American Political Science Review* Katz (1973a, 1973b) and Stokes (1973) for a "Comment." Claggett, Flanigan, and Zingale (1984) propose the more articulated reflection on the dimensions composing the concept of nationalization (see also Claggett 1987). See Carrothers and Stonecash (1985) for a methodological critique and Claggett, Flanigan, and Zingale (1985) for a "Reply." See also Kawato (1987). For a more recent comparative analysis involving U.S. elections, see Chhibber and Kollman (1998). Agnew (1987) locates these concepts within the more general field of political geography.

[4] Some of the aspects presented in this chapter were developed in two articles published in the *Rivista Italiana di Scienza Politica* (1994) and in *West European Politics* (1996a).

Exit, Voice, and the Structuring of the Space of Political Systems

Exit and voice are two alternative mechanisms for individuals' reaction to the performance and output of organizations. The first belongs to the realm of economy and the second to that of politics. Because exit is not possible in situations of pure monopoly, it is not a mechanism of reaction in a number types of groups, such as the family and the church (Hirschman 1970). Among the organizations from which exit cannot be considered a viable option, Hirschman includes the state. For a consumer, it is possible to exit from a product – even in cases where no alternative is at hand – but this option is not available in politics. Furthermore, exit in the political sphere is charged with a negative connotation synonymous with desertion, defection, and treason. To belong as a citizen/subject to a state is not a choice but a given for each member.

On the basis of this scheme, Rokkan revisited his analysis of democratization processes (see in particular 1974b). The structuring of the space of West European political systems results from the two macroprocesses of *reduction of exit options* and *development of voice*. As a consequence of a situation of no exit in politics, voice is the only alternative channel for the expression of protest. State formation, nation-building, and the consolidation of membership boundaries are historical processes that have narrowed exit possibilities. However, what makes the exit option nonapplicable to state organizations in the West is not only a situation of pure monopoly but also the third concept coined by Hirschman: *loyalty*. The presence of a feeling of loyalty to the group to which individuals belong makes the exit option less likely. Moreover, the feeling of loyalty to the group makes it difficult to enter new groups.

The relation between the two mechanisms is negative: The development of voice channels is a function of exit possibilities, and the reduction of the exit option enhances the expression of voice. The reduction of the exit option by Western nation-states occurred essentially through boundary-building (both membership boundaries and territorial borders). The consequent development of voice implies, on the one hand, the *development of institutional channels of representation* and, on the other, the *opposition among individuals and groups along specific cleavages*. As far as the territorial dimension of space is concerned, we will focus on *territorial* channels of voice and establish the extent to which functional cleavages "project" or "sediment" along *territorial* lines.

What follows develops the scheme depicted in Figure 1.1, which sketches the structuring of the territorial space of political systems. The structuring of the space of political systems will be considered along with the two dimensions that define it – *external boundaries* and *internal political structuring* – which are both defined in terms of territoriality and functionality.

- *(External) boundary-building*. Boundary-building defines the external borders of the space and occurs along two dimensions: (1) *territorial physical boundary-building* (corresponding to territorial delimitation) and (2) *functional sociocultural boundary-building* (corresponding to membership delimitation).
- *(Internal) political-institutional structuring*. The internal structuring of the political space is defined (1) by the development of *institutions for the channeling of voice (representation)* and (2) by *political cleavages*.

Figure 1.1 schematizes external boundary-building by identifying it with the process of *state formation*; the structuring of internal institutions for the representation and channeling of voice is identified with the process of *democratization*; the structuring of political cleavages is identified with the process of *nation-building*.

(External) Boundary-Building

Analyzing the structuring of the space of political systems involves first analyzing its external delimitation, that is, the borders between systems. The process of state formation consists of the closing of boundaries to reduce exit options. The concept of boundary is crucial for the social sciences since it relates to the criteria that link individuals to groups by defining insiders and outsiders. It is a mechanism for allocating persons to groups (Brubaker 1992: 31). The definition of external state boundaries is therefore a definition of *citizenship*. Furthermore, the analysis of exit options (costs and payoffs of the institution of barriers) requires the analysis of strategies of boundary-building. There are two types of boundaries that, at the same time, define two types of space:

- *Territorial, physical, or geographical* space/boundary. Territorial boundaries are typical of the modern Westphalian state. Territorial closure is the basis of national legislation and implies, for nonmembers, the impossibility of accessing a number of resources. Sovereignty and citizenship are territorially delimited. The political system – as opposed to the cultural or economic sphere – is the only one capable of controlling a territory.

- *Functional, social/cultural, or membership* space/boundary. Social boundaries are much firmer than geographical ones and more difficult to cross. It is easier to enter a territorial space than to be accepted as a member of a social or cultural group – for example, kinship, religion, national citizenship (Rokkan et al. 1987: 17–20).

In the hunting-gathering communities, the distinction between insiders and outsiders was defined independently of any territorial element. Nomad groups were defined by social boundaries. The territorial dimension of boundaries and its distinction from the social boundaries became of crucial importance with the appearance of cities and city systems and with the sedentarization during the Neolithic revolution.[5] The tension between the two dimensions became more evident first with the Roman Empire and the Germanic Holy Roman Empire – in which both the biological (or ethnic) and the physical boundaries were replaced by the social boundaries of citizenry[6] – and later with the rise of Christianity, which helped to accentuate the social dimension of membership. Christianity established a cross-territorial and cross-ethnic religion in which the sociocultural affiliation to the community defines belonging to both a community on earth and the kingdom of salvation. In the following postimperial centuries, within the new, smaller, and more compact national political units, the idea of citizenship survived but was narrowed in scope. Nation-states were able – given their reduced size and the improvement of defense means – to stabilize their territorial boundaries. Through this process, citizenship (or state membership) was merged with territorial identity. Subjects and citizens were tied to territory.

The state is an entity with a jurisdiction confined within a territory and defined by spatial borders. In this sense, state sovereignty is possible only with reference to a territory. The nation can be defined "as both inherently limited [geographically] and sovereign" (Anderson 1983: 6). Two centuries

---

[5] Fustel de Coulange in *La Cité Antique* (1957) analyzes the impact of cities on membership, and Max Weber shows how *conjurationes* and *confraternitates* (types of corporations) cut across kinship relationships and permitted the expansion of Christianity as a cross-territorial and individual religious membership (see Rokkan et al. 1987: 5–20).

[6] Social, in this respect, refers to the medieval allegiance and to the pyramidal structure of society. However, more generally, it also refers to group membership following criteria such as religion or estates rather than ethnic or racial (biological) criteria or territorial ones (living in a given area).

19

Dimensions of the space of political systems

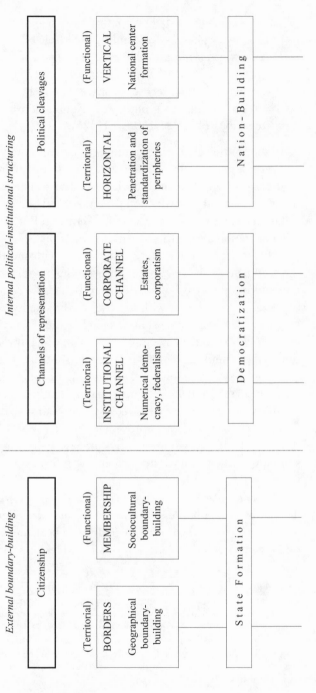

External boundary-building

Internal political-institutional structuring

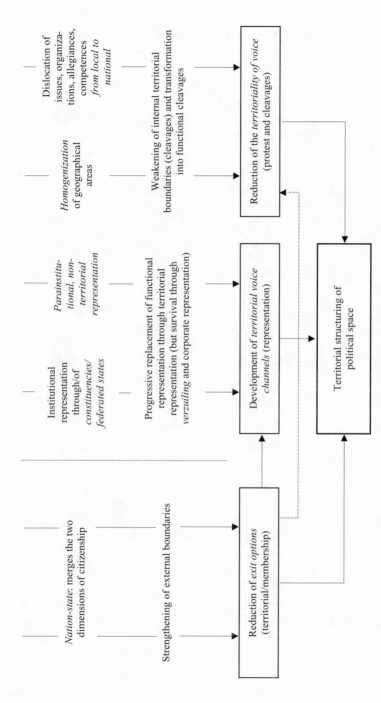

Figure 1.1 External and internal structuring of the space of political systems.

21

earlier, the Encyclopedists asserted that a nation was a group of people inhabiting a given territory and obeying the same law. States are defined by their exclusive jurisdiction over a delimited territory, and the boundaries of territorial competence define the sovereignty of a state (Sahlins 1989: 2–3). Historically, it was the French Revolution that emphasized the national meaning of territory and territorial sovereignty in the sense of an "invention of territory" (Alliès 1980). In Eugene Weber's words, peasants became national citizens when they abandoned their local sense of place centered on the village and replaced it by a feeling of belonging to a more extended territory (Weber 1976). Hence, "national identity means replacing a sense of local territory by love of national territory" (Sahlins 1989: 8).

Nation-states in Western Europe reached the closest correspondence between territorial and membership spaces, adapting the latter to the former and vice versa. In the peripheral regions of Europe, the development of a national feeling and the consolidation of the political and legal states occurred as parallel processes. By contrast, in the central areas of Europe, the latter phenomenon was delayed: "the nineteenth century saw the consolidation of the French and the construction of a German nation-state" (Brubaker 1992: 10). In the peripheral areas of Europe, the conditions existed for a fusion between the territorial-legal idea of nation and the membership to the ethnic group. Deprived of the political element of nationality, Germany (as the more typical and well-documented case) maintained and consolidated an ethnocultural meaning of the nation that did not correspond to any territorial-legal state – neither Prussia nor the *Kleinstaaterei* – until the late nineteenth century. Thus, the German understanding has been based on the idea of the *Volk* and, without a sovereign territorial assessment, was "prepolitical," organic, cultural, and racial rather than abstract, universalistic, legal, and centered on the political unit.

The nations that formed in Europe therefore maintained important differences, the most important being that between *territorial nations and ethnic nations* (Smith 1986). Although the territorial and membership dimensions of the political space both characterize Western nation-states, the combination of the two varies. Brubaker's comparison between France and Germany, for example, points out the differences between territorial and ethnic nations.[7] The French Revolution and the building of the Republic introduced territorial and institutional features. Emphasis was put on the political unit

---

[7] A comparison between these two countries can also be found in Dumont (1991), who distinguishes the German *cultural identity* from the French *political ideology*.

rather than on the cultural community. France's national identity developed within a geographical and institutional frame. The German "spirit" developed outside of, and in opposition to, the preexisting spatial organization of the states' mosaic, allowing for the emergence of an apolitical *Kulturnation*.

Thus, "the creation of the territorial state constituted one component of the modern nation-state; the emergence of national identity formed another" (Sahlins 1989: 7). "The modern state is not simply a territorial organization but a membership organization" and "is not only a territorial state . . . [but] also a nation-state" (Brubaker 1992: 21, 27). Nation-states, as such, need additional elements of solidarity and fraternity that cannot be achieved exclusively through political participation; they require attachment to the community through cultural and ethnic links. This is the reason why territorial nations foster mass education. Agencies of socialization – school, army, and so on – function as integrators to the community much more than to the political unit. On the other hand, however, there is the necessity for cultural entities to integrate political and legal elements to transform "ethnic" into "national" (Smith 1986: 137). Legal codes and institutions tend to substitute for customs and dialects, as well as for the other folk elements of the nation; that is, elements that provide the social cement for territorial nations must be used by ethic groups in order to survive in the international context. It appears, therefore, that there is a convergent process: Territorial states manifest the need for a communitarian base; ethnic groups adopt the civic model as they seek to become nations. The result of this two-way process is that modern states are characterized by the combination of the territorial and political qualities of states and the typical features of ethnic membership.

The nature of *citizenship* is the consequence of the fundamental principles that are at the basis of the nation; it is the legal dimension of nationhood. The link between a universalistic or ethnic idea of nation and the type of *jus* (*soli* or *sanguinis*) applied in order to define the members of this nation is straightforward. Territory constitutes a neutral criterion. What counts is the attachment to abstract political principles that are the basis of the territorial meaning of the nation. By contrast, an ethnic idea of the nation can conceive only a dynastic membership (a "community of descent"), by blood, and corresponds to a type of legislation that makes the acquisition of citizenship more difficult. Through the law of 1889, French citizenship was given to all individuals with foreign parents but born on French territory. According to the 1913 German law of citizenship, by contrast, there are no automatic procedures to give citizenship to immigrants' children born in Germany and long-term residents. Citizenship is founded on filiation, and naturalization is defined in restrictive terms (Brubaker 1991, 1992).

(Internal) Political-Institutional Structuring

The Reduction of Exit and the Expression of Voice

The internal aspects of the structuring of the political space concern the expression of voice. Hirschman interprets the "statelessness" (the "atrophy of voice") of several primordial tribes as a consequence of the presence of exit possibilities (Hirschman 1978). This statelessness is defined as the absence of institutional channels of voice that did not develop because of the possibility of exit for the members of these tribes.

To different types of spaces and boundaries correspond different *types of exits*. Again, we can distinguish:

- *territorial exits*: for example, secession;
- *nonterritorial* – functional or membership – *exits*: emigration (strong meaning), but also the refusal to perform military and fiscal duties (weak meaning) (Finer 1974: 82).

Emigration has been viewed in terms of nonterritorial exit. The availability of exit options makes voice less probable and is positive for the maintenance of the state and the reduction of conflicts ("safety valve"). MacDonald, for example, noted that the Italian emigration during the decade preceding World War I included many anarchists and socialists, that is, potential revolutionaries (MacDonald 1963–64, quoted in Hirschman 1978: 102).[8] A further example of nonterritorial exit is that described by Sombart and later by Lipset in the "frontier thesis" in the United States (see Sombart 1906; Lipset 1977). This thesis has often been criticized but nonetheless provides an example of the functioning of exit as a safety valve. The open frontier in the United States provided the American worker with the opportunity to escape from unsatisfactory working conditions under capitalism

---

[8] A similar case could be observed in Ireland, where emigration was conceived as a safety valve and, later, in negative terms as "blood running out of its veins." The Irish case was analyzed by N. R. Burnett in "Exit, Voice, and Ireland, 1936–58," unpublished, and in *Emigration in Modern Ireland*, the doctoral dissertation by the same author (Johns Hopkins University 1976; quoted by Hirschman 1978: 102). For a more recent contribution along these lines see Hirschman (1993).

by settling into the free land of the West. The thesis claims that this was one of the reasons why socialism did not develop (as a form of voice expression) to the same extent as in Europe. Also the great social mobility that characterizes the labor market in the United States provided the worker with the possibility of individual satisfaction, discouraging the organization of collective movements for the amelioration of poor social conditions.

From an evolutionary perspective, functional exit (emigration) replaced territorial exit (secession), since control over the territory and boundaries, as well as the degree of national integration, became strong enough to make geographical separation "unthinkable." However, exit from states and nations has not always been unthinkable. As Samuel Finer wrote, most European states in their early phases of formation were "obsessed by the demon of exit" (1974: 115), that is, by their territorial breakup. In a paired comparison between the English and French cases, Finer showed that whereas French politics had always been "obsessed by the demon of exit," English politics had been "obsessed by the angel of voice" (1974: 98–127). The history of France has been characterized by constant threats of exit of parts of the territory caused by the proximity to the city-trade belt and, therefore, the strong temptations that trade and cultural exchanges offered to border territories (the Hundred Years' War and the religious wars). By contrast, the geographical position of England accounts for the absence of such threats.

While French borders have always been extremely mobile and are highly "improbable" (Finer 1974: 121), English borders have remained almost unchanged since the tenth century. Whereas France was constructed as a link between one master system and several peripheral subsystems, the frequent invasions in England had flattened particularistic institutions and, in the long run, canceled them out. No English conflict ever involved secession. The conflict never expressed exit claims but instead always voice options, with conflicting groups attempting to control the center instead of breaking away from it.

The important elements that stand out are two. First, the *distance to the city-trade belt* is a crucial variable for understanding the threats of exit within systems or the "territorial temptations." Exit options on the European scale become a function of the geographical proximity to the core area of the Old Empire. Second, the *development of voice channels is a function of the availability of exit options.* England could smoothly develop its channels of representation because of the absence of other options of expression of discontent (it could control the borders and open up voice), while France had to pass through violent changes: To avoid exit, voice had to be kept at bay as well. However, the creation of channels of representation is only one aspect of the internal structuring of the political space. Internal space structuring consists of *political cleavages expressed through developing (institutional) channels of voice* (Figure 1.1). Therefore, two separate elements are considered next:

- the development of *channels of voice* (institutional and noninstitutional representation);
- *political cleavages*, that is, the form and the shape of voice within the space of each political system.

The Channeling of Voice (Representation)

Two different channels of representation have always coexisted, although the first in particular is associated with the process of democratization and the development of mass politics, as well as the mobilization of enfranchized electorates by political parties (Rokkan 1977). These two channels are:

- a *territorial* channel of representation: Democratization has meant the development of *territorial institutional channels of voice* (or territorial representation) in the form of numerical (electoral) democracy or other forms of territorial representation, such as federalism;
- a *functional* channel of representation, typical of predemocratic parliaments based on estates (usually nobility, clergy, burgesses, peasantry, etc.), but also of non- or parainstitutional representation of corporate interests or of subcultural segments of society (pillars or *zeuilen*, *Lager*, etc.).

The process of democratization has radically changed the modes of representation. Western "numerical democracies," since their development in the nineteenth and twentieth centuries, rely principally upon the territorial channel of representation. The territorial organization of the process of representation responded to the necessity of "unifying the national system of representation" (Bendix 1977: 91), leading to the transformation of estate political regimes into modern parliamentary systems. Although the principle of territorial representation existed throughout the feudal society – with the atomization of European territories and sovereignty after the breakdown of the Roman Empire – the firm functional segmentation was a second very significant feature of the Middle Ages, both in the horizontal (guilds, estates, corporations, etc.) and in the vertical perspective (with different social levels from nobility to serfs). In later periods, before and after absolutism, parliaments were based on estate representation. Only England maintained the system of territorial representation, allowing for a smoother transition to modern and democratic political institutions. In the English juridical context, the House of Commons has never been an assembly of estates, but rather a body of legislators representing the constituent territorial localities of the kingdom (the *communitates*).

In continental Europe, under the impulse of the French revolutionary ideals, the individual replaced estates as the basic unit of the political and social order and representation modalities were defined by territorial criteria. The French Revolution introduced the *plebiscitarian principle* (Bendix 1977: 90), that is, the principle of the direct vote by all qualified electors. According to this principle, no power, group, or association (the so-called *corps intermédiaires*) should stand between the individual and the state. The adoption of territorial criteria of representation was seen as the more neutral, universal, and egalitarian solution: *national* in a word. Politics was no longer channeled by separate functional bodies, but rather by a unified national assembly through territorial units.

The functional mode of representation has survived in two main areas. The first is the "representation of interests."[9] Work on neocorporatism has shown the extent to which functional modalities of interest representation – by trade unions, employers' organizations, and pressure groups – play an important role in decision-making processes within Western political systems (Schmitter and Lehmbruch 1979). This approach goes beyond parliamentary processes and also takes into account the extra- or parainstitutional actors such as the representation bodies of the major "social partners": government, workers' representatives, sectorial organizations, organizations of industrial entrepreneurs, and so on. The second area is that of territorial versus functional representation expressed in the defense of minority rights. One of the major issues of state and nation-building processes, as well as of democratic theory,[10] has been that of minority rights and representation – especially religious and ethnic minorities – and the

---

[9] See Rokkan (1977) for the use of this dichotomy in relation to the concept of *verzuiling* (or pillarization). See also Rokkan (1966a) for a discussion of "numerical democracy" versus "corporate pluralism" in the Norwegian case.

[10] An exhaustive treatment of minorities in the democratic theoretical literature can be found in Dahl (1957). Dahl does not limit his considerations to the *size* of the minorities (as the majoritarian principle commonly assumes) but also analyzes the *intensity* of the expression of preferences by social groups. See also Conclusion in this volume.

modalities through which they are incorporated into the decision-making process and provide the same opportunities to access the labor market. Depending on the degree of territoriality of such minorities, the praxis of elites in fragmented countries provides telling examples leading to different types of accommodation: pillarization (functional principle) versus federalism (territorial principle).[11]

Nevertheless, although the reduction of exit options caused by the strengthening of external boundaries (through the process of state formation) leads to the development of both functional and territorial voice channels, with the process of democratization it is *territorial* channels of voice in particular that are developed, responding to an individual and egalitarian principle of general representation.

The Territoriality of Political Cleavages

Political cleavages characterize the *divisions and oppositions within the space of political systems*. They determine the "internal shape" of the space of a political system and its internal boundaries. For example, a center–periphery cleavage and a rural–urban cleavage take different shapes within a system. However, although the territoriality of cleavages relates directly to the problems of this book, it would be reductive to limit the internal shape of the space of political systems to the geographical dimension.

The political space, on the contrary, is generated by both a territorial and a functional axis forming a two-dimensional abstract grid:

- *Territorial*: the two ends of this axis represent the extremes of the degree of territoriality from (1) local oppositions to centralizing and standardizing pressures to (2) cross-territorial conflicts of the system as a whole.
- *Functional*: the two ends of this axis represent (1) conflicts over the allocation of resources (economic benefits) and (2) conflicts over identity issues and definition of membership groups, mainly in terms of language and religion. Functional conflicts cut across territorial units (Lipset and Rokkan 1967a; Rokkan 1970a: 96–101).

---

[11] According to democratic theory, cross-cutting cleavages tend to weaken the intensity of conflicts. Moreover, additional territorial divisions cutting across functional ones further reduce their intensity. In Simmel's words, systems "based on territorial units are . . . the techniques for the organic integration of the whole" (Simmel 1955: 194; quoted in Lijphart 1968: 99).

The *territoriality of political cleavages* is essentially equivalent to the degree to which (linguistic, religious, economic) groups of individuals are opposed along territorial lines. Whereas the early growth of national states and bureaucracies produced mainly territorial oppositions, these developed later into a more complex constellation of cleavages in that some of them opposed territorial units and others opposed individuals and groups across units. Among the four cleavages engendered by the National and Industrial Revolutions in Rokkan's model, in two of them the territorial dimension is stronger. One is the conflict between the *central nation-building culture* and the *ethnic, linguistic, and religious resistance of peripheral populations*. The other is the conflict between the *landed interests* and the *industrial entrepreneurs*. For the other two cleavages the territorial dimension is weaker. One is the conflict between *the nation-state* and the *privileges of the church*. The other is the conflict between *employers* and *workers*. However, the territoriality of these cleavages – and of the party families stemming from each of them – varies from country to country and over time. The extent to which they vary is a matter of empirical analysis (see Chapter 5).

Center–Periphery Structures

For Rokkan, center–periphery structures are the essential features of the territorial space of political systems. The contribution of the center–periphery model is important since it clearly focuses on the integration of the peripheries, their incorporation into the national framework, and their standardization (legal and cultural). Processes of nationalization are in the first place the dynamic evolutions and transformations of such territorial structures. Referring to K. Deutsch, Rokkan writes: "his model is primarily designed to predict variations in the extent of territorial-cultural integration through the joint, but not necessarily parallel, process of national standardization" (Rokkan 1970a: 49),[12] and "the focus was primarily the incorporation of peripheral populations within some form of national community" (1970a: 51).

The model is therefore centered on the propagation of waves of political innovation from the centers of the national territory to its peripheries.

---

[12] See also Rokkan (1970a: 227), where he asks: "Did this process of mobilization and activation move forward at roughly the same rate throughout the national territory, or were there marked differences in the rate of change between the central, economically advanced localities and the geographical and economic peripheries?"

The concern is "to explore possible processes of spread from the central, highly commercialized industrialized areas, to the peripheral, economically less developed areas" (1970a: 182). And in describing "nationalization processes in the territorial peripheries" (1970a: 53), rather than peripheral variables such as cultural and physical distance and the mobilization of local resources, Rokkan points to the center-forming collectivities. The process of nationalization is associated with that of state formation.

Political mobilization is at the origin of this evolution.[13] Processes of mobilization are seen in the first place as the electoral mobilization of the peripheries in terms of electoral participation, party membership, and candidate recruitment. The purpose of the model is to explain the differences between central regions and peripheral regions in reaching the threshold of participation. These differences are considered in terms of timing. How long did it take the center and the periphery to reach similar levels of participation? How strong are the differences between regions? The indicators used by Rokkan for the empirical assessment of these phenomena are of different types. Recalling E. Faul's work on the *Bundestag* elections of the 1920s,[14] Rokkan notes that this author "has recently interpreted the data as evidence of the rapid 'nationalization' of political life in Germany"; therefore, "[i]t will be an interesting task for comparative research to assemble data for a number of countries on the rapidity of this process of mobilization and national political integration" (1970a: 186).

Particular attention must also be devoted to Rokkan's discussion of the process of "politicization." Politicization consists fundamentally in "the breakdown of the traditional systems of local rule through the entry of nationally organized parties" (1970a: 227). The relevant questions, in this respect, concern the duration of the process of establishing political parties throughout every region of the nation, the time lag of certain peripheral areas, and the factors that favored the resistance of given areas of the country. The indicator used for this analysis is "the spread of partisan competitiveness from the central to the peripheral localities" (1970a: 232). Interpreting the results, Rokkan observes that the rate of change is higher in the cities than in the rural districts. Only later, after World War I, processes of

[13] See two significant chapters in *Citizens, Elections, Parties* (1970a): "The Mobilization of the Periphery: Data on Turnout, Party Membership, and Candidate Recruitment in Norway" (Chapter 6) and "Electoral Mobilization, Party Competition, and National Integration" (Chapter 7).

[14] Faul (1960). Rokkan quotes a significant passage: "Since then there are no longer politically untouched spots in Germany" (1970a: 186; translation from original German text).

industrialization and monetarization of the primary sector – through the propagation of the socialist ideology – brought local communes to effective competition between lists. Nationalization occurs with the breakdown of local traditions of government through the development of national parties. The comparison of the results of political mobilization (turnout) in local and national elections shows that nationalization was achieved more rapidly in the latter than in the former.[15]

From Territorial to Functional Cleavages

In the process of political system-building, the territorial dimension of cleavages becomes less significant and the functional dimension becomes more important. The process of *strengthening of external boundaries*, therefore, is paralleled by the *weakening of internal (territorial) boundaries or cleavages*. This corresponds to the transformation of territorial cleavages into functional cleavages. The weakening of internal territorial divisions with the development of territorial systems is caused by the process of nation-building through political-administrative centralization, economic integration, and cultural standardization. Functional oppositions, however, can develop only after the initial consolidation of national territories. They replace territorial ones with the increasing interaction and communication across localities. The consolidation of purely functional cleavages cutting across territorial units requires a certain degree of consolidation of the national territory, that is, the consolidation of external boundaries (see the broken line in Figure 1.1).

Territorial conflicts are wiped out by the "massification" of political life (extension of suffrage), social mobilization through industrialization and urbanization, development of mass educational systems, and so on. Territorial oppositions are typical of earlier phases of electoral development. However, according to Rokkan, "[e]arly democratization will not necessarily generate clear-cut divisions on functional lines. The initial result of a widening of suffrage will often be an accentuation of the contrasts between the countryside and the urban centers and between the orthodox/ fundamentalist beliefs of the peasantry and the small-town citizens and the secularism fostered in the larger cities and the metropolis" (Lipset and

---

[15] "In a safe local election the marginal utility of mobilized votes is very small, but in the national election each vote delivered to the provincial total serves as a 'counter' in bargains for positions and for favors at the next level of the system" (Rokkan 1970a: 234).

Rokkan 1967a: 12). Internal structures of the space of political parties are influenced by *the level and the timing of consolidation of external boundaries.* These have been continuously modified (mainly by wars and secessions), especially for some countries (e.g., Germany). Furthermore, *the level and timing of consolidation of the electoral-territorial channel of representation* cause several problems for comparative analysis, in particular problems of periodization (general parliamentary elections have been held in Britain since 1832, whereas Austria since 1919 has a completely different territory with respect to the Habsburg Empire). These factors represent a series of variables whose impact will be tested empirically in the analysis that follows in Parts II and III.

This temporal shift from strong territorial oppositions to cleavages in which the functional dimensions prevails varies from country to country. Earlier territorial consolidation and the creation of national churches during the Reformation, for example, facilitated early nation-building and made it easier to overcome cultural-territorial cleavages before the age of mass mobilization. It is this aspect of transformation of cleavages – from territorial to functional – that this book is concerned with in the first place. It analyzes the evolution through *time* of the territorial structures of the political *space* mainly in Chapter 3. A *cross-country comparative analysis* is presented in Chapters 3 and 4. Chapter 5 analyzes more closely the territorial structures of support of the *party families that emerged from the main cleavages.*

The Theory of the Nationalization of Politics

Developed in the American setting, the theory of the "nationalization of politics" provides a useful instrument to investigate empirically the previously discussed issues. The process of reduction of the territoriality of cleavages occurs along the two main dimensions of the nationalization of politics (see also Figure 1.1).

- First, there is a *horizontal* process of territorial homogenization concerning political attitudes and behavior. This is a process of *penetration and standardization of peripheries* in the course of the process of nation-building.
- Second, there is a process of *vertical* dislocation of issues, organizations, allegiances, and competences from the local to the national level. This is a process of *center formation.*

These two basic elements of the nationalization of politics are outlined explicitly for the first time in Schattschneider's *The Semisovereign People* (1960). Describing the American party system in which, for more than 30 years – between 1896 and 1932 – national political life was dominated by the Republican Party, Schattschneider notes how the electoral support of the two major parties was characterized by strong territoriality ("sectionalism" in the American terminology). The support of the Republican Party was concentrated in the Northeast and Middle West and that of the Democratic Party in the South. In both areas, the opposition party was nearly nonexistent in electoral terms: "[i]n large areas of both sections the opposition party was extinguished and became ineffective."[16] Only in 1932 did this high degree of territoriality dissipate and a national political alignment emerged.

As Schattschneider observes, "before 1896 the major parties contested elections on remarkably equal terms throughout the country."[17] Not only were the two major parties – the Democrats and the Republicans – competing in equilibrium on the national level, but also in the different states this equilibrium was maintained. However, between 1892 and 1896 this situation underwent a radical change leading to the "Republican party system," which dominated the first 30 years of the twentieth century. The new political alignment created in 1896 arose from the different reactions to the agrarian protest, the "populist movement." In the South, the Democratic–Populist alliance supported the agrarian movement, which frightened the Northern business Republicans. The result of this situation was "the most sharply sectional political division in American history," with "the Democratic party in large areas of the Northeast and Middle West... wiped out whereas the Republican party consolidated its supremacy in all of the most populous areas of the country." The supremacy of the Republicans proved extremely stable and powerful. "The Solid South," Schattschneider writes, "was one of the foundation stones of the Republican system because it weakened the Democratic party disastrously and virtually destroyed for a generation the possibility of an effective national opposition party." As a consequence of the domination of one party in each section, the territorial cleavage became deeper. This created a "conflict of conflicts": The Solid South abandoned national politics to have a free

---

[16] For all quotations of Schattschneider in this chapter, see Schattschneider (1960: 79–93); original emphases are omitted.

[17] Schattschneider's reasoning is based on American presidential elections.

hand on racial issues, while the North continued to take advantage of its dominant economic position.

In 1932 this situation changed radically. The Democratic Party gained national power after more than 30 years. Electoral figures clearly show that the support for both parties became much more homogeneous compared to that of the 1896–1932 period. The "solid" sections melted down. This "revolution" was due in the first place to a deep change of political issues; that is, "the party realignment of 1932 is closely related to a deep change in the agenda of American politics." The high degree of territoriality of American politics dissipated because after 1932 it became dominated by national rather than local questions. The Depression and the New Deal had the effect of *nationalizing political issues*. This process was reinforced a decade later by international events focusing the attention of the entire nation: After the radical change occurred at the level of public policy in 1932, a change of even greater dimensions occurred with World War II and with the beginning of the Cold War. These processes had the effect of reducing local and sectional questions, that were replaced by issues shared by the whole country: "elections [were] dominated by factors that work on a national scale." Speaking about the 1952 and 1956 elections, Schattschneider notes that "[w]e are, for the first time in American history, within striking distance of a competitive two-party system throughout the country, and the nationalizing tendency has continued regardless of which of the parties is successful."

For Schattschneider, therefore, the nationalization of politics consists in the turn from sectional to national politics. It means homogeneous voting behavior throughout the country, with parties contesting elections in each state. It means, furthermore, the shifting of influences and issues from the local to the national scale. Finally, nationalization stands for similar shifts (swings) of votes between elections in all states: "[t]he universality of political trends is an index of the nationalization of the political system. Does the same trend appear throughout the country, or do conflicting trends appear?"

Since the time of Schattschneider's writings, the topic of the nationalization of politics has received constant and renewed attention. Donald E. Stokes, in his first analysis, has paid close attention "to the political level at which the forces acting on the electorate arise" (Stokes 1965: 63). The focus of the analysis is on the *location* of the forces influencing voters' behavior. The aim of Stokes's analysis is to verify the importance of national influences – the personality of the president, the performance of the party in government – on turnout rates and voting choices. The shift is vertical: Are the salient issues local, regional, or national? The investigation is based on the "variance components model" (an application of the analysis of variance), and the findings attest to a different impact of national forces on turnout levels and party votes. Whereas the decision of whether or not to participate in congressional elections seems to be determined by influences at the national level, national influences are less important when party choice is concerned.[18] Conversely, the effect of local influences on party choice is very strong, attesting to the importance of factors such as candidates, party organization, and local issues.[19] Furthermore, historical trends over a century (1870s–1950s) in the United States display a decline in local and state components, whereas the national influence on turnout rates has grown since the 1900s.

Stokes also presents data introducing a further dimension of the concept of nationalization, that is, the *correspondence* of the change from one election to the next between the national level and a given number of constituencies. The higher the number of constituencies that show a change against the national trend, the lower the level of nationalization. In a comparative analysis (1967), this evidence leads Stokes to conclude that the British electorate is more nationalized than the American one.

---

[18] Components of variance of percentage turnout and the Republican percentage of the two-party vote for the U.S. House of Representatives in the 1950s (normalized variance component) are:

Political Level	Turnout (%)	Republican Vote (%)
National (federal)	.86	.32
States	.08	.19
Local (congressional districts)	.06	.49
Total variance	1.00	1.00

Source: Stokes (1965: 75–76).

[19] The comparative analysis of the American and British cases allows Stokes to document the differences in the structure of the two electorates (Stokes 1967): The national component is more important in Britain than in the United States. The difference in the amount of influence of local politics between the two electorates is estimated through the analysis of the *swings* between subsequent elections. The change in turnout and in levels of party support between two elections is more homogeneous in Britain than in the United States. Stokes also notes that Britain had always been more nationalized than the United States.

Dimensions of Nationalization

From these works, different dimensions of the nationalization of politics stand out, which should be conceptually distinguished although they are intermingled on the empirical level. Discussing Schattschneider's and Stokes's contributions, Claggett, Flanigan, and Zingale (1984) provide the most systematic clarification of the concepts and relationships between dimensions. They note that three different aspects coexist:

- *Homogeneity of support.* The nationalization of politics is a process of *convergence in the levels of partisan support,* that is, a process of *territorial homogenization* of turnout and support for political parties.[20]
- *Source (or level) of political forces.* This dimension refers to the tendency of electorates to refer to political forces located on the national level rather than to forces situated on a local level. National political forces have a stronger and increasing impact on voting behavior compared to regional or local forces. These influences are seen as national political *stimuli* from which electoral *responses* originate. For example, voters refer to national political leaders rather than local candidates.
- *Type of response.* The responses to these stimuli, in turn, constitute a further dimension: Nationalization means *uniform responses to political forces* operationalized as *uniform swings* between two subsequent elections. For example, a party increases its support from one election to the next in all territorial units (a uniformly positive response).

The *convergence of the levels of electoral support* or *homogeneous levels of support* means that differences between areas in terms of voting behavior disappear and a similarity among regions occurs. Claggett, Flanigan, and Zingale point out that this dimension has often been confused with that of uniform responses to political forces (the third dimension). This happened

---

[20] For J. Sundquist, the nationalization of American politics basically meant "the convergence of party strength," that is – in Schattschneider's words – the progressive disappearance of "one-party states" due to the reduction of strongholds and to the diffusion of support throughout the territory. Sundquist's expression "convergence to the center" indicates that the two main parties receive a similar percentage of votes (around 50 percent each): "as the barriers weaken . . . each community can be expected to come to rest somewhere near the national average of party strength" and to see the distribution of constituency values characterized by a reduced variance around this average. This movement toward the center (the average) "will appear in favor of the minority party wherever the distribution of party strength has been unbalanced" and the more unbalanced, "the stronger its rebound toward the 50 percent level" (Sundquist 1973: 332–37).

Type of response	Location of forces (or stimuli)	
	National	Local (or regional)
Uniform swing	A: Nationalization of politics. Uniform responses of constituencies or other territorial units to national factors.	B: Coincidence. Uniform responses of constituencies or other territorial units to independent locally based factors.
Nonuniform swing	C: Mediated national influences. Nonuniform responses of constituencies or other territorial units to national factors.	D: Localization of politics. Nonuniform responses of constituencies or other territorial units to independent locally based factors.

Figure 1.2 Type of response and location of forces.
Notes: In this figure, the specific terminology referring to the American case has been adapted for the purpose of analytical generalization. The dimension of the "location of forces" (originally consisting of three levels) has been dichotomized.
Source: Adapted from Claggett, Flanigan, and Zingale (1984).

because both dimensions share the *territorial* character. In both cases, there are territorial areas that are more or less similar in terms of electoral behavior. However, the two aspects are clearly distinct. Homogeneity of the levels of electoral support can coexist with a nonuniformity of responses around these levels; that is, in some territorial units a party can increase its vote, while in others it undergoes a decrease.

The third dimension has been used by Stokes and later by Katz (1973a, 1973b) as an indicator of the second dimension (the location of political stimuli). In Stokes's model, uniform swings indicate responses to national forces. Katz's main criticism to this approach is that Stokes underestimates the amount of national effects since his method considers a response to national forces only uniform swings, whereas nonuniform swings could also be responses to national forces. There are not necessarily corresponding uniform responses to national influences; regional units could also give differentiated responses to these influences. In both cases, the electorate responds to national forces.

Claggett, Flanigan, and Zingale (1984) try to clarify the distinction between "level of influence" and "type of response." Figure 1.2 reproduces but generalizes their scheme. In this figure, one entry is the level of political stimuli (national or local) and the other is the type of response (a uniform or nonuniform increase/decrease from one election to the next). Both uniform and differentiated responses to national influences may emanate from the various geographical areas of a country. As regards case A, it is easy to imagine the electoral response given to a national political scandal (a uniformly negative response) or to a particularly appreciated government action (a uniformly positive response). Similarly, one could imagine the uniformly positive effect produced by a popular presidential candidate. However, a national influence may also result in a differentiated response (case C). A president who is very popular in some areas and less so in others is clearly a national factor to which differentiated responses correspond. By contrast, if the stimuli regarded as relevant by the electorate are situated at the level of the local community or the region, it is plausible that stimuli will be very different from area to area, producing differentiated shifts between two elections (case D). Only in coincidences (case B) does the aggregation of all local stimuli produce a uniform shift throughout the country.

The difference between case A and case C is the presence of local factors, that in the second type constitute a filter through which national influences pass. In the first case, the relationship between national factors and the type of response is *immediate*, whereas in the second case, national influences are *mediated* by local factors determining differentiated responses. In their analysis of British elections, Butler and Stokes (1974) obtain results attesting to the presence of factors that modify the uniforming effects of national influences, in particular mechanisms that increase the support of parties in constituencies in which they are already dominant and decrease their support in constituencies in which they are already weak. This may be due to the influence of the surrounding environment and the face-to-face contacts that unavoidably occur in situations of spatial proximity.[21]

However, Claggett, Flanigan, and Zingale – through an attentive evaluation of the methodology devized to distinguish empirically the four cases in Figure 1.2 – demonstrate that "there is no means in analysis of variance-based techniques to distinguish among the *types* of forces which may cause the nonuniform response by the local units" (1984: 83). It is plausible that uniform swings are caused by national influences (if one excludes the possibility of coincidences). However, *in cases of nonuniform responses, it is impossible to determine at what level the stimulus was located* (whether nationally or locally).[22] This leads Claggett, Flanigan, and Zingale to

[21] A full formulation of this hypothesis is found notably in Butler and Stokes (1974: 143ff). See also Cox (1969a), Taylor and Johnston (1979, 221–69), and Orbell (1970). For an empirical confirmation of the Butler-Stokes hypothesis in the British context, see Johnston (1981a).

[22] The model, however, distinguishes uniform from nonuniform responses.

conclude that the operationalization of the presence of national political forces is an insurmountable task with constituency-level data. The source of stimuli acting on the electorate cannot be measured through ecological data; instead, individual-level data must be collected by means of survey techniques.

The Relationship Between National Forces and Territorial Structures

Although attempts to operationalize the location of political forces on the basis of ecological data have failed, there still is a relationship between the location of political forces and the territorial configuration of electoral behavior. Claggett, Flanigan, and Zingale themselves observe that only with respect to *nonuniform* territorial configurations it is impossible to establish the location of the influence. However, it is possible to determine the national location of stimuli when uniform patterns exist.

Since local influences do not produce homogeneous territorial patterns, it follows that homogeneous distributions are an indicator of the presence of national forces. The national location of political forces can therefore be derived from a homogeneous or uniform territorial distribution of voting behavior. In this respect, Schattschneider was right in affirming that "[w]e ought to suspect that something has happened to the political system when we observe that the Republican party gained ground in every state in 1952 and lost ground in forty-five states in 1954, gained ground throughout the country in 1956 and lost ground in nearly every state in 1958. These trends are national in scope."

In the present work, nonuniform territorial configurations are assumed to be determined exclusively by local factors and therefore do not lead to a nationalization of case C but rather to a localization of politics. If territorial configurations are differentiated, this means (1) that at least some *intervening local factor* has acted to distort the homogenizing effects of national factors or (2) that *local factors have predominated over national ones*. Regionally or locally differentiated voting behavior can be explained only through the presence of forces exerting an influence at the regional or local level. Territorially diverse voting behavior, therefore, always refers in one way or the other – either directly as sources of stimuli as such or as intervening factors distorting national influences – to local factors.

Furthermore, the degree of uniformity of responses and the homogeneity of support are two types of voting behavior that can be more or less homogeneously distributed throughout the territory. The dimension of the type of response is a subdimension of the homogeneity of voting be-havior. In the first case, what is homogeneous across territorial units is the level of turnout or support for given political parties. In the case of the type of response, by contrast, what is more or less homogeneous is the *change* occurring between subsequent elections.[23] With the uniformity of swings having failed as an indicator of the location of political forces, we are left with an electoral phenomenon that can be more or less homo-geneously distributed across regions, as partisan support, turnout, volatil-ity, number of parties, levels of fractionalization, or any other electoral indicator.[24]

The Nature of National Political Forces

Besides the technical difficulties with the operationalization of the sources of influence – whether local or national – a number of other problems occur in determining which factors are considered sources of influence. First, the literature on nationalization has defined *stimuli* (or forces or in-fluences) either as issues and policies set by parties and institutions or as the influence of national political leaders such as prime ministers and presi-dents. With specific reference to locally based stimuli, stress has been placed on the effect of local issues and leaders. Such a view is, however, limited. *All* factors at the origin of the electoral choice or any other voting be-havior are political stimuli. Therefore, everything is a potential political stimulus – an issue, a political leader, a policy, but also the organizational strength of political parties in given areas or the intensity of their cam-paigning. The general socioeconomic and political characteristics of areas can influence voters' behavior. The spatially delimited social environment determines, to a large extent, voting choices through social pressure as well as political traditions (Catholic, socialist, etc.) or social conditions

---

[23] On the one hand, the similarity concerns the *direction* of change in the vote for a party from one election to the next, that is, whether a party increases or decreases its share of votes. On the other hand, the uniformity concerns the *amount* of change. In other words, one has to establish whether a party increases its support everywhere (in each territorial unit) with equivalent percentages or whether it undergoes a similar decrease throughout the country between two elections.

[24] A link between the homogenization of support and the uniformity of swings exists, for if there is no homogeneity of support, percentages of swing will not be equivalent among regions but rather will be proportional to the party's share of the votes. The uniformity of amount, therefore, manifests itself through a *nonuniformity* of values. On this point see Butler and Stokes (1974: 142–43).

(unemployment, insecurity, etc.). Finally, a particularly important element of the nationalization of politics has been identified with national symbolism and "mythologies."[25]

Second, aggregate techniques are unable to distinguish between the *subjective* and *objective* nature of the location of a political force acting on the electorate.[26] An organizationally or structurally effective transfer of political stimuli does not necessarily correspond to the *perception* that stimuli are located nationally. The problem of locating stimuli on an imaginary vertical scale therefore becomes, to a large extent, a question of *information flows* that determine the perception of the relevant forces and their location (Cox 1969b). The social and economic structure of a local community may exert a strong influence on voters if the channels of information are those of grass-roots organizations (media but also face-to-face contacts and neighborhood effects). By contrast, voters may refer to national issues simply through national channels of information.[27]

The early phases of electoral development and structuring of party systems have witnessed the centralization of partisan organizations and campaigning techniques.[28] Similarly, both political issues and policies became increasingly national in their historical development. The appearance of national media of mass communication are also objective elements of the national location of political forces. Nonetheless, this does not reveal much about the *perception* of the location of the salient political forces.

Third, the transfer of the relevant environment to which individuals refer can be considered from two different perspectives. First, this transfer can be viewed as a *historical process*. The development of national party organizations and campaigning, central information sources, the emergence of national issues, the enlargement of the scope of public policies due to

---

[25] On the impact of political symbolism on national mass movements in the German case see Mosse (1975). This work identifies the Nazi and Fascist movements as crucial in the nationalization of politics through their extremist worship of "the nation" and "the people." On the Italian case see Tobia (1996).

[26] Deutsch distinguishes subjective (state of mind) and objective (national development) dimensions of political integration. See Deutsch (1981: 52–53).

[27] Work in this direction has been carried out in the wake of contextual analyses stressing the influence of the socioeconomic environment on individuals' decisions and behavior.

[28] This is the case of the development of nationwide party organizations and the decline of strictly territorial politics. According to Rokkan, for example, processes of nationalization of political life and of integration of peripheries could be "documented statistically, from official electoral counts" (Rokkan 1970a: 226). On the nationalization of party organizations see also Mair (1987).

the interdependence of sectors, nation-building, welfare state, and so on are fundamental long-term factors of change according to which the political environment to which individuals belong, and from which they receive their socialization, is no longer the local community but the nation as a whole. By contrast, what previous literature has tried to operationalize is a *contingent* type of short-term change acting from election to election, such as the sudden emergence of an issue or the appearance of a new political leader.

Forms of Nationalization and Delimitation of the Analysis

The previous discussion leaves the nationalization of electorates and party systems with two main dimensions:

- the *territorial homogeneity/homogenization of electoral and party system features*: The homogeneity/homogenization in this work is considered mainly *horizontally* among the regional units subdividing national territories;[29]
- the *predominance of national political forces or influences* over regional ones: issues and structures (organizations, institutions).

In the present work, national political forces are derived from homogeneous electoral behavior. Uniform swings (i.e., changes between two elections) are unable to detect the location of stimuli and are therefore only one of the many aspects that can be more or less homogeneously distributed across territories; the analysis will therefore exclude this aspect. The homogeneity of electoral behavior is therefore the parsimonious indicator of the nationalization of broader political aspects. Unlike all other indices, the

---

[29] Comparative research on the *vertical* correspondence between the features of the single constituencies and those at the national level was carried out by Hearl, Budge, and Pearson (1996). The correspondence between constituencies and the national level can be described as *vertical homogeneity* (not among constituencies but between constituencies and the national level). There are two major problems when dealing with this type of homogeneity. First, it is necessary to determine whether "national level" means the average of constituency values or the actual national value. Second, it is necessary to clarify the relationship between the horizontal and vertical homogeneities. Generally, the more a party is horizontally homogeneous, the more the constituency values correspond to the national values. See Budge and Hearl (1990) and Hearl, Budge, and Pearson (1996). The second article is the English and extended version of an essay in Italian. This dimension is closely related to the horizontal homogeneity of behavior: It is a dimension, therefore, that can be derived from homogeneous behavior (see also Lee 1988).

homogeneity of electoral behavior allows for broad analysis across countries and electoral systems. The technical problems of measurement of the different indicators are discussed in the next chapter. In Part II, the homogeneity of electoral behavior – electoral participation and support for parties – will be used to analyze historical trends, country differences, and party families, as well as single political parties.

2

Data, Indices, Method

The analysis of regional variations of voting behavior (turnout and party votes) requires *territorially disaggregated data*, namely, election results at the level of *single constituencies*. Data used for analysis are those published in machine-readable form in the CD-ROM *EWE-1815* and documented in the accompanying handbook.[1] As the present book analyzes for the first time that wealth of new and unexplored data, the following section gives a summarized description of the collection and of the criteria that guided it. The rest of the chapter is concerned with methodological aspects, indicators of the formation of national electorates and party systems, and measures.

Data

Periods Covered and Data Sources

The period of time covered by the analysis is approximately 150 years, roughly from the democratic revolutions of 1848 – a crucial step toward parliamentary democracy in most West European countries – to the present. However, among the 17 countries considered, the period of time varies according to (1) patterns of state formation and (2) availability of sources (see Table I.1 in the Introduction and Table 2.1). The period of time covers all elections ending with the most recent elections published by 1999 (and does not include nondemocratic elections of the Nazi and Fascist periods between the two world wars).

---

[1] See especially the Introduction and Appendixes 1 and 2, as well as the explanatory texts in the country chapters and on CD-ROM.

As far as patterns of state formation are concerned, the starting point is determined by the timing of national *unification* or *independence* and by the definite transition from estate (or absolutist) systems to modern parliamentary systems based on general territorial representation. No estate elections are included, even though for some countries (e.g., Austria) such data would be available at the disaggregated level of the *Kronländer* (the crown states of the Habsburg Empire).

Concerning the availability of sources, the recording of election results is intrinsically linked to the bureaucratization of the nation-state. The "cybernetic capacity" of state administrations (Flora 1977: 114) has improved progressively through the organization of censuses, the publication of statistical yearbooks, and so forth. Electoral statistics appear later than other types of statistics. Whereas headings of financial or criminal statistics appear in all national yearbooks since the beginning of statistical activities, electoral information is reported only in some cases, depending upon the degree of development of representative institutions. The moment at which this type of information appears in statistical records also depends upon the stability of political regimes, the need for legitimacy of newly created institutions, secret voting, and the degree of structuration of party systems. In several cases, statistics collected by private scholars compensate for the lack of official sources.

Among the *early established states* (i.e., before or by the time of the Congress of Vienna, 1815), electoral official returns in the United Kingdom have been recorded by the Public Record Office since the 1832 reform. These data have been collected and rearranged with the addition of party affiliations by F. W. S. Craig in a series of well-known volumes. In France, the collection at the constituency level starts in 1910 with the results made available by the work of G. Lachapelle. Systematic official data on elections, however, do not appear until after World War II. In Denmark, electorate statistics have been published by the *Statens Statistiske Bureau* since 1849 (*Statistisk Tabelværk*, later *Statistisk Meddelelser*). Since 1895, data have also figured in the statistical yearbook. However, the main source for 1849–1915 is J. P. Nordengård's work (*Valgene til Rigsdagen i 100 aar*). For Sweden, data are available since 1866, when the estate system was replaced by the bicameral *Riksdag*. The *Statistiska Centralbyrån* has published the results of elections regularly since then, and the last issues include an increasing number of retrospective elections. Party affiliations, however, are available only since the introduction of PR in 1911. For the Netherlands, data are available by parties since 1888.

As far as *independence* patterns are concerned, for Ireland results are available since the first election after the signing in 1922 of the Anglo-Irish Treaty, which gave dominion status to the 26 counties of the Irish Free State. The *Dáil Éireann* and the Stationery Office have published the results of the elections since 1948. From 1922 to 1944, election results were published by W. J. Flynn (*The Irish Parliamentary Handbook*, published since 1932 by the Stationery Office). In Finland, the *Vaalitilasto XXIX* series has been published regularly since 1907, when the first election took place before the country's secession from the Russian Empire (1917). For the other Nordic countries too, independence cannot be considered the relevant starting point. Iceland became an independent republic in 1945, but elections are registered since 1874, when it was granted self-government with a representative *Alþingi*. The *Hagskýrslur Íslands* published only sporadic information until 1908; a retrospective publication appeared in 1912 covering 1874–1903. The entire 1874–1987 period is covered by a retrospective publication combining all previous ones.[2] Norway was recognized as independent by the Swedish *Riksdag* in 1905, but elections to the *Storthing* had been held and registered since 1815. Periodical series have been published since 1882 (*Statistik over Storthings- og Valgmandsvalgene*). For 1815–85 a retrospective volume was published in 1895 (*Statistik Vedkommende Valgmandsvalgene og Storthingsvalgene 1815–1885*) by J. Utheim.

For Belgium, by contrast, the starting point is 1847 even though national elections were held since independence from the Netherlands in 1830. Some election statistics have been included in the yearbook since 1841, but series have been published systematically only since 1919 by the *Institut National de Statistique*. The main source for 1847–1914 is therefore Moyne's *Résultats des Élections Belges entre 1847 et 1914*. R. E. De Smet, R. Evalenko, and W. Fraeys published a second major work on Belgium for the 1919–61 period (*Atlas des Élections Belges, 1919–1954* and the two *Suppléments* for the 1958 and 1961 elections).

In the case of *unification* patterns, the starting point for Switzerland is the creation of the federal state (1848). For some Swiss cantons, as for Denmark, elections are officially registered only since the introduction of secret ballots (1872 and 1901, respectively). Until 1917, official statistics (published in the *Bundesblatt*) were limited to the list of elected candidates indicating (only for 1881–90) the three main political tendencies (left, center, and

---

[2] *Kosningaskýrslur, Fyrsta Bindi: 1874–1946; Kosningaskýrslur, Annað Bindi: 1949–87*, Reykjavík, Hagstofu Íslands (1988).

Table 2.1. *Availability of Election Results by Party at the Constituency or Other Subnational Level*

Country	Decades (1810s–1990s)	Entries
Austria		17 Kronländer; 25 Wahlkreise; 9 Länderwahlkreise
Belgium		41 arrondissements; 30 groups of arrondissements
Denmark		113 Valkredse; 22–23 Amts- and storkredse; 17 Amts- and stork.
Finland		16–17 Vaalipiirit
France		88–100 départements
Germany		374 Wahlkreise; 35–36 Wk.; 242–328 Wahlkreise
Greece		38–56 nomoi or 98–99 provinces
Iceland		19 kjördæmi; 19–28 kjördæmi; 8 kjördæmi
Ireland		28–42 Dáil constituencies
Italy		14–16 regioni; 40–54; 31–32 circoscrizioni; 475
Netherlands		100 kiesdistricten; 123–6 distr.; 18–20 kieskringen
Norway		38–58 Amter and kjøbstæder; 29 distrikter; 19–20 fylker
Portugal		20 circulos el.
Spain		52 provincias
Sweden		173–201 Valkretsar; 56; 28–29 Valkretsar
Switzerland		49–52 Wahlkreise; 25–26 cantons
UK–Britain		335–651 parliamentary constituencies
(N.) Ireland		66–103 parliamentary consituencies (Ireland); 10–17 parliamentary constituencies (Northern Ireland)

Column headings: 1810s | 1820s | 1830s | 1840s | 1850s | 1860s | 1870s | 1880s | 1890s | 1900s | 1910s | 1920s | 1930s | 1940s | 1950s | 1960s | 1970s | 1980s | 1990s

Legend:
- Election results by party affiliation available.
- No party results available at the levels of constituencies or other subnational levels.
- Party results available but period excluded from analysis or interruption of democratic elections.

Notes: Two tiers in Austria and 43 *Wahlkreise* since 1995. France: *circonscriptions uninominales* (plurality districts) not always available. Ireland before 1922: results under the United Kingdom, but not included in computations (see instead Chapter 6). In Italy for 1946–92, data on provinces are available.

Source: *EWE-1815 : 7.*

47

right). Secondary sources, however, allow the starting point to be pushed back. Election statistics between 1848 and 1917 were made available by E. Gruner (*Die Wahlen in den Schweizerischen Nationalrat, 1848–1919*, 1978). The partisan affiliation of the candidates is indicated, and party figures are computed on the basis of candidates' votes in the various ballots that took place. For Germany and Italy the starting point is the unification of the nation-states, even though earlier data are available for some territories.

Greece was the first country to introduce universal male suffrage in 1844, but official data are not available until 1926. For the same reason, the collection of results starts only in 1975 for Portugal and in 1977 in Spain, for which material on elections from the first republic (1869) until the Civil War (1936) concerns mainly seat figures. A further specific mention concerns Austria. Results are available since 1873, when elections (under the Habsburg monarchy) were still held by estates for the entire Austrian half of the empire (Cisleithania). Nonetheless, the analysis considers Austria only since the breakdown of the empire and the first republican election in 1919, when the country was reduced to one-fifth of its former size. Because of the peculiarities of the electoral system, French elections of 1914, 1919, 1924, 1932, and 1936 are not included in the analysis, and data for the second 1946 election are missing. Similarly, data for the 1933 and 1950 Greek elections are not available for party lists or are not reliable, and the 1935 election was fixed. The 1924 Italian election is usually not considered a democratic election (although it took place before the Fascist regime had taken over), and at the 1917 Dutch election an agreement between parties was reached so that the distribution of seats would remain unchanged. These elections too have therefore been excluded.

Elections

Data include results of *general national legislative elections* (and elections of constituent assemblies). They do not include results for regional, provincial, or communal bodies or for the European Parliament. Data concern only elections of representatives and do not include referenda or other forms of direct democracy. Results have been collected for lower houses. Senates, houses of regional representation (*Bundesrat* and *Ständerat*), or chambers of higher estates have not been considered even in those cases in which the two houses have equal power. The collection considers general elections and partial elections (e.g., the renewal by half of the lower house in Belgium) but not by-elections due to vacancies occurring during legislatures.

The basic information collected for each election concerns the:

- number of persons entitled to vote (*electorate*);
- number of actual voters (*turnout*);
- total number of *valid votes*;
- number of votes cast for each party (*party votes*);
- number of dispersed votes or votes for minor lists or candidates (*other parties*).

When applicable, information has been collected for first and second ballots, direct and indirect elections (two or more steps), *Erst-* and *Zweitstimmen*, and so on. All information has been collected at the level of single constituencies and other subnational units.

Political Parties and Codes for Party Families

The criterion applied in order to select parties has been a size criterion in purely numerical terms. Parties should have a certain relevance in order to be included in the analysis and enter the computation of indices of territorial homogeneity. However, given the territorially disaggregated nature of the data, political parties have been selected when they poll *at least 5 percent of the vote within at least one territorial unit*, meaning that such parties may poll less than 5 percent of the total nationwide vote (for the same criterion, see Rose and Urwin 1975: 18; Urwin 1983: 228). Parties that do not fulfill this criterion were added to the "other parties" category.

A series of standard codes have been given to parties according to the classification used by Bartolini, Caramani, and Hug (1997, 1998) and Caramani and Hug (1998). This allows an increase in the comparability of the data across countries and time. The following shortcuts are used for each of the 10 party families: social democrats, conservatives, liberals, communists, Catholics, (interconfessional) people's parties, Protestants, regionalists, agrarians, greens. Extreme right-wing parties have been considered only occasionally.

First, the standardization of codes for political parties has been carried out *across countries*. The same code has been given to the main historical parties of the socialist family (or social democratic or labor parties) that formed at the end of the nineteenth century (e.g., the German Social Democratic Party or the British Labour Party); similarly, the same code has been given to the main historical communist parties that broke away after World War I from these socialist parties (e.g., the Italian Communist Party, the French

Communist Party), to the main denominational people's parties (e.g., the Italian Christian Democracy and the German Christian Democratic Union), and so on. Appendix 1 lists the standard codes for the 10 party families, with the parties that were included in each category. These categories do not mean that parties have been aggregated together. Each party is dealt with individually. For *each party only one code is applicable, and two parties of the same country were never given the same code*. For example, in those countries in which, in addition to the historical social democrats (code "s"), there is a second socialist party, this is coded with its acronym (e.g., the *Venstresocialisterne*–Danish Left Socialist Party is coded "vs"; the *Partito social-democratico italiano*–Italian Social Democratic Party is coded "psdi").

Second, in order to increase *historical continuity*, codes have been left unchanged when the name of the political party changed. Party codes have been standardized according to a criterion of *organizational continuity* rather than on an ideological basis. This implies that even important ideological changes reflected by a change in the name do not lead to a change of code. This has been done to increase the temporal continuity of the data and makes it easier to follow party developments through time. Codes allow for the comparison of party families carried out in Chapter 5.

Levels of Aggregation and Boundary Changes

With respect to intertemporal comparability, the *continuity of territorial units through time* represents the main problem. It is possible to create continuous time series only in those cases in which territorial units did not change. In Switzerland, for example, since 1919 the cantons have been the electoral units; only one change occurred with the creation of the canton of Jura (which seceded from Berne). In most cases, however, constituencies change more often: in Ireland at almost every election. Three types of territorial change make intertemporal comparability problematic:

- national boundary changes;
- drastic changes in the organization of constituencies;
- minor changes of constituencies within the same framework of constituency organization.

The basic files used in the analysis contain results by *constituencies* (parliamentary constituencies, *Wahlkreise, circonscriptions, collegi, valgkredse*, etc.) and correspond to periods of time characterized by *continuous national boundaries and organization of constituencies*. The period covered by the files is determined by drastic changes in constituencies or national boundaries. Within these periods, minor boundary changes often occur, which, however, do not prevent the possibility of building a continuous file. Minor boundary changes include

- *addition of new units* (the Åland Islands in Finland in 1948);
- *disappearance of units* (the German constituencies of Elsaß-Lothringen were transferred to France after World War I);
- *merged units*: Two or more units are tied together (in Austria, Nordtirol and Lienz were merged to form Tirol in 1923);
- *split of units or secession*: A unit is divided into two or more units (Jura seceded from Berne, Switzerland, in the 1970s).

To keep as much continuity as possible in the data, territorial units that did not change keep their regional code throughout the entire file. With the creation or disappearance of territorial units in given election years, units are simply added or omitted. In cases of merger, the two or more old units disappear and a new unit is created. The same applies in cases of splitting of units (the old unit disappears, and two or more new units are created).[3]

In a few cases, to increase the intertemporal comparability of units, *upper levels of aggregation* are also used in the analysis. The aggregation of data makes it possible to build longer time series. The wish to give the data historical continuity implied the choice of upper levels of aggregation that were continuously applicable throughout the electoral history of a country, in particular for earlier periods. Whereas data for the most recent periods are available at very disaggregated levels, this was not always the case before World War I. Problems of aggregation arise with a large number of uncontested constituencies and missing information or with multiple voting systems. The choice of the level of aggregation used in the analysis is in many cases – especially for earlier historical periods – determined by available sources. Furthermore, in some cases, party votes are available only for higher levels of aggregation and not for constituencies (e.g., Italy 1861–1913). Table 2.2 gives the levels of aggregation of the data for each period. These are described in further details in Appendix 2. Levels of aggregation in the table are limited to two, even when there is a third level (details are specified in due course). Minor changes explain why the number of territorial units (*N*) varies within a same period.

---

[3] No estimates have been produced at the level of constituencies to make data comparable in the case of birth and death of units, mergers, and splits. It has been preferred to maintain the actual constituencies as the basic units of analysis.

Table 2.2. *Countries, Periods Covered, and Levels of Aggregation*

Country	Basic Territorial Units (Electoral Constituencies)			Aggregated Territorial Units (Second Tier or Administr. Units)		
	Unit	Period	N	Unit	Period	N
Austria	*Wahlkreise*	1919–70	25			
	Landeswk.	1971–94	9	*Länder*	1919–95	9
	Regionalwk.	1995	43			
Belgium	*Arrondissements adm.*	1847–98	41			
		1990–91	30	*Provinces*	1847–1995	9
	Circonscrip.	1995	20			
Denmark	*Valgkredse*	1849–1915	100–13			
		1918	110	*Amter*	1849–1968	22–23
	Amt- and *Storkredse*	1920–68	22–23			
	Storkredse	1971–98	17		1971–98	17
Finland	*Vaalipiirit*	1907–95	15–16			
France	See text			*Départements*	1910–97	88–96
Germany		1871–1912	382–97	*Staaten*	1912–71	25–26
		1919	36			
		1920–33	35			
		1949–61	242–47		1949–61	9–10
	Wahlkreise	1965–72	248		1965–87	10
		1976–87	248	*Länder*		
		1990–94	328			
		1998	328		1990–98	16
	Nomoí	1926–56	38–43			
Greece	Provinces	1928–33	98	Courts	1926–96	9–13
		1952	99			
	Nomoí	1958–96	55–6			
Iceland	*Kjördæmakosningar*	1874–1959	19–28	*Landskosningar*	1874–1995	1
		1959–95	8			
Ireland		1922	28			
		1923–33	30			
		1937–44	34			
		1948–57	40			
	Dáil constituencies	1961–65	38			
		1969–73	42			
		1977	42			
		1981–89	41			
		1992	41			
		1997	41			

Table 2.2. (*continued*)

Country	Basic Territorial Units (Electoral Constituencies)			Aggregated Territorial Units (Second Tier or Administr. Units)		
	Unit	Period	N	Unit	Period	N
Italy	*Collegi* or *circoscrizioni*	1861–1913	508			
		1882–90	135	*Regioni*	1861–1921	14–16
		1919	54			
		1921	40			
		1946–92	31–32		1946–96	20
	Collegi unin.	1994–96	475			
Netherlands	*Kiesdistricten*	1888–1917	100	Provinces	1888–1998	11–13
	Kieskringen	1918–98	18–20			
Norway	*Amter* and *kjøstædter*	1815–1903	38–58			
	Landdistrikt. and *kjøstæd.*	1906–18	123–26			
	Fylker	1921–49	29	*Fylker*	1921–97	19–20
		1953–97	19–20			
Portugal	*Círculos eleitorais*	1975–95	20			
Spain	*Provincias*	1977–96	52			
Sweden	*Valkretsar*	1866–1908	173–201			
		1911–20	56	*Län*	1866–1994	25
		1921–94	28–29			
		1998	29		1998	22
Switzerland	*Bezirke*	1848–1917	47–52	Cantons	1848–1999	25–26
	Cantons	1919–99	25–26			
United Kingdom		1832–80	333–52			
		1885–1910	542			
Britain	Parliamentary constituencies	1918–45	585–609			
		1950–70	613–18			
		1974–79	623			
		1983–92	633–34			
		1997	641			
Ireland		1832–80	64–66			
		1885–1910	101			
		1918	103			
Northern Ireland		1922–45	20			
		1950–79	12			
		1983–92	17			
		1997	18			

Format of the Data

The data on which the analysis is based have been completely computerized and standardized in different programs (Excel, SPSS, SAS) and are available on CD-ROM.[4] Furthermore, data are available in different forms, which is required for the computation of the different indices used for the analysis: (1) absolute figures, (2) percentage distribution of votes by parties (computed on the number of total valid votes; turnout is computed as the percentage of voters with respect to the number of persons entitled to vote), and (3) percentages of parties' vote distribution by constituencies. However, not all percentage figures can be computed, especially for earlier periods because of:

- *Missing information*, meaning that contested elections have taken place but information on the electorate, voters, or party votes is not available. Figures of *total valid votes* are in most cases based on the original sources. When these figures were missing, the total number of valid votes has been estimated on the basis of known party votes. If among party votes some are missing, the total number of valid votes includes only known information. The percentage of the parties' strength for which information is known is, in these cases, overestimated.
- *Uncontested constituencies*, meaning that only one candidate is present in a constituency and is declared elected without election (or two candidates in a two-member constituency, and so on). In some cases, the partisan affiliation of the elected candidate(s) is known and estimates have been produced (see the following discussion and Appendix 3).

In particular, missing information and uncontested constituencies prevent the computation of national totals, affecting the computation of a certain number of indices. For this reason, the analysis of earlier periods – for which missing information and uncontested constituencies are higher – is particularly problematic.[5] In the case of uncontested constituencies,

---

[4] Data are also available in three main files structures: (1) horizontal structure (election years and parties as variables and constituencies as cases); (2) vertical structure (basic cases are parties by constituencies and election years); and (3) mixed structure (variables are election years, and cases are parties and constituencies). In the mixed structure, however, there are two substructures: (a) parties are considered by their official name, so that a party that changed its name is considered a different case, and (b) parties are considered by their standard code, so that a party that changed its name is not considered a different case.

[5] Strictly speaking, in case of missing information at the constituency level, national totals should also be set as missing (even when only one unit is missing). This rule has not always been followed rigidly to increase the length of the time series.

different types of estimates have been produced. In most cases, all votes (100 percent) have been attributed to the winning party or candidate (if the party affiliation is known).

Electoral System Specificities

The computation of indices of homogeneity is also made problematic by the many features that characterize electoral systems. Following is a list of the main and more general problems encountered (the main one being the first). Country details are given in Appendix 4.

As far as types of votes are concerned:

- *Multiple voting*. In multiple voting, each voter has as many votes as there are seats to be filled, and the number of valid *votes* largely exceeds the number of valid *ballots* (since more votes can be cast on each ballot); thus the equivalence "voters/votes" is lost. This system concerns notably Belgium and Switzerland – for which figures based on the "fictitious voter" estimate have been made available by the *Bundesamt für Statistik* – but also the United Kingdom in multimember constituencies. Two types of figures in the dataset are available:

  1. Results based on *votes*, that is, as many votes as voters were allowed to cast on their ballot;
  2. *1:1 estimates* that trace back the information available on the vote to the "one voter/one vote" equivalence. Since the 1:1 estimates are standardized, these figures are preferred for comparative analysis.

- *Partial elections* (or staggered elections) were particularly frequent in Belgium up to 1919 (*renouvellement partiel des chambres*). This means that elections did not take place in all territorial units. Elections were most often held within approximately half of the constituencies.
- *Repeated-ballot systems*. Only first ballots are used for the computation of indices of homogeneity. Specific analyses are carried out on the number of second ballots held at a given election (see Chapter 6).
- *Two-vote systems*. Since 1953 in Germany voters have had two votes: *Erststimmen* and *Zweitstimmen*. Since seats are allocated on the basis of the second vote, the *Zweitstimmen* are used for the computation of indices of homogeneity (but at the level of the 242–328 *erststimmen Wahlkreise*). Since 1994 in Italy, 75 percent of the seats in the Chamber of Deputies have been allocated by plurality in single-member constituencies. The remaining 25 percent of the seats have been allocated by

PR in 26 multimember constituencies. PR votes have been used for the computation of indices (but at the level of the 475 *collegi uninominali*).

- *Unknown votes* (where the party affiliation of candidates or lists is not known) never enter the computations: This concerns Denmark, Iceland, Italy, and Sweden; for Denmark also, the *nej* votes against unopposed candidates are excluded.

As far as parties and candidates are concerned:

- *Candidate voting*. Under plurality systems, results are available for single candidates. In the United Kingdom and Denmark there were often two, three, or more candidates of the same party contesting the same constituency. *Candidate figures have been aggregated to obtain party votes*, and indices of homogeneity have been computed on the aggregated party variables.
- *Independent candidates* are excluded.

Units of Analysis

The design of the research permits us to avoid the major problem that ecological analyses face. Problems of ecological inference arise in the attempt to infer conclusions reached on the basis of analyses with territorial units down to the individual level. Robinson's article showed the extent to which such a procedure could lead to "ecological fallacies" (Robinson 1950). Put simply, "what is true on one level of aggregation is not necessarily true on another level of aggregation" (Berglund 1990: 1).[6]

[6] "[I]n 1950 life became more difficult for social scientists attempting the quantitative study of individual behavior" (Langbein and Lichtman 1978: 9). The neologism "ecology," created by E. Häckel (Dogan and Rokkan 1969a: 3), originally designated analyses focusing on the influence of the environment on human behavior. Ecological analyses also became synonymous with analyses that could not rely on individual-level data and had to rely on data collected on more aggregated – usually spatial – units. This has been the case notably for electoral studies for which individual-level data were not available until the development of survey techniques to overcome the "central challenge" of the secrecy of vote (Rokkan and Meyriat 1969: 4; see also Rokkan 1961). Robinson's article published in 1950 in the *American Sociological Review* undermined the assumption that correlations observed at the level of aggregated units could be inferred at the individual level. The term "ecological fallacy" became popular, and analyses based on ecological data were dropped in favor of emerging survey techniques for individual data collection. Crucial events for the recovery of ecological techniques were the International Social Science Consortium (ISSC) Symposium at Yale in 1963 and the International Sociology Association (ISA) World Congress at Evian in 1966 (see Merritt and Rokkan 1966; Dogan and Rokkan 1969b). For a general discussion see also Berglund and Thomsen (1990). See Alker (1969) for a typologization of ecological fallacies.

Given the goals of this research, the "basic option" (Rokkan et al. 1987: 286) is to keep the conclusions at the level at which the analysis was run and to exclude attempts to transfer results to individuals. The research on the processes of nationalization in Western Europe is above all a historical analysis of the evolutions of the *territorial structures* of partisan support and of the *spatial organization* of electoral behavior. The entire analysis remains at the level of ecological data without inferences at the individual level, although, as mentioned in Chapter 1, there have been attempts to infer individual attitudes from territorial structures.

What is usually understood under the label of "ecological analysis" is the relationship between two or more variables whose cases are territorial units. This research design implies that both dependent and independent variables are available at the same level of aggregation (problematic in case of electoral studies with a historical perspective). Constituency-level data, however, are used here to create *national values of vote homogeneity*. For each party at each election, the levels of nationalization constitute country values, which are systemic values insofar as they concern the whole political system. Consequently, explanatory factors for the understanding of country variations are also defined as "global attributes" (Dogan and Rokkan 1969a: 5). However, whereas for the dependent variable the analysis concerns "variations of within-nation variations," for the independent factors within-country variance does not occur.

As far as the territorial homogeneity of *party votes* is concerned, three *units of analysis* can be distinguished:

- *Individual political parties* (e.g., *Fine Gael*): Values of homogeneity of the support for a given party can be synchronic (at a given election or for a given period) or diachronic (evolution over time of the values).
- *Party systems* (e.g., Ireland): Such systemic values are obtained by aggregating party values in each party system and can again be synchronic or diachronic. In this aggregation, minor parties (mainly other parties and independent candidates) are excluded.
- *Party families* (e.g., conservatives): The aggregation of parties occurs *across* – instead of *within* – systems. In this case there is no space variation, for party families are Europeanwide units of analysis. As before, values of homogeneity of the support for a given party can be either synchronic or diachronic.

Differences in the level of homogeneity of voting behavior between European countries are caused by different factors than those causing differences between party families or time variations. As far as the explanatory research design is concerned, different *sets of hypotheses* must therefore be formulated according to which *dimension of variation* is considered. Comparative research has mainly considered space as the principal dimension of variation (see Lijphart 1971; Tilly 1984; Sartori 1991). Bartolini (1993) has stressed the need for a more rigorous treatment of *time* as a dimension of variation. Values of voting homogeneity, however, vary according to an additional dimension that arises from parties as units of analysis: partisan variation as differences between *individual parties* and between *party families*. The three dimensions can be combined in various ways. For a number of hypotheses, specific cases have been deliberately identified and selected by focusing on two parties or countries whose similarities or differences offer the possibility to highlight particular relationships. These relationships do not lead to generalizable conclusions. Nonetheless, they permit progressive refinement of the analysis and the combination of "paired comparisons" with macrocomparisons.[7]

Measures and Indices

Attempts to operationalize the territorial homogenization of electorates and party systems can be subdivided into two broad categories: (1) indices and measures based on single elections; and (2) indices and measures based on the *change* that occurred between two or more elections. The first type of operationalization includes mostly measures of dispersion that are typical of descriptive statistics, as well as other indices based on the *distribution of votes across regions at a given election*. These measures will be dealt with later. The second type of operationalization has given rise, as seen in Chapter 1, to major works on the nationalization of electoral politics. Instead of considering the distribution across regions of voting behavior at a single election, this approach considers the distribution across regions of the *rate of change between two or more elections*.

---

[7] An example that well illustrates this process of inquiry is Rokkan (1970b) on the growth and structuring of mass politics in Western Europe (part of a broader $2 \times 2 \times 2 \times 2$ scheme of comparison; see Rokkan 1970a). Paired differentiations allow one to combine "the need for maximal information about concrete developments" and "the need for conceptual parsimony" (Rokkan 1970b: 66). In another publication, Rokkan underlines the "greater potential value in the development of systematic macro-theory" of "the strategy of *paired comparisons*" permitting "a deepening of insights" and offering springboards for further model building and generating hypotheses (1970a: 52).

Here three forms of analysis can be distinguished:

- The *correlation between two (subsequent) elections*: Examples are Converse (1969) on a comparison between the United States and France, Hoschka and Schunck (1976) on the evolution of regional patterns of electoral support in West Germany between 1949 and 1976, and Pavsic (1985) on the homogenization of the main Italian political parties from 1953 to 1983;[8]
- The analysis of *uniform swings between two (subsequent) elections*: Examples are, among others, Butler and Stokes (1974: 140–51), Johnston (1981a, 1981b), Johnston and Hay (1982), McLean (1973), and Taylor, Gudgin, and Johnston (1986), all mostly on British elections or those with other plurality formulas;
- Models based on *the analysis of variance*: The main example is the debate in the *American Political Science Review* based on Stokes's model (see Stokes 1965, 1967) with contributions by Katz, Claggett et al., Carrothers and Stonecash, and Stokes himself (see footnote 3 in Chapter 1).

The fundamental prerequisite for indices measuring the change in the territorial distribution of voting behavior between two elections is the identical organization of constituencies. In the long-term historical perspective, therefore, these measures cannot be applied thoroughly. For this reason, this type of operationalization has not been considered in this analysis, which instead is based on indicators of dispersion of votes across regions at single elections that also allow for the analysis of the different political cleavages.

However, measures and indices of territorial homogeneity of voting behavior have certain problems. These indicators face in particular two main sources of bias:

- the *size of political parties* (which does not concern turnout);
- the *number of territorial units* (constituencies) on which measures of homogeneity are computed.

---

[8] The territorial homogenization of the vote that occurs between two elections is measured by considering the nonstandardized parameters (beta) of the bivariate regression between the disaggregated results (constituencies) of two elections, with election t on the horizontal axis and election $t + 1$ on the vertical axis. A slope of the regression line less than 1 (which corresponds to the slope of the bisector of the graph) corresponds to an increase in homogeneity between two elections (Schadee 1987).

The following reviews the attempts to operationalize the formation of national electorates and party systems, with particular attention to these two issues.[9]

Competition

The first operative definition of the nationalization of electoral behavior was formulated by Schattschneider (1960) in terms of the "competiveness" of the political system. Before 1896, the American electorate was nationalized insofar as "the major parties contested elections on remarkably equal terms throughout the country." In "1892 there were thirty-six states in which on the face of the returns something like a competitive party situation existed." By contrast, "by 1904 there remained only six states in which the parties were evenly matched" (Schattschneider 1960: 82–83). Therefore, the more numerous the states where two parties compete with equivalent forces, the more nationalized the electorate is. Competitiveness is here an indicator of homogeneous electoral forces across the country (see also Rokkan 1970a: 232).[10]

According to Urwin too, as for Schattschneider, "the simplest indicator of nationalization is the degree of partisan competition" (Urwin 1982a: 41). To operationalize this concept Urwin uses the *number of uncontested seats*, that is, the proportion of constituencies in which only one candidate is contesting the single seat to be returned. This technique is used to analyze the homogenization of electoral politics both in the United Kingdom and in Germany (Urwin 1982a, 1982b). Cornford (1970) develops a similar methodology focusing on the proportion of the *safe seats* for each political party. The analysis of safe seats is particularly useful for the early phases of electoral development, when these types of constituencies were frequent. The higher the number of uncontested constituencies, the lower the proportion of districts covered by parties. In the present work the analysis of uncontested constituencies is carried out in Chapter 6.

[9] The discussion is limited to the measures that have been employed in electoral analyses. Other measures, such as the Schutz index (1951) and the Gini index (1933), are omitted here, as they are used mostly with individual data, especially in the fields of income inequality and poverty (Monroe 1994). For inequality indices see also Atkinson (1970), Coulter (1989), Cowell (1977), and Moulin (1988).

[10] The equivalence between homogeneous voting and competitiveness is, however, not direct, as a hypothetical homogeneous distribution of votes across the country of 80 percent for party A and 20 percent for party B shows (see also Claggett, Flanigan, and Zingale 1984). For an analysis of the birth of competitive patterns in Europe see Caramani (2003a).

Territorial Coverage by Parties

A different approach to the territorial coverage by parties consists of considering the *number of constituencies in which a party is present* as a percentage of the total number of constituencies. For example, the *Volksunie* in Belgium is present (on average in all elections) in 57 percent of the constituencies, whereas the *Parti socialiste belge* (before it split according to the linguistic cleavage) is present in 96.47 percent of the constituencies. By considering the average of values across parties, one can obtain systemic measures (e.g., in Switzerland, 43.95 percent of the territory is covered by parties on average). This type of measure will be called "presence" or "coverage" and obviously does not apply to turnout (voters always cover 100 percent of the constituencies). Uncontested constituencies are considered to be covered by the party of the unopposed candidate.

Measures of Homogeneity of Voting Behavior

Whereas territorial coverage indicates the *spread* of parties across constituencies, measures of homogenization indicate the extent to which the *levels of electoral support are homogeneous* across all constituencies. A party can be present in all constituencies and still get heterogeneous support.

Statistics provide several possible ways to measure the dispersion of values. Most measures are based on the *dispersion of regional values around the national mean*. The *mean absolute deviation* (MAD), or "index of variation" for Rose and Urwin (1975: 24), is the sum of the deviations from each single value (the party's share of votes in a region) and the mean of all these values divided by the number of regions. Deviations are summed without regard to plus and minus signs (absolute values). Another solution to the problem of plus and minus signs is to square each deviation instead of taking absolute deviations. The measure in this case is the *mean squared deviation* (MSD). Measures that are more frequently used are the variance and the standard deviation. The *variance* (S^2) is the same as the MSD, except that instead of dividing the sum of squared deviations by the number of regions (n), the sum is divided by $n - 1$. The *standard deviation* (S) is simply the square root of the variance, which is taken to compensate for having squared the deviations in the variance.

Lee (1988) proposes an index based on the differences between the percentage a party obtains in each constituency and the national value. Absolute differences are summed and then divided by 2 to avoid double counting.

61

The *Lee index* corresponds to the MAD, except for the denominator, which is 2 instead of n (number of regions). This index is used by Budge and Hearl (1990) and by Hearl, Budge, and Pearson (1996).

The literature has often emphasized the limits and failings of some of these measures (Taylor and Johnston 1979: 152–53). In particular, it has been pointed out that the standard deviation and the MAD (index of variation) attribute higher values to large parties and lower values to small parties (Blalock 1972; see also Allison 1978) since they are computed from deviations from the party's mean vote. Indices take low levels of dispersion for very regionalized but small parties. Furthermore, the standard deviation and the MAD take higher values of dispersion when the number of regions is small. Finally, both are not standardized and therefore have no upper limit.

Therefore, other measures have sometimes been preferred, such as the *variability coefficient* (CV), which divides the standard deviation by the mean in an attempt to adjust the standard deviation for the size of parties. However, it has been argued that the CV is sensitive to differences in the size of the compared samples and universes, that is, the number of regions: The values of the CV diminish when the number of units increases (Martin and Gray 1971; Smithson 1982). This makes cross-national comparisons problematic. Furthermore, this index too has no upper limit and its values are highly dispersed.[11]

Several methods have attempted to adjust indices for both party size and number of regions. Dividing the core expression of the Lee index, for example, by the sum of the shares of the vote in individual regions (the national vote, in other words) eliminates the influence of the size of parties. This index is here named *index adjusted for party size and number of regions* (IPR) (see Appendix 3 for the formula); it varies between 0 and 1 and thus permits an easy interpretation. Rose and Urwin (1975), to compensate for the drawbacks of the standard deviation, have proposed the *cumulative regional inequality index* (CRII). This index aims to take into account the influences on the degree of homogeneity of differences in size (in terms of the number of electors) of territorial units.[12] The CRII is based on *percentages of parties' vote distribution by constituencies* rather than on *percentage distribution of votes*

---

[11] Ersson, Janda, and Lane use the *standardized and weighted variability coefficient* (SCVw). Unlike the CV, this coefficient takes the size of the regions (size of the electorate) into account, but it is biased with respect to the number of units (Ersson, Janda, and Lane 1985: 176).

[12] For a more general discussion of redistricting issues, see Grofman et al. (1982) and McLean and Butler (1996).

by parties or on *absolute figures*. It is computed by subtracting the percentage of votes obtained in one region (with respect to the national score) from the percentage of voters of that region, adding the absolute values of these differences, and dividing the result by 2. If divided by 100, this index too varies between 0 and 1. This measure, however, overestimates the differences in the size of regions and is not applicable to turnout levels since its computation is based on the difference between voters and party votes in each constituency.

For party support (not applicable to turnout), all previous indices have been computed on

- the *total number of constituencies* (with constituencies in which the party was not present coded "zero percent");
- the constituencies in which the party *was present* only (with constituencies in which the party was not present excluded from the computation of indices).

Turnout values of indices computed on all constituencies or on contested constituencies only are the same. For the CRII too, the distinction is not applicable since the index is computed on the basis of the differences between party votes' and voters' distributions. For the computation of indices, unopposed parties or candidates in uncontested constituencies have been estimated as receiving 100 percent of the votes. This applies to both single-member and multimember uncontested constituencies. Since voting did not take place in such constituencies, this estimation has been extended to turnout (although 100 percent of voters is overestimated, especially in earlier periods).

Verification of the Consistency of Indicators

A test of all these measures is carried out next in order to check empirically for the influence of levels of territorial aggregation and size of political parties.

Number and Size of Territorial Units

To what extent does the level of aggregation of election results actually influence the level of homogeneity as measured by the different indicators? This issue is particularly relevant as we compare different countries over different periods during which either majoritarian systems (based on

63

a large number of constituencies) or PR systems (with fewer and larger constituencies) were in force.

Generally, statisticians expect that the lower the number of territorial units the less variation across them because of the larger size of units and the elimination – through aggregation – of extreme and outlying values. Empirically, all indices seem to be characterized by some degree of increase in the level of territorial disparity when the number of constituencies increases (Figure 2.1).[13] There are, however, important differences between the indicators considered. The IPR and the CRII both vary between 0 and 1 and – as can be seen in the top graph – take higher values as the number of constituencies increases. The pattern is parallel. The variability coefficient (CV, not displayed in the figure because of scale differences) follows a similar trend. Similarly, the territorial coverage by parties decreases with a large number of constituencies. By contrast, the standard deviation and the mean deviations (MAD and MSD) seem to be less influenced by the number of constituencies (see the lower graph). Both follow a parallel pattern, and their values rise with the increasing number of constituencies in Denmark (1849–1915), Germany (1871–1912), and the Netherlands (1888–1917). The Lee index (also not displayed in the figure because of scale differences) follows a similar but accentuated pattern.

The lesson from this first test is therefore that measures adjusted for the size of parties (IRP, CV, and CRII) are more influenced by the number of constituencies than measures that are not adjusted for the size of parties (standard deviation, MAD, and territorial coverage).

Size of Political Parties

Consequently, the second empirical test concerns the size of political parties and its influence on the indicators. Two different indices of homogeneity can be distinguished: those influenced by the size of parties and those that control for the size of parties. According to Blalock (1972: 88), the correlation between the size of the units of analysis (in this case, parties) and the standard deviation is not intrinsically linked to its statistical formula. Rather, we *expect* that for large units the deviation from the mean value is also large and that for small units the deviation is small. In other

---

[13] There are no important differences between the figures obtained for turnout and those concerning party support. For this reason, the two graphs present results for party support only.

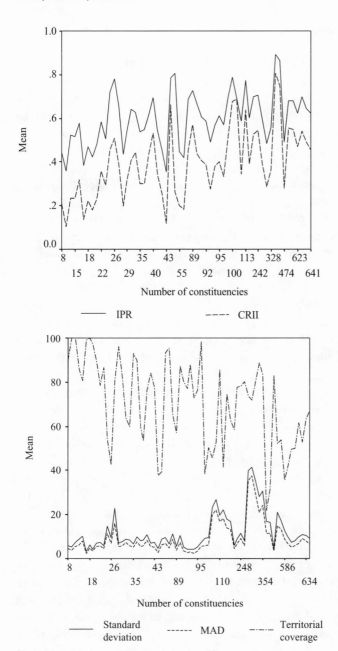

Figure 2.1 Frequency distribution of levels of territorial disparity according to the number of territorial units (8–641).

words, the correlation between the size of units and the standard deviation is empirical.

Results of the test of this relationship are displayed in Table 2.3. The correlation has been carried out for all indices used and for both party support and turnout (even though, for turnout, variations in size are less meaningful than for party figures). Party support figures are further subdivided between figures for all constituencies and figures for constituencies in which the party was present only. These latter figures are based on a smaller number of cases because, for parties that are present in one constituency only, no index has been produced since there is no variation.

According to the results, all indices appear to vary according to the size of parties (the mean votes polled across constituencies), either positively or negatively. In the first case, there are five indices that are positively correlated with party size (the larger the parties, the larger the levels of heterogeneity of regional support): MAD, MSD, standard deviation, variance, and the Lee index. In the second case, there are three indices that are (weakly) negatively correlated with party size, corresponding to the three adjusted indices: IPR, CRII, and CV. As far as the territorial coverage is concerned, the high coefficients indicate simply that the larger the party, the more territory it tends to cover and vice versa.

First, coefficients of correlation have been produced disregarding the number and size of territorial units (3,015 cases): Pearson's r values are all high, ranging between $\pm.33$ and $\pm.63$. In a second phase of the test, coefficients have been produced by controlling for the number and size of territorial units. As it appears, results do not vary drastically when the number of constituencies changes. The index that is most weakly influenced by the size of parties is the Lee index, although this changes when the number of constituencies increases. But this is true for all indices: *The higher the number of constituencies, the stronger the impact* (both positive and negative) *of the size of parties on the levels of territorial disparities* (especially when the number of constituencies is higher than 200).

As far as turnout is concerned, things look quite different. The number of cases (419) corresponds to the elections for which turnout figures are available. Territorial coverage does not apply to turnout since voters are always present in all constituencies (a constant value of 100 percent) and the CRII cannot be computed for turnout. All remaining indices are strongly negatively correlated with the size of turnout: *The larger the turnout, the smaller the differences in turnout rates between regions.* This finding must

Data, Indices, Method

Table 2.3. *Correlation (Pearson's r) Between the Size of Parties (and Levels of Turnout) and Levels of Homogeneity*

| Indices | Number of Units | National Mean of Constituency Levels of Party Votes (%) | | National Mean Of Constituency Levels of Turnout (%) |
		All Constituencies	Only Contested Constituencies	
Territorial coverage	Overall	.47 (3,015)	–	–
	1–50	.46 (1,962)		
	51–200	.47 (672)		
	Over 200	.66 (409)		
MAD	Overall	.63 (3,015)	.69 (2,930)	−.63 (419)
	1–50	.60 (1,962)	.69 (1,906)	−.73 (285)
	51–200	.69 (672)	.66 (647)	−.53 (92)
	Over 200	.69 (409)	.62 (406)	−.87 (43)
MSD	Overall	.50 (3,015)	.51 (2,930)	−.49 (419)
	1–50	.42 (1,962)	.46 (1,906)	−.63 (285)
	51–200	.59 (672)	.58 (647)	−.47 (92)
	Over 200	.63 (409)	.55 (406)	−.85 (43)
Standard deviation	Overall	.61 (3,015)	.67 (2,930)	−.66 (419)
	1–50	.57 (1,962)	.66 (1,906)	−.74 (285)
	51–200	.68 (672)	.63 (647)	−.54 (92)
	Over 200	.65 (409)	.64 (406)	−.88 (43)
Variance	Overall	.50 (3,015)	.48 (2,930)	−.49 (419)
	1–50	.42 (1,962)	.46 (1,906)	−.63 (285)
	51–200	.59 (672)	.48 (647)	−.47 (92)
	Over 200	.63 (409)	.54 (406)	−.85 (43)
Variability coefficient	Overall	−.42 (3,015)	−.38 (2,930)	−.74 (419)
	1–50	−.49 (1,962)	−.35 (1,906)	−.80 (285)
	51–200	−.51 (672)	−.46 (647)	−.63 (92)
	Over 200	−.48 (409)	−.51 (406)	−.92 (43)
Lee index	Overall	.33 (3,015)	.39 (2,930)	−.25 (419)
	1–50	.56 (1,962)	.67 (1,906)	−.62 (285)
	51–200	.65 (672)	.54 (647)	−.53 (92)
	Over 200	.69 (409)	.48 (406)	−.85 (43)
IPR	Overall	−.59 (3,015)	−.39 (2,930)	−.80 (419)
	1–50	−.58 (1,962)	−.37 (1,906)	−.85 (285)
	51–200	−.58 (672)	−.51 (647)	−.66 (92)
	Over 200	−.70 (409)	−.46 (406)	−.92 (43)
CRII	Overall	−.49 (3,015)	–	–
	1–50	−.51 (1,962)		
	51–200	−.40 (672)		
	Over 200	−.69 (409)		

Note: Computations exclude other parties and independent candidates, as well as second ballots, partial elections, *Erststimmen*, etc. The number of cases (parties for "party votes" and elections for "turnout") is given in parentheses.

be interpreted considering the generally high levels of turnout.[14] Further-more, low levels of turnout characterize earlier periods, when territorial disparities – as will be seen in the next chapter – were also stronger. Finally, these figures are strongly influenced by the low turnout rates of Switzer-land. If this country is left out, the Pearson's *r* indicate a weaker correlation (about .10 less on every index with the exception of the Lee index). However, this finding is also a first indication of the formation of mass electorates, with a parallel process of extension of voting rights to the masses and their progressive homogenization across regions.

Correlation Between Indicators

Finally, it is useful to know the degree of correlation between indicators themselves. It was seen in Figure 2.1 that the different indices follow two parallel patterns on the basis of whether or not they are adjusted for party size. This is confirmed by the correlation matrix in Table 2.4 between in-dicators for both party support (lower half of the table) and turnout (upper half).

Considering party support first, the table shows that indices that are adjusted for party size are strongly correlated with each other: The stan-dard deviation, variance, MAD, MSD, and Lee index are correlated from a minimum of .47 (between variance and the Lee index) to a maximum of .98 (between the standard deviation and the MAD). Between the variance and the MSD there is a perfect correlation of 1.00 since the two formulas are basically the same. On the other hand, these indices are weakly correlated

---

[14] The mean turnout rates computed across the constituencies of each country over the entire period are as follows:

Country	Turnout (%)	Number of Elections	Country	Turnout (%)	Number of Elections
Austria	90.81	21	Italy	72.56	33
Belgium	90.21	32	Netherlands	86.84	25
Denmark	74.39	44	Norway	67.53	24
Finland	67.58	32	Portugal	77.17	9
France	76.44	15	Spain	74.10	7
Germany	65.76	36	Sweden	76.90	29
Greece	77.61	15	Switzerland	58.11	44
Iceland	80.62	30	UK (Britain)	76.40	14
Ireland	73.16	10			

Note: The number of elections indicates those for which turnout figures are available.

Table 2.4. *Correlations (Pearson's r) Between Indicators for Party Support and Turnout*

Index	Coverage	S	Variance	CV	MAD	MSD	LEE	IPR	CRII
					Turnout				
Coverage		–	–	–	–	–	–	–	–
S	−.03		.93	.97	.99	.93	.48	.97	–
Variance	−.04	.90		.91	.96	1.00	.48	.85	–
CV	−.75	−.15	−.09		.97	.91	.43	.98	–
MAD	.03	.98	.88	−.21		.96	.50	.96	–
MSD	.03	.90	1.00	−.09	.88		.49	.84	–
LEE	−.08	.55	.47	−.05	.55	.48		.44	–
IPR	−.93	.05	.06	.72	−.01	.07	.06		–
CRII	−.93	.08	.11	.80	−.03	.11	.16	.95	
					Party Support				

Notes: N = 3,015 (party vote) and 419 (turnout). Territorial coverage and CRII are not applicable to turnout. For party support, indices have been considered for all constituencies.

with the indices that do not control for party size: CV, IPR, and CRII (from a minimum of −.01 to a maximum of .16). These indices too are strongly correlated with each other from a minimum of .72 (between CV and IPR) to a maximum of .95 (between IPR and CRII).

The percentage of territorial coverage, on the other hand, is weakly correlated with the indices not controlling for party size: standard deviation (−.03), variance (−.04), MAD (.03), MSD (.03), and Lee index (−.08). By contrast, the territorial coverage is strongly *negatively* correlated with the indices adjusted for party size: CV (−.75), IPR (−.93), and CRII (−.93). The more a party covers territory, the smaller the regional disparities. As far as turnout is concerned, all indices are strongly positively correlated, from a minimum of .43 (between the Lee index and the CV) to a maximum of .99 (between the MAD and the standard deviation).

In conclusion, all indices of territorial disparity are in some way influenced by both the number of territorial units and the size of parties. The three indices that are adjusted for party size (IPR, CRII, and CV) are more influenced by the number of territorial units and are negatively – but weakly – correlated with party size. The nonadjusted indices are less influenced by the number of territorial units and are positively correlated with party size. Furthermore, the impact of the size of parties is stronger with large numbers of constituencies. Finally, indices are strongly correlated with the other indices of the same group. This information is summarized in Figure 2.2.

Size of political parties (mean votes across constituencies)

		Sensible (positively)	Sensible (negatively)
Number of constituencies	Sensible	Territorial coverage (number of constituencies in which party is present as a percentage of the total number of constituencies)	Index adjusted for party size and number of regions (IPR), cumulative regional inequality index (CRII), and variability coefficient (CV)
	Non-sensible	Standard deviation (S), mean absolute deviation (MAD), mean sum deviation (MSD), variance (S^2), Lee index	—

Figure 2.2 Typology of indicators on the basis of their sensitivity to party size and number and size of territorial units.
Note: Only party support figures. Typology does not apply to electoral participation (turnout) figures.

The lesson of these three different empirical tests is that indicators must be used carefully and that they serve different purposes. The *comparison of parties and party families* (both synchronically and diachronically) necessitates indicators that are "blind" as much as possible to the size of parties; otherwise, the largest political families (e.g., socialists, Catholics) would always look less nationalized than the smaller ones (e.g., agrarians, communists, etc.). Furthermore, the comparison of parties belonging to the same family or within the same country must be based on indices controlling for their size.

On the other hand, in *the comparison of party systems*, that is, *elections or countries* (both synchronically and diachronically), the impact on regionalism of a large party should be considered more important than the impact of a small party. Conversely, the limited regionalization of a large party should be considered more important than the strong regionalization of a small party. In other words, in comparing countries, it is important to weight the size of parties. As will be seen, an important consequence concerns regionalist parties. These parties have a major influence on country values since their levels of territorial disparity are very high. In most cases, however, these parties are small and their impact on the party system is limited. If their importance is overestimated by using a technique that establishes the one-to-one equivalence between parties of very different sizes, the actual fragmentation of a system may be overlooked.

PART II

Evidence

3

Time and Space

EVIDENCE FROM THE HISTORICAL COMPARISON

Historical Trends in Europe

Figures 3.1 to 3.4 display the general historical evolution of the levels of territorial homogeneity of party support and turnout (for all countries) from the 1830s to the present, as measured by different indicators weighting for the size of parties. They show the basic result of this broad exploration: a *clear trend toward increasing nationally integrated electorates and homogeneous party systems over the past 150 years.*

As mentioned earlier, figures of turnout and party support measure distinct aspects of the nationalization of politics:

* *Turnout*: High territorial disparities in turnout indicate the survival of marginal areas in terms of socioeconomic development: economic structure – for example, the persistence of traditional society (an economically backward periphery) – literacy, certain forms of political culture (local clientelism or patronage), and so on; a pattern of homogeneous turnout rates, on the other hand, indicates how these marginal groups have been mobilized and integrated into the national political system.
* *Party support*: This is an indicator of the strength of the *territoriality of political cleavages* that emerged from the National and Industrial Revolutions: center–periphery and cultural cleavages (ethnolinguistic and religious cleavages in particular) and socioeconomic cleavages such as the urban–rural cleavage and the left–right opposition between wage earners on the one hand and employers and owners on the other.

The shape of the curves in these figures toward a reduction of territorial disparities indicates therefore *both the integration of electorates of peripheral regions and the reduction of the territoriality of political cleavages* over the nineteenth and twentieth centuries. During the period of time covered, territorial differences in electoral behavior within countries constantly decrease, and parties cover an increasing proportion of national territories with candidates and organizations. The fact that the same shape appears in the curves drawn using different indicators strengthens this basic finding. The empirical question of whether processes of territorial integration actually took place in Western Europe is therefore answered in the affirmative.

On the whole, the territorial heterogeneity of voting behavior decreased continuously from the 1850s to the 1990s; however, since the interwar period, the decrease of regional disparities has slowed (the Lee index and the variance even show a perfect stability of territorial configurations). On the one hand, the period up to World War I is characterized by *radical changes* in the territorial structuring of voting behaviour and partisan strength. On the other, the period since the 1920s is characterized by *stable territorial configurations* of party support and voter turnout.

To reduce the erratic shifts of measures based on single elections, data have been aggregated by decades. The number of countries included in the indices displayed in these figures increases progressively from 1 to 17 (as the dates in Table I.1 indicate). In Figures 3.1 and 3.2 the two solid lines represent values computed on all constituencies, whereas the two dashed lines represent values only for constituencies in which parties are present (the upper lines are the standard deviations and the lower ones are the MAD). Similarly, in Figure 3.2 the upper lines are the Lee index.

The two curves for all constituencies are parallel over the entire period, and so are the two curves for only the constituencies in which parties are present. Since the 1870s, the two groups of curves become increasingly close to each other. This is true for all four indicators. From the 1830s to the 1860s, the two types of measures are distinct because of the larger number of constituencies in which parties were not present. The approaching of the two types of measures is therefore an indication of the *increasing spread of parties across constituencies in the early phases of electoral history*. This evidence is confirmed by the average percentage of constituencies in which parties are present over the total number of constituencies (Figure 3.4). For two decades – from the 1840s to the 1860s – there is a reduction of the share of constituencies in which parties are present, mainly as a result of the inclusion of data from Belgium, Denmark, and Switzerland in 1847–48 and from Germany in 1871. From the 1870s and 1880s until World War I, however, there is a rapid and constant increase in the share of constituencies in which parties contest elections.

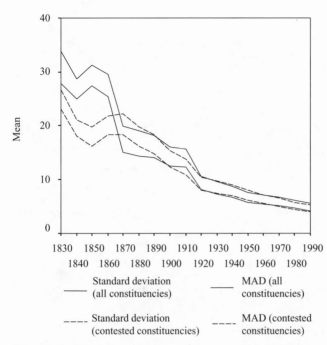

Figure 3.1 The reduction of territorial heterogeneity of party support in Europe: 1830s–1990s (standard deviation and MAD).

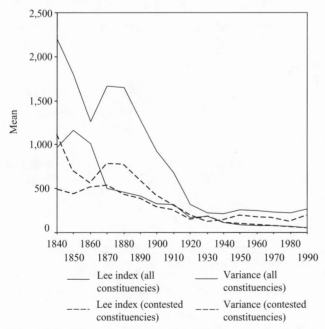

Figure 3.2 The reduction of territorial heterogeneity of party support in Europe: 1830s–1990s (Lee index and variance).

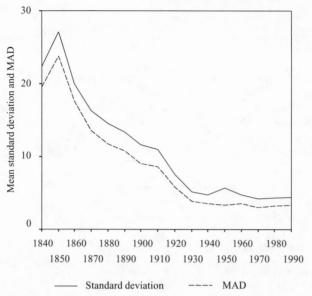

Figure 3.3 The reduction of territorial heterogeneity of turnout in Europe: 1830s–1990s.

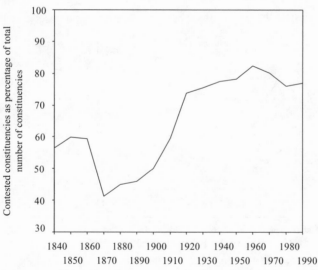

Figure 3.4 Evolution of the territorial coverage by parties in Europe: 1830s–1990s.

The numerical data on which these curves are based are presented in Table 3.1. The whole period is subdivided into three main periods corresponding to:

- 1830s–1910s: *restricted suffrage and majoritarian electoral systems*;
- 1920s–40s: major *massification of politics* in Europe (extension of voting rights, PR, mass parties);
- 1950s–90s: *stable mass democracies*, ending with the most recent elections published by 1999.

In this table the overall number of cases for party votes is 3,015 (each party is a case at a given election). The number of cases is slightly smaller for measures based on contested constituencies only, since parties that are present in only one constituency are excluded from computation (there is no territorial variation). The number of such cases is 180 over the entire period and for all countries. The overall number of cases for turnout corresponds to that of elections.[1] Most elections considered took place after World War II (219 elections). Voting always takes place in all constituencies (there are almost no uncontested constituencies during this period). Table 3.1 confirms through all indicators the general temporal trend over the three periods of time distinguished: There is *a constant decrease in the values of territorial heterogeneity of voting behavior from the first to the third period*. This is true for both party vote and turnout and for the two types of indices. The two main exceptions are the CV, on which the mean size of the party has a strong influence (as well as the IPR as far as contested constituencies are concerned), and the percentage of territory covered by parties. According to the latter indicator, the level of territorial coverage stabilizes after World War I.

Furthermore, *electoral participation displays lower levels of territorial disparities compared to party vote*. European voting behavior is more nationalized as far as turnout is concerned than party support. All indices show a significant discrepancy between the degree of territorial homogeneity of turnout and the electoral support for political parties. While party vote reflects the existence of cleavages attesting to differences in interests and values among territorially divided social groups, regional differences in turnout levels attest to marginal and peripheral positions of certain cultural and

---

[1] The number of elections considered is 535. However, given a certain amount of missing data, the number of elections for which turnout figures are available is 419.

economic groups and, more generally, to a lower degree of integration in the institutionalized forms of political participation.

Finally, there are no significant differences between the values of indices computed only on constituencies in which a party is present (leaving out the constituencies in which the party was not present) and the values of indices computed with these constituencies (with a value of zero percent of support). Although one may have expected greater homogeneity of support among contested constituencies only, it should be considered that these measures leave out the 180 highly regionalized parties that contested one constituency only (for which no territorial variation applies).

Although the process of nationalization of voting behavior is *continuous* – starting with the beginning of competitive parliamentary elections – what appears from this evidence is that the formation of national electorates and party systems took place "early" in the electoral and political history of Europe, that is, before World War I. This means that it is a typical process of the *first phases of the structuring of cleavage constellations and party systems*. All figures show that the nationalization of voting behavior took place before World War I. What we observe, therefore, is that the erosion of territorial cleavages is a process occurring in *two phases*. Territorial diversity of voting behavior decreases until World War I and then remains stable. As will be seen in Chapter 6 on the interpretation of these trends, from the mid-nineteenth century until World War I, European societies – and their electorates and party systems – became increasingly homogeneous under the pressure of macroprocesses, among which the most important are:

- the social and spatial mobility created by *industrialization and urbanization*, which led to the hegemony of the left–right cleavage;
- the processes of *state formation* and *nation-building*, that is, the construction of national citizenship, the standardization of language (compulsory education), national religions (in the Protestant countries), and the increasing intervention of states in various spheres of the national economies and welfare policies;
- the development of *communication technologies*.

These are all processes of the nineteenth century. However, World War I appears as the moment of conclusion of these nationalizing trends. It is the moment in which the major steps and progress of democratization and enlargement of mass participation – a process displayed throughout the nineteenth century – took a crucial turn. This historical turn corresponds

Table 3.1. *Levels of Territorial Disparities in Three Different Historical Periods (Several Indices)*

	Party Vote				Turnout			
Indices	1830s–1910s	1920s–40s	1950s–90s	Entire Period	1830s–1910s	1920s–40s	1950s–90s	Entire Period
	All Constituencies							
Coverage (%)	52.19	75.04	77.73	70.70	100.00	100.00	100.00	100.00
Standard dev.	18.49	9.59	6.58	10.10	14.35	5.96	4.43	7.58
Variance	461.81	151.19	70.81	180.77	263.61	53.44	30.69	102.24
CV	1.89	1.45	1.24	1.45	.24	.09	.06	.12
MAD	14.65	7.25	4.98	7.14	11.76	4.56	3.24	5.95
MSD	453.38	145.73	68.41	176.23	256.82	51.32	29.64	99.33
Lee	1,162.10	248.60	231.99	450.50	504.19	69.94	165.88	245.49
IPR	.72	.61	.54	.60	.30	.17	.14	.19
CRII	.55	.36	.32	.38	–	–	–	–
N	(695)	(744)	(1,576)	(3,015)	(121)	(79)	(219)	(419)
	Only Contested Constituencies							
Standard dev.	17.43	9.86	6.54	9.87	–	–	–	–
Variance	364.61	154.11	75.09	161.38	–	–	–	–
CV	.58	.63	.49	.55	–	–	–	–
MAD	14.15	7.54	5.00	7.74	–	–	–	–
MSD	345.95	141.67	65.41	148.82	–	–	–	–
Lee	560.49	167.57	173.42	261.28	–	–	–	–
IPR	.49	.50	.43	.46	–	–	–	–
N	(678)	(719)	(1,534)	(2,931)	–	–	–	–

Notes: Territorial coverage is not applicable to turnout and identical between "all constituencies" and "only contested constituencies." CRII is not applicable to both turnout and "only contested constituencies." Cases: parties for "party vote" and elections for "turnout."

to the "massification" of politics: first, the almost general introduction of *male universal suffrage* and the enfranchisement of women in several cases; second, the organization of *mass parties for the mobilization of electorates*; third, the almost general introduction of *PR* as a strong incentive for parties to spread in all constituencies of a country, also in those in which they had weak support; and, finally, the use of campaign techniques based on *mass communication*.

The process of nationalization of electorates and party systems, therefore, took place mainly *before World War I and stabilized with the full mobilization and integration of the newly enfranchised electorates* during the interwar period. By contrast, *the period after World War II is a period of fundamental stability of territorial configurations*. The period from 1945 to the present has been characterized by great stability in the levels of territorial disparity. The curves displayed in Figures 3.1 to 3.4 indicate the impossibility of compressing further the already small territorial diversity in preferences, attitudes, and behavior. This also means that no factor intervening after World War II was able to modify the territorial structures: (1) neither the *further development of communication technologies* (through electronic media); (2) nor the *transformation of social structures* from agrarian societies to postindustrial and service economies or the process of secularisation of Western societies; (3) nor, finally, the *transformation of political parties* from mass into broader catchall parties deprived of solid socioelectoral bases and ideologies.

All these macrotransformations did not affect the structure of consolidated territorial configurations, confirming results of other long-term electoral analyses, namely, those of the "freezing hypothesis" (Lipset and Rokkan 1967a; Pedersen 1983; Bartolini and Mair 1990). Territorial configurations and electoral behavior crystallized after World War I and remained stable in the following decades. These findings are also supported by results of previous research conducted on the territoriality of cleavages: "the evidence refutes the hypothesis asserting that nationalizing trends have followed from affluence as envisaged in the social science literature of a decade ago.... [T]he amount of change in the [second] post-war era has been very limited in magnitude" (Rose and Urwin 1975: 45). This hypothesis had been formulated on the basis of American research (Stokes 1967; Claggett, Flanigan, and Zingale 1984). Indeed, in Europe too the levels of diversity continued to decrease after World War II. Previous work, however, was limited to the post–World War II period. The empirical data presented in this chapter not only reject the hypothesis that affluence after World War II was a major determinant of the nationalization of electorates and party systems, but in addition reveal that nationalization processes occurred *from the very beginning of competitive elections* up to World War I, that is, before the major steps toward the full democratization of Western electorates. Changes after World War I were minor compared to the processes of the nineteenth and early twentieth centuries, showing that other factors have shaped European electorates.

As far as the more recent developments of electorates and party systems are concerned, renewed attention in the literature has recently been devoted to the recrudescence of regionalism and to a process of denationalization of political identities and attitudes. This has been caused partly by the democratic transitions in Central and Eastern Europe, territories characterized by strong ethnic and linguistic diversity, historically even stronger than the cultural diversity of Western Europe (Flora 1999: 88). In several cases, the end of communist rule has meant a reawakening of ethnic and nationalist identities. In Western Europe, however, recent trends since the 1960s do not indicate drastic increases in regionalization as far as party votes are concerned (see Figure 3.5). In this figure, elections have been grouped by five-year intervals, and the 1995 value includes elections up to 1999. Whereas from the 1960s to the end of the 1990s the curve for party support slightly declines, the curve for turnout remains fundamentally stable since the 1970s.

Among the countries considered here, three in particular have been characterized in recent times by trends toward increasing regional diversity: Belgium, Italy, and Britain. However, they do not affect the general European trends displayed in Figures 3.1 to 3.4. These countries are the only ones displaying in the past decades trends toward more territorial heterogeneity of electoral behavior among the 17 countries considered in this study. In Belgium, the main political parties divided along linguistic lines (Walloon vs. Flemish) during the 1960s and 1970s: The Catholics divided in 1968, the Liberals in 1974, and the Socialists in 1977. Even the Greens were formed as two separate parties: *Ecolo* (1978) and *Agalev* (1982). Since then these linguistic wings have been dealt with separately, which influences the levels of territorial diversity in this country. In Italy, the 1990s were characterized by the rise of one main large regionalist party (the *Lega Nord*) and by several minor parties such as the *Lega di azione meridionale*, besides the traditional regional parties of the French-speaking minority in

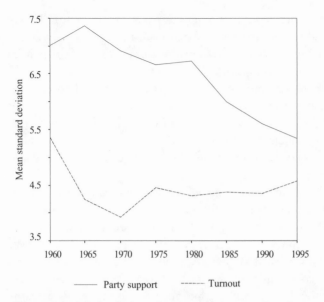

Figure 3.5 The evolution of territorial heterogeneity of turnout and party support in Europe: 1960s–90s.

Valle d'Aosta and in South Tyrol. In Britain, finally, both the impact of a reterritorialization of the Labour and Conservative parties and the increase of support for the Scottish National Party and *Plaid Cymru* have led to an increase in territorial politics, although the merger between the Liberals and the Social Democrats has reduced the territoriality of a great deal of electoral behavior in this country.

Furthermore, since the 1970s, figures for Spain have been included. However, in Spain regionalist parties are numerous but small. The main parties of the Spanish system are nationalized parties (*Partido popular, Partido socialista obrero español, Izquierda unida*, and, until 1982, the *Unión del centro democrático*), and a measure adjusted for the size of parties strongly reduces the impact of regionalized but small parties. The specificities of each national case lead us to the comparative investigation in the remainder of this chapter and in the next.

The Comparative Study of Countries: From Party to Party System Measures

The rest of this chapter deals primarily with the descriptive aspects of the differences and similarities between countries and with the transformations of their territorial structures of electoral behavior over time. The following chapter is devoted to the country description and to typologies of territorial configurations. Chapter 7 considers more systematically the explanatory factors accounting for the similarities and differences between systems. First, however, a brief discussion about the appropriate measures to be used in cross-national comparison is necessary.

Having seen in Chapter 2 how the homogeneity of the vote for single parties can be measured, we must consider how these indices can be used for the measurement of *systemic values* of homogeneity, that is, the extent to which an *entire party system* is homogeneous or territorially fragmented. This is crucial for comparing countries. The fundamental principle is that, to compare countries, within each system *small parties and large parties should have different weights*. The aggregation of measures from individual parties into systemic values must therefore adjust for the size of parties. This is not a problem for those indices that, as seen in Chapter 2, are adjusted for party size: MAD, MSD, variance, standard deviation, and Lee index. For indices that do not weight the size of parties (CV, IPR, CRII), however, the values of each party must be multiplied by the mean share of its vote in the regions.

Second, to obtain the level of homogeneity of a party system, we put together party values, as many as there are parties according to the 5 percent criterion at each election.[2] There are many ways of computing party system values. The most straightforward way is to take the *mean* of party values (e.g., of the standard deviation: *mean standard deviation*). In this way, however, small parties (which have small values of territorial differentiation because they are weighted by size) have a strong homogenizing effect on the overall system figure. This chapter therefore also includes different aggregated partisan figures, namely, through the *sum* (the *cumulative standard deviation*). This approach has the advantage of reducing the homogenizing effect of small parties on the party system as a whole and, consequently, controls for the format of party systems: A system with many small parties (a fragmented party system) will always appear more homogeneous than a system with few large parties (a two-party system).[3]

The sum of individual party values too, however, is sensitive to the number of parties. The greater the number of parties, the higher systems'

[2] This criterion is that only parties receiving at least 5 percent of the vote within at least one constituency (meaning that they may receive less than 5 percent nationwide) have been considered in the computation of indices at each single election.
[3] The sum must, of course, be divided by the number of elections.

measures of territorial differentiation. Therefore, although the sum is useful to compare systems within the same periods of time, it is not appropriate in a *historical perspective* (the number of parties increases toward the end of the nineteenth century and with the introduction of PR).[4]

Homogeneous versus Heterogeneous Territorial Systems

The first part of this chapter has shown a clear evolution of electorates and party systems toward increasingly homogeneous electoral behavior across regions before World War I. The period before the war was characterized by higher levels of territorial differentiation. Including countries for which data are available before World War I would therefore distort the comparison with countries for which data are available only for more recent times. Also the interruption of democratic life in several countries and the suspension of elections that affected other countries during the interwar period because of war and occupation (Austria 1930–45, Finland 1939–45, France 1936–45, Germany 1933–49, Greece 1936–46, Italy 1922–46, the Netherlands 1937–46, Norway 1936–45, the United Kingdom 1935–45) would alter the overall comparison of systemic values of territorial heterogeneity. For these reasons, to carry out the comparison of countries, the period from World War II to the present has been considered first instead of the entire period. After this first exploration, evidence will be broken down for earlier periods as well.

Overall Comparative Figures Since World War II

The main results of the country comparison are presented in Table 3.2 and Table 3.3 (for party support and electoral participation respectively). In both tables, countries are ordered on the basis of the standard deviation computed on all constituencies. According to the cumulative standard deviation, the most regionalized country in Europe since 1945 for party support is Switzerland, with an average value over elections of 98.30.[5] By contrast, the

---

[4] To avoid this, the threshold for inclusion in the computation of indices has been increased from 5 percent within at least one constituency to 7 percent nationwide. This seems to be the best compromise to control for differences in the number of parties (over time and across countries) as well as party turnover, i.e., the influence of sporadic parties.

[5] The territoriality of the Swiss party system is partly increased by the correspondence between historically and culturally defined cantons, on the one hand, and electoral constituencies, on the other. In all other cases, constituencies cut across historical and cultural boundaries.

most nationalized country is Sweden, with a value corresponding roughly to a fourth of the Swiss one: 24.32. Among the countries with the most heterogeneous party support, there are four additional countries for which the standard deviation is above 50.00: Belgium, Finland, Spain, and Germany. Italy and Britain approach this group. On the other hand, Greece, Denmark, and Austria approach Sweden as the most homogeneous countries, with values below 30.00. Between these two groups there is an intermediate group of countries displaying values ranging from 32.88 for Ireland to 42.35 for Portugal (this group also includes the Netherlands, Iceland, Norway, and France).

In addition to the standard deviation, Table 3.2 includes two measures weighted according to the size of parties: IPRw and CRIIw. The two indices present few differences with respect to the rank ordering of the standard deviation (mainly Germany and Britain, which appear more regionalized according to the IPR, and Belgium and Germany according to the CRII).

Larger discrepancies with the ranking of the standard deviations can be observed when one considers the *number of constituencies in which parties are present as a percentage of the total number of constituencies* (territorial coverage). According to this measure, which – unlike the other measures considered here – does not take into account the size of the parties, the two systems that appear most regionalized are Spain and Switzerland, the only two countries for which the average percentage of territorial coverage is below the half of the constituencies. In the case of Spain, the proportion of territory covered by parties on average is only 37.81 percent and, in the case of Switzerland, 42.09 percent. The most nationalized party systems, according to this measure, are Austria, the Netherlands, Norway, and Sweden, where parties, on average, cover more than 95 percent of the constituencies.

Spain is characterized by a more homogeneous territorial structure when measures of homogeneity are considered, whereas it appears as a highly regionalized country when the degree of territorial coverage is taken as an indicator. This can be explained by the large number of territorially concentrated regionalist parties, which, however, are very small and have a small weight in the aggregated measures of dispersion controlling for the size of parties. By contrast, for Switzerland there is no inconsistency between the degree of territorial coverage and the measures of homogeneity, both indicating a regionalized structure. It is the larger parties of the system that are characterized by very diverse support across regions. Among the

Table 3.2. Levels of Territorial Heterogeneity by Country (Party Support): World War II–Present

Country	First Election Considered	All Constituencies					Contested Constituencies Only			Number of Elections
		Coverage (Mean %)	S	IPRw	CRIIw	N	S	IPRw	N	
Switzerland	1947	42.09	98.30	57.20	26.40	(128)	95.20	76.60	(120)	13
Belgium	1946	59.42	78.12	56.67	33.04	(123)	46.91	54.93	(122)	17
Finland	1945	85.52	66.06	47.75	20.00	(96)	70.65	57.65	(96)	15
Spain	1977	37.81	56.67	38.05	17.83	(86)	65.07	72.72	(81)	7
Germany	1949	77.87	55.67	42.40	21.10	(78)	36.56	45.36	(78)	14
Italy	1946	76.51	48.25	37.61	14.99	(134)	70.57	61.38	(124)	14
UK-Britain	1945	55.09	47.37	40.56	17.79	(73)	54.98	52.54	(73)	15
Portugal	1975	90.73	42.35	38.09	13.32	(41)	37.87	40.03	(41)	9
Netherlands	1946	99.90	37.74	36.56	14.35	(100)	37.74	36.56	(100)	16
Iceland	1946	91.80	37.47	38.59	16.05	(76)	35.70	38.19	(71)	16
Norway	1945	95.63	34.29	36.23	13.38	(84)	32.94	36.23	(83)	14
France	1946	96.12	34.23	31.61	12.35	(122)	32.90	31.74	(122)	15
Ireland	1944	71.15	32.88	32.08	12.65	(75)	32.78	37.14	(75)	16
Greece	1946	90.17	29.12	30.56	9.64	(78)	29.06	32.21	(77)	18
Denmark	1945	94.88	28.41	31.88	10.72	(152)	27.72	31.75	(145)	22
Austria	1945	96.75	24.86	31.68	9.11	(59)	24.73	31.66	(59)	16
Sweden	1944	98.64	24.32	30.27	10.31	(92)	24.61	30.47	(92)	18

Notes: The number of cases (parties) is given in parentheses. The number of constituencies in which parties are presentas a percentage of the total number of constituencies is not applicable to "contested constituencies only." The same applies to the CRII.

Legend: S = standard deviation; IPRw and CRIIw = weighted measures. For other abbreviations see Abbreviations and Symbols in the front matter.

Table 3.3. *Levels of Territorial Heterogeneity by Country (Turnout): World War II–Present*

Country	First Election Considered	Standard Deviation	Variance	MAD	MSD	N
Switzerland	1947	14.32	212.66	10.59	205.88	(12)
Finland	1945	7.82	64.29	3.90	60.08	(13)
Germany	1949	6.49	23.02	2.55	22.15	(13)
Greece	1946	6.47	43.44	4.94	42.66	(15)
Spain	1977	6.01	36.68	4.48	35.98	(7)
UK-Britain	1945	5.75	34.51	4.14	34.46	(14)
Italy	1946	5.62	33.67	4.59	33.40	(12)
Portugal	1975	4.88	33.52	3.34	31.84	(9)
Ireland	1944	4.85	24.14	3.79	23.55	(10)
Norway	1945	3.79	15.37	2.84	14.58	(12)
France	1946	3.40	11.82	2.56	11.69	(13)
Austria	1945	3.37	13.24	2.69	12.06	(14)
Netherlands	1946	3.20	12.74	2.52	12.07	(14)
Denmark	1945	1.99	4.02	1.45	3.79	(16)
Sweden	1944	1.54	2.91	1.21	2.81	(16)
Belgium	1946	1.47	2.25	1.19	2.17	(15)
Iceland	1946	1.47	2.64	1.13	2.44	(14)

Notes: For UK (Britain), the computation of turnout rates is based on valid votes instead of voters.
Legend: N = number of elections (not necessarily identical to number of elections for party votes due to missing information).

countries in which, on average, parties cover a reduced portion of the territory, Belgium (59.42 percent) and Britain (55.09 percent) must also be included. For all other countries, the percentage of constituencies contested by parties as a percentage of the total number of constituencies is above 70 percent.

If we now look at the right-hand half of Table 3.2, where values computed on the contested constituencies only are displayed, we see that for Belgium and Germany party support across regions is significantly more homogeneous. This indicates clear territorial sections with large differences *between* solid areas and small disparities *within* these areas. This is not the case for those countries in which the differences within areas are as large as (Switzerland) or even larger than (Italy, Finland, Britain, and Spain) those between areas, indicating territorial differences but no large solid zones. For Spain, the fact that the standard deviation remains low when contested constituencies alone are considered confirms the limited influence on the entire system of the many but small regionalist parties.

As it clearly stands out in Table 3.3, Switzerland is the territorial system with the most regionalized *turnout rates* (according to the mean standard deviation), with a score of 14.32. Because of the large differences in electoral participation from canton to canton, Switzerland displays disparities almost twice as high as those of Finland, which is the most regionalized of the remaining countries on the basis of this indicator. This table also confirms that *turnout levels are more homogeneous than levels of party support*. In reality, the difference between the nationalization of party support and turnout would be even larger if Switzerland did not influence the overall disparity of electoral participation so strongly. Furthermore, leaving aside the outlier Switzerland, the levels of nationalization of turnout are concentrated within a more restricted range of values compared to party support. The remaining indicators strengthen this finding with the exception of the variance and MSD (two very similar measures), according to which Germany appears as more uniform.

Trends in the 1990s

In spite of general stability in the levels of territorial homogeneity of voting behavior since World War II, a closer analysis of the period after 1945 reveals a certain number of shifts in the rank ordering between countries. Table 3.4 considers the levels of regionalization in the 1990s. The number of elections that have been considered to compose this table varies according to countries, between two and three in the past decade. The most regionalized country in the past 10 years is Belgium, which is much more regionalized than it was in the past and compared to most other countries (the values of territorial disparity are slightly larger than those for Switzerland). For the remaining countries, the rank order does not change drastically.

As far as territorial coverage by the parties is concerned, there are five countries for which all parties cover 100 percent of the constituencies in the 1990s (Austria, Denmark, Norway, Portugal, and Sweden) and two for which the percentage is almost the highest (Greece and the Netherlands). For Germany the number of contested constituencies by parties on average increased in the past decade despite the presence of one main new regionalized party (the *Partei des demokratischen Sozialismus*), which receives its support mainly in the new *Länder* as a consequence of reunification in 1990. The lowest degree of territorial coverage again characterizes Belgium,

Table 3.4. *Levels of Territorial Heterogeneity by Country in the 1990s (Party Support)*

Country	Period of Elections	Coverage (Mean %)	All Constituencies				Contested Constituencies Only			Number of Elections
			S	IPRw	CRIIw	N	S	IPRw	N	
Belgium	1991–95	51.08	102.91	68.91	43.84	(23)	54.99	64.16	(23)	2
Switzerland	1991–95	41.62	102.02	57.84	26.86	(28)	95.12	72.96	(24)	2
Finland	1991–95	85.33	67.82	47.34	19.84	(15)	75.50	60.20	(15)	2
Spain	1993–96	27.42	57.58	36.57	17.56	(27)	64.52	76.27	(24)	2
Italy	1992–96	77.01	55.82	41.41	19.10	(39)	63.32	53.26	(37)	3
Germany	1990–98	80.19	55.08	40.86	20.22	(20)	35.89	43.08	(20)	3
UK-Britain	1992–97	65.32	53.95	43.90	20.64	(11)	63.74	56.05	(11)	2
Ireland	1992–97	65.24	44.19	37.74	16.54	(16)	45.14	43.19	(16)	2
France	1993–97	98.02	34.20	32.19	12.07	(15)	32.90	32.30	(15)	2
Iceland	1991–95	86.53	31.87	35.57	13.38	(13)	28.05	34.22	(11)	2
Norway	1993–97	100.00	28.52	33.03	10.90	(15)	28.52	33.03	(15)	2
Netherlands	1994–98	99.44	28.32	31.41	8.63	(18)	28.32	31.41	(18)	2
Portugal	1991–95	100.00	26.11	30.48	7.91	(8)	26.11	30.48	(8)	2
Austria	1990–95	100.00	24.60	31.27	8.09	(15)	24.60	31.27	(15)	3
Denmark	1990–98	100.00	23.28	28.41	7.66	(24)	23.28	28.41	(24)	3
Sweden	1991–98	100.00	22.28	29.12	9.52	(22)	22.28	29.12	(22)	3
Greece	1990–96	98.88	18.90	24.92	5.99	(16)	16.32	23.81	(16)	3

Notes: The number of cases (parties) is given in parentheses. The number of constituencies in which parties are present as a percentage of the total number of constituencies not applicable to "contested constituencies only." The same applies to the CRII.

Legend: S = standard deviation; IPRw and CRIIw = weighted measures. For other abbreviations see Abbreviations and Symbols in the front matter.

Switzerland, and, above all, Spain, for which the value is 27.42 percent in the two elections of 1993 and 1996.

Finally, if we look at the values computed on contested constituencies only, Belgium is characterized by strong territoriality of the ethnolinguistic cleavage. Two solid regions appear very distinctively (the right-hand side of Table 3.4) that are very homogeneous internally (the cumulative standard deviation computed on contested constituencies only is 54.99 against 102.91). A similar case is represented by Germany, whose value (35.89) reflects more the territorial distinctiveness of Bavaria than that of eastern Germany.

In Figure 3.6 the overall post–World War II figures have been broken down by decade to show the comparative evolution of the countries during this period. In this figure the distribution of the cumulative standard deviation has been standardized to vary between 0 and 1.[6] The figure confirms in the first place the stability of most countries, with a slight tendency toward nationalization. The most dramatic cases of nationalization are those of Greece (between the 1940s and the 1960s), France (from the 1950s on), the Netherlands, and Iceland. Higher levels of territoriality in the 1940s can also be noted for Britain (and Germany, where, however, only the 1949 election took place during this decade). In general, there is a stabilizing pattern after World War II, with many small and sporadic parties making a brief appearance (this was the case notably in Germany, but also in France with the *Poujadistes* and in Italy with the *Uomo qualunque*). The last country for which rapid nationalization can be observed is Portugal, although this occurs in a later period, as the first election took place in 1975. Spain, the other Iberian country, by contrast, remains stable after the 1970s as a regionalized country. For two countries, the level of regionalization is stable and high: Switzerland and Finland. In three cases we see that countries have become more regionalized in recent decades: Belgium, Italy, and Britain (as well as Ireland).

The Historical Evolution Toward More Homogeneous Territorial Systems

The small range in levels of regionalization between countries in recent periods suggests an earlier convergence toward more similar and homogeneous territorial structures. It is therefore interesting to analyze earlier

[6] Although the scale has in principle no upper limit.

90

periods of electoral history and the historical evolution of these structures. The analysis now turns to the long-term dynamic comparison of the nationalization of electoral politics.

Plotting the curves for each country allows for the description of the peculiarities of each national evolution. In several cases, the presence of outliers can influence the shape of the curve, hindering the detection of the overall trend. Outlying cases are small parties that – according to the 5 percent criterion – were grouped into the "other parties/dispersed votes" category (thus not entering the computation of indices) for some elections but not for all. To avoid these erratic movements of the curves, data have been presented for five-year intervals instead of single elections. Furthermore, the analysis in this section is limited to figures based on all constituencies (to reduce the complexity and amount of information) and only the standard deviation is used, leaving aside other indices. To analyze the historical evolution of territorial structures, the overall temporal period covered by this analysis is subdivided into the three main periods distinguished earlier: 1840s–1910s (restricted suffrage and majoritarian elections), 1920s–40s (massification of politics), and 1950s–90s (stable democracies). Since data are not available for all countries during the first period, four groups of countries are distinguished:

- first, four "early democracies" (Belgium, Denmark, Switzerland, and Britain) since the 1830s–40s;
- second, three countries for which data are available from the 1870s–80s (Germany, the Netherlands, and in part Italy);
- third, Finland, Norway, and Sweden (information available since the beginning of the twentieth century);
- fourth, countries for which data are available since the beginning of the 1920s (Austria, France, Greece, Iceland, and Ireland).

Since the 1920s, therefore, most countries can be included in the comparisons. For Portugal and Spain no historical evolution is displayed since data are available on a regional basis only since the 1970s.

In Figure 3.7, for the sake of comparison, the scale of the vertical axis (mean standard deviation) has been kept at a constant value of 50 for the four graphs. The main result is that *no country displays a long-term trend toward regionalization*, neither during the 1840s–World War I period nor for the period since 1918, which confirms the thesis of the nationalization of electoral politics as a *general* phenomenon. Only Finland displays a basic stability of the territorial configurations from 1907 to the present, while

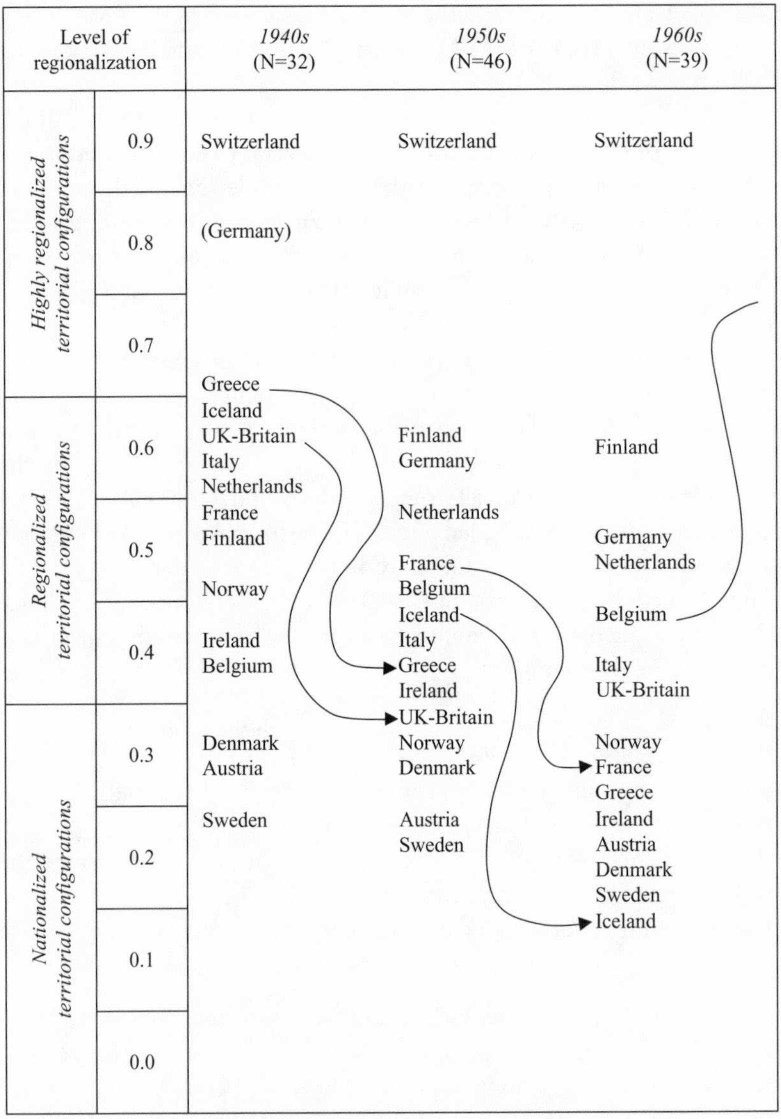

Level of regionalization		1940s (N=32)	1950s (N=46)	1960s (N=39)
Highly regionalized territorial configurations	0.9	Switzerland	Switzerland	Switzerland
	0.8	(Germany)		
	0.7			
Regionalized territorial configurations	0.6	Greece Iceland UK-Britain Italy Netherlands	Finland Germany	Finland
	0.5	France Finland Norway	Netherlands France Belgium Iceland	Germany Netherlands Belgium
	0.4	Ireland Belgium	Italy Greece Ireland UK-Britain	Italy UK-Britain
Nationalized territorial configurations	0.3	Denmark Austria	Norway Denmark	Norway France Greece
	0.2	Sweden	Austria Sweden	Ireland Austria Denmark Sweden Iceland
	0.1			
	0.0			

Figure 3.6 The comparative evolution of territorial heterogeneity in Europe: World War II–present.

Notes: Arrows indicate main changes over time. *N* indicates the overall number of elections in all countries per decade. Germany in the 1940s had only one election (1949). Measures indicate a standardized index of the cumulative standard deviation varying from 0 to 1.

1970s (N=52)	1980s (N=51)	1990s (N=40)	Level of regionalization	
Switzerland	Switzerland Belgium	Belgium Switzerland	0.9	Highly regionalized territorial configurations
Belgium			0.8	
			0.7	
Finland	Finland	Finland	0.6	Regionalized territorial configurations
	UK-Britain	UK-Britain Spain		
Spain Germany Portugal	Spain Germany	Italy Germany	0.5	
UK-Britain Italy	Italy Portugal	Ireland	0.4	
Netherlands Norway France Greece	Iceland Norway France	France Iceland Norway	0.3	Nationalized territorial configurations
Denmark Ireland Sweden Austria	Ireland Denmark Netherlands Austria Sweden Greece	Netherlands Portugal Austria Denmark	0.2	
		Sweden Greece	0.1	
			0.0	

Figure 3.6 (*continued*)
Legend: Italics are used for countries included since the 1970s: Portugal and Spain.

Belgium and Britain show a renewed but weak reterritorialization of electoral behavior during the period following World War II. For Germany, the increase in regionalization after World War II is due to the *Christlich-Soziale Union* and to the decision to treat it as a separate party from the *Christlich-Demokratische Union*. What follows is a more detailed analysis of the evolution by country.

Four "Early Democracies": 1840s–Present

Data for Britain are available since the time of the First Reform Bill of 1832. Elections have always been held by plurality in single- and multimember constituencies and multiple voting (as many votes as seats to be returned in each constituency). Multimember constituencies were abolished in 1950, and the number of seats in the House of Commons equals since then the number of constituencies. In the remaining three countries, by contrast, voting was held in single-member constituencies until the introduction of PR (Belgium in 1900; Denmark in 1918, limited to the constituencies of Copenhagen and Frederiksberg; and Switzerland in 1919). In all these countries, repeated-ballot formulas and uncontested constituencies have been dealt with as described in Appendix 4.

Figure 3.7 shows a convergence between the countries from the 1840s to the 1880s. Since this time, patterns for the four countries display a similar trend toward nationalization until World War I and then a basic stability of the territorial configurations of the vote until the present. These trends also confirm the independence of the processes of nationalization from the levels of aggregation of the data and from electoral systems. The progressive reduction of territorial diversity takes place before the introduction of PR in all countries. Denmark and Britain follow a parallel trend, with high territorial heterogeneity in the 1840s (standard deviation above 40) that decreases steadily until World War I. This is also the case for Belgium, although the level of heterogeneity is less marked during the early elections (standard deviation of about 30).

By contrast, Switzerland – in the period before the 1880s – is characterized by a comparatively high level of homogeneity of voting behavior. Its values then converge with those of the other three countries after this period. From the 1850s to the 1880s, mainly as a consequence of the civil war (*Sonderbundkrieg*) and the following retrenchment of the Catholics in their strongholds, the electoral base becomes more differentiated between regions. During the 1860s, furthermore, two minor political parties increase the general level of territorial heterogeneity. These are the *Dissidente Radikale*, a cantonal splinter in Basel-Land of the Radical Party (*Freisinnig-Demokratische Partei*), and the *Gemässigte Konservative*, a conservative group in the canton of Schwyz. Also the increasing disparities of 1887, 1890, and 1893 are due to a minor group of moderate conservatives active in the cantons of Berne, Basel-Stadt, and St. Gallen. During the first decade of the twentieth century, the level of disparity remains high because of the presence of a series of local splinter groups and cantonal formations: the *Dissidente Radikale* in 1902, the *Bernische Volkspartei* in 1905, and the *Jungfreisinnige* with the *Fortschrittliche Bürgerpartei* in 1911. Since World War I the pattern remained stable until the beginning of the 1980s, when another period of growing disparity among cantons began because of the appearance of several small parties concentrating their efforts in given cantons: the *Parti chrétien-social indépendant* in Jura, the *Partito socialista autonomo* in the Italian-speaking canton of Ticino, the *Mouvement national d'action républicaine et sociale* (a right-wing group active in Geneva), and, since 1995, the *Lega dei ticinesi*. Nevertheless, since the beginning of the 1970s, the level of territorial disparity has decreased in Switzerland.

In Denmark, the crucial periods of the nationalization of electoral politics are the 1860s and 1870s. As will be seen in Chapter 4, these are the periods in which the two main parties of the time before World War I spread throughout the territory: the *Venstre* (Left-Liberals) and the *Højre* (Right-Conservatives). In 1918, when the curve of territorial disparities dropped again, only the region of Copenhagen elected its representatives by PR. Since 1920, when PR was extended to the entire country, the small, erratic movements of the curve have been caused by the only regionalist party of Denmark, the *Schleswigsche Partei* or *Slesvigske parti*, representing the German-speaking minority.[7] This small party does not fulfill the 5 percent criterion for all elections and, therefore, does not enter systemic figures at every election. Nevertheless, as a confirmation of the small impact of this party on the entire system, from the 1920s to the 1990s the low level of disparity of party support that characterizes Denmark constantly decreases.

As far as Britain is concerned, the two main parties of the nineteenth century, the Conservatives and the Liberals, underwent a process of territorial homogenization from the 1830s–40s to the 1920s, which was sporadically interrupted by localized political forces such as the Liberal Unionists at the

---

[7] Because of the annexation of Schleswig-Holstein by Germany, this party did not run for elections in Denmark during World War II.

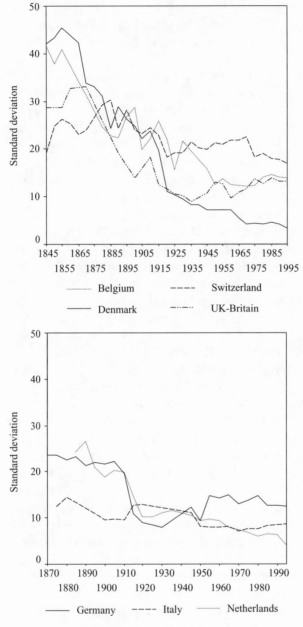

Figure 3.7 The levels of territorial disparity of party support in 15 European countries: 1847–present.

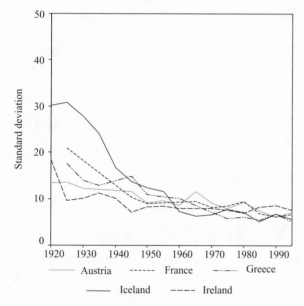

Figure 3.7 (*continued*)

beginning of the twentieth century (see the peak of the curve in Figure 3.7). By contrast, the Chartists from 1837 to 1859, the Social Democratic Federation from 1885 to 1910, and the many small regionalist formations (Scottish United Trades Councils Labour Party, Scottish Land Restoration League, Scottish Workers Representation Committee, etc.) had no impact on the overall degree of territoriality of the British system. After the 1920s, the Liberals were replaced by the Labour Party as the second major party. This favored the progression toward a more homogeneous territorial configuration until World War II. Since then, the pattern shows an increase in territoriality since the 1950s corresponding to the growth of the two main British regionalist parties: the Scottish National Party and the Welsh *Plaid Cymru*. The other regionalist parties did not affect significantly the level of territoriality of the system (the Cornish Nationalist Party and *Mebyon Kernow* in Cornwall, the Wessex Regionalists, *Mudiad Gweriniaethol Cymru* in Wales, the Orkney and Shetland Movement, etc.).[8]

The Belgian party system underwent a rapid nationalization of electoral politics between the 1860s and the end of the nineteenth century, that is, before the introduction of PR – as the first country – in 1900, with the accompanying reduction of the number of constituencies from 41 to 30. During this period only general elections were considered in drawing the curve (which were held only after dissolution of the parliament) and not partial elections, that is, the renewal of only half of the seats every two years. The temporal distance between elections until World War I is therefore larger than for other countries. The two main parties before World War I were the Catholics (*Parti catholique belge*) and the Liberals (*Parti libéral*). With the introduction of universal male suffrage in 1893, new parties enter the electoral stage, in particular three new groups characterized by initial territorial heterogeneity: the *Parti ouvrier belge*, the *Partisans de Daens*, and the *Cartel libéral-socialiste* (a provincial-level alliance between the Liberals and the Socialists).

The division of the main parties (Catholics, Liberals, and Socialists; as well as the Greens) into two linguistic wings, Walloon and Flemish, occurred between the 1960s and the end of the 1970s. Furthermore, the

---

[8] As far as Ireland is concerned, during the 1832–1918 period (the last all-Ireland election before the adoption of the Government of Ireland Act by the Commons establishing an independent *Dáil Éireann* in 26 Southern counties), voting was held in mostly single-member constituencies (64–66 until 1880, then 101 and 103 in 1918) by plurality, as in the rest of the United Kingdom. Data for this period – not displayed in the figures – are characterized by overall stability, as for the period since the establishment of the Irish Free State in 1921.

growth of other regionalist parties influenced to a great extent the degree of territoriality of the Belgian system. Since the early 1930s, the *Partis pro-allemand* (Pro-German Parties) have included different groups of the German-speaking minority of the *arrondissement* of Verviers (the main one being the *Partei der deutschsprachigen Belgier*–Party of the German-Speaking Belgians). The other main regionalist party since 1919 is the Flemish *Volksunie* (People's Union). Since 1968 the *Front démocratique des Bruxellois francophones* (FDF) and the *Cartel van de Boeynants* have contested mainly the constituencies of Brussels. Since 1968, also the *Rassemblement wallon* (often in alliance with the FDF) has been active in the French-speaking provinces. Finally, since 1991 (before this date it does not fulfill the 5 percent criterion), the *Vlaamse bloc*, a splinter group since 1977 of the *Volksunie*, has appeared as a radical Flemish nationalist party.[9]

By World War I, Belgium, Denmark, Switzerland, and Britain had reached a similar level of nationalization with standard deviation values around 10, after which only Denmark seemed to be characterized by a further reduction in territorial diversity. This country has become increasingly distinct with respect to the other three, as its levels of nationalization progressively increase. This is noted in the rank ordering of the countries in Table 3.2, where Denmark appears as one of the most nationalized countries, whereas Belgium, Switzerland, and Britain are among the most regionalized countries. Table 3.5, however, shows that the rank ordering of the countries has been varying over time. In this table the four early democracies are ordered according to the level of standard deviations (party vote). For all three periods the most regionalized country is Switzerland.

Three Countries Since the 1870s

As the second graph in Figure 3.7 shows, at the time of the first democratic elections in Germany and the Netherlands, the levels of territorial heterogeneity are similar to those of the four "early democracies" in the same period of time. For both countries from the 1870s until World War I, there is a trend toward increasing uniformity in electoral behavior. Italy is characterized by a more stable territorial configuration and Germany by renewed territorialization during the Federal Republic. Data on legislative

---

[9] The curves for Belgium, Italy, and Ireland do not display the same sharp increase as in Figure 3.6 because of the use of the mean standard deviation instead of the cumulative standard deviation. As mentioned, this choice is preferable in a long-term historical perspective.

elections are available for Italy since 1860. For party votes, however, the only level of aggregation at which these data are available is 14–16 large regions. Furthermore, results are not available for all elections. For Germany and the Netherlands, by contrast, election results are fully documented by party and constituency since 1871 and 1888, respectively. In all three countries, elections were held by a two-ballot majoritarian electoral formula in single-member constituencies.

Italy appears to be the most homogeneous country of those compared up to World War I, and the evolution of the territorial structure of this country is toward increasing homogeneity until the 1913 election (the last one before the war). The party system during the period from national unification in the 1860s to World War I is characterized by the weakness of the party organizations, with the large Liberal party family divided into several internal factions but dominating the entire political spectrum. Available data for this period do not include results for parties proper, but rather for the *Destra* (Right), *Ministeriali* (candidates supporting the government), *Opposizione* (candidates of the opposition), and *Sinistra ministeriale* and *Sinistra dissidente* (that is, left liberal candidates either supporting or opposing the government). Only with the introduction of (almost) universal suffrage before the 1913 election did parties start to appear on the political stage: the *Partito cattolico* (the Catholic Party, later *Partito popolare* and *Democrazia cristiana*, which did not participate in the previous elections because of the papal ban), the *Partito liberale*, the *Partito radicale*, the *Partito socialista ufficiale* (which contested elections under this label in 1895), the *Partito socialista indipendente*, and the *Partito socialista riformista*.

With the two elections of 1919 and 1921 (after the introduction of universal suffrage and PR), the territoriality of elections increases, although only slightly. This is caused mainly by parties representing minorities of newly annexed territories after World War I: *Deutscher Verband* (an alliance of German parties), *Concentrazione slava* (Slavic Concentration, a Slovene minority in Istria), and the *Partito sardo d'azione* (Sardinian Action Party), which appears in 1921. Despite the strong emphasis in the literature on "red" and "white" zones during the Republican period after 1946 (Communist areas in central Italy and Catholic areas in the Northeast), it is only recently that Italy appears more regionalized as a consequence of the appearance of the *Lega lombarda* (later transformed into the *Lega Nord*). Two main parties in defense of linguistic minorities existed earlier: the *Union valdotaine* (of the French-speaking minority of the Valle d'Aosta, the only constituency in which elections were held by plurality between 1946 and 1992), and the *Südtiroler Volkspartei* (of the German-speaking minority of Alto Adige). More recently, several local parties have been created, but without a strong impact on the territorial configuration of the system (in particular the *Lega d'azione meridionale* and the *Associazione per Trieste*).

As far as the German *Reich* is concerned (1871–1912), Figure 3.7 shows strong territoriality of elections during this period despite the spread of the *Deutsche Volkspartei* and the weakening of the several regionalist-agrarian parties such as the *Bayerischer Bauernbund*, the *Bund der Land-wirte*, the *Dänen*, the particularists of Elsaß-Lothringen (Alsace-Lorraine), the *Welfen* (a regional party of Hannover), the *Polen*, the *Süddeutsche Volkspartei*, and so on. Only during the Weimar Republic does the German system reach a higher level of nationalization. The reterritorialization of elections during the Federal Republic is mainly a consequence of the territorial-religious cleavage within the party system between the mostly Catholic *Christlich-Soziale Union* (CSU) in Bavaria and the interconfessional *Christlich-Demokratische Union* (CDU) in the rest of the country (only in 1953 did the two parties present a common list throughout the territory).[10] The increasing territorial distinctiveness until the 1970s is due to the growth of the CSU and the consequent increase of its weight in the system's average (as well as the presence of the *Südschlewsigscher Wählerbund* in some elections). The reunification of 1990 introduced a further party with strong territorial roots in the new *Länder*: the *Partei des demokratischen Sozialismus*.

The process of nationalization that takes place in the Netherlands from 1888 until 1913 is mainly due to two factors. In the first place, the *Conservativen*, who were characterized by a very high level of territorial disparity of their support, disappear on the basis of the 5 percent criterion. Second, the process of nationalization is to a large extent determined by the homogenization of support of the *Sociaal-democratische arbeiders partij*, whose disparity of support decreases considerably after the 1897 election. After World War I, the evolution stabilizes, with few increases in the territoriality of voting behavior due to the presence of smaller parties such as the *Staatkundig gereformeerde partij* (a splinter group of the *Anti-revolutionaire partij* in 1918). The merger in 1975 of the major confessional parties (*Anti-revolutionaire partij, Christelijk-historische unie, Katholieke volkspartij*) into the interconfessional *Christen democratisch appèl* does not affect the slope of the

---

[10] The *Christlich-Soziale Union* is here considered mainly a Catholic party given the predominance of Catholics in Bavaria, although this label could be questioned, as this party represents a broader confessional electorate, both Catholic and Protestant.

curve, meaning that these parties were less territorially segmented than religious parties in other countries (e.g., in Switzerland and Germany).

Table 3.5 permits a comparison of Germany, Italy, and the Netherlands with the four "early democracies" over the period 1870s–1910s. The most regionalized countries are Germany and the Netherlands, followed by Switzerland (which ranks high according to turnout differences among cantons). Germany, in particular, is characterized by a very low percentage of territorial coverage (33.36 percent on average). Italy, by contrast, appears as a very homogeneous country, considering both party support and turnout, with a cumulative standard deviation half that of other countries.

Since the Beginning of the Twentieth Century

For Finland, Norway, and Sweden, results by parties are available at the constituency level since the first decade of the twentieth century. In Norway a two-ballot majoritarian system in single-member constituencies was in force until 1918. For Finland data are available since 1907, the year of the first election after the abolition of estate representation. The system introduced was PR as for the first election in Sweden (1911) after the abolition of indirect elections, for which only votes for elected candidates are available.

During the 1900s, these three countries are characterized by levels of territorial heterogeneity of party support similar to those reached at that point by the seven countries for which data are available earlier. For all four countries the trend until the 1990s is then clearly stable, with only a slight move toward increased homogeneity until World War II for Norway and Sweden. Finland, by contrast, maintains a more stable pattern. The source of territoriality in Finnish politics is mainly the presence of the *Ruotsalainen kansanpuolue* or *Svenska folkspartiet* (the Swedish People's Party), representing the Swedish-speaking minority mainly in the constituencies of Uudenmaan, Turun, Vaasan, and above all in the Åland Islands. From 1907 until 1995 this party contested all elections, and its success was always sufficient to fulfill the 5 percent criterion for inclusion in the systemic averages.

Norway and Sweden are characterized by a parallel pattern, which displays a trend toward nationalization until World War II and then a fundamental stability of the territorial configurations. The party support in the Norwegian *fylker* has undergone a marked nationalization, although some instability can be observed during the interwar period. Between 1921 and 1933 the erratic movements are caused by the values of the *Radikale folkeparti*, a local party of small farmers that draws its support from the constituencies of Akershus, Hedmark, and Opland and from the *fylke* of Trøndelag. This party no longer enters the computations in 1936, but territoriality is increased by the *Frisinnede folkepartiet* in Bergen. Up to the present, however, the levels of homogeneity have been stable in spite of the local breakaway group from *Det norske arbeiderparti* of the region of Finnmark named *Framtid for Finnmark* (which has been considered a separate party with respect to the Social Democrats).

In Sweden, besides the main parties of the early system (the *Socialdemokratistiska arbetareparti*, the *Liberala*, and the *Högerpartiet*), several small parties were characterized by territorially diverse support, although their reduced size did not affect the overall homogeneity of the system and the basic stability since the 1940s. This is true of the agrarian party *Bondeförbundet*, whose support is characterized by disparities between the rural and urban areas. Furthermore, the support for the *Vänstersocialister* (Left Socialists) and the *Jordbrukarnas riksförbund* (Farmers' Union) is unevenly spread across the constituencies (*valkretsar*). After 1924 the Liberals themselves become less homogeneous. This, however, does not hinder the process of nationalization until the 1940s, after which the pattern remains stable despite the territorialized confessional party *Kristen demokratisk samlig* in 1982 and 1988.

Since the 1900s and 1910s we can compare up to 11 countries (party data for Iceland are available only since 1916). Table 3.5 shows that the most regionalized countries are again Germany and the Netherlands, with Italy and Sweden ranking as the most homogeneous countries as far as party vote is concerned. Three of the countries for which data are available since the beginning of the twentieth century are rather homogeneous (Norway, Finland, and Sweden).

After World War I

The second half (right-hand page) of Table 3.5 displays the comparative values of territorial homogeneity of party vote after World War I, that is, after the introduction of major changes in electoral formulas and franchise. With the addition of Austria, France, Greece, Iceland, and Ireland, the comparison takes into account 15 countries, that is, all those considered in this book except Portugal and Spain. By the end of World War I all countries had introduced (male) universal suffrage, and most countries (the

Table 3.5. *Levels of Territorial Heterogeneity Before and After World War I*

		Party Vote			Turnout		
Countries	Coverage (%)	S	IPRw	*N*	S	MAD	*N*
			Before World War I				
			1840s–1910s				
Switzerland	48.87	103.20	63.39	(141)	19.64	16.03	(25)
Denmark	48.83	88.81	58.88	(108)	21.72	18.48	(33)
UK-Britain	61.67	73.02	52.99	(58)	...	...	(20)
Belgium	68.50	59.40	47.58	(31)	9.26	7.31	(9)
			1870s–1910s				
Germany	33.36	177.80	78.01	(140)	10.09	8.04	(14)
Netherlands	47.66	111.60	62.73	(72)	12.77	10.17	(10)
Switzerland	45.58	106.77	66.10	(99)	18.41	14.99	(17)
Denmark	47.75	78.00	54.04	(82)	17.47	13.78	(20)
UK-Britain	53.17	62.18	46.40	(38)	...	...	(10)
Belgium	83.00	60.01	47.62	(25)	7.66	6.05	(6)
Italy	78.14	35.54	37.12	(44)	7.52	6.19	(15)
			1900s–10s				
Germany	46.30	120.60	63.06	(34)	6.59	4.82	(1)
Netherlands	45.91	120.52	67.75	(44)	11.00	8.42	(5)
Denmark	45.56	108.30	65.76	(40)	12.72	9.32	(3)
Switzerland	42.70	106.28	63.05	(46)	19.63	16.18	(4)
France	65.26	101.35	63.23	(9)	6.49	4.81	(9)
UK-Britain	41.40	82.98	51.17	(23)	...	...	(4)
Norway	71.73	70.90	51.24	(20)	14.40	12.10	(6)
Finland	73.68	66.02	50.12	(52)	9.79	6.88	(8)
Belgium	64.17	58.15	46.37	(16)	3.35	1.99	(1)
Italy	73.06	53.74	43.97	(35)	5.34	3.99	(9)
Sweden	95.79	46.57	43.23	(14)	5.62	4.38	(5)

Notes: Territorial coverage is not applicable to turnout. The number of cases (*N*) for party vote refers to political parties; the number of cases for turnout refers to elections. The number of elections is not necessarily applicable to the party vote because of missing data. Concerning the period 1950s–90s, Portugal and Spain only since 1975 and 1977, respectively. For Greece and Ireland (1920s–40s), and Britain (1840s–1940s) turnout figures are missing. For Belgium until World War I, only general renewals of the *Chambre des Représentants* and not partial elections are presented. The IPR is preferred to the CRII because data on voters are missing in several cases.

Table 3.5 (*continued*)

Countries	Party Vote				Turnout		
	Coverage (%)	S	IPRw	N	S	MAD	N
			After World War I				
			1920s–40s				
Switzerland	45.87	95.99	56.46	(60)	15.32	11.29	(8)
Iceland	80.65	91.13	62.67	(44)	7.74	6.32	(14)
Greece	55.52	85.54	52.49	(45)	...	...	(5)
Italy	53.17	80.01	49.37	(35)	5.57	4.63	(3)
France	82.29	75.53	47.88	(22)	4.70	3.32	(3)
Finland	83.08	65.10	50.19	(65)	6.29	4.33	(10)
UK-Britain	51.54	64.02	46.95	(31)	...	...	(7)
Germany	85.62	59.06	45.22	(79)	4.34	3.37	(9)
Netherlands	99.79	59.01	46.67	(54)	1.16	.83	(7)
Norway	77.39	57.42	46.80	(52)	7.54	6.09	(8)
Belgium	68.89	49.22	43.18	(57)	1.58	1.05	(8)
Ireland	64.72	48.26	39.16	(58)	...	...	(11)
Denmark	84.61	42.46	40.12	(70)	1.87	1.27	(12)
Sweden	93.49	41.21	39.27	(51)	3.99	3.09	(9)
Austria	96.57	38.13	39.69	(21)	3.69	2.94	(6)
			1950s–90s				
Switzerland	42.09	98.30	57.20	(123)	14.32	10.59	(12)
Belgium	59.42	78.12	56.67	(41)	1.47	1.19	(15)
Finland	85.52	66.06	47.75	(128)	7.82	3.90	(13)
Spain	37.81	56.67	38.05	(78)	6.02	4.48	(7)
Germany	77.87	55.67	42.40	(73)	2.80	2.20	(13)
Italy	76.51	48.25	37.61	(96)	5.62	4.59	(12)
UK-Britain	55.09	47.37	40.56	(76)	5.75	4.15	(14)
Portugal	90.73	42.35	38.09	(101)	4.88	3.34	(9)
Netherlands	99.90	37.74	36.56	(75)	3.20	2.52	(14)
Iceland	91.80	37.47	38.59	(78)	1.47	1.13	(14)
Norway	95.63	34.29	36.23	(59)	3.79	2.84	(12)
France	96.12	34.23	31.61	(100)	3.40	2.56	(13)
Ireland	71.15	32.88	32.08	(84)	4.85	3.79	(15)
Greece	90.17	29.12	30.56	(86)	6.47	4.94	(16)
Denmark	94.88	28.41	31.88	(134)	1.99	1.45	(20)
Austria	96.75	24.86	31.68	(92)	3.37	2.69	(14)
Sweden	98.64	24.32	30.27	(152)	1.54	1.21	(16)

Legend: S = standard deviation. IPRw refers to the weighted index. For other abbreviations see the list of Abbreviations and Symbols in the front matter.

main exception being Britain) changed from a majoritarian electoral system to PR. Several countries introduced mixed systems (Iceland, France) or oscillated between PR and plurality elections from one election to the next (Greece). The newly formed Irish Free State adopted the single transferable vote (STV) which is still in use. The change to similar electoral systems in most countries allows for a more direct comparison between countries.

For all countries since World War I, including Austria, France, Greece, Iceland, and Ireland, the period up to the present has been characterized by a general stability of the territorial structures. In the 1920s, Austria, Greece, and Ireland display similar levels of territorial diversity in comparison to the levels reached by the other 11 countries at that time. In Ireland the presence throughout its electoral history since 1922 of small, regionalized parties (such as the National League, the Independent Farmers, the National Labour, and the *Aontacht Éireann*–Unified Ireland from 1923 to 1973) did not affect the overall stability of the territorial configuration based on the three main parties of the Irish system: *Fianna Fáil, Fine Gael*, and the Irish Labour Party. Only in more recent times did the appearance of several new parties (Progressive Democrats, the Workers' Party, and the Democratic Left in particular) increase the territorial fragmentation of the system.

The territorial structure of voting support in Austria and France is characterized by a regular and slight decline in disparity between constituencies. Only in 1959 did a weak reterritorialization take place with the formation of the *Bunddemokratischer Sozialisten*, whose support is concentrated in the constituency of Kärnten (Carinthia), and in 1966 the *Kommunisten-Linkssozialisten* contested the constituency of Wien Nordost, giving up the remaining 24 constituencies in which it had previously presented a list. For France the trend is one of basic stability, except for the period between the 1930s and the 1950s, when a process of nationalization takes place.

In Iceland the level of regionalization is very high in comparison to all other countries in the 1920s (a mean standard deviation of about 30). This system is characterized by a steady decline of regional disparities until the 1950s, when it reaches the average level of the other European countries. From the 1920s to the 1940s, Iceland is one of the most regionalized countries. Nonetheless, during this period – and in spite of a system that remains to a large extent majoritarian – Icelandic parties cover about 80 percent of the constituencies, a much higher degree of territorial coverage than that of Britain, Switzerland, Italy, and Greece. The regionalization of the interwar period for this country is caused mainly by the appearance during the 1927–31 elections of two less homogeneous parties: the Liberal Party (*Frjálslyndi flokkurinn*) and the Communist Party (*Kommúnistaflokkur*). In 1929 the Liberals merge with the Conservative Party (*Íhaldsflokkur*) to form the Independence Party (*Sjálfstæðisflokkur*), which, by covering a greater part of the territory, is more homogeneous than the two parties separately. In 1937, however, the Nationalist Party (*Flokkur þjóðernissinna*, a right-wing splinter group of the Independence Party), which receives all of its support from the Gullbringu-Kiosarysla constituency, again causes higher values of territorial disparity. And again, in the second election of 1942 (October), the Republican Party (*Landsmálaflokkur þjóðveldismanna*) increases the levels of disparity, receiving all of its support from the constituency of Reykjavík.

After World War II, the process of homogenization stabilizes into structured territorial configurations that the appearance of new parties did not change: For example, in 1987 both the Association for Equality and Justice (*Samtök um jafnrétti og félagshyggu*), which contested only the constituency of Nordurlandskjordaemi eystra, and the Populist Party (*Þjóðarflokkur*), which contested five constituencies out of eight, are characterized by strong disparity of support. The important changes in constituencies in 1959 and the introduction of PR throughout the country did not affect the level of nationalization. The Icelandic party system had already reached the maximum level of territorial homogeneity, with the main parties spread uniformly across constituencies: the Independence Party, the Social Democrats, the Communist Party, and the Agrarians (Progressive Party).

Turnout

As for party support, for turnout too the curves of territorial heterogeneity begin at different points in time, according to the democratic evolution of the countries. This appears in Figure 3.8. Again, Portugal and Spain have not been included because of the short period of time covered. Historically, Table 3.5 confirms the high levels of regionalization of electoral participation in Switzerland, which, however, do not seem to represent an exception as far as the earliest periods (up to the 1910s) are concerned. The values of heterogeneity are also very high for Denmark before World War I (see also the values for Germany and the Netherlands during this period). However, since World War I, Switzerland appears as an exception to the patterns of all other countries. After World War II, the standard deviation for this country (14.42) is twice as high as that of Finland (7.82), the second most

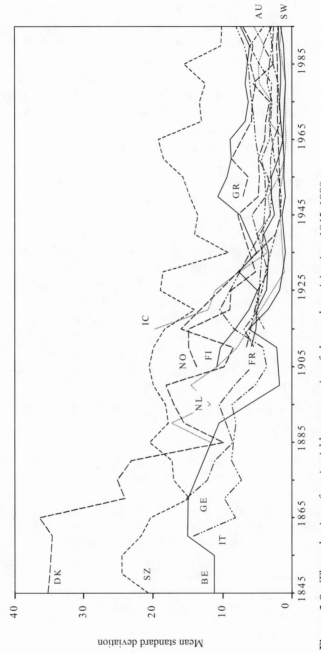

Figure 3.8 The reduction of territorial heterogeneity of electoral participation: 1845–1998.
Notes: Portugal and Spain not included in the figure because of the short time period; Ireland and UK (Britain) not included because of missing data. Data grouped by five-year intervals (e.g.: 1845–49 = 1845).

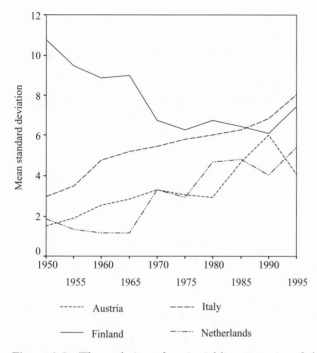

Figure 3.9 The evolution of territorial heterogeneity of electoral participation since World War II in four countries.

regionalized country as far as turnout is concerned.[11] The level of territorial disparities is low in Britain, although plurality systems are expected to cause differentiated levels of participation in relation to the competitiveness or marginality of the constituency.[12] As for party support, therefore, the evolution of the territorial structures of electoral participation of the countries displays a basic convergence toward high levels of homogeneity. This progressive convergence is complete by 1930. From then on, European electorates seem to have reached a definite point of nationalization.

In analyzing the homogenization of electoral participation, it is important to consider *compulsory voting*. Belgium was the first country to introduce compulsory voting simultaneously with universal suffrage in 1894. From

---

[11] Switzerland is also the country characterized by the lowest turnout rates (see footnote 14 in Chapter 2).

[12] See Denver and Hands (1974).

Figure 3.8 it appears that the territorial diversity of turnout in Belgium drops after 1894 and remains among the lowest after that time. Table 3.5 confirms that Belgium has the lowest turnout diversity in Europe (a standard deviation of 1.47).[13]

To clarify the more recent period, Figure 3.9 focuses on the evolution of territorial disparities in turnout rates since World War II. Switzerland has been excluded to avoid an unnecessary enlargement of the scale of the vertical axis. Furthermore, all countries for which the trend is one of stability, without a clear increase or decrease in territorial heterogeneity of electoral participation since the 1950s, have also been excluded. This leaves four cases, three of which display a trend toward a renewed territorialization of electorates (Austria, Italy, and the Netherlands after the abolition of compulsory voting in 1967) and one with a marked reduction of territoriality (Finland). As can be seen, the scale is quite small, ranging only up to a mean standard deviation of 12.0. These trends are therefore significant, but their scope is limited within the overall homogeneity of the most recent periods.

---

[13] In Austria and Switzerland compulsory voting exists on *Land* and cantonal bases. Periods of compulsory voting also existed in Greece and Spain, as well as on a regional basis in Germany. In the Netherlands compulsory voting existed until 1967. Concerning Italy, it has long been debated whether voting from 1946 to 1992 should be considered compulsory or not. Indirect electoral systems were often accompanied by compulsory voting for great electors. On these points, and for a history of the introduction of compulsory voting, see Caramani (2000: 57–58).

4

Types of Territorial Configurations

NATIONAL VARIATIONS

This chapter compares the territorial configurations of electoral support for the political parties of each country and highlights their specificities, the final aim being the identification of *types* of territorial configurations on the basis of two dimensions: (1) How *regionalized* is the support for the *main parties* of a system? (2) What is the impact of *regionalist parties*, that is, parties specifically created for territorial defense on the basis of linguistic, religious, or economic distinctiveness?[1] To do this, the level of analysis shifts from party systems to *single parties*. A series of tables on all countries (limited to the post–World War II period) display the values of homogeneity for each political party (based on measures controlling for their size). Diachronically, the analysis describes the historical evolution through time of the levels of nationalization for all major parties.

This country-by-country analysis cannot incorporate – in the frame of a broad comparative and historical work – the large amount of literature produced in each national system on the *geography of the vote*. Instead, the analysis presented here is based on a great deal of new data on the territoriality of each party requiring a first *défrichement* and a systematic exploration. In Figure 4.1 – placed in the middle of this chapter since it includes graphs for all countries[2] – to improve the visibility of the graphs, only major parties have been considered as well as parties significantly affecting the territorial configuration of the vote in a given system (e.g., green parties for which

---

[1] The other strong element of territoriality is the *urban–rural cleavage*. However, as will become clear, since World War II the agrarian element of territoriality in politics has weakened, even in those countries – such as the Scandinavian – in which it was stronger.

[2] Given the short period of time covered, figures for Portugal and Spain are omitted.

the evolution over time is limited have been omitted).[3] Furthermore, to increase the comparability of temporal patterns, the scale for all countries is the same (from 0 to 1 according to the IPR). Time points are five-year intervals. Dates therefore do not correspond to election years. Further details on each country are given in due course.

Countries with reduced territorial coverage are compared first: Belgium, Spain, Switzerland, and Britain. Three countries – Germany, Ireland, and Italy – in which parties cover no more than three-quarters of the constituencies are then considered. For these two groups of countries both types of figures, computed on all constituencies and on contested constituencies only, are given. Finally, in the remaining nine countries, parties cover most geographical areas. For these countries, as well as for Finland, where only the Swedish People's Party covers less than 90 percent of the territory, only figures computed on all units are given.

Regionalist versus Regionalized Parties

The first group of countries permits us to address the question of the impact of small regionalist parties on the territorial configuration of the entire party system. Chapter 3 underlined the discrepancy between a very low degree of territorial coverage in Spain and a higher level of overall homogeneity of the vote. On the other hand, for Belgium and Switzerland in particular (but also for Britain), there is no inconsistency between the degree of territorial coverage and the measures of homogeneity, both indicating territorially fragmented electoral behavior. A closer comparison of these cases will shed some light on this point.

Small Regionalist Parties: Spain

The Spanish party system is characterized by the lowest degree of territorial coverage (on average, parties contest only 37.81 percent of the constituencies). However, on the basis of an index of homogeneity of voting behavior as the standard deviation, Spain appears much more homogeneous. How can this discrepancy be explained? First, if parties are weighted by size, the large number of regionalist parties (21 since 1977 according to the 5 percent criterion) does not affect significantly the overall homogeneity of the system

---

[3] To make it easier to follow the temporal pattern of each party, lines in the graphs have not been broken when elections were not applicable.

because of their small size. Whereas the main Spanish parties are present in almost all *provincias* (see Table 4.1), all other parties cover no more than 15 percent of the territory. In the computation of the country average for territorial coverage, the large *Partido socialista obrero español* and the small *Unión valenciana*, for example, are weighted one-to-one. By contrast, by taking larger values with larger parties, an adjusted index weights the first more than the second on the basis of their average size across constituencies.

Second, for regionalist parties contesting one or a few constituencies, indices display low values of dispersion because the percentage of votes is homogeneously zero except in a few constituencies. For example, the *Unión valenciana* receives a very homogeneous zero vote all over the country except in the provinces of Alicante (.52 percent at the 1996 election), Castellon (1.98), and Valencia (5.67).

These points confirm the reduced systemic impact of the many but small regionalist parties in Spain.[4] Of the 16 parties in Table 4.1, 11 are regionalist parties. Indices show a clear gap between these parties and the five national parties. The five main parties of the system, which are present on average in almost all constituencies (at least 97 percent of them), are the *Partido socialista obrero español, Partido popular, Centro democrático y social, Izquierda unida* (communist), and *Unión del centro democrático*. For all these parties an index controlling for party size such as the CRII is below .20. For all remaining regionalist parties, by contrast, the index ranges between a minimum of .83 (*Partido andalucista*) and a maximum of .97 (regionalist parties of the Canary Islands and the *Partido aragonés regionalista*). The remaining larger parties of the Basque Country (*Partido nacionalista vasco, Herri batasuna*) and Catalonia (*Convergencia y unió*, etc.) range between these values. All these parties cover no more than 9 percent of the territory with the exception of the *Partido andalucista*, which covers 15.3 percent.

On the right-hand side of Table 4.1 – with values of heterogeneity computed on contested constituencies only – it appears, first, that these parties are very strong in their areas (up to a maximum of 31.87 percent of the votes for *Convergencia y unió*) and, second, that they are fairly homogeneous within their regions – with the exception of the *Agrupaciones canarias*, which are strong in Santa Cruz de Tenerife (18.60 percent in 1989) but weak in Las Palmas (1.79).

---

[4] Values for Spain are computed on a much shorter time period by comparison to all other countries (except Portugal). Disparity scores of this country may therefore also be lower because of the general trend toward nationalization.

Table 4.1. *Levels of Territorial Heterogeneity for Spanish Parties: 1977–Present*

Parties	All Constituencies							Contested Constituencies Only					
	Mean Votes	Coverage (%)	S	IPR	LEE	CV	CRII	Mean Votes	S	IPR	LEE	CV	N
Partido soc. obrero esp.	37.34	100.0	8.30	.16	174.1	.23	.08	37.34	8.30	.31	174.1	.23	(7)
Unión del centro democ.	31.14	97.4	10.62	.40	224.8	.41	.19	31.61	10.10	.39	213.0	.37	(3)
Partido popular	26.23	99.1	9.09	.40	188.9	.40	.17	26.30	9.05	.40	187.7	.39	(7)
Centro democ. y social	7.49	100.0	4.81	.46	77.4	.69	.20	7.49	4.81	.43	77.4	.69	(3)
Izquierda unida	6.35	98.0	3.50	.48	71.5	.58	.19	6.47	3.42	.47	68.9	.56	(7)
Convergencia y unió	2.45	7.6	8.73	.97	117.6	3.57	.84	31.87	6.69	.34	10.7	.22	(6)
Partido nacional. vasco	1.46	7.1	5.96	.97	70.5	4.10	.94	20.84	10.26	.49	13.8	.53	(7)
Herri batasuna	1.10	7.6	3.87	.97	50.6	3.67	.93	13.72	4.74	.41	6.9	.35	(6)
Coalición canaria	.98	3.8	4.96	.99	49.1	5.05	.97	25.53	1.58	.21	1.1	.06	(2)
Eusko alkartasuna	.66	7.6	2.67	.97	31.9	4.03	.94	8.64	5.40	.56	7.8	.63	(2)
Partido andalucista	.65	15.3	1.76	.93	28.4	2.71	.83	4.20	2.36	.48	6.8	.55	(2)
Partido aragonés region.	.60	4.8	2.62	.99	29.6	4.88	.97	11.97	1.84	.27	2.0	.13	(4)
Euskadiko ezkerra	.51	7.3	2.10	.97	24.6	4.21	.93	7.07	4.04	.53	5.6	.60	(6)
Esquerra rep. Catalunya	.43	9.1	1.51	.96	20.2	3.55	.84	4.77	2.17	.48	4.2	.47	(4)
Agrupaciones canarias	.39	3.8	2.59	.99	19.7	6.56	.97	10.24	11.80	.91	8.3	1.15	(2)
Unión valenciana	.18	5.7	1.10	.98	8.8	5.85	.90	3.12	3.82	.83	4.3	1.22	(4)

Notes: Only parties contesting at least two elections are included in the table. Parties are ordered by size. The number of constituencies in which parties are present as a percentage of the total number of constituencies and CRII is not applicable to "contested constituencies only." Party names are shortened. For changes of names, splits, mergers, and alliances between parties see Synopses 3 and 4 (Spain) in *EWE-1815*.

Legend: N = number of contested elections; S = standard deviation. For other abbreviations see Abbreviations and Symbols in the front matter.

Table 4.2. *Levels of Territorial Heterogeneity for Swiss Parties: World War II–Present*

Parties	All Constituencies							Contested Constituencies Only					
	Mean Votes	Coverage (%)	S	IPR	LEE	CV	CRII	Mean Votes	S	IPR	LEE	CV	N
Christlich Demok. Partei	29.64	82.2	28.75	.64	285.7	.97	.36	36.11	27.73	.56	218.8	.77	(12)
Freisinnig-Demok. Partei	23.89	84.5	18.40	.52	151.0	.77	.15	28.29	16.55	.44	110.9	.58	(12)
Sozialdemokrat. Partei	19.12	78.3	13.45	.54	133.3	.71	.13	24.39	9.88	.40	73.8	.40	(12)
Schweizer. Volkspartei	6.69	40.1	11.48	.81	104.2	1.74	.41	16.50	12.61	.53	46.4	.74	(12)
Freie Liste	4.02	78.4	3.21	.58	33.3	.79	.20	5.14	2.70	.48	22.1	.52	(2)
Grüne Partei	2.73	45.1	3.47	.77	37.9	1.39	.36	6.04	2.81	.44	12.7	.46	(4)
Auto-Partei	2.72	42.3	3.79	.78	40.6	1.39	.40	6.35	3.13	.47	14.9	.47	(3)
Liberale Partei	2.69	17.3	6.55	.93	57.0	2.43	.83	15.83	5.86	.41	10.2	.38	(12)
Landesring der Unabh.	2.39	31.7	4.09	.84	40.2	1.80	.42	7.54	3.96	.49	12.3	.53	(12)
Partei der Arbeit	1.77	24.9	4.21	.90	34.3	2.42	.69	7.46	5.80	.61	13.6	.85	(12)
Nationale Aktion (SD)	1.74	43.4	2.44	.77	24.9	1.42	.34	3.99	2.13	.47	9.3	.53	(5)
Gruppe der Demokraten	1.67	10.0	6.38	.97	37.3	3.96	.81	18.86	15.05	.76	14.8	.94	(6)
Republikaner	.95	14.5	2.43	.94	17.9	3.85	.73	7.48	3.85	.71	6.7	.86	(3)
POCH	.87	15.3	2.34	.94	17.9	3.38	.75	6.19	3.89	.61	8.6	.72	(3)
Lega dei Ticinesi	.81	3.8	4.13	1.00	20.2	5.10	.95	21.06	–	–	–	–	(2)
Evangelische Volksp.	.69	16.3	1.62	.93	14.3	2.47	.56	4.16	1.19	.38	1.8	.30	(6)
Christlich-Soziale Partei	.56	7.6	2.11	.99	8.9	3.93	.94	7.21	2.62	.61	1.5	.47	(4)
Partito social. autonomo	.40	3.8	2.06	1.00	10.0	5.10	.95	10.51	–	–	–	–	(3)

Notes: Party names are shortened (and only German names are given). For changes of names, splits, mergers, and alliances between parties see Synopses 3 and 4 (Switzerland) in *EWE-1815. Grün-Alternative* is not included in the table. See also notes to Table 4.1. For other abbreviations see Abbreviations and Symbols in the front matter.

Legend: N = number of contested elections; S = standard deviation.

Large Regionalized Parties: Switzerland

In contrast to Spain, in Switzerland it is the largest parties that are characterized by a reduced territorial coverage. As Table 4.2 shows, all parties – even the larger ones – are characterized by strong regional disparities (especially the Catholic *Christlich Demokratische Partei* and the Agrarian *Schweizerische Volkspartei*, with an IPR of .64 and .81, respectively). Even the Social Democrats and the Radicals (*Freisinnig Demokratische Partei*) display high scores. Other indices controlling for party size (CV and CRII) support these results. Unlike the situation in Spain, furthermore, the Swiss party system has been characterized by long-term continuity in which the basic alignments have remained stable and the availability of election results permits the whole period of time since 1848 to be covered.

The uniqueness of the processes of state formation and nation-building in Switzerland produced an extremely complex pattern of cleavages and divisions (Steinberg 1996). The linguistic east–west division between the two main languages became stronger after 1815 with the addition of the French-speaking cantons. The religious north–south division, by contrast, dates back to the religious wars between 1529 and 1712 that caused bitter conflicts both within and between cantons. Religious tensions exploded again during the transformation of a loose *Staatenbund* (confederation) into the federal state in the 1840s (the *Sonderbund* war of November 1847) when the Catholic cantons allied against the secularizing-Protestant center in defense of their confessional rights. From 1848 to 1891 – as a consequence of the victory in the *Sonderbund* war – the Radicals dominated the political scene and were the only national party. By contrast, the severe defeat delayed the national organization of the Catholics that concentrated in the Catholic cantons (Gruner 1969; Gruner et al. 1978). Besides these two "civil war" parties, the liberal tendency of the Protestant bourgeoisie of the French-speaking cantons and Basel (becoming the *Liberale Partei* in 1894) and the *Sozialdemokratische Partei* (since 1887) were the other main elements of the system in the nineteenth century. After World War I, two other parties were created from the Radical stock: the Agrarians (as *Bauern-, Gewerbe-, und Bürgerpartei*, today *Schweizerische Volkspartei*) and the *Evangelische Partei* (a Protestant confessional party).

The territorial configurations of voting behavior up to the present reflect the complexity of the cleavage system. Since World War II, only four parties have been present in more than the half of the cantons. Of these, three have formed since 1959 the governmental coalition named "magic formula": Radicals (84.5 percent of cantons), Catholics (82.2 percent), and Social Democrats (78.3 percent) – together with the Agrarians, who cover only 40.1 percent of the territory. All other parties (with the exception of the small *Freie Liste*) cover less than 50 percent of the constituencies. According to indicators of homogeneity, the two more nationalized parties are the Radicals and the Social Democrats.

Yet, only two parties in Switzerland are explicitly regionalist: the *Lega dei ticinesi* and the *Parti chrétien-social indépendant du Jura* (each contests one constituency only). The *Partito socialista autonomo* too can be considered a regionalist party since (as the *Lega dei ticinesi*) this party contests elections only in the Italian-speaking canton of Ticino (as the IPR shows by taking the value of 1.00).[5] None of the remaining parties concentrating in given regions is a regionalist party. This is the case with the Communist Party (*Partei der Arbeit*), which concentrates most of its political support in the cantons of Geneva, Vaud, and Neuchâtel in the French-speaking part of the country (IPR of .90). The Liberals, too, since the beginning of the twentieth century have concentrated their support in these cantons and in Basel Stadt. These cantons correspond to those in which the early liberal tendency of the Radical was predominant by 1848. The *Landesring der Unabhängigen* has contested elections since 1935, with a support based initially in the cantons of Zurich and St. Gallen.

The evolution through time of the territorial configuration displayed in Figure 4.1 shows that the levels of electoral heterogeneity generally have remained high during the 150 years covered. The levels of territorial heterogeneity of Catholic and radical support have remained stable, whereas liberal support underwent a rapid process of retrenchment from the late nineteenth century until World War II. By contrast, the Social Democrats expanded their electoral support from 1887 until World War I (PR in 1919). Since then, their level of heterogeneity has remained unchanged. Finally, Agrarians are characterized by a higher level of regional disparity, although more recently the trend has turned toward a more uniform pattern with the transformation of this party into a populist/nationalist protest party of the right, which has increased its support outside the traditional rural areas of support in Protestant cantons such as Berne.

---

[5] One regionalist party in particular, not included in the table, was important in previous periods: the *Bernische Volkspartei* in the canton of Bern.

Table 4.3. *Levels of Territorial Heterogeneity for British Parties: World War II–Present*

Parties	All Constituencies							Contested Constituencies Only					
	Mean Votes	Coverage (%)	S	IPR	LEE	CV	CRII	Mean Votes	S	IPR	LEE	CV	N
Labour Party	42.28	99.9	15.55	.40	4,048.1	.38	.15	42.30	15.52	.40	4,041.1	.38	(14)
Conservative Party	42.10	99.6	12.67	.35	3,197.7	.30	.13	42.26	12.40	.35	3,144.4	.30	(14)
Liberal Democrat Party	17.05	99.4	10.53	.49	2,631.3	.62	.26	17.14	10.48	.49	2,611.0	.61	(2)
Social Democratic Party	10.99	48.8	12.29	.72	3,564.0	1.12	.52	22.46	6.98	.35	810.7	.32	(2)
Liberal Party	10.44	57.2	10.19	.67	2,460.3	1.31	.46	18.24	9.11	.43	1,076.1	.53	(12)
Referendum Party	2.61	85.3	1.67	.50	422.4	.64	.26	3.06	1.38	.42	291.7	.45	(1)
Scottish National Party	1.31	6.9	4.54	.96	732.7	7.63	.94	15.87	8.51	.50	149.9	.57	(14)
Plaid Cymru	.43	4.3	2.68	.98	252.8	7.12	.96	9.44	8.24	.55	91.3	.87	(14)

Notes: The Liberal Party in 1983 and 1987 was allied with the Social Democratic Party (The Alliance), a breakaway group of the Labour Party, but votes are considered separately for the two parties. The two parties merged in 1992 to form the Liberal Democrat Party. For further details see Synopses 3 and 4 (United Kingdom) in *EWE-1815*. See also notes to Table 4.1.

Legend: *N* = number of contested elections; S = standard deviation. For other abbreviations see Abbreviations and Symbols in the front matter.

118

Table 4.4. *Levels of Territorial Heterogeneity for Belgium Parties: World War II–Present*

Parties	All Constituencies							Contested Constituencies Only					
	Mean Votes	Coverage (%)	S	IPR	LEE	CV	CRII	Mean Votes	S	IPR	LEE	CV	N
Catholics	*45.53*	*100.0*	*14.86*	*.38*	*184.2*	*.33*	*.14*	*45.53*	*14.86*	*.38*	*184.2*	*.33*	*(5)*
Chriselijke volkspartij	19.60	53.8	19.02	.69	266.0	.97	.44	36.49	5.83	.26	35.8	.16	(10)
Parti social-chrétien	11.40	47.0	13.56	.74	177.7	1.19	.56	24.29	8.23	.37	42.2	.34	(10)
Socialists	*30.09*	*94.8*	*11.75*	*.39*	*136.4*	*.39*	*.13*	*31.95*	*9.84*	*.36*	*113.9*	*.31*	*(9)*
Belg. socialistische partij	11.79	54.1	11.42	.69	155.6	.97	.42	21.80	3.64	.26	19.8	.17	(6)
Parti socialiste belge	16.61	47.2	19.16	.74	251.8	1.15	.56	35.22	10.10	.36	56.2	.29	(6)
Liberals	*14.76*	*94.2*	*6.30*	*.43*	*75.5*	*.46*	*.16*	*15.45*	*5.77*	*.40*	*66.1*	*.38*	*(7)*
Partij voor vrijheid en v.	10.08	53.9	10.29	.69	133.0	1.02	.43	18.67	5.45	.35	32.8	.30	(8)
Parti de la liberté et du p.	9.84	47.0	11.23	.74	148.4	1.15	.55	20.87	5.38	.33	28.8	.27	(8)
Agalev	3.24	53.0	3.26	.70	42.0	1.02	.42	6.04	1.53	.32	8.6	.25	(5)
Ecolo	3.92	47.3	4.32	.74	56.6	1.11	.56	8.25	1.50	.27	7.5	.18	(5)
Volksunie	6.29	57.7	6.07	.68	82.0	.98	.36	10.86	3.46	.36	21.5	.34	(14)
Vlaamse bloc	5.39	55.8	5.89	.69	59.2	1.10	.34	9.67	4.40	.41	21.5	.46	(2)
Cartel libéral-socialiste	4.07	13.3	10.93	.95	105.8	2.68	.93	30.53	8.71	.40	14.5	.29	(3)
Parti communiste de B.	2.99	78.6	3.21	.67	37.6	1.12	.36	3.83	3.20	.59	30.5	.84	(10)
UDRT	2.05	65.5	1.62	.69	18.4	1.21	.48	2.33	1.59	.50	15.8	.64	(3)
FDF/RW	.43	11.1	1.62	.96	11.2	3.98	.80	4.06	3.90	.74	4.4	.99	(3)

Notes: Only parties contesting at least two elections are included in the table. The data in italics are for main parties before splits along linguistic cleavage lines. For changes of names, splits, mergers, and alliances between parties see Synopses 3 and 4 (Belgium) in *EWE-1815*. See also notes to Table 4.1.

Legend: *N* = number of contested elections; S = standard deviation. For other abbreviations see Abbreviations and Symbols in the front matter.

A Two-Party System: Britain

Two other countries display low territorial coverage on average by parties: Britain (55.09 percent) and Belgium (59.42 percent). For both countries, there are no large discrepancies with the values of the remaining indicators of heterogeneity, meaning that the main parties too are weakly nationalized.

In Britain the only two parties covering almost the entire territory since World War II are the Conservative and Labour parties, the two main parties of the system receiving on average more then 80 percent of the vote – clearly *a two-party system* (Table 4.3). Notwithstanding their diffuse presence (both parties contest practically all constituencies), the levels of inequality of support are high for both parties, especially according to the standard deviation, which is influenced by their particularly large size.[6] The three indicators controlling for the size of the compared units show a much more reduced level of heterogeneity for these two parties. The Liberal Democrat Party – which has contested elections only since 1992 – is the only other party that is present in almost all constituencies, although its support is more diverse across regions, as it is the result of a merger of two parties that covered about half of the constituencies each: the Liberal Party and the Social Democratic Party. The right-hand side of Table 4.3 shows that both parties formerly received congruous and quite homogeneous support within their strongholds (22.46 and 18.24 percent of votes, respectively).

The two major regionalist parties are the Scottish National Party, which contests 6.9 percent of the constituencies (the Scottish ones), and the *Plaid Cymru*, which contests 4.3 percent of the constituencies (the Welsh ones).[7] The levels of disparity are high when measured with indices controlling for the size of parties (IPR of .96 and .98 for the Scottish National Party and *Plaid Cymru*, respectively). Both parties are weak nationwide (with only 1.31 and .43 percent of the votes, respectively). In the contested constituencies,

---

[6] Literature on the voting distribution in Britain has widely documented the strength of the Conservatives in the south east and the concentration of the early liberal vote and, later, labor support in the areas on the remove from the center (see, e.g., Pelling 1967; Cornford 1970; Johnston 1985). On the emergence of liberalism and after the 1890s of labor, see Cox (1970) and Morgan (1980) for Wales and Mackenzie (1981) for Scotland. Bogdanor and Field (1993) have argued that recent elections in Britain replicate the pre-1914 electoral alignments, and they present historical data that highlight the core–periphery dimension in British politics.

[7] Britain is characterized by a number of regionalist parties that have not been included in the analysis on the basis of the 5 percent criterion: the Scottish Labour Party, *Mudiad Gw-eriniaethol Cymru* (Welsh Republican Movement), the Cornish National Party, and *Mebyon Kernow* (Sons of Cornwall), among others.

however, the level of support reaches 15.87 percent for the Scottish National Party and 9.44 percent for the *Plaid Cymru*. Within their areas of support the level of heterogeneity is almost halved.

In a dynamic perspective (Figure 4.1), we see that the Conservative support (solid line) has remained stable over the period from 1832 to the present. By contrast, the Liberals are replaced by the Labour Party as the "second party" of the British party system after World War I. The Liberals decline but do not disappear. They undergo a process of retrenchment, covering a diminishing number of constituencies (see also Chapter 6 for a comparison with Switzerland) and relying on increasingly regionalized electoral support. The opposite trend characterizes the Labour Party, which undergoes a rapid process of nationalization from the beginning of the twentieth century until the 1930s and then stabilizes. Finally, the two parties of the Celtic fringe – the Scottish National Party and *Plaid Cymru* – appear in the 1920s. Both are characterized by stable regionalized support.

Two Party Systems: Belgium

Whereas Britain can be described as *a two-party system*, Belgium seems rather to have *two party systems*. Since the 1960s–70s this country has been divided into two main homogeneous parts. The main Belgian parties (Socialist, Christian Democrats, and Liberals, as well as the Greens) divided into two parties (Walloon and Flemish). In this work, the two linguistic "wings" of the previously unitary parties are considered separate parties (see Appendix 1). The consequence of this choice is not only that since the 1960s–70s Belgium has been characterized by two party systems – a Walloon one and a Flemish one – but, in addition, that the party system(s) that emerged from this process of separation along linguistic lines is completely different from the Belgian system that formed in the nineteenth century.

Figure 4.1 shows that the territorial configuration of electoral behavior changes radically with the division of the main parties. Catholics (the early *Union* or *Parti catholique belge*) and Liberals (*Parti libéral*) are the two historical parties that were present throughout the country since 1847 (the first election for which party results are available at the level of the *arrondissements administratifs*). They dominated the party system until the emergence of the Socialists (*Parti ouvrier belge*) in 1894. These three parties together have gained around 80 percent of the votes on average. As for Switzerland and Britain, the conservative and liberal-radical parties have been able to spread throughout the territory since the

beginning of democratic elections, whereas the social democrats nationalize their electoral support more rapidly until the introduction of PR (1900).
The introduction of PR also favors small regionalist parties, the main one
being the Flemish *Volksunie* since 1919. The high levels of territoriality of
this party have remained stable up to the present.

In the 1960s–70s the curves for the three main Catholic, Liberal, and
Socialist parties are interrupted and replaced by two curves for each of
them, corresponding to the Flemish and Walloon wings. The two groups
of three curves are superimposed because, from this time on, each party contests roughly half of the constituencies. The Walloon curves for Catholics,
Liberals, and Socialists are higher than the Flemish curves because of the
smaller area covered by these parties with respect to Flanders.

All indices are affected by these major transformations of the Belgian
party system. Before the 1960s–70s, the indices take high values of homogeneity for Catholics (IPR of .38), Liberals (.43), and Socialists (.39). After
the division of the parties, the IPR values for the Catholics, for example,
increase to .69 and .74 for the Flemish and Walloon Catholic parties, respectively (see Table 4.4). It is interesting to note that IPR values for the
Flemish Catholics, Liberals, and Socialists are identical (.69), as well as
the IPR values for the corresponding Walloon parties (.74), meaning that
the support for these parties is characterized by the same degree of territoriality determined by the linguistic cleavage. This is confirmed by the
percentage of territorial coverage: 53–54 percent for the Flemish wings and
about 47 percent of the Walloon ones. This also applies to the two Green
parties, *Anders gaan level* (or *Agalev*, Flemish) and *Ecologistes confédérés pour
l'organisation de luttes originales* (or *Ecolo*, Walloon), which were created as
two separate parties.

As in the case of Switzerland, in Belgium it is not the presence of regionalist parties that makes the system regionalized but rather the regionalization of the main parties themselves. The strength of the linguistic-ethnic
cleavage in the Belgian case transformed each of the main parties in two different parties.[8] Presently, the parties that cover most constituencies are the
left-wing *Parti communiste de Belgique* (78.6 percent of the *arrondissements*)
and the *Union démocratique pour le respect du travail* (UDRT) (65.5 percent).
No other party covers more than 57.7 percent of the territory (this value

---

[8] The same problem occurs with Switzerland, another very decentralized country, whose
parties have strong ideological and programmatic differences from canton to canton. In this
case, however, parties have been considered national because there is no clear-cut linguistic
or religious division but rather strong cantonal variations.

being, paradoxically, that of the regionalist *Volksunie*). In addition, however, a number of more specifically regionalist parties exist in Belgium. Among these, the two main ones are the previously mentioned *Volksunie* (a party existing since World War I) and the *Vlaamse bloc*, a party that does not affect strongly the overall levels of regionalization since it does not fulfil the 5 percent criterion for all elections (and therefore does not enter the computations of indices). On the other hand, the *Rassemblement wallon* fulfills the criterion only when in alliance with the *Front démocratique des Bruxellois francophones* (FDF/RW) (which occurs from 1968 to 1981) and the *Parti libéral de Bruxelles* (in 1974). These parties contest the *arrondissements* of Bruxelles and Nivelles only. Finally, the *Partei der deutschspachigen Belgier* (formerly the *Parti pro-allemands*), a party of the German-speaking minority of Verviers, affects the levels of regionalization mainly in the interwar period and therefore is not included in Table 4.4.[9]

If the values computed on all constituencies are compared with the values computed on the contested constituencies only, it appears that the disparities in Belgium are therefore primarily *between* regions in which parties are present and regions in which parties are not present (the Flemish and Walloon sections of the country). By contrast, in Switzerland and Britain (as well as in Spain), there are strong differences in support among the constituencies in which parties are present.

Incomplete Territorial Coverage

For three additional countries, territorial coverage ranges between 70 and 80 percent (Table 3.2): Ireland (71.15 percent), Italy (76.51 percent), and Germany (77.87 percent). Whereas Germany and Italy are characterized by the presence of large regionalist parties, this type of party is absent in the Irish party system. On the other hand, Ireland appears as one of the nationalized countries, whereas Germany and Italy are among the rather regionalized countries.

Many Small Parties: Italy

The basic features of the Italian party system were set in 1919 with the introduction of PR and the birth of mass parties. Before this date, political

[9] As noted by Lorwin, the Flemish identity has been stronger than the Walloon consciousness since the 1930s, when Flemish parties peaked, and also later on the school issue (Lorwin 1966: 163, 171).

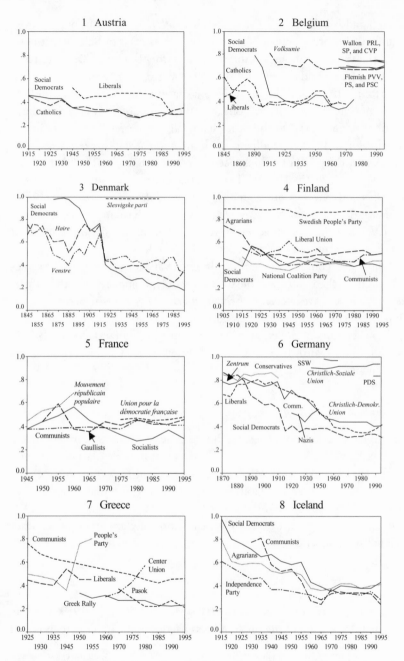

Figure 4.1 The evolution of territorial configurations in 15 European countries (mean IPR).

Types of Territorial Configurations

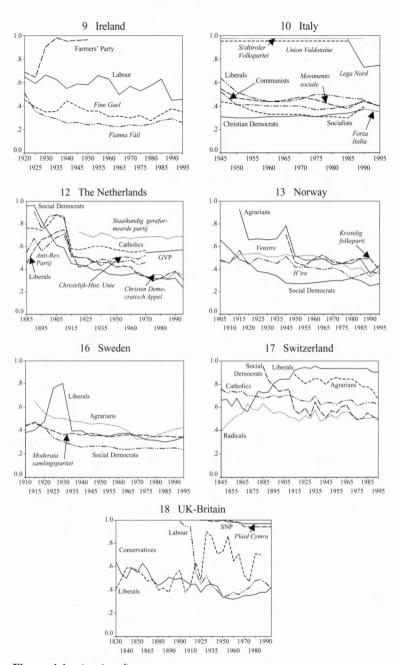

Figure 4.1   *(continued)*

125

parties hardly existed and parliamentary groups were highly fluid and unstable. Given the long interruption of democratic life after 1922, figures and curves for Italy are therefore displayed only since 1946 (see Figure 4.1), the year of the election to the Constituent Assembly, in which parties reorganized as legacies of the organizations existing before the time of Fascist rule, with the Catholic *Partito popolare* reconstituted as *Democrazia cristiana* and the *Partito socialista* (PSI) and *Partito comunista* (PCI) as the main parties of the left (the PCI and PSI allied in the *Fronte democratico popolare* in the 1948 election). Later, after a long period of electoral stability, the Italian party system underwent a drastic transformation between the 1992 and 1994 elections. First, since 1994 elections have been held with a new mixed electoral system that replaced PR. Second, the *Democrazia cristiana* divided into several splinter groups, the main one being the *Partito popolare italiano* (PPI). Third, new parties emerged, mainly *Forza Italia* and the *Lega Nord*.

The comparison with other European cases disconfirms to a certain extent the traditional literature on the Italian political geography, which emphasized the differences between "red" (socialist-communist) and "white" (Catholic) zones.[10] From World War II until the 1992 election the electoral support for the main Italian parties was homogeneous, the most uniform support being for the predominant Catholic party *Democrazia cristiana* (IPR of .30 and CRII of .09, as shown in Table 4.5). Support for the other main party before 1992, the *Partito comunista italiano*, is also relatively homogeneous (IPR of .40 and CRII of .15). Also *Forza Italia* today is characterized by homogeneous support (IPR of .37 and CRII of .13). Furthermore, the main Italian parties cover basically all constituencies with the exception of the Valle d'Aosta, where – since the single seat has always been allocated by plurality – local alliances were formed. This is why, for most parties, the percentage of territorial coverage is very high but never 100 percent.

Italian electoral regionalism seems rather to be caused by the presence of a number of regionalist parties. The most important of these parties is the *Lega Nord*, which, since the late 1980s (when it first appeared as *Lega lombarda*), covers approximately half of the territory (52.90 percent of territorial coverage).[11] However, given its reduced size on a national scale (8.31 percent of the votes on average over four elections: 1987–96), its effect on the systemic values is limited. As far as the other main regional parties

---

[10] For the first use of this expression see Compagna (1950) and Compagna and de Caprariis (1954). For an overview see Bartolini (1976). For a more recent analysis see Brusa (1984).

[11] On the early evolution of the *Lega* see Biorcio (1991).

are concerned, their national impact is even more reduced. The most regionalized parties are the *Südtiroler Volkspartei* (IPR of .99 support limited to Alto Adige) and the *Union valdotaîne* (IPR and CRII of 1.00 since it is present only in Valle d'Aosta). The *Liga veneta* (which merged before 1987 with the *Lega lombarda* and other regionalist parties to form the *Lega Nord*) and, more recently, the *Lega d'azione meridionale*, in the southern part of the country, are present in a reduced number of constituencies. The *Partito sardo d'azione*, by contrast, is also present outside Sardinia in 34.33 percent of the territory. The figures computed on contested constituencies only (the right-hand side of Table 4.5), appear to indicate that the only two regionalist parties that really dominate their territories are the *Südtiroler Volkspartei* and the *Union valdotaîne* (30.30 and 46.43 percent, respectively). The *Lega Nord* itself does not go beyond 11.05 percent of the vote on average in the constituencies it contests.

The stable pattern since 1945 observed at the systemic level is confirmed in Figure 4.1 for the main parties. Overall, in a long-term and comparative perspective, the trend also appears stable since the late 1980s with the appearance of the *Lega Nord* and after 1992 with the breakup of the *Democrazia cristiana* and the birth of *Forza Italia*. The support for the two main ethnic parties representing the French- and German-speaking minorities maintains its regionalized configuration.[12] By contrast, the support of the *Lega* has expanded territorially with the change from *Lega lombarda* to *Lega Nord*.

From Many Small to Few Large Parties: Germany

In spite of the differences between the German party systems during the three main periods into which the electoral history of the unified country can be subdivided – *Reich*, Weimar, and Federal Republic – regional distinctiveness is a well-known aspect throughout German electoral history.[13] In particular during the empire period, the degree of "nationness" of Germany was low and political particularism was one of the main features of the system. The political system of the *Reich* included a large number of regionalist groups that, with the consolidation of the nation-state and the subsequent

---

[12] The new electoral system prevents Valle d'Aosta from participating in the PR vote, and therefore the curve for the *Union valdotaîne* is interrupted; the *Südtiroler Volkspartei* allies with other parties.

[13] See Oberndörfer and Schmitt (1991) and Rohe (1990). Immerfall (1992) presents an interpretation based on the strength of the city network and the barriers to the construction of a political center.

Table 4.5. *Levels of Territorial Heterogeneity for Italian Parties: World War II–Present*

Parties	All Constituencies							Contested Constituencies Only					
	Mean Votes	Coverage (%)	S	IPR	LEE	CV	CRII	Mean Votes	S	IPR	LEE	CV	N
Democrazia cristiana/PPI	33.20	99.5	8.80	.30	410.1	.29	.09	33.36	8.50	.30	402.1	.28	(12)
Partito comunista/PDS	25.40	99.2	10.13	.40	595.0	.41	.15	25.61	9.90	.39	585.9	.40	(12)
Forza Italia	20.87	96.4	7.43	.37	1,334.5	.36	.13	21.68	6.38	.34	1,147.5	.29	(2)
Partito socialista/PSIUP	10.96	99.1	3.22	.35	136.0	.32	.11	11.07	3.04	.34	131.5	.31	(12)
Movimento sociale/AN	7.11	99.9	3.43	.44	316.2	.48	.20	7.11	3.43	.44	316.1	.48	(12)
Rifondazione comunista	6.82	97.1	2.73	.41	391.7	.41	.16	7.01	2.54	.39	349.6	.36	(3)
Lega Lombarda/Nord	6.24	52.9	8.31	.80	1,247.5	2.03	.61	11.05	8.53	.60	679.0	.80	(4)
Partito social-democrat.	4.04	98.6	1.88	.43	68.7	.48	.17	4.09	1.84	.42	66.6	.46	(9)
Partito liberale italiano	2.99	99.0	1.87	.48	60.3	.67	.20	3.01	1.86	.47	59.3	.65	(10)
Partito repubblicano it.	2.74	98.9	2.02	.51	61.2	.86	.24	2.77	2.01	.51	60.1	.84	(10)
Partito radicale	2.73	89.0	1.40	.45	199.4	.51	.20	3.10	1.07	.37	121.0	.35	(3)
Monarchici	2.72	97.2	2.63	.59	89.6	.99	.34	2.78	2.63	.58	87.9	.97	(4)
Verdi	2.51	96.4	1.13	.41	116.6	.45	.16	2.60	1.04	.39	101.5	.40	(4)
Rete	1.80	77.3	2.91	.68	254.3	1.61	.41	2.32	3.10	.64	232.8	1.33	(2)
Südtiroler Volkspartei	.69	2.4	6.15	.99	62.9	8.93	.98	30.30	37.03	.92	28.9	1.27	(10)
Union valdôtaine	.50	1.0	4.80	1.00	45.9	9.67	1.00	46.43	–	–	–	–	(7)
Partito sardo d'azione	.35	34.3	1.61	.96	42.9	5.25	.90	4.61	1.85	.53	19.5	1.47	(3)
Liga veneta	.31	8.4	1.20	.97	26.8	3.90	.92	3.89	1.59	.44	6.0	.50	(2)
Lega azione meridionale	.17	12.5	1.52	.95	51.5	8.61	.86	1.83	4.85	.85	40.8	2.74	(2)

Notes: Only parties contesting at least two elections are included in the table. For changes of names, splits, mergers, and alliances between parties see Synopses 3 and 4 (Italy) in *EWE-1815*. See also notes of Table 4.1.

Legend: N = number of contested elections; S = standard deviation. For other abbreviations Abbreviations and Symbols in the front matter.

Table 4.6. *Levels of Territorial Heterogeneity for German Parties: World War II–Present*

Parties	All Constituencies							Contested Constituencies Only					
	Mean Votes	Coverage (%)	S	IPR	LEE	CV	CRII	Mean Votes	S	IPR	LEE	CV	N
Sozialdemokrat. Partei	37.99	100.0	9.24	.32	1,001.2	.25	.10	37.95	9.24	.32	1,001.2	.25	(13)
Christlich-Dem. Union	35.59	82.9	18.11	.44	1,784.3	.51	.19	42.99	8.80	.28	762.8	.20	(12)
Christlich-Soz. Union	9.53	17.2	21.13	.91	2,064.5	2.25	.83	54.93	8.90	.26	168.3	.16	(12)
Freie Demokrat. Partei	8.58	100.0	3.17	.38	323.1	.37	.14	8.58	3.17	.38	323.1	.37	(13)
Die Grünen	6.25	95.9	2.58	.40	290.4	.43	.15	6.45	2.44	.37	263.7	.38	(5)
Heimatvertriebenen	5.55	100.0	3.67	.54	386.1	.66	.30	5.55	3.67	.54	386.1	.66	(2)
Partei des demok. Sozial.	4.46	100.0	7.23	.80	928.6	1.66	.65	4.46	7.23	.80	928.6	1.66	(3)
Deutsche Partei	3.40	100.0	5.06	.69	387.0	1.49	.47	3.40	5.06	.69	387.0	1.49	(2)
Nationaldemok. Partei D.	3.18	100.0	1.24	.41	119.7	.43	.17	3.18	1.24	.41	119.7	.43	(2)
Republikaner	2.12	100.0	1.45	.52	183.7	.69	.27	2.12	1.45	.52	183.7	.69	(1)
Kommunistische Partei	2.09	100.0	1.63	.55	151.4	.78	.31	2.09	1.63	.55	151.4	.78	(1)
Gesamtdeutscher Volks.	2.07	100.0	1.88	.57	166.4	.90	.33	2.07	1.88	.57	166.4	.90	(2)
Bayernpartei	1.82	19.4	4.31	.90	355.8	2.36	.82	9.39	4.98	.48	98.1	.53	(1)
Bündnis '90	1.34	24.3	2.59	.88	336.7	1.93	.78	5.51	2.13	.37	60.6	.39	(1)
Deutsche Reformpartei	1.00	83.3	1.20	.62	96.9	1.18	.39	1.36	1.25	.56	76.0	.94	(3)
Föderalistische Union	.90	59.5	1.69	.80	142.1	1.88	.63	1.51	1.97	.70	108.7	1.30	(1)
Zentrum	.73	27.2	1.89	.88	135.7	2.57	.76	2.69	2.81	.65	74.2	1.04	(1)
Südschleswigscher W.b.	.17	5.7	1.60	.98	40.8	9.19	.97	3.04	6.20	.88	30.3	2.04	(3)

Notes: For changes of names, splits, mergers, and alliances between parties see Synopses 3 and 4 (Germany) in *EWE, 1815*. See also notes to Table 4.1.
Legend: *N* = number of contested elections; *S* = standard deviation. For other abbreviations see Abbreviations and Symbols in the front matter.

changes of border lines, disappeared in subsequent periods. These parties represented mainly the Polish, Danish, Alsace-Lorraine (under the name of *Partikularisten*), and Hannover minorities. In addition, among the less nationalized parties, the system included a group of parties stemming from the urban–rural cleavage such as the *Bayerische Bauernbund* and the *Bund der Landwirte*.

During the Empire period, major parties did not have uniform support. The *Sozialdemokratische Partei Deutschland* itself cannot be defined as fully national during this period. As Urwin (1982b: 189) notes, the real nationalization of the Social Democrats starts at the beginning of the twentieth century. The curve in Figure 4.1 confirms this view but – as will become clear in the party family comparison – this is the case for most social democratic parties. As far as the *Zentrum* is concerned – the only other party to present candidates in more than half of the constituencies by 1907 – its nationalization occurs later, during the Weimar Republic, in particular when it allies with the *Bayerische Volkspartei*. Among the most important parties, finally, the Nazis, the Nationalists, the Communists, and the People's Party also receive homogeneous support.

During the Federal Republic the number of parties decreases. The *Christlich-Demokratische Union* (CDU) and the *Sozialdemokratische Partei Deutschlands* together achieve over 70 percent of the votes. Among the most important parties, the Social Democrats and the Liberals (*Freie Demokratische Partei*) are the most homogeneous (IPR of .32 and .38, respectively), together with *Die Grünen* (see Table 4.6). Social Democrats and Liberals are present in all constituencies. A somewhat less nationalized support, but still strongly homogeneous (IPR of .44 and territorial coverage of 82.9 percent), can be observed for the Christian Democrats. This party is not present in Bavaria, whose *Wahlkreise* are contested by the *Christlich-Soziale Union* (CSU), the mostly Catholic party of Bavaria allied with the CDU.

The presence of the CSU is limited to the 45 constituencies of Bavaria and, therefore, is characterized by highly concentrated support (IPR of .91). As the right-hand side of Table 4.6 shows, support for this party is very homogeneous within the Bavarian territory (the same applies to the CDU for the remaining areas of the country; see the IPR values). The CSU is the main factor in the regionalism of German elections since World War II if it is considered separately from the CDU. The comparatively high level of heterogeneity in the voting behavior of Germany is therefore influenced by the choice to consider the CDU and CSU as separate parties. If these two parties were considered a single unit, the level of territorial diversity in German elections would have been lower.[14] The other party of regional distinctiveness is the *Südschleswigscher Wählerverband* (or *Sydslesvigsk vælger-forening* in Danish), which, however, fulfills the 5 percent criterion only in three elections, from 1949 to 1957. This party represents the Danish minority of Schleswig-Holstein, and its support is limited to a few constituencies.

Figure 4.1 confirms that the process of nationalization took place during the empire period and the Weimar Republic. However, the territorial configuration of voting behavior during the Federal Republic maintains elements of regionalism, confirming the results of other analyses (see, e.g., Hoschka and Schunck 1976). Unique since World War II, Germany is the only country for which territory changed radically with the reunification in 1990 of the Federal Republic of Germany and the German Democratic Republic (GDR) (from 248 to 328 *Wahlkreise*). The impact of this major change in the territorial configuration of the vote was nevertheless limited. The major parties expanded into the new *Länder*: the *Sozialdemokratische Partei Deutschlands* and the *Freie Demokratische Partei* (which maintained their territorial coverage of 100 percent), as well as the *Christlich-Demokratische Union* and *Die Grünen*.[15] The *Christlich-Soziale Union*, by contrast, remained confined within the borders of Bavaria.[16]

The major change resulting from reunification is the new *Partei des demokratischen Sozialismus* (PDS) (the heir of the ruling communist party in the in the former GDR) and *Bündnis '90* (expression of the movements for civil rights), with their electoral strongholds in the new *Länder*. The PDS receives highly regionalized electoral support, as shown in Figure 4.1, although it is present in all German constituencies (100 percent of coverage), with an IPR of .80 and a CRII of .65. Nevertheless, its small national size

---

[14] It is an oversimplification to say that Bavaria is Catholic. The most Catholic areas are located between the Danube and the Alps (where there is also a large number of monasteries). However, the cities (Nürnberg, Augsburg) and the north (Franken) were strongly invested by Reformist movements in the sixteenth century, and the *Sozialdemokratische Partei Deutschlands* receives stable and conspicuous electoral support, in particular in Munich (Mintzel 1990).

[15] The presence of the Greens across the territory was reduced after reunification (from 100 percent to about 80 percent) and the indicators of homogeneity decreased in 1990. The party expanded in the new *Länder* since 1994 through its alliance with *Bündnis '90*.

[16] The percentage of territorial coverage diminished after 1990 for the CSU since the overall number of constituencies increased. By contrast, the percentage increased for the CDU. Before reunification the CDU was present in 203 constituencies out of 248, that is, all constituencies except the 45 Bavarian constituencies covered by the CSU. In 1990 it was present in 283 constituencies out of 328.

(4.46 percent on average over three elections: 1990, 1994, and 1998) limits its impact on the overall systemic level of regionalization. As indicated on the right-hand side of Table 4.6, the support for this party is also diverse within the territory of the former GDR. By contrast, *Bündnis '90* contested only the constituencies of the new *Länder* before it allied with the Greens in 1994, and in these areas its vote is fairly homogeneous.[17]

The Influence of Small Parties: Ireland

Since 1922, the territorial configuration of Irish electoral behavior, like that of Italy, has been influenced by the presence of a number of small parties. Although, in contrast to Italy, these parties appear sporadically and usually contest a reduced number of elections before disappearing, they are responsible for the incomplete territorial coverage in this system (71.15 percent of coverage on average). The three main parties of the system – contesting all elections since World War II, whereas all others have not contested more than five – are the two sui generis parties created by the cleavage over the Anglo-Irish Treaty of 1921 and the Irish Labour Party. *Fianna Fáil* (Warriors of Destiny) and *Fine Gael* (Tribe of the Gael) were born from the division of *Sinn Féin* (Ourselves) over acceptance of the treaty and the degree of independence of the Irish Free State (*Anti-* and *Pro-Treaty Sinn Féin*).

The many short-lived small parties appeared at two different times. First, after 1922 and until World War II, several parties threatened the domination of the "treaty cleavage": the Farmers' Party, *Clann na Talmhan* (Family of the Land), and the National Coalition Party before it merged in 1933 with the *Cumann na nGaedheal* (Family of the Gael) to form what is now called *Fine Gael*. Second, since the early 1980s, several new parties have entered the electoral arena. Among the most important are *Sinn Féin*-Workers' Party (WP), the Democratic Left (a breakaway group from the WP), and the Progressive Democratic Party (a breakaway group from *Fianna Fáil*).

The two main parties in the Irish system are characterized by very homogeneous support. They are always present in practically all constituencies.

---

[17] Several other parties display strong regional support. However, these parties are small and are present in only a few elections. This is the case of the disappearing parties soon after World War II – the Bavarian *Bayernpartei*, *Hannoversche Landspartei* (which formed the *Föderalistische Union* in 1957) – the right-wing *Nationaldemokratische Partei Deutschlands*, *Die Republikaner*, etc. In 1990 *Die Republikaner* were included for the first time in the computations according to the 5 percent criterion. This party is present in all constituencies, with homogeneous (although limited) electoral support.

Table 4.7. *Levels of Territorial Heterogeneity for Irish Parties: World War II–Present*

Parties	Mean Votes	Coverage (%)	All Constituencies					Contested Constituencies Only					
			S	IPR	LEE	CV	CRII	Mean Votes	S	IPR	LEE	CV	N
Fianna Fáil	45.32	100.0	6.89	.25	111.6	.15	.06	45.32	6.89	.25	111.6	.15	(15)
Fine Gael	31.45	99.8	8.05	.32	128.2	.26	.10	31.49	7.99	.32	127.4	.26	(15)
Irish Labour Party	11.64	82.6	8.42	.56	141.6	.75	.30	14.05	7.33	.47	100.3	.53	(15)
Progressive Dem. Party	6.25	67.0	5.90	.63	91.5	1.03	.38	9.16	5.13	.47	52.5	.59	(4)
Workers' Party	3.03	43.9	4.56	.80	68.7	2.06	.62	6.04	5.18	.60	40.2	.92	(3)
Sinn Féin	2.96	40.1	4.15	.78	67.2	1.53	.60	7.14	3.57	.44	21.7	.50	(4)
Green Alliance	2.72	63.4	3.05	.65	46.0	1.12	.40	4.29	2.81	.46	23.1	.66	(1)
Clann na Talmhan	2.67	12.6	7.93	.95	93.1	2.96	.89	22.26	9.34	.47	19.4	.45	(4)
Democratic Left	2.54	40.2	4.13	.81	66.6	1.63	.63	6.57	4.14	.55	29.4	.65	(2)
Clann na Poblachta	2.37	29.7	4.09	.85	59.0	2.20	.71	7.98	4.66	.51	20.7	.59	(5)
National Party	1.12	39.0	1.64	.79	28.0	1.46	.61	2.88	1.33	.44	8.4	.46	(1)
Aontacht Éireann	.91	28.5	1.76	.86	27.4	1.93	.71	3.20	1.90	.51	9.0	.60	(1)
National Democr. Party	.90	7.8	3.51	.97	31.5	3.89	.91	11.41	6.91	.59	7.9	.61	(1)
Farmers' Party	.80	7.5	3.10	.97	29.7	3.86	.94	10.73	5.20	.53	5.9	.49	(2)
Socialist Party	.74	12.2	2.82	.95	26.4	3.83	.88	6.03	6.29	.69	11.3	1.04	(1)

Notes: For changes of names, splits, mergers, and alliances between parties see Synopses 3 and 4 (Ireland) in *EWE-1815*. See also notes to Table 4.1.

Legend: N = number of contested elections; S = standard deviation. For other abbreviations see Abbreviations and Symbols in the front matter.

Taking the IPR as an indicator, *Fianna Fáil* and *Fine Gael* score .25 and .32, respectively, whereas no other party has a value below .56 (Labour Party). As far as territorial coverage is concerned, besides these two parties and the Labour Party, with 82.6 percent of coverage, all other parties cover no more than 67 percent of *Dáil* constituencies. The evolution of the party system shown in Figure 4.1 displays the fundamental stability of the territorial homogeneity of support for the three main parties. As for the period before World War II, the Farmers' Party is characterized by a curve toward regionalization corresponding to its electoral decline.

A Regionalized Nordic Country: Finland

Finland – where parties are present in about 85 percent of electoral districts – represents an intermediary case between incomplete and national territorial coverage. Figure 4.1 shows that after 1907 – when the unicameral parliament *Eduskunta* replaced the four-estate Diet – the main factor in regionalism is the Swedish People's Party (*Ruotsalainen kansanpuolue* or *Svenska folkspartiet* in Swedish), representing the Swedish-speaking minority in particular from the *lääni* of Uudenamaan, Vasaan, and the Åland Islands, inhabited by a Swedish minority (which since 1948 have been represented in the Finnish parliament and where elections are held by plurality, as in Lapland). This party also receives important support from the province of Helsinki and parts of Turun-Porin. The area covered by the Swedish People's Party is therefore quite large (around 38 percent of the *vaalipiirit* or electoral areas). The graph in Figure 4.1 also shows that the territoriality of the electoral support for this party has been stable, with an IPR of about .86 from 1907 until the present. All other Finnish parties cover an important number of constituencies (see Table 4.8). Nevertheless, given the domination of the Swedish People's Party in the Åland Islands (it receives always more than 90 percent of the votes), none reaches 100 percent of territorial coverage. The only parties that contested all constituencies were the historical nationalist parties that contested elections until 1917: the Old Finns (*Vanhasuomalaiset*) and the Young Finns (*Nuorsuomalsiienen puolue*).[18]

However, the support for Finnish parties is generally not homogeneous, as the IPR in Table 4.8 shows. Considering all parties, this index is never

---

[18] At the time, the Åland Islands were not yet part of Finland. These two parties have not been included in the graph in Figure 4.1. On the evolution of the Finnish party system see Pesonen (1974).

Types of Territorial Configurations

Table 4.8. *Levels of Territorial Heterogeneity for Finnish Parties: World War II–Present*

Parties	Mean Votes	Coverage (%)	S	IPR	LEE	CV	CRII	N
Sosialdemokr. puolue	23.12	93.8	9.56	.42	58.0	.41	.12	(13)
Maalausk./Keskustap.	21.19	93.4	11.75	.49	72.7	.56	.23	(12)
Komm./Vasemmistol.	16.46	96.9	7.17	.44	42.8	.45	.14	(13)
Kansallinen kokoom.	15.87	93.3	6.59	.41	38.2	.42	.12	(13)
Svenska folkspartiet	10.29	38.0	24.63	.86	107.3	2.41	.60	(13)
Suomen maaseudun p.	6.45	93.3	3.56	.49	20.0	.59	.20	(8)
Vihreä liitto	4.93	93.3	2.83	.46	14.3	.58	.18	(3)
Liberaalinern kansanp.	4.90	92.6	2.83	.48	16.3	.57	.19	(9)
Demokraattinen vaiht.	4.12	93.3	2.98	.50	14.6	.72	.18	(1)
Työväen-pienviljelijäin	3.38	93.3	1.90	.49	10.7	.59	.19	(2)
Suomen kristillinen t.	3.38	93.3	1.67	.46	9.6	.50	.15	(5)
Kansalaisvallan liitto	1.78	93.3	1.57	.62	9.6	.88	.34	(1)
Sosialdem. oppositio	1.51	25.0	2.79	.89	18.1	1.84	.71	(1)
Perustuslaillinen oik.	1.09	80.0	1.60	.70	7.5	1.47	.44	(1)

Notes: For changes of names, splits, mergers, and alliances between parties see Synopses 3 and 4 (Finland) in *EWE-1815*. See also notes to Table 4.1.
Legend: N = number of contested elections; S = standard deviation. For other abbreviations see Abbreviations and Symbols in the front matter.

below .41–.42 for the *Kansallinen kokoomuspuolue* (National Coalition Party) and the *Sosialdemokraattinen puolue* (Social Democrats). Overall, as the graph in Figure 4.1 shows, these values remained stable throughout the twentieth century. Besides the Swedish minority, another major factor in the territoriality of the Finnish party system is the different agrarian parties, in particular the large *Maalaisliitto* (Agrarian Union), established in 1906 and later transformed into the *Keskustapuolue* (Center Party). Since World War II, the agrarian Center Party has relied on support that is comparable – as far as its homogeneity is concerned – to that of the other major parties. This also applies to the other major agrarian party, *Suomen maaseudun puolue* (the Finnish Rural Party). However, it appears that the Agrarian Union-Center Party became increasingly nationalized between 1907 – when its rural character was stronger – and the 1930s. Since then, the territorial configuration of its electoral support has stabilized.

The levels of homogeneity of the Communist Party and the conservative National Coalition Party are similar to those of the Agrarians and the Social Democrats. The Greens (*Vihreä liitto*) and the Christian Labour Party (*Suomen kristillinen työväen puolue*) are smaller parties (with less than

135

5 percent of the vote nationwide) with comparable levels of homogeneity of support. The temporal pattern is one of basic stability, with the exception of the Agrarians. The Social Democrats are an interesting case since the levels of disparity of the vote peak suddenly in 1922, when this party suffered from a loss of support (from about 38 to 25 percent nationwide). This was due to the founding of the Communist Party (as the Finnish Socialist Workers' Party), which relied initially on support limited to a few regions.[19]

The Nationalized Territorial Configurations

In all of the remaining nine countries, parties cover most national territories: In Austria, Denmark, France, Greece, Iceland, the Netherlands, Norway, Portugal, and Sweden, territorial coverage by parties involves more than 90 percent of the constituencies (see also Table 3.2). In all these countries, furthermore, electoral behavior is homogeneous.

Homogeneous Nordic Countries: Denmark, Iceland, Norway, Sweden

In all respects (territorial coverage by parties and uniformity of electoral behavior), Denmark appears to be an extremely homogeneous country. Table 4.9 illustrates this result. Almost all parties have contested all constituencies (*storkredse* and *amtskredse*) since World War II, and the values for all other indices are low. The most homogeneous party is the *Socialdemokrater*, the dominant party of the system. The IPR and CRII values are very low (.25 and .05, respectively), as is the standard deviation (5.19), despite its large size in terms of votes. The other main party is the Liberal Party (*Venstre* or Left), which, notwithstanding the electoral decline since World War I, is still the second largest party after World War II. This party, like most Scandinavian liberal parties, has strong agrarian connotations and is particularly weak in the city *storkredse* of Copenhagen (Søndre, Østre, and Vestre) and in all of the capital *amtskredse*, while it collects most votes in the areas of Ribe, Ringkøbing, and Viborg. Its support is therefore less homogeneous than that of the Social Democrats even though it is present throughout the country. Finally, the last major party of the system is the *Konservative folkeparti* (Conservative People's Party), the successor of *Højre* (or Right), which also displays homogeneous support throughout

[19] These constituencies are Uudenmaan lääni, Turun-Porin lääni eteläinen, Kuopion lääni läntinen, Oulun lääni eteläinen, Oulun lääni pohjoinen, and Lapland.

the country. Other homogeneous parties are *Det radikale venstre* (an agrarian splinter group of the Venstre in 1905) and *Fremskridtspartiet* (Progress Party), the new right-wing party established in 1972.

The less nationalized parties include the Communist Party (*Danmarks kommunistiske parti*) and the Christian People's Party (*Kristeligt folkepartiet*), as well as the small green party (*Grønne*). The most regionalized party is the *Slesvigske parti* (or *Schleswigsche Partei* in German) of the German-speaking minority, which was established after the third 1920 election. It receives all its support from a single constituency (as the IPR of 1.00 shows): Haderslev according to the districts of 1918 and Sønderjyllands according to the districts of 1971.[20]

The evolution of the territorial configuration of the main parties (Figure 4.1) shows an early process of nationalization of the two main parties of the nineteenth century: *Venstre* and *Højre*. This is similar to the patterns seen in Belgium (Catholics and Liberals), Switzerland (Radicals and Liberals), and Britain (Conservatives and Liberals). Furthermore, the Social Democrats undergo a faster and more abrupt process of nationalization in the late nineteenth and early twentieth centuries. Since the 1920s the pattern has stabilized with the introduction of PR, although a slower evolution towards uniformity of voting behavior occurs afterward.

For Iceland, party results are available only since 1916, which explains why the curves in Figure 4.1 start only at this date. Until the first (June) of the two elections of 1959, the electoral system of Iceland was a complicated mixture of plurality and PR formulas, and of *Kjördæmakosningar* (elections by plurality held either in single-member or two-member constituencies) and *Landskosningar* (supplementary seats with national lists). The system changed radically at the October 1959 election, when plurality was completely abandoned and PR extended to the entire country. As indicated in Figure 4.1, this change has had a stabilizing effect on the territorial configuration of the support for the main parties since the 1950s. Nevertheless, during the previous period, there was a clear trend toward increasing homogeneity of support across the regions. This is true for all four main parties of the Icelandic system.

These four parties are the ones participating in all 14 elections since World War II. No other party has participated in more than four elections (according to the 5 percent criterion). All four parties are fairly

---

[20] The curve in Figure 4.1 of the *Slesvigske parti* is perfectly flat at the IPR level of 1.00, although it appears a bit lower to avoid superimposition with the frame of the graph. This party does not fulfill the 5 percent criterion for every election, in particular since 1973.

Table 4.9. *Levels of Territorial Heterogeneity for Danish Parties: World War II–Present*

Parties	Mean Votes	Coverage (%)	S	IPR	LEE	CV	CRII	N
Socialdemokrater	35.58	100.0	5.19	.25	41.8	.15	.05	(20)
Venstre	19.60	100.0	8.47	.42	66.0	.44	.18	(20)
Konser. Folkep. (Højre)	14.71	100.0	3.89	.33	30.2	.27	.10	(20)
Fremskridtspartiet	8.87	99.4	2.36	.35	15.5	.33	.12	(11)
Socialistisk folkeparti	7.93	100.0	3.84	.45	27.1	.51	.16	(16)
Danks folkeparti	7.41	100.0	1.44	.27	8.7	.19	.08	(1)
Det radikale venstre	7.26	100.0	2.27	.36	18.5	.32	.11	(19)
Retsforbundet	5.59	100.0	1.55	.34	13.9	.28	.10	(4)
Centrum demokraterne	5.48	100.0	1.47	.33	9.5	.27	.10	(8)
Kristeligt folkepartiet	3.37	100.0	2.03	.52	14.0	.63	.24	(6)
D. Kommunistiske p.	3.32	100.0	2.47	.54	18.7	.74	.25	(8)
De uafhængige	2.79	97.1	1.65	.51	15.6	.60	.22	(3)
Grønne	2.78	100.0	2.27	.56	13.7	.83	.23	(3)
Venstresocialisterne	2.64	100.0	2.11	.58	13.6	.82	.26	(5)
Slesvigske parti	.34	4.5	1.61	1.00	7.2	4.71	.95	(8)

Notes: For changes of names, splits, mergers, and alliances between parties see Synopses 3 and 4 (Denmark) in *EWE-1815*. See also notes to Table 4.1.
Legend: N = number of contested elections; S = standard deviation. For other abbreviations see Abbreviations and Symbols in the front matter.

homogeneous. The two most homogeneous parties are the conservative Independence Party (*Sjálfstæðisflokkur*) and the Communist Party (now the People's Alliance or *Alþiðubandalag*). The two other main parties are the agrarian Progressive Party (*Framsóknarflokkur*) and the Social Democratic Party (*Alþýðuflokkur*). In more recent times new parties have appeared, the most continuous of which is the *Samtök um kvennalista* (Women's List) since 1983. Three lists in particular are territorially concentrated in a single constituency (as the IPR of 1.00 in Table 4.10 indicates): the *Vestfjarðalistinn* (the Westfiord Candidacy) and *Suðurlandslistinn* (the Southern Icelandic Candidacy) in 1995, and the *Samtök um jafnrétti og félagshyggu* (Association for Equality and Social Justice), which contested only the 1987 election in the Nordurlandskjördæmi. In neither case, however, is it possible to speak of regionalist parties proper.

The agrarian element in Icelandic politics was much stronger before World War II, although the Farmers' Party (1) (*Bændaflokkur*) and the Independent Farmers (*Óháðir bændur*) merged in 1916 to form the Progressive Party (a change of name that occurred much later in other Scandinavian

Types of Territorial Configurations

Table 4.10. *Levels of Territorial Heterogeneity for Icelandic Parties: World War II–Present*

Parties	Mean Votes	Coverage (%)	S	IPR	LEE	CV	CRII	N
Sjálfstæðisflokkur	33.43	100.0	8.41	.33	45.3	.25	.09	(14)
Framsóknarflokkur	31.79	100.0	13.27	.42	83.2	.42	.27	(14)
Komm./Alþiðubandal.	15.35	100.0	4.76	.36	27.7	.33	.09	(14)
Alþýðuflokkur	12.72	99.7	6.35	.45	41.6	.50	.12	(14)
Borgaraflokkur	8.01	100.0	4.52	.52	15.2	.56	.15	(1)
Samtök frjálslyndra	7.53	93.7	5.54	.52	14.5	.72	.16	(2)
Þióðvaki, hreyfing fól.	6.12	100.0	2.01	.38	6.3	.33	.11	(1)
Bandalag jafnaðarman.	5.55	100.0	2.29	.43	7.2	.41	.14	(1)
Kvennalista	5.21	84.3	2.80	.53	9.0	.66	.20	(4)
Þióðarflokkur	3.22	62.5	3.77	.70	11.1	1.17	.70	(1)
Þióðvarnaflokkur	2.46	82.5	2.03	.61	17.7	.90	.27	(4)
Vestfjarðalistinn	1.63	12.5	4.62	1.00	11.4	2.83	.97	(1)
Samtök jafnrétti og f.	1.51	12.5	4.28	1.00	10.6	2.83	.90	(1)
Lýðveldisflokkur	1.25	100.0	1.46	.64	13.6	1.17	.38	(1)
Suðurlandslistinn	1.07	12.5	3.01	1.00	7.4	2.83	.92	(1)

Notes: For changes of names, splits, mergers, and alliances between parties see Synopses 3 and 4 (Iceland) in *EWE-1815*. See also notes to Table 4.1.

Legend: N = number of contested elections; S = standard deviation. For other abbreviations see Abbreviations and Symbols in the front matter.

countries). Furthermore, in 1934 the Farmers' Party (2) formed as a splinter group of the Progressive Party but contested only two elections.

Norway's parties too – despite the strong emphasis in the literature on territorial countercultures[21] – rely on homogeneous support. The combination of countercultural movements has produced the distinctiveness of some regions, such as the *fylker* of the West. However, these cleavages have not produced deep regional differences in party strength. As can be seen in Table 4.11, on a comparative basis all major parties display high nationalization of electoral support.

[21] Norwegian regionalism has been widely documented in the wake of S. Rokkan and H. Valen's efforts to collect and systematize socioeconomic, cultural, and electoral data at the communal level (Valen and Katz 1961, 1964; Rokkan and Lipset 1967; Rokkan and Aarebrot 1969; Rokkan and Valen 1970; Valen and Converse 1971; Valen and Rokkan 1974; Valen 1976). Norway is characterized by three main countercultures: (a) a religious counterculture that opposes the west and the south of the country to the secularized central and urban areas, (b) a linguistic counterculture according to which the *nynorsk* movement created a written language out of oral dialects, and (c) the temperance movement (or "teetotalism") attempting to limit the consumption of spirits.

Table 4.11. *Levels of Territorial Heterogeneity for Norwegian Parties: World War II–Present*

Parties	Mean Votes	Coverage (%)	S	IPR	LEE	CV	CRII	N
Det norske arbeiderp.	41.28	100.0	8.00	.29	63.3	.19	.07	(12)
Høire	19.11	100.0	6.96	.38	50.4	.38	.16	(12)
Kristelig folkeparti	10.49	97.5	5.36	.47	42.7	.52	.22	(12)
Bonde/Senterpartiet	10.44	93.3	5.67	.47	40.7	.56	.21	(12)
Fremskrittspartiet	7.31	100.0	2.47	.41	19.9	.39	.15	(6)
Venstre	6.57	100.0	3.42	.45	27.8	.49	.20	(12)
Sosialistisk folkeparti	5.48	91.6	2.25	.45	17.4	.52	.18	(9)
Norske kommun. parti	3.28	91.2	2.83	.56	18.1	.93	.23	(4)
Det liberale folkeparti	1.64	73.6	1.20	.66	9.3	.94	.35	(2)
Framtid for Finnmark	1.13	5.2	4.93	1.00	20.3	4.36	.98	(1)
Rød Valgallianse	.74	100.0	1.11	.63	5.2	1.49	.45	(1)

Notes: For changes of names, splits, mergers, and alliances between parties see Synopses 3 and 4 (Norway) in *EWE-1815*. See also notes to Table 4.1.

Legend: N = number of contested elections; S = standard deviation. For other abbreviations see Abbreviations and Symbols in the front matter.

In Figure 4.1 the curves of territorial heterogeneity of support for the main Norwegian parties start in 1903, with the introduction of a two-ballot majoritarian formula in 123–26 single-member constituencies (PR is introduced at the 1921 election with 29 *valgdistrikter*). The graph shows fundamental stability of the level of regionalism for all parties. Support for the Labor Party (*Det norske arbeiderparti*) becomes more uniform between 1903 and 1945 and then stabilizes. From the 1920s to the 1940s, the most regionalized party was the agrarian *Bondepartiet*, which became more na-tionalized after World War II with its transformation into the Center Party (*Senderpartiet*) in 1961. In the 1950s another party appeared and spread throughout the country: the Christian People's Party (*Kristelig folkeparti*). For the two main parties of the nineteenth century, the Liberals (*Venstre*) and Conservatives (*Høire*), the pattern was nationalized in the 1900s and remained stable afterward.

After World War II, the Norwegian party system is dominated by the Labor Party, which receives on average (12 elections) 41.28 percent of the votes. The support for this party is very homogeneously distributed across regions (IPR of .29), although it has traditional strongholds in the north and the east (with the exception of the cities, Oslo in particular, where *Høire* is stronger). The Labor Party is weakest in the west, where

Table 4.12. *Levels of Territorial Heterogeneity for Swedish Parties: World War II–Present*

Parties	Mean Votes	Coverage (%)	S	IPR	LEE	CV	CRII	N
Sv. sociald. arbetarep.	44.92	100.0	5.87	.24	71.7	.13	.06	(16)
Moderata samlingsp.	16.76	100.0	4.95	.35	54.4	.30	.13	(16)
Bondef./Centerpartiet	16.04	100.0	5.87	.39	62.6	.40	.18	(15)
Folkspartiet liberalerna	12.73	100.0	3.73	.33	39.2	.28	.11	(16)
Ny demokrati	6.55	100.0	1.37	.29	14.8	.21	.07	(1)
Kristdem. Samhällsp.	4.96	98.2	1.96	.43	19.6	.52	.18	(6)
Vänsterp. Kommunist.	4.93	97.3	2.58	.45	25.7	.59	.21	(16)
Miljöpartiet de Gröna	4.51	100.0	.80	.27	9.0	.18	.07	(4)
Medborgelig samling	.99	28.5	5.26	1.00	26.8	5.29	.94	(1)

Notes: For changes of names, splits, mergers, and alliances between parties see Synopses 3 and 4 (Sweden) in *EWE-1815*. In 1985 *Centerpartiet* allied with *Kristdemokratiska samhällspartiet* (the Christian Democratic Community Party). See also notes to Table 4.1.

Legend: N = number of contested elections; S = standard deviation. For other abbreviations see Abbreviations and Symbols in the front matter.

the countercultures dominate and where the Christian People's Party relies on the Lutheran fundamentalist support. Finally, the right-wing Progress Party (*Fremskrittspartiet*), which has been contesting the past six elections, is homogeneously present in all constituencies. The only party for which the indicators of heterogeneity are high is the *Framtid for Finnmark* (Future for Finnmark), a recent regional splinter of the Labour Party, which has been considered separately. This party is present in one *fylke* (Finnmark) and fulfills the 5 percent criterion only in 1989.

Sweden, like Norway, has been dominated by the Social Democratic Workers' Party (*Socialdemokratistiska arbetareparti*), which since World War II has received almost 45 percent of the votes on average (Table 4.12). The Swedish Social Democratic Workers' Party is extremely homogeneous across the country (IPR of .24). Support for all other parties is also distributed homogeneously across regions. The IPR is never above .45 (for the Communists), with the exception of the Citizens' Union (*Medgorgelig samling*), which contested the only 1964 election and whose support comes from a single *län* (constituency) (Malmö/Fyrstadskretsen). All of the main parties are present in all constituencies: the conservative *Moderata sam-lingspartiet* (Moderate Alliance Party, formerly the *Högerpartiet* or Right Party), the liberal *Folkspartiet liberalerna* (Liberal People's Party) – which split between 1923 and 1934 into the *Frisinnade folkepartiet* (prohibitionist liberals) and the *Sweriges liberale parti* – and the agrarian *Bondeförbundet* (Agrarian League), renamed the *Centerpartiet* (Center Party) in 1957. The three more recent parties – *Miljö partiet de gröna* (Greens), *Kristdemokratiska samhällspartiet* (Christian Democratic Community Party), and the right-wing *Ny demokrati* (New Democracy) – are also very homogeneous. The pattern for all parties is stable, with the notable exception of the Liberals during the 1920s and 1930s, corresponding to their division along the prohibitionist cleavage. As far as the more recent decades are concerned, only the Center Party seems to indicate a renewed regionalization of its support, due mainly to the loss of support this party encountered in the cities.

Nonterritorial Cleavages: The Netherlands and Austria

The Dutch case is particularly interesting, for it combines a high level of social segmentation with a low level of territorial heterogeneity. Political parties are the expression of three main "pillars" (*zuilen*) – closed networks of social organization based on religion and ideology – to which a great deal of work has been devoted (Daalder 1971a, 1971b; Lijphart 1968): the Catholic and Protestant pillars, culturally more closed and organizationally more structured, and the *algemene* or general pillar (which includes the social-democratic and liberal subcultures), with a more fluid organization and a less rigid ideology. The links between subcultures and electoral behavior have always been very close, with voting patterns reproducing the segmentation of the society. Only by the end of the 1960s has the *verzuiling* started to melt down (*ontzuiling*), weakened by the process of secularization and challenged by new parties such as *Democraten '66*.

Whereas the unity of the Roman Catholic Church discouraged the fragmentation of the Catholic camp, two main Calvinist parties existed. The first is the *Anti-revolutionaire partij* (Anti-Revolutionary Party), founded in 1879 in opposition to the Liberals and the ideals of the French Revolution. The second is the *Christelijke-historische unie* (Christian Historical Union), formed in 1908 as a breakaway from the Anti-Revolutionary Party. The *Katholieke volkspartij* (Catholic People's Party) first formed as an electoral league (*Rooms-katholieke bond van kiesverenigingen*). The two main parties of the general pillar are the Liberals (since 1946 the *Volkspartij voor vrijheid en democratie*) and the *Partij van der arbeid* (Labor Party), founded in 1946 in a merger between the small *Vrijzinning-democratische bond* (Liberal Democratic League), *Christelijk-democratische unie* (Christian Democratic

Union), and the historical labor party *Sociaal-democratische arbeiders partij* (established in 1894).

In 1919 PR was introduced with 18 *kamerkieskringen* (constituencies) (19 since 1986 with the addition of Flevoland) for the presentation of lists. The single national constituency explains to a certain extent why all parties are present in all *kamerkieskringen* since World War II (see Table 4.13) with the exception of the *Centrumdemocraten* (Center Democrats), who in 1998 do not present lists in Drenthe and Nijmegen. According to the remaining indicators, the support for all parties is extremely homogeneous; no CRII value is above .42. Even values of the standard deviation – influenced by the size of parties – are very low with the exception of the Catholic People's Party, whose support is concentrated mainly in the provinces of 's-Hertogenbosch, Tilburg, and Limburg (almost 80 percent of the votes), whereas in the provinces of Groningen, Friesland, and Drenthe its support is rarely above 5 percent. The remaining largest confessional parties are more evenly distributed across provinces, as the indicators show, even though the support for the Protestant Anti-Revolutionary Party and the Christian Historical Union is stronger in provinces such as Friesland, Dordrecht, Zeeland, Arnhem, and so on. Support for the Social Democrats and the Liberals is weaker in 's-Hertogenbosch, Tilburg, and Limburg, where the Catholics dominate.[22] Among the large number of smaller confessional parties (see Table 4.13 and Table 5.7 in the next chapter), the least nationalized is the Calvinist *Staatkundig Gereformeerde Partij* (Political Reformed Party), a very persistent independent party that was established in 1918 and that relies on support mainly from the province of Zeeland.

As the Dutch graph in Figure 4.1 shows, since World War I this party has been the most regionalized party in the Netherlands. Whereas the period from 1888 to 1918 displays quite erratic curves of territorial disparities, since the introduction of PR the pattern has become more stable, with the notable change in the party system occurring between the 1972 and 1977 elections, when the three main confessional parties (Catholic People's Party, Anti-Revolutionary Party, and Christian Historical Union) merged to form the *Christen democratisch appèl* (Christian Democrat Appeal). The curves for

---

[22] As far as the Liberals are concerned, Daalder notes that they were overrepresented in the international-commercially oriented northwest. Before World War I, part of the nonterritorial nature of the Catholic and Protestant distribution of votes can be attributed to different franchise provisions between areas (rural and urban in particular) and to gerrymandering (Daalder 1966: 204).

Table 4.13. *Levels of Territorial Heterogeneity for Dutch Parties: World War II–Present*

Parties	Mean Votes	Coverage (%)	S	IPR	LEE	CV	CRII	N
Partij van de Arbeid	29.74	100.0	7.67	.33	54.9	.26	.09	(14)
Christen Dem. Appèl	27.46	100.0	7.96	.34	57.7	.30	.10	(7)
Katholieke Volksp.	25.56	100.0	19.88	.56	136.0	.78	.30	(7)
Liberale P./VVD	15.46	100.0	4.76	.36	34.2	.33	.12	(14)
Anti-Revolut. Partij	10.13	100.0	5.27	.46	36.6	.52	.21	(7)
Christ.-Historische U.	8.10	100.0	4.61	.51	35.1	.57	.26	(7)
Democraten '66	7.86	100.0	1.71	.31	12.3	.23	.08	(9)
Boerenpartij	4.75	100.0	1.65	.40	12.6	.35	.15	(1)
Polit. Partij Radicalen	4.67	100.0	.95	.30	6.9	.20	.07	(1)
Dem. Socialisten '70	4.66	100.0	1.73	.41	13.0	.37	.16	(2)
Communistische Partij	4.23	100.0	3.47	.56	21.0	.90	.31	(8)
Socialistische Partij	3.47	100.0	1.25	.39	10.2	.36	.15	(1)
Pacifistisch-Soc. Partij	2.85	100.0	1.77	.52	12.9	.62	.25	(2)
Katholieke Nat. Partij	2.56	100.0	1.95	.56	13.7	.76	.27	(1)
Staatkundig Geref. P.	2.15	100.0	2.42	.68	17.3	1.12	.42	(11)
Algemeen Ouderen V.	2.09	100.0	.70	.38	5.6	.35	.14	(2)
Rerformat. Pol. Feder.	1.94	100.0	1.17	.52	10.0	.60	.28	(1)
Gereformeerd Polit. V.	1.65	100.0	1.22	.55	8.8	.75	.29	(3)
Centrumdemocraten	1.63	95.0	.85	.45	6.1	.53	.16	(2)

Notes: For changes of names, splits, mergers, and alliances between parties see Synopses 3 and 4 (The Netherlands) in *EWE-1815*. See also notes to Table 4.1.

Legend: N = number of contested elections; S = standard deviation. For other abbreviations see Abbreviations and Symbols in the front matter.

the Catholic party and the two Calvinist parties are therefore interrupted and replaced by the homogeneous curve of the new party. This party, by incorporating the main religious segments of the population, covers the entire territory homogeneously.

As shown in the country comparison, Austria belongs to the most nationalized systems. Table 4.14 confirms that all parties are present in all constituencies for every election (coverage of 100 percent).[23] Since 1919, the Austrian party system has been dominated by two main parties: the *Österreichische Volkspartei* (Austrian People's Party) and the *Sozialistische Partei Österreichs* (Austrian Socialist Party). The two parties, on average, receive more than 80 percent of the vote. The third party of the system

[23] Only the Communists have a more limited presence. Their score would be 100 percent, but in 1966 this party contested a single constituency (Wien Nordost), so the overall mean is reduced to the values appearing in Table 4.14.

Table 4.14. *Levels of Territorial Heterogeneity for Austrian Parties: World War II–Present*

Parties	Mean Votes	Coverage (%)	S	IPR	LEE	CV	CRII	N
Sozialistische P. Öst.	42.74	100.0	9.07	.30	70.2	.21	.07	(14)
Österr. Volkspartei	42.14	100.0	9.82	.31	76.6	.24	.09	(14)
Freiheitliche Partei	10.21	100.0	3.88	.43	27.9	.44	.16	(14)
Die Grünen	5.73	100.0	1.90	.38	15.2	.34	.12	(3)
Liberales Forum	5.53	100.0	2.20	.40	24.7	.40	.16	(2)
Grüne Alternative	4.81	100.0	1.90	.43	7.2	.39	.16	(1)
Dem. Fortschrittliche	3.34	100.0	2.48	.57	26.0	.74	.29	(1)
Kommunistische Part.	2.24	88.0	1.68	.56	13.8	1.16	.31	(8)
Vereinte Grüne	2.08	100.0	1.21	.51	4.2	.58	.18	(1)

Notes: For changes of names, splits, mergers, and alliances between parties see Synopses 3 and 4 (Austria) in *EWE-1815*. See also notes to Table 4.1.
Legend: N = number of contested elections; S = standard deviation. For other abbreviations see Abbreviations and Symbols in the front matter.

is the *Freiheitliche Partei Österreichs* (Austrian Liberal Party). These are the only three parties contesting all 14 elections since World War II, as shown in Table 4.14 (according to the 5 percent criterion).

The early literature on the Austrian party system described the main political cleavage between the socialist, Catholic-conservative (represented by the *Christlich-Soziale Partei* after World War I, which led to the corporatist state), and German-national-liberal camps (in the 1930 the *Großdeutsche Volkspartei* and after World War II the Independents, which eventually formed the Liberal Party) in terms of *Lager* (see, e.g., Lehmbruch 1967). Traditionally, the Socialists were stronger in Vienna, so that this cleavage assumed to some extent a center–periphery dimension (Gerlich 1987). Furthermore, in the Catholic-conservative *Lager*, a number of agrarian elements existed (represented during the same periods by the *Landbund für Österreich*).

Nevertheless, the *Lager* are not territorial but rather functional alignments, similar to the *zeuilen* in the Netherlands. As the data show, the two most nationalized parties are the People's Party and the Socialist Party (IPR of .31 and .30, respectively). The Greens (*Die Grünen*) are also homogeneously distributed across the constituencies. The temporal evolution of the three main Austrian parties (Figure 4.1) shows a fundamental stability of the levels of territoriality, with a smooth trend toward increasing nationalization and with the Liberals spreading throughout the country since the

1980s (a process similar to that of the Swiss Agrarians after the ideological change).

Homogeneous Systems: France, Greece, and Portugal

The French party system has traditionally been characterized by fluid and unstable electoral alignments, with a delayed structuring of party organizations and parliamentary groups. For this reason, works attempting to reconstruct the party affiliation of candidates are rare until 1910 (see Chapter 2).[24] The continuity of party organizations since World War II itself is very insecure, with – as an example – the Gaullist party changing its name seven times since its foundation in 1951.

One aspect of the unstructured character of French party organizations is the weak control of the territory by parties that build differentiated alliances from constituency to constituency (not last because of the frequent changes in the electoral legislation), very much influenced by local personalities. Since this analysis concentrates as much as possible on parties, regional alliances have been omitted in Table 4.15. This is notably the case for alliances at the constituency level between the *Mouvement républicain populaire* and the *Union démocratique et socialiste de la résistance*, between the Socialists and the *Parti républicain radical et radical socialiste*, and between the various radical and independent republican parties.

At the beginning of the Third Republic, the Right (conservatives) was stronger in the western regions of France, whereas the Left (the Republicans and, later, the Radicals and Socialists) dominated in the eastern half, in particular the industrial districts of the northeast as well as the rural areas of the southeast (with the exception of the Massif Central). Conservative support has a strong correlation with Catholicism in the west (Brittany), and Alsace-Lorraine. In the Fourth and Fifth Republics these distributions were inherited by the *Mouvement républicain populaire* (MPR), (the Christian-democrats of the Fourth Republic) and the Gaullists. Whereas the Socialists

---

[24] Parliamentary registrations have played an important role. Until 1906 party groups in the *Chambre des députés* hardly existed on a juridical basis. Representatives were allowed to enroll in up to three different groups at the same time, and no official registers were held (Bomier-Landowski 1951). In 1910 the *Règlement de la Chambre* introduced the rule of the *groupes fermés*, according to which representatives could belong to no more than one parliamentary group.

Table 4.15. *Levels of Territorial Heterogeneity for French Parties: World War II–Present*

Parties	Mean Votes	Coverage (%)	S	IPR	LEE	CV	CRII	N
Gaullistes	22.03	94.0	9.66	.44	355.9	.52	.17	(12)
Parti socialiste	21.91	98.0	7.93	.40	291.8	.41	.16	(13)
Union pour la dém. fr.	19.30	95.2	10.95	.46	395.0	.56	.18	(5)
Parti communiste	16.90	99.9	6.57	.40	247.7	.41	.16	(13)
Mouv. rép. populaire	11.39	85.2	10.01	.59	339.2	.91	.33	(4)
Centre démocrates soc.	9.81	76.8	8.43	.61	308.4	1.01	.36	(3)
Front national	8.76	89.3	3.49	.48	131.7	.67	.23	(5)
Républicains indépend.	6.87	49.7	9.92	.76	343.5	1.70	.56	(4)
Conservateurs	6.32	71.1	6.17	.68	207.5	1.40	.41	(12)
Parti radical-socialiste	6.08	57.4	5.70	.71	190.8	1.96	.54	(5)
Radicaux de droite	3.89	39.4	7.91	.84	241.5	2.05	.63	(2)
Ecologistes	2.73	69.3	1.58	.60	60.2	.96	.32	(5)
Rass. des gauches rép.	2.51	26.1	6.03	.88	167.3	2.61	.69	(2)
Mouv. rad. de gauche	2.12	35.8	4.99	.87	145.5	2.66	.71	(6)
Extrême droite	1.00	36.3	1.58	.82	48.9	2.28	.61	(5)

Notes: For changes of names, splits, mergers, and alliances between parties see Synopses 3 and 4 (France) in *EWE-1815*. See also notes to Table 4.1.
Legend: N = number of contested elections; S = standard deviation. For other abbreviations see Abbreviations and Symbols in the front matter.

were traditionally strong in the south, the Communists had strongholds around Paris.[25]

In spite of this diversity, Table 4.15 shows that the major French parties are rather nationalized. Parties characterised by some organizational continuity since World War II are, first, the *Parti socialiste* and the *Parti communiste français*. The other parties are the Gaullists (the largest party in France on average in 13 elections) and the *Union pour la démocratie française* (UDF), which, however, has existed only since 1978.[26] These are the most homogeneous parties in France (IPR between .40 and .46), covering more than 95 percent of the constituencies. Another quite homogeneous party is the *Front national* (IPR of .48), a recent party in its current form that contested five elections. The evolution since 1945 of the levels of territorial heterogeneity displayed in Figure 4.1 shows fundamental stability, disregarding the frequent changes of electoral law, from PR to two-ballot

[25] See Sternberger and Vogel (1969: 480 and 508) for a historical overview.
[26] The Gaullists and the UDF have merged to form the *Union pour un Mouvement Populaire* after the 2002 presidential and parliamentary elections.

Table 4.16. *Levels of Territorial Heterogeneity for Greek Parties: World War II–Present*

Parties	Mean Votes	Coverage (%)	S	IPR	LEE	CV	CRII	N
Nea demokratia	44.18	100.0	8.50	.27	188.1	.19	.08	(16)
PASOK	37.45	98.8	6.48	.25	124.0	.19	.06	(9)
Eniaia dim. aristera	31.40	84.8	16.63	.46	652.4	.53	.14	(2)
Enosi kentrou	27.44	100.0	7.54	.38	151.6	.54	.13	(6)
Komma filelefheron	21.71	100.0	12.72	.45	207.3	.59	.19	(2)
Prood. agrotiki enosi	10.93	98.1	8.69	.57	188.6	.79	.28	(1)
Ethniki prood. enosis	9.84	89.2	7.37	.56	168.9	.82	.29	(8)
Kommun. k. elladas	8.24	98.6	4.09	.45	88.9	.51	.17	(8)
Inomeni parataxis eth.	3.67	51.4	5.93	.77	100.8	2.62	.60	(3)
Politiki anixi	3.66	100.0	1.50	.38	28.0	.42	.13	(2)
Syn. aristeras proodou	3.37	100.0	1.41	.39	28.3	.42	.20	(2)
Agrotikon ergatikon	.97	10.0	4.27	.96	50.6	5.36	.90	(2)
Ikologi enallaktiki	.53	100.0	.23	.38	4.1	.44	.23	(2)
Ethniki polit. enosi	.46	98.2	.23	.46	5.3	.51	.17	(2)

Notes: For changes of names, splits, mergers, and alliances between parties see Synopses 3 and 4 (Greece) in *EWE-1815*. See also notes to Table 4.1.
Legend: N = number of contested elections; S = standard deviation. For other abbreviations see Abbreviations and Symbols in the front matter.

majoritarian systems and back. The only exception is the MRP, which, like other Catholic parties, has retrenched as a consequence of its weakening.[27]

The Greek party system was formed along the cleavages that emerged from the two main national conflicts of the twentieth century, that is, the "National Schism" of 1915–17 (Venezelists and Anti-Venezelists) and the civil war of 1947–49 (Nicolacopoulos 1984). These two cleavages structured the three-party system, with a "center" opposed to the Left on the basis of the civil war and opposed to the Right on the basis of the National Schism. The National Progressive Center Union progressively incorporated liberal and agrarian parties (*Komma fileleftheron*, *Agrotikon kai ergatikon komma*, etc.) to form the larger *Enosi kentrou* (Center Union in 1961). The Right reorganized as Greek Rally (*Ellenikos synagermos* in 1951, renamed later New Democracy, *Nea demokratia*, in 1974). The Center Union included all

---

[27] The *Poujadistes* (i.e., the *Union pour la défense des commerçants et des artisans*) and the *Centre national des indépendants et des paysans* (a liberal–agrarian party) have not been included since both contested only one election according to the 5 percent criterion. Other parties not considered include the *Groupement des contribuables* and minor Marxist-Leninist formations.

Table 4.17. *Levels of Territorial Heterogeneity for Portuguese Parties: World War II–Present*

Parties	Mean Votes	Coverage (%)	S	IPR	LEE	CV	CRII	N
Aliança democrática	43.27	90.0	20.27	.44	160.6	.47	.12	(2)
P. popular democrático	30.86	80.0	13.84	.51	101.2	.96	.31	(9)
P. socialista português	30.78	100.0	5.68	.28	46.2	.18	.06	(9)
P. comunista portug.	13.48	100.0	13.06	.63	101.3	.99	.30	(9)
P. renovador democ.	10.46	100.0	3.74	.43	30.8	.41	.15	(2)
P. centro dem. social	7.77	80.0	4.19	.56	33.2	1.06	.33	(9)
Mov. democr. portug.	4.72	100.0	2.17	.42	15.5	.46	.13	(1)

Notes: For party alliances see Appendix 4. For changes of names, splits, mergers, and alliances between parties see Synopses 3 and 4 (Portugal) in *EWE-1815*. See also notes to Table 4.1. *Legend:* N = number of contested elections; S = standard deviation. For other abbreviations see Abbreviations and Symbols in the front matter.

forces opposed to the Greek Rally, with the exception of the Communists (*Kommounistiko komma elladas*). The old People's Party (*Laikon komma*), which together with the Liberals dominated the party system before World War II, joined the Greek Rally in 1951 (except in four departments, which explains its curve in Figure 4.1).

The electoral support for these different forces – and, later, for the main party of the left (*PASOK*) – was characterized by a clear geographical segmentation based on the scheme of "old versus new provinces." The Greek Rally was, however, able to conquer the largest of the new provinces (Epirus, Macedonia, and Thrace), and to a lesser extent Crete and the eastern isles of the Aegean, replacing the old territorial cleavage with an urban–rural one. The rural areas supported the Center Union, which included agrarian parties. Therefore, whereas the liberal Venezelists were distributed unequally throughout the regions, the influence of the Center Union became much more homogeneous. The evolution of the main parties displayed in Figure 4.1 supports this view of a general trend toward the homogenization of electoral support.

Finally, the last among the most homogeneous party systems is the Portuguese one. As for Spain, results for elections to the Portuguese *Assembleia da República* are available for a shorter period of time (from 1975 to the present). The analysis has been carried out on the 20 *círculos eleitorais* (constituencies): 18 mainland *distritos administrativos* and 2 autonomous regions, the *Região autónoma dos Açores* and *Região autónoma da Madeira* (see Appendix 2).[28] All Portuguese parties are present in all constituencies (see Table 4.17). *Aliança democrática* is the result of an alliance in 1979 and 1980 between the *Partido popular democrático* (later the *Partido social democráta*, actually the Liberals) and the *Partido do centro democrático social*. Since this alliance was not extended to the entire country, the coverage is not 100 percent for the entire period since 1975 (see Appendix 4). Nevertheless, what appears in Table 4.17 is a highly nationalized political system with few regional differences in the levels of support between parties. The main party that displays higher levels of regionalization is the Communist Party, which is particularly strong in Beja, Évora, and Setúbal (its support is also stronger in the capital and in Portalegre). In the remaining constituencies, this party rarely receives more than 3 percent of the vote. The Portuguese political system does not include regionalist and agrarian parties, and the *Partido da democracia crista* never reached the 5 percent threshold for inclusion in the computations.

A Typology of Territorial Configurations

The previous country-by-country description has the function of pointing out the many specificities of the territorial configuration of European party systems. Furthermore, it allows one to identify the features that distinguish and assimilate countries. In other words, it clarifies the "composition" of regionalism in those countries in which the territorial element is stronger in voting behavior. These elements can be used to classify countries according to two dimensions distinguished earlier, each of which has been roughly dichotomized in Figure 4.2.

The *first dimension* – how regionalized is the support for the *main parties* of each system? – divides the main parties of each system into heterogeneous versus homogeneous groups by including in the analysis only those parties collecting at least 15 percent of the nationwide vote on average over all elections since World War II. National systems are then classified according to the average IPR value of these parties. IPR values range from a maximum of .72 in the case of the major Belgian parties (after their division along the linguistic cleavage) to a minimum of .29 (Greece). The median value of .40 has therefore been chosen to dichotomize this dimension.

[28] In 1975 and 1976 the two autonomous regions constituted four districts: Angra do Heroísmo, Horta, Ponta Delgada (Açores), and Funchal (Madeira). These can be aggregated for the period 1979–present into the two autonomous regions.

The *second dimension* – what is the impact of *regionalist parties*, that is, parties specifically created for territorial defense? – distinguishes the small from the large regionalist parties. Large regionalist parties are those that cover at least 10 percent of the national territory and receive strong support within the areas they cover. "Strong" support here means that the party receives at least 10 percent of the vote in the constituencies it contests. There are not many such parties in Europe: the *Volksunie* and the *Vlaamse bloc* in Belgium (to which it is possible to add the *Rassemblement wallon* when it is allied with the FDF), the *Christlich-Soziale Union* in Germany (which has here been considered a regionalist party), the *Svenska folkspartiet* in Finland, and more recently the *Lega Nord* in Italy. Other parties covering large areas exist but usually have weak support (e.g., the *Partito sardo d'azione* in Italy). Most regionalist parties are small, covering less than 10 percent of the national territory.

On the basis of this twofold dichotomy, four types of territorial configurations can be distinguished. In Figure 4.2 the most regionalized countries according to the ranking of Chapter 3, based on the cumulative standard deviation, are presented in boldface. The figure shows that the most regionalized systems are those in which either (1) *the main parties rely on regionalized support* (Belgium, Finland, Switzerland, in part Britain) or (2) *there is a large regionalist party* (Germany, in part Italy), with (3) one exception (Spain). The four types are the following.

1. *Nationalized party systems.* These systems are characterized by homogeneous support for all parties and by the absence of regionalist parties.

These countries are characterized first by territorially homogeneous support for the main parties (IPR values reach a maximum of .37). Second, there are no large regionalist parties except for *Framtid for Finnmark* in Norway, the two independent candidacies in Iceland, and the German-speaking minority party in Denmark. In this group *Spain* stands out as the outlier. What characterizes Spain is not the regionalization of the large parties or the size of the regionalist parties, but the extremely large *number* of regionalist parties in most of the ethnically distinct regions.

2. *Segmented party systems.* The term "segmented" indicates the presence of mainly one distinct "solid" region represented by a strong regionalist party with homogeneous support.[29]

In the *German* case the support for the main parties (CDU and *Sozialdemokratische Partei*) is uniform (.37 on average since World War II),

[29] See the preceding analysis of contested constituencies only.

Electoral support for main parties (>15% nationwide) is:

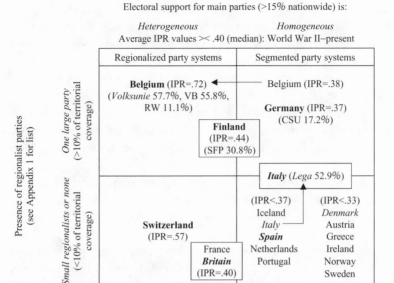

Figure 4.2 A classification of party systems on the basis of the territorial configurations of party support.

Notes: The following regionalist parties have not been considered in the classification of countries: *Lega dei ticinesi* (Switzerland), *Framtid for Finnmark* (Norway), *Vestfjarðalistinn* and *Suðurlandslistinn* (Iceland), *Partito sardo d'azione* and *Lega d'azione meridionale* (Italy), and *Slesvigske parti* (Germany). In Portugal alliances in Açores are not considered. In Spain, *Partido andalucista* actually covers 15.3 percent of constituencies.

Legend: Italics are used for the presence of small regionalist parties. Bold characters are used for regionalized territorial configurations of party systems (above European mean of 45.65, see Table 3.2) on the basis of cumulative standard deviation. CSU = *Christlich-Soziale Union*, SFP = *Svenska folkspartiet*, RW = *Rassemblement wallon*, VB = *Vlaamse bloc*.

although the alliance between the CSU and the CDU also affects the CDU in that this party does not present its own candidates in the 45 Bavarian *Wahlkreise*. Instead, regionalism in Germany since World War II is characterized by the distinctive vote for the CSU in Bavaria, which can therefore be considered a confessional (mostly Catholic) party with strong regionalist connotations. A similar case is *Belgium before* the division of the main parties along the linguistic cleavage. Socialists, Catholics, and Liberals were highly nationalized parties with homogeneous support (IPR of .38 on average), whereas there were a number of larger and smaller regionalist parties (the *Volksunie* being the main one). Overall, however, these regionalist parties were unable to make the Belgian territorial configuration of voting behavior highly regionalized. In *Italy* too, the main parties are nationalized and the system includes a number of small regionalist parties. Since the beginning of the 1990s, in addition, one large regionalist party exists. This party is the *Lega Nord*, which covers more than half of the constituencies and receives about 11 percent of the votes within these areas.

3. *Territorialized party systems.* The main parties of the system are heterogeneously distributed across the territory because of cultural cleavages, but there are no strong regionalist parties.

In contrast to Germany and Finland, *Switzerland* is characterized by the absence of regionalist parties (the *Lega dei ticinesi* and the *Parti social-chrétien indépendant du Jura* are recent and limited regionalist phenomena). The regionalist territorial configuration in this fragmented country is caused instead by the diversity of support for the main parties, for which, on average since 1945, the IPR is .57. In *France and Britain* the degree of regionalism of the support for the larger parties corresponds to the median (.40). In Britain a number of small regionalist parties exist, the main ones being the Scottish National Party and the *Plaid Cymru*. The effect on the rather regionalized territorial configuration of these two parties is, however, limited.

4. *Regionalized party systems.* Not only are the main parties unevenly distributed across the territory because of cultural cleavages, but regional identities give rise to strong regionalist parties.

Two countries combine the diversity of support for the main parties and the presence of a large regionalist party. In *Belgium after* the division of the main parties along the linguistic cleavage, electoral support for the main Socialist, Catholic, and Liberal parties is extremely regionalized and the IPR ranges from .38 to .72. In addition, the *Volksunie* and, more recently, the *Vlaamse bloc* are two strong regionalist parties covering a large part of the national territory (the Flemish *arrondissements*), both receiving about 10 percent of the vote in those areas. In *Finland*, support for the main parties is more regionalized than in most other countries, especially compared to the other Nordic countries (IPR of .44 as opposed to values below .33 for the Scandinavian territories). No party covers the territory entirely because of the presence of the Swedish minority on the Åland Islands. Furthermore, the *Svenska folkspartiet* is a large regionalist party covering more than 30 percent of the national territory.

5

The Comparative Study of Cleavages and Party Families

The third main axis of comparison – after time and countries – is that of *cleavages* and, in particular, the *party families* that stemmed from them. This chapter compares the overall European levels of homogeneity of support of party families across countries, as well as their evolution over time.

Cleavages and Party Families

For the sake of cross-national and cross-temporal comparison, a series of standard codes have been given to parties. Appendix 1 lists the standard codes and the abbreviations, as well as the parties included in each of the following 10 party families: (1) social democrats, (2) conservatives, (3) liberals (and radicals), (4) communists, (5) Catholics, (6) interconfessional people's parties, (7) Protestants, (8) regionalists, (9) agrarians (and center parties), and (10) greens (ecological parties).[1]

The aggregation of national parties into European families raises a number of problems due to the differences existing between parties of the same family but of different countries. Which national parties have been included in each family? It would be a mistake to include all national parties belonging to a given ideological area (e.g., one could consider including in the social democratic category all Austrian, Belgian, and other national

---

[1] Nationalist parties (which had an important role particularly during the interwar period) and the more recent extreme right-wing parties *Fremskridtspartiet* (DK), *Front national* (FR), *Republikaner* (GE), *Movimento sociale italiano* (IT), *Fremskrittspartiet* (NO), *Nationale Aktion*, and *Republikanische Bewegung* (CH) have not been considered systematically. The same applies to monarchic parties, as well as Fascist and Nazi parties between World Wars I and II. See Appendix 1, as well as Chapter 2, for special cases (e.g., Irish parties) and for the division of Belgian parties along the linguistic cleavage in the 1960s–70s.

socialist parties). For some families in particular, it is important to distinguish parties and include only parties that are relevant from an *ideological, historical, and organizational* point of view. The first term defines the political family of parties. The second allows one to distinguish, within the same family, parties that had a relevant role in the phases of the formation and structuring of party systems from small parties that sporadically contested elections (e.g., the Danish *Socialdemokratiet* from the *Venstresocialisterne*, the Austrian *Sozialistische Partei Österreichs* from the *Bunddemokratische Sozialisten*). Clearly, the inclusion of such parties would distort the analysis to an important extent given their short-term existence, the erratic nature of their temporal evolution, and their number in each country at different times. Furthermore, the level of international comparability is very low for these parties, while for "official" parties it is much higher. From the organizational point of view, finally, relevance means a structured organization for the mobilization of electoral support and a leading role in international party organizations. The organizational strength of these parties led to a long-term and continuous presence throughout the period covered.

The aggregation of parties into families has been carried out as follows:

- *Conservative, liberal, and social democrat families*. These are the three main historical party families that formed during the nineteenth century and structured most European party systems until World War I. For each of these families, only the main party of each country has been included. The same applies to *communist* parties: Only communist parties that formed at the end of World War I – as splinters from the large working-class parties (social democrats, labor, etc.) – have been included in this party family.
- As far as *agrarian, green,* and *regionalist families* are concerned, all parties fulfilling the 5 percent criterion have been included. The family of *agrarian* parties includes two types of parties: (1) the large Nordic (and Swiss) agrarian parties that changed into center parties after World War II and (2) the smaller peasants' and farmers' parties that – at one time or another – existed in most countries.
- In the case of the *confessional family* too, all parties are included. Confessional parties have been divided into *Catholics, Protestants,* and *(interconfessional) people's parties*, but in some cases the three types have been included in a single category. Furthermore, some confessional parties have been grouped together as people's parties. This category includes the

155

Österreichische Volkspartei (Austria), *Parti social chrétien-Christelijke Volkspartij* (Belgium), *Mouvement républicain populaire* (France), *Christlich-Demokratische Union* (Germany), *Democrazia cristiana* (Italy), and *Christen democratisch appèl* (the Netherlands). The main problems with this category arise from mergers between different parties (e.g., in the Netherlands in the 1970s). Parties were kept separate until mergers occurred and then were classified differently. Another problem is that in several countries (Austria, Belgium, Switzerland, etc.) the *conservative party* was Catholic.

As mentioned in Chapter 2, to increase historical continuity, codes have been left unchanged when the name of the political party changed as a consequence of modified ideological positions. The comparison is therefore carried out following the organizational continuity rather than the ideological orientation of parties. This implies that even when important ideological changes occurred, codes do not change.

The Homogeneity of European Party Families

The Comparison of Party Families

Results of the comparison of the levels of heterogeneity of support between party families appear in Table 5.1, which is divided into three main periods and is based on indices controlling for party size (the standard deviation is included for reference). The least homogeneous party type is the *regionalist family*. Values of the indicators for this type of party are clearly outlying with respect to the values of other types. These parties cover on average about 16 percent of national territories. Also, the three indices that are appropriate for party comparison (IPR, CV, and CRII) display values that are much higher than those of the second, more regionalized party type since World War II (Protestant parties according to the IPR and the CV, and Catholic parties according to the CRII). During this period, for all other families, the percentage of constituencies in which parties are present is above 73 percent.

Regionalist parties also receive the most sectional support in the periods before World War I and during the interwar period. However, the gap between the values of regionalist parties and other party families is reduced compared to the period after World War II. From the 1840s until the 1910s, regionalist parties cover on average 14.37 percent of the territory. There are two more families for which the percentage is below 50: Agrarian parties are present in 37.96 percent and Protestant parties in 41.65 percent of the constituencies. The remaining indicators also display a smaller range between party families. In general, all party families are more regionalized in the earlier phases of electoral development. After World War I, however, the regionalists are the only party type covering less than half of the constituencies, and the gap in values according to all indicators increases.

The support *within* the territory covered by these parties on average is relatively homogeneous, indicating the existence of *solid sectional cleavages*. For all three periods of time, the IPR and CV computed on contested constituencies only (see the right-hand side of Table 5.1) display lower values for regionalist parties than to the same indices computed on all constituencies (contested and not). As far as the IPR is concerned, for example, during the first period the value is .47 as opposed to .94.

Despite the outlying values for the regionalist parties, the variation among the other party families remains quite important. It ranges from the less homogeneous agrarian and religious parties (Protestants and Catholics in particular) to the most uniform social democratic and conservative parties. By their nature, both agrarian and Catholic-Protestant parties refer to territorially defined electorates.

Historically, *agrarian parties* have based their claims upon defending agricultural interests against those of the industrialized areas and financial centers. The urban–rural cleavage from which these parties originate – as a legacy of the Industrial Revolution and of the estate system in which peasants elected their own representatives – has a strong territorial connotation. This is especially true for the nineteenth century. Before World War I, these parties cover on average a third of the territory, with values of disparity approaching those of regionalist parties. For these parties too, a sectional territorial structure can be observed during this period: Values computed on contested constituencies only show much greater homogeneity. During the interwar period they spread throughout constituencies, being present in 68.18 percent of them. Since World War II, finally, these parties continue to spread across national territories, reaching 84.38 percent, not least as a consequence of the transformation of the major Nordic agrarian parties into center parties during the 1950s–60s. Values of the measures of dispersion for these parties are also more homogeneous (IPR of .53 and CRII of .28).

Table 5.1. *The Territorial Heterogeneity of Party Families in Europe Subdivided by Periods*

Code	Party Families	Coverage (%)	All Constituencies					Only Contested Constituencies			
			IPR	CV	CRII	S	N	IPR	CV	S	N
					Before World War I (1840s–1910s)						
C	Conservatives	71.73	.60	1.02	.42	24.95	(124)	.44	.46	19.53	(124)
L	Liberals	70.73	.60	.90	.45	25.58	(124)	.42	.45	18.83	(123)
CC	Catholics	64.14	.69	1.95	.49	17.99	(63)	.53	.66	26.57	(62)
S	Social democrats	58.46	.71	2.00	.48	13.82	(93)	.52	.65	14.88	(89)
–	Religious parties	55.14	.73	1.40	.52	21.36	(105)	.53	.64	20.07	(102)
PROT	Protestants	41.65	.79	1.72	.58	10.47	(42)	.52	.61	10.01	(40)
A	Agrarians	37.96	.82	2.72	.66	12.21	(22)	.56	.72	14.78	(20)
REG	Regionalists	14.37	.94	3.76	.84	13.00	(31)	.47	.51	17.80	(30)
					Interwar Period (1920s–40s)						
C	Conservatives	93.43	.43	.53	.15	13.63	(94)	.39	.41	12.45	(94)
S	Social democrats	92.05	.46	.55	.18	12.65	(111)	.42	.44	11.80	(111)
NAZ	National-socialists/fascists	91.47	.46	.56	.21	4.98	(11)	.40	.44	4.63	(11)
CC	Catholics	91.79	.54	.77	.30	18.04	(45)	.51	.65	17.74	(45)
–	Religious parties	92.66	.55	.78	.30	14.02	(68)	.52	.67	13.73	(68)
PROT	Protestants	95.11	.56	.79	.29	5.56	(22)	.54	.72	5.45	(22)
L	Liberals	82.38	.56	.89	.32	9.62	(80)	.45	.50	8.94	(80)
K	Communists	85.24	.61	1.09	.33	5.78	(70)	.57	.83	6.12	(70)
A	Agrarians	68.18	.69	1.52	.46	11.19	(85)	.54	.81	10.80	(84)
REG	Regionalists	18.79	.92	5.82	.77	7.22	(49)	.54	.67	13.00	(32)

World War II–Present

	Party family										
S	Social democrats	94.32	.38	.37	.13	8.65 (227)	.34	.29	7.68	(227)
C	Conservatives	94.59	.39	.47	.15	7.96 (190)	.37	.36	7.68	(190)
ICP	Interconfessional parties	89.75	.40	.42	.16	14.30 (20)	.31	.24	8.72	(20)
–	Denomin. people's parties	82.73	.47	.56	.24	13.17 (73)	.33	.28	9.04	(73)
L	Liberals	85.22	.50	.72	.27	6.46 (177)	.40	.41	5.64	(177)
EX	Extreme right-wing parties	84.62	.50	.84	.24	2.65 (39)	.43	.47	2.67	(38)
K	Communists	90.40	.52	.80	.25	5.29 (151)	.48	.61	5.36	(150)
A	Agrarians	84.38	.53	.81	.28	8.39 (80)	.45	.51	8.31	(80)
G	Greens	78.14	.54	.75	.28	2.38 (44)	.38	.39	1.73	(44)
–	Religious parties	79.97	.56	.90	.32	11.05 (174)	.42	.46	8.39	(174)
CC	Catholics	73.17	.57	.92	.36	16.35 (87)	.38	.39	12.35	(87)
PROT	Protestants	85.90	.58	1.02	.33	3.20 (67)	.50	.61	3.14	(67)
REG	Regionalists	16.76	.93	4.90	.83	5.58 (172)	.56	.79	10.59	(143)

Notes: Party families are ordered from most to least homogeneous support based on the IPR. Territorial coverage (the number of constituencies in which parties are present on average as a percentage of the total number of constituencies) and CRII are applicable only to "all constituencies." The number of cases refers to parties at single elections. Depending on the missingness of voters' figures, the *N* for the CRII (see the formula in Appendix 3) can be less than the number indicated in the table. Italics are used for measures not appropriate for party comparison.

Legend: See Abbreviations and Symbols in the front matter.

In religiously mixed countries, *Catholic parties* – one of the most regionalized party types after World War II – base their electoral support in
the Catholic areas. Catholic minorities in mixed countries are often territorially concentrated: in Germany and Switzerland as well as, to a lesser
extent, in the Netherlands. In homogeneous Catholic countries such as
Austria, Belgium, France, and Italy, the distributions are more nationalized.
In these countries too, however, Catholic parties have strongholds causing
a certain degree of territorial disparity. Similarly, there is a distinction between *Protestant parties* in homogeneous Protestant countries (the Nordic
ones) and Protestant parties in religiously divided countries (Switzerland
and the Netherlands). Unlike Protestant parties, Catholic parties appear
to be homogeneous during the nineteenth and early twentieth centuries.
Figures for these periods, however, are limited to two parties, namely, the
Union catholique belge (as the Catholic party was called at the time) and the
Swiss *Katholische Konservative*.

Compared to the Catholic and Protestant parties, the interconfessional
people's parties after World War II – the Dutch *Christen democratisch appèl*
and the German *Christlich-Demokratische Union* – are characterized by
greater territorial homogeneity. The reasons for their more diffuse support lie not only in the general trend toward nationalization, but also in the
geographical distribution of the electorate. These parties overcome terri-
torial/religious cleavages and cover nearly 90 percent of the constituencies.
Indicators of dispersion have values similar to those of the conservatives
and the social democrats, that is, the most nationalized party types.

After World War I the main new parties that appear are *communist parties*, mostly as breakaways from the socialist and social democratic parties.
Furthermore, in addition to the political families listed in Appendix 1, for
the interwar period the *national-socialist and fascist family* has been created
and includes the German and Italian parties in the 1920s and 1930s as
well as the Danish *Danmarks nationalsocialistiske arbejderparti*, the Dutch
Nationaal-socialistische beveging, and the Norwegian *Nasjonal samling*. Communist parties are characterized by a medium level of homogeneity. Like
agrarians and religious parties, communist parties rely on rather concentrated support (namely, from the urban and industrialized zones or, as in
Italy, from given regions), although they tend to be present in a large number of constituencies (90.40 percent in the last period). In most countries,
communists are not the main party of the left, as is the case in Finland,
France, or Italy. Their support is more limited and less evenly spread geographically. A less diffuse and structured political organization concentrates

its efforts in the traditional areas of communist support.[2] By contrast, when they first appeared, national-socialist and fascist parties were homogeneous and covered more than 90 percent of the territory, with levels of nationalization similar to those of social democrats and conservatives.

The remaining parties display a much more homogenous pattern. *Liberal and conservative parties* are the political families that have dominated the electoral history of the nineteenth century and have been – together with the *social democrats* – the main elements of the structure of West European party systems since the 1850s. Conservatives (in some countries as Catholics) and liberals have existed since the earliest phases of constitutionalism and parliamentary life, and they figure as the first actors in the game of free elections. These parties are the state- and nation-builders of the political systems that emerged from the revolutions of the nineteenth century. Social democratic parties, on the other hand, represented the link between the newly enfranchised masses mobilized through the Industrial Revolution and the political system at the moment of the extension of suffrage. The claims and ideologies of all these party types do not address territorially segmented groups of the European electorates, and the spatial configuration of the support for these parties appears as the most homogeneous.

During the first of the three periods distinguished in Table 5.1, conservatives and liberals are the two most nationalized party families according to all indicators. Both parties are the only ones to cover more than 70 percent of national territories on average. Having appeared later, the social democrats cover a shorter period of time. Their support is initially more concentrated. After World War I, however, and the enfranchisement of the masses, social democrats appear as the most nationalized type of party after the conservatives. By contrast, the liberal family during the last two periods of time does not range among the most uniform families. This is also the effect of the general trend toward nationalization of the other families rather than reflecting exclusively a regionalization of support for the liberal parties (IPR values decrease constantly from .60 to .56 to .50 over the three periods). Since World War II, conservatives and social democrats are the most nationalized parties together with the larger interconfessional people's parties.

---

[2] The overall level of nationalization of communist parties is strongly influenced by the score of the Swiss *Partei der Arbeit*, whose electoral support is almost exclusively confined to the canton of Geneva.

Another type of party, which has appeared more recently, is the *ecological or green party family*. These usually small parties do not belong to the most nationalized category of parties. They are present in 84.38 percent of the constituencies on average and display medium levels of territorial disparity. Finally, in the last period (1945–present), one more family has been created: the *extreme right-wing party family*. This family includes the main new right-wing parties since the 1960s–70s such as the Progress parties in the Scandinavian countries (namely, the Danish *Fremskridtspartiet*, the Swedish *Ny Demokrati*, and the Norwegian *Fremskrittspartiet*), the *Front national* in France, the *Republikaner* in Germany, the *Movimento sociale italiano*, and the *Republikanische Bewegung* and *Nationale Aktion* (since 1990 *Schweizer Demokraten*) in Switzerland. Like the green parties, the extreme right-wing parties do not belong to the most nationalized group of families. They cover on average 84.62 percent of national territories, and the other indicators display medium levels of disparity of electoral support.

The Path Toward the Nationalization of Historical Parties

The comparison of the evolution over time is limited to the most important families and leaves out those for which the time span is too short: that is, greens, national-socialists, and fascist parties, as well as extreme right-wing parties.

Figure 5.1 shows that *all families tend toward the nationalization of support* in the course of the nineteenth and twentieth centuries with the *exception of the regionalist party family*. This indicates a progressive reduction of territorial disparities in voting support for all party families in Europe, except for those parties based on linguistic, territorial, and ethnic claims that refer specifically to the distinctiveness of the cultural and economic region from which they draw support. In Figure 5.1, the different types of denominational parties (Protestants, Catholics, etc.) have been aggregated together (see Figure 5.3 for the evolution of these types of parties).[3] For communist parties, the period of time that is covered is shorter since these parties

---

[3] The indicator that has been used is the IPR (appropriate for party comparisons since it controls for the size of parties and party families). Curves for other indicators (CV and CRII) have been omitted to avoid redundancy. Part of the information referred to in the text is not displayed in the tables and graphs.

appear in the wake of the International (Soviet) Revolution of 1917 in the aftermath of World War I. There is a move toward increased homogeneity of support after World War II due in part to the growth of these parties (namely, in France and Italy).

Besides regionalist and communist parties, the remaining five types of parties can be grouped into two categories:

- *Agrarian and social democratic parties*: sudden, steep evolution toward the uniformity of electoral support during the last decades of the nineteenth century and the first decades of the twentieth century;
- *Conservative, liberal, and confessional parties*: continuous, smooth evolution toward nationalization of voting support during the second half of the nineteenth century (since the beginning of competitive elections) and the twentieth century.

Agrarian parties, mostly those of the Nordic countries and Switzerland, clearly tend toward homogeneity (Figure 5.2). The support for this type of party becomes more uniform in all countries except Switzerland, whose *Schweizerische Volkspartei* (or *Union démocratique du centre*) is characterized by a rather stable geographical configuration until the mid-1980s, after which support becomes markedly diffused. The reduction of territoriality in the support for agrarian parties is particularly marked between the 1890s (when, in the graph, this type of party appears with the extension of suffrage) and World War I. During the 1890s the level of territoriality of agrarian parties – reflecting differences in support between rural and urban areas – is particularly high, equivalent to the levels of territorial disparity of regionalist parties.

Another family that stemmed from the cleavages created by the Industrial Revolution and urbanization processes is the *social democratic family* in the last decades of the nineteenth century. As with agrarians, the process of nationalization of the social democrats is rapid. In the space of three decades the territorial disparities that characterized these parties in the 1880s are more than halved. This process characterizes all countries for which data are available since the nineteenth century: Belgium, Denmark, Germany, Italy, the Netherlands, Switzerland, and the United Kingdom (see also Figure 6.5 in the next chapter). Notwithstanding the inclusion of additional countries in the first decades of the twentieth century and after World War I, the support for this type of party has remained extremely homogeneous in subsequent periods.

Conservative and liberal parties display a similar pattern through time. The level of nationalization of these electorates progressively increases during the nineteenth century and, during the twentieth century, the level reached by the end of World War I is maintained. In both cases the process of nationalization takes place early. Both types of parties are already nationalized in the nineteenth century. Particularly in the countries for which data are available since the mid-nineteenth century – Belgium, Denmark, Switzerland, and Britain – these parties are already structured organizations at the moment of the inclusion of the newly enfranchised masses and during the periods of greater democratization with the extension of suffrage and the equalization of voting conditions.[4]

The analysis of these four party families (agrarians, conservatives, liberals, and social democrats) confirms what was noted earlier: that the most important moments in the nationalization of electoral politics must be located in the first periods of West European electoral history, that is, during *the phases of first mobilization and formation of cleavage constellations and party systems.* These four types of parties could mobilize – through their organization and ideology – the electorates appearing for the first time on the political stage with the progressive extension of suffrage. This process was projected onto the spatial dimension. Territorial configurations assumed a definite form for the existing parties very early and remained stable in the second half of the twentieth century (as seen in Chapter 3). Parties that for the first time could create allegiances within newly enfranchised masses also produced an organizational effort that permitted their control over the territory. Since the process of nationalization for these parties took place early, it occurred in a phase of great opportunity for parties to mobilize and control the masses.

There are therefore important differences in the *timing* of the process of increasing nationalization of electorates. Compared to the conservatives and liberals, whose curves date back to the 1840s, the agrarian and social democratic curves appear steeper, *closely related to the rapid mobilization of the masses and linked to the rapid extension of political rights toward the end of the nineteenth century and the beginning of the twentieth century.* The slopes are particularly steep between the 1880s and 1910s because of the possibility – both organizationally and ideologically – of controlling growing parts of new electorates. Conservatives and liberals developed their

---

[4] This is less true for France, Italy, Spain, and also Germany, where the structures of the party systems were much more fluid.

164

Cleavages and Party Families

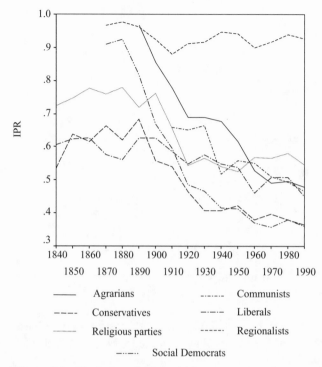

Figure 5.1 Evolution of territorial heterogeneity of support for main party families in Europe: 1840s–present.

organizational and electoral machineries, as well as their belief systems, at a time of *restricted electorates*. They were the first parties to occupy the ideological and geographical political space before new masses entered the political scene. These masses, by contrast, seem to have been controlled mostly, although not exclusively, by the workers' organizations.[5]

As for the more recent periods, since World War II most political families seem to have been characterized by stable territorial configurations; that is, the high levels of homogeneity remained constant. However, in the case of the agrarian family, after World War II the trend toward more homogeneous support remains comparatively strong. Figures for the agrarian parties of Finland, Iceland, Norway, and Sweden show a similar evolution toward more diffused electoral support across national territories after these parties transformed into center parties in which the rural element

---

[5] See the next chapter. For an analysis of the mobilization of the working class by the Conservatives in England, see McKenzie and Silver (1967).

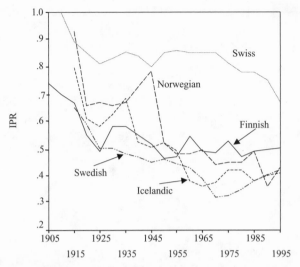

Figure 5.2 Evolution of territorial heterogeneity of support for five major agrarian parties.

is less marked (see Figure 5.2).[6] The Icelandic Progressive Party adopted its name in 1916 after the Farmers' Party merged with the Independent Farmers. In Sweden the change occurred in 1957, in Norway in 1959, and in Finland in 1965. In Switzerland, the Swiss Farmers', Artisans', and Bourgeois' Party became the Swiss People's Party of the Center in 1971. This party was active almost exclusively in the canton of Berne (and in some other Protestant cantons). Only a rightward move under its new leadership (on immigration issues and European integration) allowed its support to expand territorially.

Patterns of Reterritorialization

By contrast, the most recent period of time highlights the bifurcation since the 1920s between the highly nationalized conservatives and social democrats on the one hand, and the liberals on the other, that is, a party family that historically always ranged among the most homogeneous types of parties but that in recent times – due to the electoral decline of many

[6] Denmark had an agrarian party contesting elections from 1935 to 1943 (*Bondepartiet*, formerly *Frie folkeparti*) and a minor *Landmanspartiet*, but neither one ever constituted a central element of the party system of this country.

of these parties (the British Liberal Party during the interwar period, the *Venstre* parties of Denmark and Norway, etc.) – were not able to achieve the continuous territorial expansion and homogenization of the conservatives and the social democrats.

Another case of reterritorialization is that of the religious parties. These are characterized by a resurgence of regionalization since the 1950s. Denominational parties have been subdivided according to whether or not the country to which they belong is homogeneous. Five types of religious parties have been distinguished:

- Catholic parties

  In religiously homogeneous countries: *Österreichische Volkspartei* (AU), *Parti social chrétien* (Walloon)/*Christelijke volkspartij* (Flemish), *Mouvement républicain populaire* (FR), *Democrazia cristiana* (IT); In religiously mixed countries: *Zentrum, Christlich-Soziale Union* (GE), *Katholieke volkspartij* (NL), *Schweizerische Christlich-Demokratische Volkspartei* (SZ).

- Protestant parties

  In religiously homogeneous countries: *Kristeligt folkeparti* (DK), *Suomen kristillinen työväen puolue, Suomen kristillinen litto* (FI), *Kristelig folkeparti* (NO), *Kristen demokratisk samling* (SW); In religiously mixed countries: *Christlich-Sozialer Volkdienst-Evangelische Bewegung* (GE), *Gereformeerd politiek verbond, Anti-revolutionaire partij, Christelijk-historische unie, Chistelijk democratische unie, Staatkundig gereformeerde partij* (NL), *Evangelische Konservative, Evangelische Volkspartei* (SZ).

- Interconfessional people's parties

  In religiously mixed countries: *Christen democratisch appèl* (NL), *Christlich-Demokratische Union* (GE).

1. Figure 5.3 shows that *the slopes of the Catholic and Protestant parties in religiously mixed countries are parallel*. Both types of parties become more homogeneous until the middle of the twentieth century but *a resurgence of regionalization takes place since then*, meaning a retrenchment of these parties in the Catholic and Protestant areas of the respective countries. This explains the increase in the curve of religious parties in Figure 5.1.

In the case of Catholic parties, this resurgence is caused by the growth of the German *Christlich-Soziale Union* (based exclusively in Bavaria) since the 1950s but also by the retrenchment in the Catholic cantons of the Swiss *Christlich-Demokratische Volkspartei*. For the Protestant parties, the process of regionalization takes place in spite of the disappearance of a large number of Reformist and Calvinist parties in the Netherlands (as a consequence of their merger into the *Christen democratisch appèl* in 1975). First, in the Netherlands, not all Protestant parties joined the CDA, namely, the *Staatkundig gereformeerde partij* and the *Gereformeerd politiek verbond*. Second, in Switzerland, the *Evangelische Volkspartei* increased its support and therefore enters the computations (on the basis of the 5 percent criterion) since 1959.

2. Figure 5.3 also shows *the evolution toward uniform support across regions of Protestant parties in homogeneously Protestant countries*: Denmark, Finland, Norway, and Sweden. In these four countries Christian parties are small parties compared to the social democrats, conservatives, liberals, and agrarians, but their support becomes increasingly homogeneous. By contrast, *Catholic parties in homogeneously Catholic countries display a strong trend toward regionalization since 1950*. Unlike Protestant parties, these parties are large people's parties (in Austria, Belgium, France, and Italy). However, this is a trend toward regionalization that is caused mainly by the split of the Belgian Catholics into the *Parti social chrétien* and the *Christelijke Volkspartij* in 1968. If this case is omitted, the curve is flat after the 1960s.

3. *Interconfessional parties in religiously mixed countries tend to become homogenized*. The subdivision of confessional parties into five families leaves this category with only two cases: the German *Christlich-Demokratische Union* and the Dutch *Christen democratisch appèl* (formed in 1975 as a merger of the main Calvinist and Catholic parties). Given their interconfessional nature, these parties are able to overcome territorially based religious cleavages. Of the two, the former is less diffuse than the latter, mainly because of the decision to treat the *Christlich-Soziale Union* (the Bavarian "sister party" of the CDU) as a separate party.

Whereas, therefore, the support for confessional parties in the religiously homogeneous countries remains uniform across regions after World War II (with the notable exception of Belgium, whose Catholic party divides along the linguistic cleavage), the support for confessional parties in the mixed countries tends toward a retrenchment in the respective Protestant and Catholic areas. This is true in all three mixed countries

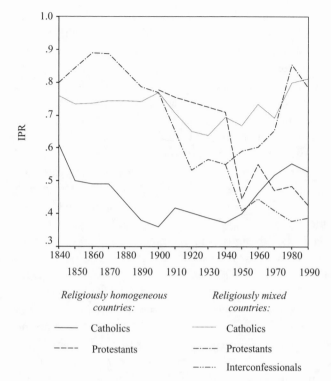

Figure 5.3 Evolution of territorial heterogeneity of support for types of confessional parties: 1840s–present.

considered – Germany, the Netherlands, and Switzerland – although in the first two cases, two large interconfessional parties spread uniformly.

Comparing Party Families Across Countries

The comparison of party families in the previous section has not only shown differences between families but also strong variations *within families*, that is, between national parties belonging to the same European party type. This section therefore compares parties of the same type across nations to give a more precise idea of the degree of cohesion of each party family, whether parties in the same family are very different from each other or whether all parties in the same family have the same type of territorial structure. Again, given the large amount of information at this level of detail of the analysis, the focus will be on the more recent periods of time, namely, since

World War II. The choice of a reduced temporal period affects primarily the agrarian party family, for – with the exception of the main Nordic parties – most smaller farmers' and peasants' parties that appeared at some point in all countries no longer exist.

First, party systems differ according to whether or not given party families exist.[7] Not all party families exist in each country, as can be seen in Table 5.2 from the number of countries for which a given type of party exists (see the N columns). The only party type that exists in all 17 countries is the social democratic type. Communists too exist everywhere, although according to the 5 percent criterion they are not counted for Ireland and the United Kingdom. Interconfessional parties, as defined here (*Christlich-Demokratische Union* and *Christen democratisch appèl*), exist only in Germany and the Netherlands. Catholic and Protestant parties exist only in seven and six countries respectively, although in some countries (e.g., the Netherlands) there is more than one. Agrarians since World War II exist in 10 countries. In some cases, however, there are several agrarian parties in one country (e.g., Finland). The same applies to regionalists: There are many such parties, but they concentrate in only 10 countries, mostly in Spain, Italy, and Belgium. Conservatives do not exist in all 17 countries; they are not found where Catholic or interconfessional people's parties take their place (Austria, Belgium, Italy, etc.). Finally, liberal parties in many countries declined during the interwar period and were replaced by social democratic parties or never had a major role in the party system.

Second, European party systems differ in that the levels of homogeneity are similar across countries for some partisan families but are very different for others. There are three families in which parties display (homogeneous) territorial structures of support – the *conservatives, liberals, and social democrats* – confirming that *these political families are an element of similarity among European party families* (see Table 5.2, right-hand side, where the main outliers have been omitted). The range between the most and least homogeneous liberal parties is .09, and for conservative and social democratic parties it is only .11 (on the basis of the CRII, which also takes into account the size of electorates). To these three families we can add the two broad *interconfessional people's parties*. Two additional families do not differ much: *communists and greens*. The families that, by contrast, distinguish the

---

[7] This variation – which is not the object of the present work – is best explained in Rokkan's model of the genesis of European party systems.

Table 5.2. *Party Families by Differences in Heterogeneity Across Countries: World War II–Present*

		All Parties						Excluding Outliers (Italics Used When Applicable)					
		Minimum (Most Diffused National Parties)		Maximum (Least Diffused National Parties)				Minimum (Most Diffused National Parties)		Maximum (Least Diffused National Parties)			
Code	Party Family	CRII	Country	CRII	Country	Range	N	CRII	Country	CRII	Country	Range	N
IC	Interconfessionals	.11	NL	.19	GE	.08	2/2	.11	NL	.19	GE	.08	2/2
L	Liberals	.11	SW	.83	SZ	.72	14/14	*.11*	*SW*	*.20*	*IT*	*.09*	*12/12*
S	Social democrats	.05	DK	.30	IR	.25	17/17	*.05*	*DK*	*.16*	*FR*	*.11*	*15/15*
C	Conservatives	.06	IR	.17	FR	.11	13/12	.06	IR	.17	FR	.11	13/12
K	Communists	.09	IC	.69	SZ	.60	15/15	*.09*	*IC*	*.36*	*BE*	*.27*	*14/14*
G	Greens	.07	SW	.40	IR	.33	12/11	.07	SW	.40	IR	.33	12/11
PR	Protestants	.15	FI	.56	SZ	.41	9/6	.15	FI	.56	SZ	.41	9/6
REG	Regionalists	.34	BE	1.00	SP	.66	46/10	.34	BE	1.00	SP	.66	46/10
–	All religious	.09	AU	.83	GE	.74	18/11	.09	AU	.83	GE	.74	18/11
CC	Catholics	.09	AU	.83	GE	.74	7/7	.09	AU	.83	GE	.74	7/7
A	Agrarians	.15	NL	.97	FR	.82	12/10	*.18*	*SW*	*.97*	*FR*	*.79*	*11/9*

Notes: Party families are ordered according to the range between the minimum and maximum diffusion of support, excluding outlying cases (right-hand side of the table). *N* refers to the number of parties taken into account for each family for the period since World War II. After the slash, the number of countries for which the party family is applicable is given. For Belgium, parties that divided along the linguistic cleavage in the 1960s–70s were counted only once and as one party (except for the Greens, which were born as two different parties).

Legend: See Abbreviations and Symbols in the front matter.

171

European party systems in regard to territorial structures are the *regionalist, Catholic, and agrarian* party families. The range between the most and least homogeneous party is .66, .74, and .79, respectively. These appear as the *families that make European territorial systems differ*, confirming – in the territorial dimension – Rokkan's idea of a "deviation" from the party system development in Europe (Lipset and Rokkan 1967a: 35–46; Rokkan 1970a: 113–29).

Accordingly, in the tables for each party family that follow, parties that are similar across countries are considered first. Then parties that differ from country to country are considered – that is, parties that cause the *diversity of the territorial structure of party systems in Europe* – religious parties, agrarians, and regionalists.[8]

Homogeneity and Similarity: Families of the Left–Right Dimension

Social democratic parties exist in all European countries. Stemming from the class cleavage between owners and employers on the one hand, and workers, tenants, and laborers on the other, this political family has often been considered a fundamental but *constant* feature of European party systems.[9] Variations in the type and format of party systems do not originate from the class cleavage, although in several countries (Finland, France, and Italy primarily) social democrats have been flanked by strong communist parties.

Table 5.3 supports the hypothesis of a basic homogeneity in the territorial structure of European social democratic parties. This family is one of the strongly homogeneous ones, and its parties in the different countries have similar levels of homogeneity. There is little difference between the most and least homogeneous social democratic parties in Europe. For the period since 1945, the Swedish, Danish, and Greek social democrats are the most homogeneous (IPR below .25), whereas the Irish and Swiss are the least homogeneous (.56 and .54).[10] Other indices confirm these

---

[8] In all tables, parties covering at least 90 percent of the constituencies are grouped together and ordered from most to least homogeneous support based on IPR levels. Parties covering less than 90 percent of the territory are ordered separately according to the percentage of coverage.

[9] For Rokkan, cultural cleavages – religion and language – have a relative predominance over economic cleavages in explaining party systems *variations*.

[10] See Chapter 7 for an explanation of these differences through the interaction between cleavages.

172

figures, although the CRII displays a much higher value for the Irish Labour Party. The Irish and Swiss parties also appear as the main outliers of the social democratic family in regard to the portion of territory covered. The Swiss *Sozialdemokratische Partei* covers no more than 78.32 percent of the constituencies (cantons) since World War II and the Irish Labour Party 82.64 percent of the *Dáil* constituencies. All other European social democrats, by contrast, cover at least 93 percent of their national territories. If these two parties are excluded, the range between the most and least nationalized parties is reduced to .11 according to the IPR (see the right-hand half of Table 5.2). This ranking of social democratic parties does not consider the two parties that emerged from the linguistic split of the Belgian Social Democrats into the Walloon *Parti socialiste belge* and the Flemish *Belgische socialistische partij* in 1977. The territorial coverage of these two parties is far below the approximately 80 percent of the Irish Labour Party and the Swiss *Sozialdemokratische Partei*, so that they appear as the least nationalized parties of all European social democrats – with 47.22 percent of the Walloon party and 54.17 of the Flemish party. Other indices also display much higher values of territorial disparity for these two linguistically – or ethnically – defined social democratic parties since the first election contested as separate formations in 1978. Before the linguistic split, the Belgian Social Democrats were characterized by a medium level of territorial diversity compared to their European counterparts.

For the *conservatives*, as for the social democrats, the structure of support is similar for all European parties, with a small difference between the most nationalized party (the Irish *Fianna Fáil*, with a CRII of .06) and the most regionalized party (the French Gaullists, with a CRII of .17). All parties cover at least 93 percent of the constituencies, with the exception of the Swiss Radical Party (see Table 5.4). The *Freisinnig-Demokratische Partei* covers only 84.56 percent of the cantons. This party does not contest the cantons of Obwalden and Nidwalden and, occasionally, the two Appenzell.

In several countries the conservative or center or right-wing party is a Catholic formation, namely, in the homogeneously Catholic countries (Austria, Belgium, Italy) or is an interconfessional people's party in religiously mixed countries (Germany, the Netherlands). The scores for these parties are displayed in Table 5.7. Only the German CDU's figure is outside the range of conservatives, with a CRII of .19 (higher than the Gaullists' .17).

Table 5.3. *The Territorial Heterogeneity of European Socialists, Social Democrats, and Labor Parties: World War II–Present*

Country Code	National Party	Period	Coverage (%)	IPR	CV	CRII	S	N
SW	Sveriges socialdemokratistiska arbetareparti	1948–98	100.00	.24	.13	.06	5.87	(17)
DK	Socialdemokratiet	1945–98	100.00	.25	.15	.05	5.19	(22)
GR	PASOK	1974–96	98.81	.25	.19	.06	6.48	(9)
PT	Partido socialista português	1975–95	100.00	.28	.18	.06	5.68	(9)
NO	Det norske arbeiderparti	1949–97	100.00	.29	.19	.07	8.00	(13)
AU	Sozialistische Partei Österreich	1945–95	100.00	.30	.21	.07	9.07	(16)
SP	Partido socialista obrero español	1977–96	100.00	.31	.23	.08	8.30	(7)
GE	Sozialistische Partei Deutschlands	1949–98	100.00	.32	.25	.10	9.24	(14)
NL	Partij van der arbeid	1946–98	100.00	.33	.26	.10	7.67	(16)
IT	Partito socialista italiano	1946–96	99.14	.35	.32	.11	3.22	(13)
BE	Parti socialiste belge/Belgische socialistische partij	1946–77	94.81	.39	.39	.13	11.75	(11)
	Parti socialiste belge (Walloon)	*(1978–95)*	*(47.22)*	*(.74)*	*(1.15)*	*(.56)*	*(19.16)*	*(6)*
	Belgische socialistische partij (Flemish)	*(1978–95)*	*(54.17)*	*(.69)*	*(.97)*	*(.42)*	*(11.42)*	*(6)*
GB	Labour Party	1945–97	99.95	.40	.38	.15	15.55	(15)
FR	Parti socialiste	1945–97	98.05	.40	.41	.16	7.93	(15)
FI	Suomen sosialdemokraattinen puolue	1945–95	93.88	.42	.41	.12	9.56	(15)
IC	Alþýðuflokkur	1946–95	99.74	.45	.50	.12	6.35	(16)
IR	Irish Labour Party	1948–97	82.64	.56	.75	.30	8.42	(16)
SZ	Sozialdemokr. Partei der Schweiz/Parti socialiste suisse	1947–95	78.32	.54	.71	.13	13.45	(13)

Notes: Parties covering at least 90 percent of the constituencies (coverage) are ordered from most to least homogeneous support based on the levels of IPR. Other parties are ordered on the basis of territorial coverage. Full formulas are given in Appendix 3. The number of cases (N) refers to single elections (not all elections were contested within the period). Italics are used for measures not appropriate for party comparison.
The Belgian socialists, the *Parti socialiste belge–Belgische socialistische partij*, divided in 1977 along the linguistic cleavage into the *Parti socialiste* and the *Belgische socialistische partij*.
Legend: See Abbreviations and Symbols in the front matter.

Table 5.4. *The Territorial Heterogeneity of European Conservative Parties: World War II–Present*

Country Code	National Party	Period	Coverage (%)	IPR	CV	CRII	S	N
IR	Fianna Fáil	1948–97	100.00	.25	.15	.06	6.89	(16)
GR	Ellinikos synagermos	1951–96	100.00	.27	.19	.08	8.50	(16)
IR	Fine Gael	1948–97	99.83	.32	.26	.10	8.47	(16)
DK	Højre-Konservative folkeparti	1945–98	100.00	.33	.27	.11	3.89	(22)
IC	Sjálfstæðisflokkur	1946–95	100.00	.33	.25	.09	8.41	(16)
PT	Partido do centro democrático social	1975–95	100.00	.34	.28	.08	2.50	(9)
SW	Högerpartiet-Moderata samlingspartiet	1948–98	100.00	.35	.30	.13	4.95	(17)
GB	Conservative Party	1945–97	99.65	.35	.30	.13	12.67	(15)
NO	Høire	1945–97	100.00	.38	.38	.16	6.96	(14)
SP	Alianza popular	1977–96	99.18	.40	.40	.17	9.09	(7)
FI	Kansallinen kokoomuspuolue	1945–95	93.40	.41	.42	.12	6.59	(15)
FR	Gaullists	1951–97	94.02	.44	.52	.17	9.66	(12)
SZ	Schweizerische Freisinnig-Demokratische Partei	1947–95	84.56	.52	.77	.16	18.40	(13)

Notes: This table considers conservatives other than Catholics and interconfessional people's parties in Table 5.7. See also the notes to Table 5.3. Swiss radicals (*Freisinnig-Demokratische Partei*) appear in this table since they are considered conservatives rather than liberals.
Legend: See Abbreviations and Symbols in the front matter.

175

The *liberals* (Table 5.5) are the last family among those displaying reduced variance across countries in terms of territorial homogeneity. There are two main outliers in this family that are characterised by high territoriality of support compared to other liberal parties. The first is the British Liberal Party, which covers only 57.21 percent of the constituencies. As seen, this retrenchment occurs between World Wars I and II (see also Figure 6.4). The second is the Swiss *Liberale Partei* or, better, *Parti libéral*, since it covers only 17.35 percent of the constituencies corresponding to the French-speaking cantons of Geneva, Neutchâtel, and Valais (partly German-speaking), as well as Basel Stadt and the Italian-speaking canton Ticino.[11] Apart from these outliers, the liberal parties of Europe are grouped within a very limited range of values, with the most and the least homogeneous being the Swedish *Folkspartiet liberalerna* (.33) and the Finnish *Liberaalinen kansanpuolue* (.48), respectively.

Again, Belgian liberals present the specificity of being divided along the linguistic cleavage since 1974: the *Parti de la liberté et du progrès* (Walloon) and the *Partij voor vrijheid en vooruitgang* (Flemish). The first covers 47.08 percent of the *arrondissements administratifs*, the second 54.96 percent. The other indices for these two parties also increase since 1974. In both cases, however, they are inferior to the Swiss indices since both parties are present in roughly half of the country, whereas the Swiss Liberals contest elections in only 5 cantons out of 25–26.

Finally, there are two more families that are quite similar across countries in regard to their homogeneous structure of support: the *greens* and the *communists* (see Table 5.6). For the communist family, the variance in the level of homogeneity across countries is increased mainly by 1 outlying case, while the remaining 14 parties display greater similarity in their territorial distributions. The outlier is the Swiss *Partei der Arbeit*, which has very concentrated support in a few cantons (in particular, Geneva). Its values of disparity are higher than those of all other communist parties in Europe, and the percentage of territory covered is only a fourth. If this outlying case is left out, the range of values between parties is reduced to .27 from .60 (CRII). Among the least homogeneous communist parties in Europe are also the Belgian, Austrian, and Portuguese parties. The Swiss,

[11] Similarly to the *Partido do centro democrático social*, the Portuguese *Partido popular democrático* (later the *Partido social democráta*) contested in 1979 and 1980 the two constituencies of *região autónoma dos Açores* and of *região autónoma da Madeira* outside the electoral alliance *Aliança democrática*, but it has been considered together with the Alliance for the computation of indicators.

Belgian, and Austrian parties are the only ones covering less than 90 percent of the constituencies. By contrast, among the most homogeneous parties, there are parties that play or played an important role in the national party systems (see, as a rough indicator, the number of contested elections).[12] The Icelandic *Alþýðubandalag* is by far the most homogeneous communist party in Europe, followed by the French *Parti communiste*, the Italian *Partito comunista*, and the Finnish *Vasemmistoliitto*.

The greens – for which no table has been produced – are a smaller party family, which, however, meets the 5 percent criterion in most countries (11 countries, with two parties in Belgium). The level of homogeneity of support for these parties ranges from the highest, displayed by the Swedish *Miljöpartiet de gröna* (CRII of .07), to the lowest, that of the Irish *Comhaontás glas* (.40); the exceptions are the two linguistically based Belgian green parties, *Agalev* (Flemish) and *Ecolo* (Walloon).

Heterogeneity and Difference: Families of Religious, Agrarian, and Regional Defense

We now turn to the aspects of European politics that are the main causes of *diversity*. The political families for which territorial structures differ most across European countries are:

- *confessional parties* (state–church and religious cleavages);
- *agrarian parties* (rural–urban cleavage); and
- *regionalist parties* (center–periphery, linguistic, and ethnic cleavages).

Following is a description of the party families that are at the origin of the "deviation" of some countries from others, causing the fundamental diversity of the territorial structures of European party systems.

Deviation I: Christian Parties and Religious Differentiation

The most homogeneous religious parties are the Austrian *Österreichische Volkspartei*, the Italian *Democrazia cristiana* (considered up to 1992), the Dutch *Christen democratisch appèl*, and the Belgian Catholics before their split in 1968 into two parties along the linguistic cleavage. On the other hand, two parties stand out for their high levels of territorial disparity:

---

[12] The N in this series of tables is important because it indicates the continuous presence of parties (and their relevance according to the 5 percent criterion).

Table 5.5. *The Territorial Heterogeneity of European Liberal and Radical Parties: World War II–Present*

Country Code	National Party	Period	Coverage (%)	IPR	CV	CRII	S	N
SW	Folkspartiet liberalerna	1948–98	100.00	.33	.28	.11	*3.73*	(17)
NL	Volkspartij voor vrijheid en democratie	1946–98	100.00	.36	.33	.12	*4.76*	(16)
GR	Enosi kentrou	1961–81	100.00	.38	.54	.13	*7.54*	(6)
GE	Freie Demokratische Partei	1949–98	100.00	.38	.37	.14	*3.17*	(14)
PT	Partido popular democrático–Partido social democráta	1975–95	100.00	.40	.39	.12	*12.16*	(9)
DK	Venstre	1945–98	100.00	.42	.44	.18	*8.47*	(22)
AU	Freiheitliche Partei Österreichs	1949–95	100.00	.43	.44	.16	*3.88*	(15)
BE	Parti de la liberté et du progrès/Partij voor vrijheid en voor.	1946–71	94.29	.43	.46	.16	*6.30*	(9)
	Parti de la liberté et du progrès (Walloon)	(1974–95)	(47.08)	(.74)	(1.15)	(.55)	*(11.23)*	(8)
	Partij voor vrijheid en vooruitgang (Flemish)	(1974–95)	(54.96)	(.69)	(1.03)	(.43)	*(10.29)*	(8)
NO	Venstre	1945–97	100.00	.45	.49	.20	*3.42*	(14)
FR	Union démocratique française	1978–97	95.21	.46	.57	.19	*10.96*	(5)
IT	Partito liberale italiano	1946–92	99.04	.48	.67	.20	*1.87*	(12)
FI	Liberaalinen kansanpuolue	1945–79	92.69	.48	.57	.19	*2.83*	(11)
GB	Liberal Party	1945–87	57.21	.67	1.31	.46	*10.19*	(13)
SZ	Liberale Partei der Schweiz–Parti libéral suisse	1947–95	17.35	.93	2.43	.83	*17.35*	(13)

Notes: The Belgian liberal *Parti de la liberté et du progrès–Partij voor vrijheid en vooruitgang* divided in 1974 along the linguistic cleavage into the *Parti réformateur libéral* and the *Partij voor vrijheid en vooruitgang*. For Switzerland the *Liberale Partei der Schweiz–Parti libéral suisse* is considered rather than the *Schweizerische Freisinnig-Demokratische Partei–Parti radical-démocratique suisse* (see Table 5.4). See also notes to Table 5.3.

Legend: See Abbreviations and Symbols in the front matter.

Table 5.6. *The Territorial Heterogeneity of European Communist Parties: World War II–Present*

Country Code	National Party	Period	Coverage (%)	IPR	CV	CRII	S	N
IC	Kommúnistaflokkur-Alþýðubandalag	1946–95	100.00	.36	.33	.09	4.76	(16)
FR	Parti communiste français	1945–97	99.91	.40	.40	.16	6.57	(15)
IT	Partito comunista italiano	1946–96	99.20	.40	.41	.15	10.13	(14)
FI	Suomen kansan demokraattinen liitto-Vasemmistoliitto	1945–95	96.92	.44	.45	.14	7.17	(15)
SW	Sveriges kommunistiska parti-Vänsterpartiet	1948–98	97.32	.45	.59	.21	2.58	(17)
GR	Kommounistiko komma-Elladas-Enomeni aristera	1946–96	98.66	.45	.51	.17	4.09	(9)
SP	Izquierda unida	1977–96	98.08	.48	.58	.19	3.50	(7)
DK	Danmarks kommunistiske parti	1945–79	100.00	.54	.74	.25	2.47	(10)
GE	Kommunistische Partei Deutschlands	1949–53	100.00	.55	.78	.31	1.63	(2)
NL	Communistische partij Nederland	1946–72	100.00	.56	.90	.31	3.47	(10)
NO	Norske communistiske parti	1945–75	91.25	.56	.93	.23	2.83	(6)
PT	Partido comunista português	1975–95	100.00	.63	.99	.31	13.06	(9)
AU	Kommunistische Partei Österreichs	1945–79	88.00	.56	1.16	.31	1.68	(10)
BE	Parti communiste de Belgique/Komm. partij van België	1946–78	78.67	.67	1.12	.36	3.21	(12)
SZ	Partei der Arbeit der Schweiz/Parti suisse du travail	1947–95	24.90	.90	2.42	.69	4.21	(13)

Notes: See notes to Table 5.3.
Legend: See Abbreviations and Symbols in the front matter.

the Bavarian *Christlich-Soziale Union* and the Swiss Protestant party *Evangelische Volkspartei* (see Table 5.7).

Among Catholic parties, what distinguishes the *Österreichische Volkspartei*, the *Democrazia cristiana*, and the *Parti social-chrétien/Christelijke volkspartij*, on the one hand, from the German *Christlich-Soziale Union*, the Dutch *Katholieke volkspartij*, and the Swiss *Christlich Demokratische Volkspartei*, on the other, is the religious structure of the counties, whether homogeneously Catholic (Austria, Belgium, Italy) or religiously mixed (Germany, the Netherlands, Switzerland). The Austrian, Belgian, and Italian parties all cover 100 percent of their national territories. Catholic populations in the three mixed countries considered here are territorially concentrated, although the general movement of the population due to the processes of industrialization and urbanization diluted them throughout the territories. As a result, Catholic electoral support suffers from religious segmentation and is therefore confined to areas such as the Catholic cantons of Switzerland (Luzern, Obwald, Nidwald, Appenzell Inner-Rhoden, Wallis, etc.), Bavaria in Germany, and the provinces of Limburg and Northern Brabant in the Netherlands. The main exception is the French *Mouvement républicain populaire*, which, under the Fourth Republic, is characterized by a relatively higher level of territorial disparity than other Catholic parties in homogeneously Catholic countries.

Since 1968, the Belgian Catholics have been divided into the Walloon *Parti social-chrétien* and the Flemish *Christelijke volkspartij*. From 1847 on, the Catholics had been a main component of the party system together with the Liberals and the Socialists, and were present throughout the territory. Figures for the two ethnic wings of the party since 1968 show that each covers either the Walloon or the Flemish provinces – around 47.00 and 53.00 percent of the constituencies, respectively. Accordingly, the other indicators of territorial disparity also have higher values. The IPR values (.74 and .69) are among the highest of all religious parties, not because of the territorial distribution of religiosity but as a consequence of the *linguistic* divide.

The divided pattern between religiously homogeneous countries and mixed countries is less clear in the case of Protestant parties. This is due first to the existence of two large interconfessional parties in Germany and the Netherlands, the *Christlich-Demokratische Union* and the *Christen democratisch appèl*. Both are among the most nationalized parties despite the divided religious structure of the countries they operate in. Both parties are broad Christian formations, covering both the Catholic and the

Protestant segments. The *Christen democratisch appèl* was formed before the 1975 election as a result of the merger among the main denominational parties of the Netherlands in response to a decline in support. Among these parties, the *Anti-revolutionaire partij*, the *Christelijk-historische unie*, the *Gereformeerd politiek verbond* (Protestant), and the *Katholieke volkspartij* (Catholic) were the four largest. The *Staatkundig gereformeerde partij* (a Calvinist party) did not join the union.

Out of nine major Protestant parties, four are Dutch. Among these, the most homogeneous party was the *Anti-revolutionaire partij*, an old party contesting elections since the transition to general parliamentary representation. This party covered 100 percent of the national territory – like all other Dutch parties – and displays medium levels of territorial disparity, whereas the other Dutch Protestant parties are more regionalized. The Swiss *Evangelische Volkspartei* stands out for its high values of disparity. Its case is similar to that of the Catholic parties in mixed countries. The *Evangelische Volkspartei* draws its support from few constituencies, although in the last few elections it expanded its influence. Traditionally, the main cantons are the largest Protestant cantons of Zurich, Berne, Basel-Stadt, and so on. The four remaining Protestant parties belong to homogeneously Protestant Nordic countries (except Iceland): *Kristeligt folkepartiet* (Denmark), *Kristillinen työväen puolue* (Finland), *Kristelig folkeparti* (Norway), and *Kristen demokratisk samlig* (Sweden). Given their smaller size and their marginal role in the party system (if compared to the large Catholic parties in Austria, Belgium, and Italy), their level of territorial disparity is higher.

Deviation II: Parties for Agrarian Defense

Most farmers' and peasants' parties that existed at some point in all European countries disappeared after World War II, and only the large Nordic and Swiss agrarian parties survived in more recent decades – with some exceptions. Notes to Table 5.8 show how many agrarian parties disappeared after World War II. As the number of contested elections in the table indicates, there are two distinct groups of agrarian parties in Europe. On the one hand, the agrarian parties of the Nordic countries (excluding Denmark) and of Switzerland contested between 13 and 16 elections during the post–World War II period. On the other hand, there are a number of smaller farmers' and peasants' parties. The difference between the two groups is that while the former were long-term relevant elements in the party

181

Table 5.7. *The Territorial Heterogeneity of European Catholic, Interconfessional, and Protestant Parties: World War II–Present*

Country Code	National Party	Period	Coverage (%)	IPR	CV	CRII	S	N
AU	Österreichische Volkspartei	1945–95	100.00	.31	.24	.09	9.82	(16)
IT	Democrazia cristiana	1946–92	99.47	.32	.26	.10	9.77	(12)
NL	Christen democratisch appèl	1977–98	100.00	.34	.30	.11	7.96	(7)
BE	Parti social-chrétien/Christelijke volkspartij	1946–65	100.00	.38	.33	.14	14.86	(7)
	Parti social-chrétien (Walloon)	(1968–95)	(47.00)	(.74)	(1.19)	(.56)	(13.56)	(10)
	Christelijke volkspartij (Flemish)	(1968–95)	(53.83)	(.69)	(.97)	(.44)	(19.02)	(10)
SW	*Kristen demokratisk samlig*	1964–94	98.21	.43	.52	.18	*1.96*	(6)
NL	*Anti-Revolutionaire Partij*	1946–72	100.00	.46	.52	.21	*5.27*	(9)
FI	*Suomen kristillinen työväen puolue*	1975–95	93.33	.46	.50	.15	*1.67*	(5)
NO	*Kristelig folkeparti*	1945–97	97.50	.47	.52	.22	*5.36*	(14)
NL	*Christelijk-Historische Unie*	1946–72	100.00	.51	.57	.26	*4.61*	(9)
DK	*Kristeligt folkepartiet*	1975–90	100.00	.52	.63	.24	*2.03*	(6)
NL	*Gereformeerd Politiek Verbond (Calvinist)*	1971–72	100.00	.55	.71	.29	*1.28*	(2)
NL	Katholieke Volkspartij	1946–72	100.00	.56	.78	.30	19.88	(9)
NL	*Staatkundig Gereformeerde Partij (Calvinist)*	1946–98	100.00	.68	1.13	.42	*2.42*	(13)
FR	Mouvement républicain populaire	1945–62	85.28	.59	.91	.33	10.01	(6)
GE	Christlich-Demokratische Union	1949–98	82.91	.44	.51	.19	18.11	(13)
SZ	Schweizerische Christlich Demokratische Volkspartei/PDC	1947–95	82.26	.64	.97	.36	28.75	(13)
GE	Christlich-Soziale Union	1949–98	17.25	.91	2.25	.83	21.13	(13)
SZ	*Schweiz. Evangelische Volkspartei/ Parti évangelique pop.*	1959–83	16.38	.93	2.47	.56	*1.62*	(6)

Notes: The Belgian Catholics divided in 1968 along the linguistic cleavage into the *Parti social-chrétien* and the *Christelijke volkspartij*. In Germany, *Zentrum* (1949 and 1953) is not considered. In the Netherlands, *Reformatorische Politieke Federatie, Katholieke Nationale Partij, Vrije Anti-Revolutionaire Partij*, and *Hervormd-Gereformeerde Staatspartij* are not considered. In Switzerland, the *Christlich-Soziale Partei* is not considered. See also notes to Table 5.3.

Legend: Italics used for Protestant/Calvinist (Reformed) parties. See also Abbreviations and Symbols in the front matter.

Table 5.8. *The Territorial Heterogeneity of European Agrarian Parties: World War II–Present*

Country Code	National Party	Period	Coverage (%)	IPR	CV	CRII	S	N
SW	Bondeförbundet-Centerpartiet	1948–98	100.00	.39	.40	.18	5.87	(16)
NL	Boerenpartij-Rechtse Volkspartij	1967	100.00	.40	.35	.15	1.65	(1)
IC	Bændaflokkur-Framsóknarflokkur	1946–95	100.00	.42	.42	.27	13.27	(16)
NO	Bondepartiet-Senderpartiet	1945–97	93.33	.47	.56	.21	5.67	(14)
FI	Maalaisliitto-Keskustapuolue-Suomen keskusta	1945–95	93.40	.49	.56	.23	11.75	(14)
FI	Suomen maaseudun puolue	1962–91	93.33	.49	.59	.20	3.56	(8)
IT	Concentrazione di unità rurale	1963	46.74	.80	1.83	.60	.58	(1)
SZ	Schweiz. Bauern-, Gewerbe-, und Bürgerpartei-Sc. Volkspartei	1947–95	40.14	.81	1.74	.41	11.48	(13)
IT	Partito agrario	1946–58	32.61	.85	2.64	.65	1.32	(3)
GR	Synagermos agroton kai ergazomenon	1951–52	10.05	.96	5.36	.90	4.27	(2)
IR	Farmers' Party	1944–54	7.50	.97	3.86	.94	3.10	(4)
FR	Parti paysan-Centre national des indépendants et des paysans	1945	6.23	.97	6.43	...	6.23	(2)

Notes: In France, for 1945 and 1946 the CRII is not computable because voters' figures are missing. In Iceland the *Bændaflokkur* of 1934–37 (the old agrarian party not in the table) divides from the Progressive Party. The following parties have not been included because they existed only until World War II: Austria: *Landbund für Österreich* (1927); Denmark: *Bondepartiet* (1935–37); Finland: *Suomen pientiljeljäin puolue* (1930–45); Germany: *Deutsche Bauernpartei* (1898–1933), *Bund der Landwirte* (1898–1903), *Landbund* (1928), and *Deutsches Landvolk* (1930); Greece: *Agrotikon-Ergatikon komma* (1926–32), and *Agrotikon komma* (1926–36); Iceland (apart from the previously mentioned *Bændaflokkur*): *Óbúðir bændur* (1916, two elections): Sweden: *Jordbrukarnas riksförbund* (1920); Switzerland: *Landwirtschaft/Gewerbevereins*; and Britain: Ariculturists and Farmers' candidates. See also notes to Table 5.3.

Legend: See Abbreviations and Symbols in the front matter.

systems, the latter appeared sporadically and had a marginal position. This applies also to previous periods.

In the section on "Developments and Deviations" of his model of party system development devoted to parties for agrarian defense, Stein Rokkan argues that the rural–urban cleavage in all countries of Europe "continued to assert itself in national politics far into the twentieth century, but the political expressions of the cleavages varied widely. . . . In the Low Countries, France, Italy and Spain, rural–urban cleavages rarely found direct expression in the development of party oppositions. Other cleavages, particularly between the state and the churches and between owners and tenants, had greater impact on the alignments of the electorates" (1970a: 195).[13]

Table 5.8 confirms that only in few cases did the urban–rural cleavage produce nationwide alignments. If we leave aside the Dutch agrarian party (*Boerenpartij*), which is homogeneously present throughout the country but which meets the 5 percent criterion for one election only, the most diffuse agrarian parties are Nordic parties that transformed later into center parties. These parties cover a large proportion of constituencies, and their degree of homogeneity is high. The Nordic agrarian parties are the only parties covering more than 90 percent of the constituencies over a large number of elections. Furthermore, the differences in homogeneity between countries are small: In the Swedish and Finnish agrarian parties, the IPR is only .10 and the CRII is .09.

The Swiss *Bauern-, Gewerbe- und Bürgerpartei*, notwithstanding its central role in the party system – and in the executive since 1959 – has a more regionalized electoral base. Its territorial coverage is much more reduced (only 40.14 percent on average), causing the other indicators of territorial disparity to be almost double those of the Nordic parties. In the remaining countries, the urban–rural cleavage was incorporated into other party alignments – state–church and left–right in particular – and did not give rise to specific political parties. Among the remaining small peasants' parties, the most important ones are the Irish Farmers' Party – which received relevant regional support (mainly in the area surrounding Cork) during the first decade after World War II – and the Italian *Partito agrario* (with strongholds in Piedmont) – which also contested elections in the same period. For all these parties, however, territorial coverage is very limited, ranging from 6.23 percent for the French *Centre national des indépendants et des paysans*

---

[13] See Chapter 6 in the present volume for an analysis of the evolution of agrarian politics in Western Europe.

to 46.74 percent for the Italian *Concentrazione di unità rurale* (in the only election of 1963).

Deviation III: Parties for Territorial Defense

Regionalist parties include:

- parties stemming from center–periphery cleavages that emerged in the process of state formation and nation-building (e.g., the Spanish *Partido nacionalista vasco*);
- parties born from ethnolinguistic cleavages (the Belgian *Volksunie*);
- parties claiming stronger administrative autonomy but not based on cultural identity (the Italian *Lega Nord*);
- parties created as local branches of larger national parties (the Norwegian *Framtid for Finnmark*, originally a local branch of the Social Democrats; the Swiss *Partito socialista autonomo* in Ticino; and the Icelandic local candidacies of the regions Suðurland and Vestfjaro).[14]

As for agrarian and religious parties, European regionalist parties differ from each other in the territorial configuration of their support. The range in Table 5.2 between the most and least regionalized parties is .66 (CRII). Regionalist parties are all characterized by a territorially concentrated support in a few regions. Nevertheless, Chapter 4 has shown that they differ in strength and territorial coverage. The most important differences between these parties can be summarized as follows.

1. It is possible to distinguish between the *number* of such parties in each country: 46 parties counted during the World War II–present period do not gather equally in the 10 countries in which they exist. There are 23 regionalist parties (given the decision to include parties on the basis of the 5 percent criterion) contesting at least one election in Spain since 1977; 8 in Italy since the end of World War II; 4 in Belgium; 2 in Iceland, Germany, Switzerland, and Britain; and 1 in Denmark, Finland, and Norway.

2. Many of these parties are *sporadic*. If one observes the *N* column of Table 5.9 indicating the number of elections for which the 5 percent criterion is fulfilled, it appears that the long-lived regionalist parties are few: the Flemish *Volksunie* (since 1919, even though the table is limited to the period since 1945), the Scottish National Party and *Plaid Cymru* (both since 1929),

---

[14] The Flemish and Walloon Catholic, Liberal, and Social Democrat parties are *not* considered regionalist parties.

Table 5.9. *The Territorial Heterogeneity of European Regionalist and Ethnic Parties: World War II–Present*

Country Code	National Party	Period	Coverage (%)	IPR	CV	CRII	S	N
BE	(Christelijke vlaamse) Volksunie-Vrije demokraten	1949–95	57.74	.68	.98	.36	*6.07*	(15)
BE	Vlaamse bloc	1991–95	55.83	.69	1.10	.34	*5.89*	(2)
IT	Lega lombarda-Lega Nord	1987–96	52.90	.80	2.03	.61	*8.31*	(4)
BE	Parti wallon-Rassemblement wallon	1968–81	47.33	.75	1.38	.55	*7.17*	(6)
IT	Associazione per Trieste	1979–83	45.21	.90	7.46	.76	*2.49*	(2)
FI	Svenska folkspartiet-Ruotsalainen kansanpuolue	1945–95	38.08	.86	2.41	.60	*24.63*	(15)
IT	Partito sardo d'azione	1946–96	34.33	.96	5.25	.90	*1.61*	(5)
GE	Bayernpartei	1949–53	19.42	.90	2.36	.82	*4.31*	(2)
SP	Partido andalucista	1989–96	15.38	.93	2.71	.83	*1.76*	(2)
SP	Partido socialista de Andalusía-Partido andaluz	1979	15.38	.93	2.76	.84	*4.16*	(1)
IT	Lega d'azione meridionale	1996	12.53	.95	8.61	.86	*1.52*	(1)
IC	Suðurlandslistinn	1995	12.50	1.00	2.83	.92	*3.01*	(1)
IC	Vestfjarðalistinn	1995	12.50	1.00	2.83	.97	*4.62*	(1)
IT	Movimento per l'indipendenza della Sicilia	1946	12.35	.95	3.41	.90	*2.82*	(1)
BE	Front démocratique des Bruxellois francophones	1968–91	11.11	.96	.98	.80	*1.62*	(3)
SP	Esquerra republicana de Catalunya	1979–96	9.13	.96	3.55	.84	*1.51*	(4)
IT	Liga veneta	1983	8.48	.97	3.90	.92	*1.20*	(1)
SP	Bloque nacionalista gallego	1996	7.69	.97	3.53	.93	*3.38*	(1)
SP	Convergencia y unió	1979–96	7.69	.97	3.57	.84	*8.73*	(6)
SP	Unió del centre i la democracia cristiana de Catalunya	1977	7.69	.97	3.63	.83	*1.81*	(1)
SP	Pacte democratic per Catalunya	1977	7.69	.97	3.63	.83	*5.73*	(1)
SP	Herri batasuna	1979–96	7.69	.97	3.67	.93	*3.87*	(6)
SP	Coalición electoral esquerra de Cataluña	1977	7.69	.97	3.76	.83	*1.39*	(1)
SP	Eusko alkartasuna-Euskal ezkerra	1989–96	7.69	.97	4.03	.94	*2.67*	(2)

	Party	Years					
SP	Euskadiko ezkerra	1977–93	7.37	.97	4.21	.93	2.10 (6)
SP	Partido nacionalista vasco-Eusko alderdi jeltzalea	1977–96	7.14	.97	4.10	.94	5.96 (7)
GB	Scottish National Party	1945–97	6.99	.96	7.63	.94	4.54 (15)
SP	Chunta aragonesista	1996	5.77	.98	4.78	.97	1.22 (1)
SP	Unión valenciana	1986–96	5.77	.98	5.85	.90	1.06 (4)
GE	Südschleswigscher Wählerverband-Sydslesvigsk vælgerforening	1949–57	5.73	.98	9.19	.97	1.60 (3)
NO	Framtid for Finnmark (local branch of Det norske arbeiderparti)	1989	5.26	1.00	4.36	.98	4.93 (1)
SP	Partido aragonés regionalista	1979–93	4.81	.99	4.88	.97	2.62 (4)
DK	Slesvigske parti-Schleswigsche Partei	1945–71	4.54	1.00	4.71	.95	1.61 (9)
GB	Plaid Cymru	1945–97	4.36	.98	7.12	.96	2.68 (15)
SZ	Lega dei ticinesi	1991–95	3.85	1.00	5.10	.95	4.13 (2)
SZ	Partito socialista autonomo	1983–91	3.85	1.00	5.10	.95	2.06 (3)
SP	Unión del pueblo canario	1979	3.85	.99	5.18	.97	2.17 (1)
SP	Agrupaciones independientes de Canarias-Coalición canaria	1986–89	3.85	.99	6.56	.97	2.59 (2)
SP	Coalición canária	1993–96	3.85	.99	5.05	.97	4.96 (2)
IT	Südtiroler Volkspartei	1948–92	2.43	.99	8.93	.98	6.15 (12)
SP	Partido socialista del pueblo de Ceuta	1996	1.92	1.00	7.21	1.00	1.02 (1)
SP	Unión del pueblo navarro	1979	1.92	1.00	7.21	.99	1.55 (1)
SP	Candidatura aragonesa independiente de centro	1977	1.92	1.00	7.21	.98	1.19 (1)
SP	Coalición electoral PSM-ENE (Baleares)	1996	1.92	1.00	7.21	.98	.80 (1)
SP	Convergencia demócrata de Navarra	1996	1.92	1.00	7.21	.99	.74 (1)
IT	Union valdôtaine	1946–96	1.07	1.00	9.67	1.00	4.80 (8)

Notes: For the United Kingdom, Northern Ireland is not considered. *Rassemblement wallon* was allied with *Front démocratique des Bruxellois francophones* (FDF) in five elections and with FDF and *Parti libéral démocrate et pluraliste* in one. See also notes to Table 5.3.

Legend: See Abbreviations and Symbols in the front matter.

the Finnish *Svenska folkspartiet* since 1907 (the first election after the transition from estate representation to the *Eduskunta*), the Danish *Slesvigske* since 1920, and the Italian *Union valdotâine* and *Südtiroler Volkspartei* (since 1946 and 1948, respectively). For Spanish parties, given the recent transition to democracy, the criterion must be different. The durable parties are mainly the three Basque parties – *Partido nacionalista vasco* (seven elections), *Herri batasuna*, and *Euskadiko ezkerra* – and the Catalan *Convergencia i unió* (all six elections). Among the remaining parties, the most important ones according to the simple criterion of duration are the Belgian *Rassemblement wallon* and the Italian *Lega Nord*.

3. Regionalist parties differ in regard to their *territorial structure*, that is, whether they draw support from a limited area or from larger geographical regions (the percentage of territorial coverage). The IPR is useful in that it takes the value of 1.00 when all the support for a party comes from a single unit (constituency). According to these two indicators, two distinct groups of regionalist parties emerge: (a) those covering large areas of the countries and (b) those drawing their support from narrower regions. Figure 5.4 sums up this information.

First, in four countries, both types of parties are present. Most *Spanish* regionalist parties present their candidates in one single constituency (an IPR of 1.00 in Table 5.9), although parties representing regions like Catalonia or the Basque countries rely on a wider electoral reservoir. *Belgian* regionalist parties mainly contest half of the constituencies. The only parties with a more restricted support are the *Fédération démocratique des Bruxellois francophones* (*arrondissements* of Bruxelles, Nivelles, and, to a certain extent, Louvain) when not allied with the *Rassemblement wallon*. The *Rassemblement wallon*, *Volksunie*, and *Vlaamse bloc* contest mainly the half of the country whose linguistic groups they represent, with Bruxelles, Louvain, and Nivelles for the *Volksunie* and the *Rassemblement wallon* (but not the *Vlaamse bloc*). Their coverage is therefore higher than that of any other European regionalist party.[15] Also in the case of *Italian* regionalist parties, there are those that act in larger areas (the *Lega Nord*, the most important party) and those that stem from small linguistic niches, such as the French-speaking Valle d'Aosta (*Union valdotâine*) and the German-speaking Alto Adige (*Südtiroler Volkspartei*). In *Germany*, since World War II the

---

[15] As seen in Chapter 4, before World War II there was a *Parti pro-allemand* or *Partei der Deutschsprachigen Belgier* (elections of 1929 and 1932) contesting the *arrondissement* of Verviers.

Countries (Overall number of regionalist parties)	Regions of electoral support by size	
	Narrow regions (1–few constituencies)	Larger geographical areas (coverage > 5%)
Spain (23)	Aragón (3), Baleares, Canarias (3), Ceuta, Navarra (2), Valencia	Andalusia (2), País vascos (4), Catalunya (5), Galicia
Italy (8)	Alto Adige (South Tirol), Trieste, Valle d'Aosta	'Padania' (North), Mezzogiorno (South), Sardegna, Sicilia, Triveneto
Belgium (4)	Bruxelles-Brussel	Vlaanderen (2), Wallonie
Germany (2)	Schleswig-Holstein	Bayern
UK/Britain (2)		Scotland, Wales, (Northern Ireland)
Finland (1)		Swedish-speaking minority (mainly provinces of Udenmaa, Turun-Porin, Åland Islands, Vaasan)
Iceland (2)	Suðurland, Vestfjarð	
Norway (1)	Finnmark	
Denmark (1)	Haderslev, Åbenrå, Sønderborg, Tønder (annexed 1920)	
Switzerland (2)	Ticino (2)	

Figure 5.4   Types of territorial structures of electoral support for regionalist parties: World War II–present.
Notes: More than one party can represent one region (the number of parties when there are more than one is given in parentheses). Trieste and Finnmark cover more than 5 percent but electoral support is very regionalized, wheareas Wales covers less than 5 percent. Belgian Flemish/Walloon Catholics, Liberals, and Social Democrats are not considered regionalists.

only party is the *Südschleswigscher Wählerverband* of the Danish population in Schleswig-Holstein (a very minor party). More problematic is Bavaria, which in the past was represented by strong regionalist parties. Today, the *Christlich-Soziale Union* – the sister party of the CDU based exclusively in Bavaria – is very much a regionalist party as well as a confessional people's party.

Second, in *Finland* and *Britain*, regionalist parties cover larger geographical areas. In Finland, the *Svenska folkspartiet* covers 38.08 percent of the *vaalipiirit* on average. In the United Kingdom, the main regionalists originate from the so-called Celtic fringe, Scotland, Wales – although these represent only 5–6 percent of constituencies – and Northern Ireland.

Third, in four other countries, by contrast, all regionalist parties draw their support from one or a few constituencies: *Iceland* (two local candidacies), *Denmark* (the party representing the German-speaking minority),

189

Norway (the local branch of the Social Democrats), and *Switzerland* (two parties from the Italian-speaking Ticino).

Two Conclusions

1. Are *country differences* in degree of homogeneity reflected *in each party family*? During the period since World War II, they are not. The first conclusion of this party family comparison is therefore that *most party families do not reflect the overall classification of the countries on the basis of level of homogeneity of national electoral support*. First, the fact that within several party families values of homogeneity are very close and their range is limited – mainly liberals conservatives, and social democrats – indicates that their values of disparity are *independent* of those of the countries in which they are located. This conclusion has emerged from the family-by-family analysis, which made it clear that the variance between countries is greatly reduced, especially once the main outlying cases have been documented and excluded. Since for these families the variance among the main parties is limited, it can be concluded that the important difference is *between families* and not between parties of the same family in different countries.

Second, the remaining party families that show strong variations among their parties – confessional parties, agrarians, and regionalists – are all characterized by *peculiar patterns not reflecting the overall ranking of countries on the basis of their degree of homogeneity*: Nordic versus other countries in the case of agrarian parties; homogeneous versus mixed religious structures in the case of Catholic and Protestant parties; small regionalist parties representing small territories in highly regionalized countries (Switzerland) versus strong regionalist parties stemming from broader geographical areas in Italy and Spain versus strong regionalist parties in highly regionalized countries (Belgium), and so on.

The simple one-way analysis of variance in Table 5.10 confirms that *the differences between European parties are caused less by their nationality* – that is, by the fact that they belong to more or less homogeneous countries – than by their *genealogy* – that is, by the fact that they belong to more or less homogeneous party families. The table sums up the country-by-country analysis presented in Chapter 4 and the family-by-family analysis carried out in this chapter. According to indicators that control for the size of parties,[16] the *differences between the types of parties are larger than the differences between*

[16] The standard deviation is included for reference.

Table 5.10. *One-Way Analysis of Variance of Country versus Family Impact on Party Levels of Territorial Homogeneity: World War II–Present*

Indicators	Differences Between Families		Differences Between Countries	
	Eta	Eta Squared	Eta	Eta Squared
Territorial coverage	.75	.57	.63	.39
Standard deviation	.60	.36	.42	.18
CV	.75	.56	.51	.26
IPR	.74	.55	.60	.36
CRII	.78	.61	.57	.32
Significance		.000		.000
N		(1,252)		(1,252)

Notes: Religious parties have been classified into Catholics, Protestants, and interconfessionals, without subdivision according to religious homogeneity/heterogeneity of countries. The analysis was performed on all constituencies.
Legend: See Abbreviations and Symbols in the front matter.

countries. The homogeneity within families is larger than the homogeneity within countries. The differences between party families are even higher if Catholic and Protestant parties are each subdivided into two categories reflecting the homogeneity versus heterogeneity of the societies they act in. All coefficients (not displayed in the table) are slightly higher than the classification presented in the table.

2. Territorial structures of the vote in European party systems are very similar with regard to the liberal, conservative, social democratic, and – to a lesser extent – communist and green party families (once the main outliers are excluded). European party systems differ from each other because of the "deviating" patterns on the three dimensions of the defense of agrarian interests, the defense of regional specificities, and religious differentiation – in particular that of Catholic populations in religiously mixed nations. In Part III the different degree of homogeneity between party families is used to interpret both the temporal evolution of nationalization patterns (Chapter 6) and the differences between countries (Chapter 7).

Toward an Explanation

6

<hr>

The Dynamic Perspective

STATE FORMATION AND MASS DEMOCRATIZATION

Guidelines for Interpretation

Part III combines the three dimensions of variation – time, space (countries), and cleavages (party families) – along which evidence has been described in Part II and introduces a series of explanatory factors based on the three dimensions of the structuring of political spaces displayed in the theoretical scheme sketched in Figure 1.1 (Chapter 1):

- *State Formation*: (1) Processes of *centralization* in opposition to cultural resistance from ethnically and religiously distinct peripheries; (2) *state–church relationships* and secularized political cultures of nation-builders (National Revolution).[1]
- *Democratization*: Development of *mass politics* and *party competition* with the progressive extension/equalization of voting rights to the working (and peasant) population mobilized during the Industrial Revolution.
- *Nation-Building*: Differentiated patterns of *cultural standardization* versus *social fragmentation*, with religious and ethnic resistance leading to differentiated center–periphery relationships.

The explanatory factors introduced in this part of the book are meant to account for the variations in the levels of integration and types of territorial configurations of national electorates and party systems in Europe. The scheme attempts to simplify a very complex story and considers two types of variations. The first are *time variations* – that is, the general pattern toward

<hr>

[1] In Lipset and Rokkan's model (1967a: 35–50, in particular the scheme on page 37), conservative and liberal parties appear as the main "N" parties together with Christian parties in some countries, that is, the core of nation-builders controlling the machinery of the state, against the "P" parties, that is, movements of resistance in subject peripheries.

the nationalization of politics in Europe. This aspect focuses on the *commonalities* between national cases. The second are *cross-national variations* – that is, *differences* between countries in regard to the level of nationalization. This aspect focuses on the resistance to – and deviations from – the main evolution toward nationalization.

Temporal and cross-country variations are interpreted through the presence/predominance of given political cleavages produced by the two revolutions of the West – the political and the industrial (Bendix 1977: 67) – and through the degree of territorial homogeneity of cleavages. This chapter includes the first two dimensions of Figure 1.1 – state formation and democratization. The working hypothesis is that processes of center-building and massification of politics through the inclusion of newly enfranchised working classes (mobilized through the Industrial Revolution) have brought about the supremacy of the left–right cleavage – a *homogenizing* cleavage. Processes of industrialization and mobilization led in all countries to predominant functional left–right cleavages, that is, nonterritorial nationwide alignments that are expressed in nationalized party families (liberals, conservatives, social democrats). In comparison with the other cleavages presented in this book, the class cleavage appears as an element of similarity between countries (Lipset and Rokkan 1967a: 46).[2]

On the other hand, in spite of this general dynamic evolution toward nationalization, differences between countries in levels of territorial diversity persist. Factors accounting for the deviations from the main pattern toward increasingly nationalized party systems are dealt with in Chapter 7, as well as factors accounting for the diversity and differences between countries in the survival of territorial politics. Chapter 7 focuses on the third dimension of Figure 1.1 (nation-building) and adopts a comparative cross-country perspective. The guiding hypothesis is that the survival of territorial politics is due principally to the presence of a series of cultural cleavages, in

---

[2] This is especially true before the International Revolution. Whereas after 1917 the birth of strong communist parties in some countries differentiated to some extent the configuration of the left in Europe, before this date – when processes of nationalization took place – the configuration of the left was much more homogeneous among countries. Instead of looking at the left–right cleavage in terms of variations – timing, electoral strength, division between social democrats and communists – the approach taken here focuses on its general development. As confirmed by the analysis of Bartolini, the variables pertaining to the Industrial Revolution have a stronger explicative potential concerning the temporal development of the class cleavage, and a weaker one concerning cross-country differences which are rather due to cultural heterogeneity (2000b: 200).

particular ethnolinguistic and religious cleavages expressed in territorialized party families (regionalists, Catholics, and Protestants, as well as agrarian parties due to the rural–urban cleavage until the 1950s–60s). These are *dishomogenizing* cleavages resulting from differentiated patterns of nation-building that survived the wave of mass and class politics.

Evidence in Chapter 3 suggests that the crucial moment of integration of national electorates was reached shortly after World War I. The curves for party support display an evolution in two phases: a sharp *decline of regional heterogeneity up to World War I* and a basic *stability of the territorial patterns of party support since the 1920s*. The changes that occurred with World War I therefore concluded a process that took place during the second half of the nineteenth century and stabilized the territorial configurations of party systems. As for the "freezing" of political alignments since the 1920s (Lipset and Rokkan 1967a; Bartolini and Mair 1990), the flatter slope of the curves after the 1920s supports the hypothesis of basic stability of the territorial patterns of electoral behavior. The territorial configurations of party support settle at the levels attained in the first postwar period and change only slightly toward more homogeneity after that time. This finding extends the conclusions reached by previous research limited to more recent periods. As the study on territorial homogenization carried out by Rose and Urwin (1975) emphasizes, the nationalization of elections must be situated before World War II.[3] Therefore, "[i]n order to explain the causes of nationalization of political competition, one would need to analyze much earlier periods in European history" (Rose and Urwin 1975: 45).

This chapter deals with three main factors temporally located before or near World War I: (1) the early mobilization of restricted electorates on nation-building and democratization issues by *liberal* and *conservative* party families; (2) the impact of *mass and class politics* toward the end of the nineteenth century, leading to the emergence of social democratic and labor parties (as well as agrarian parties in some countries); and (3) the drive toward nationwide electoral *competition*.

---

[3] The "nationalization of party competition had already occurred by the start of the [first] postwar era. The most noteworthy general finding in the figures for Western nations after more than a decade of depression and years of war is that every country, except Switzerland . . . , had already achieved the nationalization of party conflict three decades ago" (Rose and Urwin 1975: 45).

State Formation: Center-Building and State–Church Relationships

The process of nationalization can be described as a general move from territorial–cultural cleavages toward a functional left–right alignment. First, the left–right opposition includes the liberal and conservative party families that emerged from the *center–periphery* and *state–church cleavages* during the first phases of competitive elections with restricted electorates. These are the old party families that formed from the National Revolution and represent the fundamental opposition between the supporters of change and the principles of the Enlightment that acquired political significance after the French Revolution[4] and those of the maintenance of the old regime (this section). Second, the left–right functional opposition includes the social democratic party family that emerged from the *class cleavage* after the Industrial Revolution in opposition to both liberal and conservative parties (next section).

Center-Building and Secularization

The broad liberal and conservative party families dominated the political and electoral life until the emergence of social democratic parties. They were the first to form with constitutional regimes and parliamentarism, and the first parties to create organizational infrastructures (Kirchner 1988a: 9). Even before the extension of suffrage, the ideological positions of these parties were referred to in terms of "left" and "right" – where the former term identified the propensity to reform (parliamentarism and equal political rights) and the latter the propensity to maintain the status quo of the old sociopolitical order, traditions, and authority. Historically, liberals and conservatives originate from the National Revolution that created two major cleavages:

- *Center–periphery cleavage*: Conflict between the national standardizing center-building culture and the resistance of ethnolinguistically and/or religiously distinct regional populations.
- *State–church cleavage*: Conflict between the secularized center-builders of the nation-state and the claims and corporate privileges of the aristocracy and the church – in particular the Roman Catholic Church.[5]

---

[4] See von Beyme (1985: 31–32), as well as Manning (1976), Salvadori (1977), and Bogdanor (1983).

[5] The nationwide confrontation between the aspirations of the secularized radical-liberal builders of the mobilizing nation-state on the one hand, and the corporate claims of the

The liberals were the motor of the National Revolution and of the radical change from the *ancien régime* to modern states based on constitutionalism, parliamentarism, and mass democracy. The liberals, furthermore, were the main actors in the centralization of Western nation-states and their secularization in the nineteenth century, with the separation of political institutions from religious influences.[6] In all European countries this party family includes the group of state-builders, as well as the political cultures, that carried out the National Revolution – centralization/rationalization of state administration, democratization of political institutions, secularization and separation between state and church, and cultural standardization.

The origin of liberalism lies therefore both in the constitutional and democratic principles (mainly of the British political culture) and in the process of nation-building after the French Revolution, whose principles of the nation-state (*nation une et indivisible*) were exported all over Europe through the Napoleonic wars. As far as the first aspect – democratization – is concerned, liberal principles are at the origin of parliamentary general representation and mass participation. Liberals opposed the principles of the old order and were strong elements of change in most old European monarchies: Denmark, France, the Netherlands, Spain, Sweden, and the United Kingdom.[7] The "internal" origin of liberal parties (see Duverger 1951a: 3–20; La Palombara and Weiner 1966a) indicates that they developed from the early parliamentary groups and electoral committees that formed after the introduction of general representation. They participated

churches on the other, is a factor in the nationalization of liberal and conservative parties. This is true, however, mostly for homogeneous Catholic countries. In religiously mixed countries, the relationship between state and church results in protracted territorialized politics.

[6] Among the several ideological areas existing within liberalism, the radicals were more strongly in favor of universal suffrage and the abolition of the monarchy (republicanism). Radicals were also more anticlerical. The term "radical" is sometimes used interchangeably with "liberal." In Switzerland, for example, it is used in the French- and Italian-speaking cantons, whereas *Freisinnig* or *Liberal* is used in the German-speaking cantons. In the Catholic countries in particular, but also in the countries with strong Catholic minorities (Germany, the Netherlands, Switzerland), liberalism took the form of republicanism or radicalism (von Beyme 1985: 43).

[7] The name originates from *liberales*, the constitutionalists in the *Córtes* of Cadiz (1812). The label emphasized freedom, and in England it replaced that of Whig, the political grouping based on the principles of the 1688 Revolution. The term was adopted in most countries except for some Scandinavian countries, such as Denmark and Norway, where *Venstre* (Left) was used.

in the first phases of parliamentary life and were able to mobilize restricted electorates that participated in the first competitive elections. Liberals were therefore the first to mobilize nationwide for the organization of elections and the management of candidates' finance, and to compete nationally for votes with a view to obtaining the necessary parliamentary majority to support cabinets.

As far as the processes of state formation and nation-building are concerned, in many cases liberal groups promoted, and were involved in, the struggles for national independence from foreign domination and/or national unification. In the countries where the nation-building process was incomplete and that formed during the nineteenth and early twentieth centuries, liberals played an important role as nationalist mobilizing forces (Laski 1936: 15; Smith 1988: 19). In many countries, the democratization of the political system went hand in hand with movements of national independence and/or unification. Liberals played an important role in most secession states such as Norway, Finland, Iceland, and Belgium, as well as in states undergoing unification: Germany and Switzerland – where the Radicals pushed for the creation of the sovereign confederation against the resistance of Catholic cantons (eventually leading to the *Sonderbund* war). In Italy, processes of both democratization and unification – with the extension of the *Statuto albertino* (the only constitution of 1848 to survive the reaction in the peninsula) – paralleled the process of independence (in particular from the Habsburg in the north).

The rationalization of state structures and the creation of an equal citizenship against both aristocratic privileges and the consolidated prerogatives of the clergy led to a strong conflict between the liberal state and the church. The nation-state rested on a secularized ideology inspired by the principles of the French Revolution. Especially in the Roman Catholic countries, the opposition of liberals to any privilege by the *pouvoirs intermédiaires* led to violent confrontations in particular over education. The creation of an equal citizenship meant the socialization of children through universal schooling systems based on universal principles.[8] In Italy, the contrast between state and church was even deeper, as the process of state formation implied the end of the temporal power of the pope through the annexation of the papal territories by the Savoy. In the Protestant countries,

---

[8] State control over all aspects of life previously in the hands of the church was extended to the family (e.g., through civic marriage) and, later, to the welfare state and the provision for poor relief (see, e.g., Alber 1982).

the state–church conflict had been resolved long before democratization, with nationalizing consequences. The Reformation meant a nationalization of churches opposed to the supranational Roman Catholic Church. National churches were incorporated in state structures, and the move away from Rome had important cultural repercussions, in particular with the development of national linguistic standards (starting with the translation of the Bible).[9]

As seen in Chapter 5, the liberal party family appears to have been highly nationalized since the earliest elections after the main revolutionary waves. Since the mid-nineteenth century, therefore, the central position of liberals within European party systems stands out as an important factor in the nationalization of politics. First, liberals were the political force promoting the parliamentarization and democratization of political systems. They were able to mobilize nationwide candidates and electorates and to rely on state-administrative structures. Second, liberals were at the origin of the rationalization-homogenization of administrative state structures. Liberal parties emerged from, and simultaneously pursued, the centralization of both state structures and culture – language (in particular through national compulsory schooling) – initiated by older monarchies. Although the center–periphery cleavage is highly territorial, for marginal provinces and territories resist national integration protracted by the center, liberals were the parties of the center and were the agents of centralization and penetration in peripheral areas. Third, liberals were the partisan-organizational expression of the secularized-rationalistic side of the state–church conflict. In most cases, state–church oppositions cut across the territorial units of the country. On the one hand, in the Protestant countries the alliance between church and state proved to be a strong factor in cultural nationalization. On the other hand, in the Catholic countries of the Counter-Reformation church–state conflicts brought territorial areas into opposition only in rare cases: Whether through specifically Catholic parties or within broader conservative fronts, church interests were inserted in nationwide alignments, first during the periods of restricted suffrage and later – after enfranchisement – when parties of religious defense developed into mass movements. Where – as in the religiously mixed countries – Catholic resistance became retrenched in given areas, this had little effect on the

---

[9] Minor Christian parties developed later for religious defense to oppose the progressive secularization of the state and an increasingly permissive society. Historically, however, they never represented relevant elements of the party systems in these countries.

territorial diffusion of the secularized liberal nation-builders (with the exception of Switzerland).

Conservative and Catholic People's Parties

As a consequence, also the other "side" of the liberal–conservative opposition proved territorially very homogeneous. The state–church cleavage is part of a broader opposition between liberals and conservatives and concerns primarily Catholic conservative parties in Catholic or religiously mixed countries. Like liberal parties, the conservative family belongs to the first phases of electoral competition during the period of restricted electorates, and since the beginning they were able to mobilize electorates and appear as highly nationalized parties in most countries.

Conservative parties are the second party family to form ideologically in reaction to liberalism.[10] This family developed in response to the threat to aristocratic and clerical powers (Layton-Henry 1982) and aimed to restore the royal authority weakened by constitutionalism and parliamentarism. Where the old order had survived, conservatives attempted to maintain the status quo and were hostile to liberal reforms. The very philosophical principles on which liberalism rested were contested. The need of a ruling aristocracy was legitimized by arguing the natural inequality between individuals. The rule of law was considered unable to force equality upon individuals, and conservatives supported the religious moral order against the faith in reason, and the stability of traditions and institutions against the uncertainty of progress. In many countries, conservatives were identified with the right.[11] This broad label ranged from extreme reactionary positions aiming at the full restoration of the *ancien régime*, to the conservation of the status quo, to a moderate conservative reformism allowing for change but maintaining the traditional institutions and privileges (Rossiter 1968).

The establishment of a political party was for many conservatives a temporary matter, that is, an organization that would dissolve once the old order would have been reestablished. With the consolidation of the liberal state, however, conservatives and Catholics eventually accepted constitutionalism and human rights, popular sovereignty and – where the monarchy could not

---

[10] The term "conservative" appeared at the beginning of the nineteenth century, when Chateaubriand edited the ultraroyalist paper *Le conservateur*. In the 1830s the term replaced the label "Tory" also used in England, to designate the ideological area more favorable to royal authority.

[11] See, for example, the names of conservatives in Denmark and Norway: *Højre* or *Høire*.

be restored – even the republic. With the consolidation of parliamentary democracy, conservative parties not only did not disappear, but established themselves as central actors in the emerging party systems, and were successful in many cases in challenging liberals through the mobilization of restricted electorates.

The religious component of conservativism has always been very strong, both in the Catholic countries such as Austria, Belgium, France, Italy, and Spain and in the religiously mixed countries such as Germany, the Netherlands, and Switzerland. Whereas in some countries the defense of Catholic interests was represented by specific parties (Austria, Belgium, Italy), in others the opposition to liberalism was incorporated into broader conservative fronts. Conservative parties appeared notably in the states that formed early, where the state–church conflict was particularly deep and protracted. In France and Spain the defense of Catholic interests was inserted in broader fronts of the right.[12] By contrast, there are Catholic parties – later developing into people's parties – in the states born out of the national revolutions in the nineteenth century, in particular in Germany, Italy, Switzerland (unification states), Belgium (secession state from a Protestant monarchy), and in Austria. In Ireland, another secession state from a Protestant center, there is no specific Catholic party, and the case is more similar to the Protestant secession states of the North, where the alliance between state and church prevented the creation of a party for religious defense.[13]

Catholic parties developed later than conservative parties, that is, with the massification of politics. The reason lies in the difficult relationship between the church and Catholic political organizations. These parties were suspect in the eyes of the church. Rather than being an expression of the clergy, Catholic parties emerged from the doctrine of Christian

---

[12] In Spain, Catholic loyalties were transferred to and incorporated by other groups, in particular Carlism and Integrism and, later, in the more religious areas such as the Basque and Catalan regions, to the nationalist causes. Peripheral nationalism therefore overlapped with the resistance of Catholic areas to the secularizing tendencies of the Spanish center. The support for peripheral forces weakened the possibility of a Catholic party. As Linz (1967a: 229) notes, this is a major difference with Italy.

[13] The usual explanations for the absence of a specifically Catholic party in Ireland relate to the deep cleavage in 1922 over the acceptance of the treaty. Furthermore, it is often argued that anticlericalism was less likely to develop in Ireland, where the Catholic Church was a strong actor in the struggle for independence and had always been a popular institution allied to the peasants (the church in Ireland has never been a great landowner). See Rokkan (1970a: 124–26).

social groups that accepted parliamentary democracy much earlier than the Vatican[14] and that attempted to bring Christian values into democracy (the so-called *démocratie chrétienne*). Furthermore, Catholic parties in the homogeneously Catholic countries that transformed after World War II into broad confessional people's parties (e.g., the *Österreichische Volkspartei*, the *Parti social-chrétien-Christelijke volkspartij*, the *Democrazia cristiana*, and the *Mouvement republicain populaire* in France, later absorbed by the Gaullist movement) were rarely conservative but rather center parties with many progressive stands inherited from the social doctrine of Leo XIII and Pius XI and the role played by the church against totalitarian regimes. This is also the case for the interconfessional parties in the mixed countries, such as the *Christlich-Demokratische Union* in Germany, which inherited the democratic spirit of the *Zentrum* (although this party was long opposed to the Weimar Republic) and, later, of the Dutch *Christen democratisch appèl*.

Like liberal parties, the conservative party family in most countries has displayed high levels of nationalization since the beginning of competitive elections. The early opposition of conservative parties created to counter the progression of liberal reforms was of a nonterritorial nature: the defense of aristocratic and ecclesiastic privileges. Before the inclusion of mass working electorates toward the end of the nineteenth century, the mainly functional opposition between liberals and conservatives dominated the party systems under restricted voting rights, with both party families progressively competing nationwide. With the consolidation of the state and its internal standardization through processes of penetration/integration of peripheries and the reduction of center–periphery tensions – as well as the acceptance of the liberal-democratic rules of the game – the opposition between liberals and conservatives moved toward an interest-based alignment. In this regard, the emergence of a left–right alignment has also been a consequence of the development of parties for the mobilization of working electorates – social democrats and labor parties.

---

[14] The Vatican accepted democracy as an "established fact" in 1918 (von Beyme 1985: 40). In Italy, but to a certain extent also in France (Anderson 1974: 170), the papal ban (*non expedit*) against the participation of Catholics in the political life in the newly created state postponed the foundation of a Catholic party to the early twentieth century. From 1860 until the 1910s, the political scene was dominated by the broad liberal galaxy. In 1876 the liberal camp divided into the left and the right when right-wing dissidents (mainly Tuscans) split away and were referred to as *Destra* (Right) or sometimes *Conservatori*.

Democratization: Mass Politics and the Industrial Revolution

This section analyzes the impact of democratization and mass politics on the formation of territorially homogeneous electorates and party systems: the extension of the franchise and the development of parties for mass mobilization. The democratization or "massification" of politics toward the end of the nineteenth century, however, is closely related to another major social change: the Industrial Revolution and the political mobilization of the working class. The mobilization of working masses led new political forces against the dominant – liberal and conservative – elites under restricted suffrage. This conflict goes under the label of *class cleavage*, between owners and employers on the one hand, and between workers, tenants, and laborers on the other.

The entry of social democratic parties for the mobilization of newly enfranchised working masses consolidated the supremacy of the functional cleavage. The predominance of the left–right dimension can be observed in all countries and is a factor of convergence and similarity between countries. In all party systems the hegemony of the class cleavage over the others – mainly the cultural and center–periphery dimensions – has been an important step toward the nationalization of Western party systems. Social democratic parties are among the most homogeneous party families together with the two other main families of the left–right cleavage described earlier that homogenized during the early phases of restricted suffrage.

Social Mobilization and Electoral Participation

Work on political integration assumed that ethnic and territorial identity would wither away in the process of modernization.[15] The early work of Karl W. Deutsch is emblematic of the association between social mobilization triggered by the Industrial Revolution and "national assimilation."[16] Assimilation is the result of modernization in the form of increasing urbanization, industrialization, schooling, communication, and transportation: "[a] decisive factor in national assimilation or differentiation was found to be the process of social mobilization which accompanies the growth of markets, industries, and towns, and eventually of literacy and mass

---

[15] See the discussion in Introduction.
[16] See Chapter 6 on "National Assimilation or Differentiation. Some Quantitative Relationships" (Deutsch 1953: 123–52).

communication" (1953: 188).[17] In addition to increasing social and geographical mobility, industrialization led to changing perceptions. Individuals became more similar in their behavior, attitudes, and beliefs. Through a spatially static process that does not necessarily require geographic mobility, communication produces territorially integrated communities. It is functional divisions themselves that are eroded and, simultaneously, their territorial projection.[18] The Industrial Revolution therefore had a strong impact on all social divisions. Social mobility is concomitant with industrialization (Lipset and Bendix 1992: 11), and it is at the origin of the "fundamental democratization" of society as meant by Karl Mannheim (1940): the uprooting of old settings and habits, and the socialization of mobilized masses in new group memberships and commitments.[19]

The impact of social mobilization appears clearly in the effects of literacy on the nationalization of electorates. The reading and writing skills of vast sectors of the population are an important aspect of the formation of electorates, for they created the conditions for the mobilization of the lower strata and their incorporation into mass politics. Literacy, further, is an indicator of the more general process of nation-building fostered by the state and of social mobilization during the nineteenth century through obligatory school attendance and universal conscription (not surprisingly, many literacy statistics are available for army recruits), as well as the creation of national communication systems (on the French case, see Weber 1976).

The early development of literacy created the conditions for the mobilization and participation of the lower strata in mass politics.[20] This occurred especially in the Protestant regions of the Northeast, where the established churches fostered mass education and acted as strong agencies of nationalization through their alliance with nation-builders. Census statistics show, for example, that by the end of the nineteenth century in Finland,

[17] On the role of education and literacy see Cipolla (1969), Flora (1972), Coleman (1965), and Ulich (1961).

[18] As Sundquist noted about the United States: "[w]ith the upward social and economic mobility, intermarriage, and the movement from ethnic neighbourhoods to heterogeneous suburbs, some Irishmen may feel less Irish, Jews less Jewish, Poles less Polish and so on" (1973: 337).

[19] For a similar interpretation of this fundamental process of change from a traditional to a modern way of life, see also Lasswell (1951) and Lerner (1958).

[20] See Gellner (1983). For an analysis of the role of literacy and printing in the emergence of national languages and "imagined communities" during the first phases of capitalism see Anderson (1983: 38–40).

206

97.5 percent of the population over age 10 was able to read compared to 38.4 percent in Italy (over age 12), 65.6 percent in Austria (over age 6), 69.2 percent in France (over age 5), and 77.9 percent in Ireland (over age 10).

Lack of data on literacy preclude a thorough comparative verification of its impact on the nationalization of electorates, especially since the relationship between literacy and national electorates has to be analyzed with disaggregated data rather than through national levels of literacy. The mobilizing impact of literacy on the masses in relation to electoral participation can however be shown taking two countries as an example: the Austrian half of the Habsburg Empire (Cisleithania), for which data on literacy are available for the 17 *Kronlander*, and Italy, for which the same data are available for the 16 regions in which the kingdom was divided until World War I. In both countries, the first elections after the massification of politics have been considered: 1911 in the case of Austria, that is, the second election after the abolition of the first four curiae and the maintenance of the fifth general curia, for which all men over 24 were entitled to vote (although voting was still mainly indirect); 1919 in the case of Italy, the first election with PR after the full introduction of universal male suffrage (for men aged 21 and those aged 18 who had served during the war). For Italy, furthermore, a second year has been considered, 1861, when suffrage was restricted by census (based on the amount of paid direct taxes, in practice an electorate of 7.9 percent of the enfranchised group over age 25). For Austria this comparison is not possible because of the curial system before 1907 (large landowners; chambers of commerce and trade; cities, markets and industrial areas; and rural communes).

It appears from Figures 6.1 and 6.2 that in both Austria and Italy there is a close relationship between literacy and level of electoral participation after the introduction of universal suffrage (correlation coefficients of .60). What is more significant in both cases, however, is the distribution of regions, with a *clear indication of not yet formed electorates and a distinction between central and peripheral areas*. The centers of the territorial systems are those in which literacy and electoral mobilization are highest. For the Habsburg Empire these regions are those of today's Austria (Lower and Upper Austria, Salzburg, Vorarlberg), as well as the wealthy regions of Bohemia, Silesia, and Moravia, which – after World War I – make up Czechoslovakia together with the more backward regions of Slovakia and "Subcarpathian Russia" (Deutsch 1953: 209). By contrast, the peripheral regions of Dalmatia and Istria (later Yugoslavia) are those for which both literacy

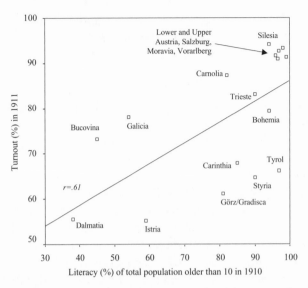

Figure 6.1 Correlation between levels of literacy and turnout in the Austrian Empire (Cisleithania, 1911).

and electoral participation are weaker. Three states display high levels of literacy but low electoral participation: These are the three more peripheral states within the core Austrian area (Styria, Carinthia, and Tyrol), whereas the two Russian states of Bucovina and Galicia are characterized by high turnout rates despite very low levels of literacy. Finally, it is interesting to note the central position of Trieste, the harbor of the Austrian Empire.

A very similar pattern appears in the graph for Italy (Figure 6.2). There is a group of regions that compose the most developed economic nucleus of the country from which the unification process started. The two Savoy regions of Piedmont and Liguria belong to this group, together with Lombardy, Emilia (partly a papal territory in which strong anticlerical mobilization took place), and Tuscany (from which, with Piedmont, most political personnel stemmed with the unification), as well as Veneto (formerly Austria). On the other hand, a number of regions display the opposite pattern. These are mostly the backward southern regions that formerly made up the Kingdom of the Two Sicilies (Sicily, Calabria, Lucania – today Basilicata – Abruzzo and Molise, and the Puglie), but also the regions formerly belonging to the Papal States (Umbria and Marche, as well as Latium, the region surrounding Rome). To this group also belongs Sardinia,

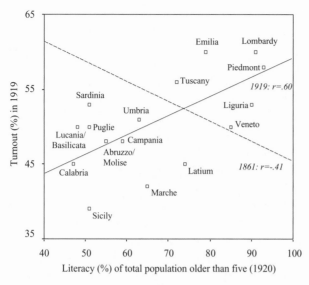

Figure 6.2 Correlation between levels of literacy and turnout in Italy: 1919 (and 1861).

the island belonging to Piedmont that, given its geographical position, has always been a periphery.

Figure 6.2 displays a second dashed line that refers to the same correlation computed for the 1861 election with data on literacy in 1871. The correlation between literacy and turnout is negative (−.41), meaning that the modalities of mobilization of the "electorate" in a time of restricted franchise were fundamentally different from those in a time of mass politics, with a much stronger role for clientelistic relationships within the elite of local *notabili*. Although in a context of restricted franchise these relationships prove highly mobilizing, they tend to reduce the participation of the masses after the introduction of universal suffrage. In Italy in particular, to the present day, the electorate is still mobilized by ideological and subcultural factors in the north and center, but by clientelistic factors in the South (see Caramani 1996b).

Class Politics: The Impact of the Left–Right Cleavage

From a developmental perspective the assimilation and integration of national communities have often been interpreted as stages. The first stage

209

is characterized by open or latent resistance to political amalgamation into a common national state. Second, integration is limited to passive compliance with orders from the center. Third, ethnoterritorial and religious group cohesion persists, but there is deeper support for the common state. Finally, national amalgamation produces the assimilation of all groups into a common language and culture (Deutsch 1966). Industrialization led to reduction of the territoriality of social segmentations. The social and geographical mobility engendered by industrialization and urbanization reduced the territoriality of political cleavages. Territorial segmentation became more fluid through a process of "social entropy" (Gellner 1983: Chapter 6). This spatially dynamic process does not necessarily imply a change in individual behavior, attitudes, and beliefs. It is rather the territorial mixing of different individuals that makes geographical areas increasingly similar. It is a modality of change in the territorial distribution of individuals, according to which functional divisions remain but do not project themselves on the territory.

Along these lines, Kevin R. Cox (1969c; see also Taylor and Johnston 1979: 107–63) has suggested a three-phase model of the evolution of cleavages. In the first, territorial phase, at the beginning of competitive elections and during the phase of the structuring of the party systems, the vote is geographically segmented, with disproportionately concentrated patterns of party support. This is closely associated with the economic, ethnic, and religious attributes that divide regions. In the second functional phase, industrialization and consequent urbanization lead to the development of communication networks and to important migrations. During this phase, territorial cleavages are replaced by oppositions between urban and rural interests and by divisions on economic and religious issues.[21] Finally, in a further functional phase, the cleavage between urban and rural areas is replaced by the class cleavage in which the rising masses of wage earners are opposed by the employers or propertied classes in general. From the electoral point of view, there is an erosion of territorial disparities. Local networks are replaced by national ones, leading to the creation of national political and economic organizations.[22]

---

[21] A classical example is the work of V. O. Key, Jr. (1964), who explains the evolution from sectionalism to class politics in the United States through the process of urbanization. In his view, however, the nationalization of electoral alignments has been hindered by party encapsulation and political socialization.

[22] See Williamson (1965) for a similar interpretation of the evolution of industrialization. For a comparative work on the emergence of industrial societies see Cipolla (1973).

Industrialization produced a general movement from the peripheries toward urban and industrial centers, bringing into contact populations in a mixed environment. Industrialization produced a more atomized spatial pattern compared to regional segmentation. Also, the parallel development of new forms of mass communications opened up by the Industrial Revolution has had a strong impact on the transformation of cleavages from territorial into functional. The growth of mass communication led to the annulment of physical space. With the "Media Revolution" – comparable in its scope and effects to the National and Industrial Revolutions of the nineteenth century – territorial aspects lost relevance. Access to information and the physical location of the main channels of communication became independent of geographic distance. Aspects of solidarity, socialization, and conflict lost specific territorial connotations. Spatial proximity (face-to-face contacts, meetings, demonstrations) no longer mediated patterns of socialization. These forms were replaced by atomized relationships between individuals and sources of information. The influence of groups, social context, and economic environments weakened, making "place" a secondary variable in determining individuals' political behavior.

In addition to the homogenizing and assimilating effects of social mobilization, however, a number of dishomogenizing and differentiating effects have been also noted. Deutsch himself acknowledges that increasing contacts between persons with diverse identities might increase groups' self-consciousness: "technological and economic processes are forcing them [the members of each group] together, into acute recognition of their differences and their common, mutual experience of strangeness, and more conspicuous differentiation and conflict may result" (1953: 126). Especially in plural societies, rapid social mobilization tends to further undermine the unity of the state whose populations are already divided into ethnic, linguistic, and religious groups (see, in particular, Deutsch 1961). Rather than being linked by a causal relationship, therefore, mobilization and assimilation are seen as two isolated processes with no other connection than a chronological one (Deutsch 1969).

Therefore, in order to test whether social mobilization has led primarily to more assimilation or to the strengthening of ethnolinguistic and religious conflict – that is, a direct impact of the Industrial Revolution on nationalization processes (see also Figure 6.12) – this subsection analyzes the impact of industrialization processes through the emergence of a cross-local functional class cleavage that came to dominate the political space through the opposition of social democrats to the old liberal and conservative elites.

Most of the research on the determinants of the reduced territoriality of sociopolitical cleavages stresses the increasing importance of functional class politics compared to cultural, rural–urban, and center–periphery cleavages. The predominance of the left–right cleavage and its homogenizing effects on European party systems were an important element of the integration of the nations during the nineteenth century. Even though in several cases the economic cleavage overlaps with former territorial configurations,[23] the advent of social democratic and labor parties as specific class parties had standardizing implications (Urwin 1982a: 47). The class cleavage and its impact on democratization overshadowed cultural and territorial cleavages. Class politics is the result of industrialization processes leading to the basic left–right opposition that marked "the decline of local politics and an increasing accentuation of functional cleavages" (Rokkan 1970a: 323); and "[t]he economic-functional salience reflects class alliance overcoming geographically delimitated units and tends to erode the structures of the local institutional leadership" (Rokkan 1970a: 336).

The important socioeconomic transformations engendered by the Industrial Revolution were translated in the party system through the electoral channel and imposed the hegemony of the left–right cleavage. This appears clearly in Figure 6.3 on the growth of social democratic parties in Europe. This figure shows the strong "clash" produced in the European party systems by industrialization and social democracy. The social democratic vote as a percentage of the total number of valid votes between the 1880s and World War I reaches a stable level of around 30 percent (which includes the votes for the main socialist and social democratic parties in each country only, not communist votes). Social democratic parties – and their opponents on the other side of the cleavage (liberals and conservatives in particular) – have since then occupied most of the political-ideological space, thus reducing the cultural-territorial dimensions.[24]

---

[23] See, for example, the British case, where the territorial configuration of the left–right cleavage corresponds to the previous geography of the vote, which helped the "survival of geographical politics" (Urwin 1980a: 147). Historically, liberal support (and later the vote for Labour) corresponded to the distribution of English Nonconformism, whereas Anglican religiosity tended to be associated with conservative support in the regions of the southeast and around London. Liberal support was therefore stronger in the areas removed from the center.

[24] For a similar curve see Bartolini (2000b: 59), where, however, the whole vote for left parties is taken instead of the social democratic vote alone.

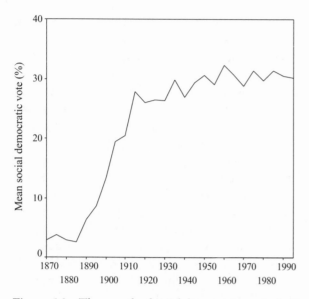

Figure 6.3   The growth of social democratic parties in Europe, 1870s–present. *Note*: 15 countries included (Portugal and Spain omitted). For Italy, Communist Party considered instead of Socialists.

The entry of new left parties and their homogenizing effect can be shown for four countries for which the time series of electoral results by parties is longer: Belgium, Denmark, Switzerland, and Britain in the nineteenth century and the beginning of the twentieth (Figure 6.4).[25] In all four countries, the territorial spread of three main party families are displayed: two old established families (conservatives or Catholics on the one hand and liberals on the other) and one new family (the social democrats).[26] Figure 6.4 shows dramatically the simultaneous appearance and territorial spread of

[25] Similar figures, not reproduced here, can be obtained for Germany, Italy, and the Netherlands since the 1870s–80s.

[26] In Belgium the parties considered are the *Union catholique belge*, the *Parti libéral*, and the *Parti ouvrier belge*. In Denmark *Højre* and *Venstre* have been considered conservative and liberal, respectively. The *Socialdemokrater* represent the new entrant. In Switzerland the Radicals (*Freisinnig-Demokratische Partei*) have been considered instead of the liberal wing (*Liberal-Demokratische Partei*), together with the *Katholische Konservative* and the *Sozialdemokratische Partei der Schweiz*. Finally, in Britain, the Conservative Party, Liberal Party, and Labour Party have been considered. In all these countries, majoritarian formulas (the two/three-ballot formula in Belgium and Switzerland, and plurality in Denmark and Britain) made the existence of other parties difficult and sporadic.

213

social democratic parties in Europe.[27] In all countries, the social democrats spread through national territories in the last decades of the nineteenth century and in the first decades of the twentieth. This occurred together with the mobilization of new working populations – either already enfranchised (as in Switzerland) or still deprived of the right to vote. Mass parties of the working class, along with agrarian parties in the Nordic countries, were able – also because of preexisting social organizations (namely, unions) – to mobilize rapidly the new working-class and peasant electorates.

Whereas in the four countries considered we find conservatives and liberals covering most of the constituencies since the major transitions toward democratic elections with restricted electorates, social democratic and labor parties arise from the socioeconomic transformations resulting from industrialization and urbanization. This occurs toward the end of the nineteenth century, and the territorial spread of this party family is sudden and rapid, as the solid lines in Figure 6.4 show. Among the four countries considered, the spread of workers' candidates was faster in Belgium and Britain, whereas it was more gradual in Denmark and Switzerland.

In Belgium, Catholics and Liberals are present in more than 80 percent of the constituencies; since the 1880s, Catholics have been present in all constituencies. The share of constituencies in which conservatives and liberals present candidates is approximately the same in Switzerland – although the cleavage between Radicals and Catholics after the *Sonderbundkrieg* is reflected in a clear-cut territorial segmentation of the vote. British parties too were constantly present in 70–90 percent of the constituencies, with no significant variations over time. The coverage of territory was also very large for both Conservatives and Liberals before the electoral reforms of 1867–68 and 1884–85 (the Franchise Act and the Redistribution Act, respectively) that stimulated the national organization of political parties.

Whereas in Belgium, Switzerland, and Britain the proportion of territorial coverage by conservatives-Catholics and liberals is stable over time, in Denmark the Right and the Left over the decades increased the number of constituencies in which they presented candidates. In the early elections after the sudden transition from absolutism to democratic representation, the two parties were present in around half of the *valgkredse*. Both parties

---

[27] The measure is the number of constituencies in which a party is present (nominator) as a percentage of the total number of constituencies (denominator). To adjust for missing data, the number of missing constituencies has been subtracted from the total number of constituencies. Furthermore, uncontested constituencies have been considered as constituencies in which the unopposed party is present.

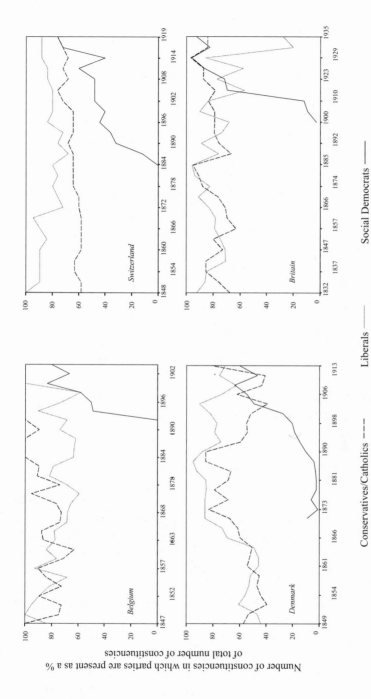

Figure 6.4 The presence in constituencies of conservatives, liberals, and social democrats in four countries, 1832–1935.

Conservatives/Catholics — — —   Liberals ·········   Social Democrats ————

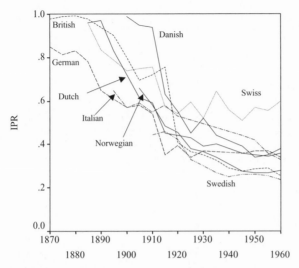

Figure 6.5 The homogenization of support for eight social democratic and labor parties in Europe: 1870s–1960s.

expanded in the 1860s–70s, reaching around 80 percent of the constituencies. A retrenchment then occurred to some extent in the 1890s and 1900 for the *Højre* and later also for the *Venstre* as a consequence of the growth of the Social Democrats.

Not only did social democratic parties spread suddenly and rapidly across territory but, in addition, evidence confirms that the electoral support of these parties homogenized rapidly. In Chapter 5 it has been shown that social democrats underwent strong homogenization. The rapid territorial homogenization of class politics appears clearly for all countries in Figure 6.5, where the patterns for eight social democratic parties are presented historically. The period between the main phases of industrialization and World War I (when male universal suffrage was introduced everywhere) witnessed the territorial homogenization of the social democratic parties in Europe, with the main exception of Switzerland.

What was the impact of the growth of class politics on the whole party system? The relationship displayed in the upper-left graph in Figure 6.6 shows a significant correlation between the level of the social democratic vote – taken as an indicator of class politics as a percentage of the total number of valid votes – and the level of nationalization of the whole party system. The higher the percentage of the social democratic vote, the greater the weight of its level of homogeneity in the overall system's average

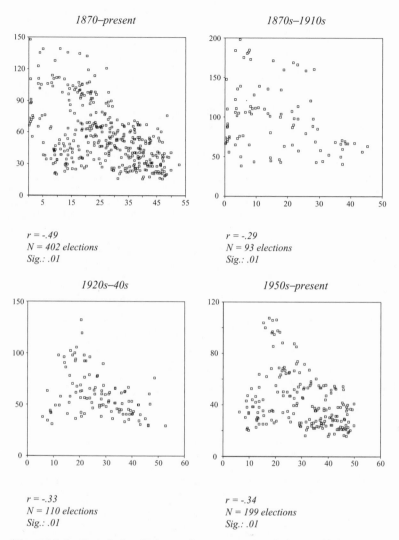

1870–present

1870s–1910s

r = -.49
N = 402 elections
Sig.: .01

r = -.29
N = 93 elections
Sig.: .01

1920s–40s

1950s–present

r = -.33
N = 110 elections
Sig.: .01

r = -.34
N = 199 elections
Sig.: .01

Figure 6.6 Correlation between the percentage of the social democratic vote (X axis) and the level of territorial heterogeneity (standard deviation) subdivided by periods.

for each election. For the overall period from the first appearance of social democratic candidates in the 1870s to the present, the correlation coefficient between the level of territorial heterogeneity (measured by the standard deviation) and social democratic vote is −.49 (with 402 elections in

15 countries).[28] This means that the stronger the social democrats, the more nationalized the whole party system.

However, this relationship presents the typical problems of historical multicollinearity, meaning that temporal series of information – especially those relating to *allgemeine Entwicklungen* of "modernization" in Western societies after the Industrial and French Revolutions – tend to be strongly associated with one another.[29] In the other three graphs in Figure 6.6, the relationship has therefore been broken down into three time slices corresponding to the main periods distinguished in the previous chapters. The subdivision into three periods controls for the time evolution of both nationalization and the social democratic vote, especially for the last period, for which evidence in Chapter 3 (and in Figure 6.3) shows a fundamental stability of both the levels of territorial heterogeneity and the social democratic vote. The correlation coefficients are weaker within the three periods: $-.29$ for the period up to World War I, $-.33$ for the decades 1920s–40s, and $-.34$ for the period since World War II, but they nonetheless show a strong impact of left–right voting on the overall levels of homogeneity of the party system. Furthermore, it appears that correlation coefficients increase between the first and third periods, confirming that the increase in the social democratic vote between the beginning of the twentieth century and the aftermath of World War I implies a higher weight on the entire party system of this homogeneous party family.

The Decline and Transformation of Agrarian Politics

Besides the development of social democratic parties, the Industrial Revolution led to the development – especially in some countries – of agra-

---

[28] Portuguese and Spanish elections since the mid-1970s have been excluded from the correlation.

[29] Historical multicollinearity is a correlation between two variables that covary over time. See Bartolini (1993: 157–60). As the author notes, the problem of historical multicollinearity is particularly acute with general and ubiquitous phenomena, as are the nationalization of elections and the increase in the social democratic vote; in other words, "wherever no cross-unit variance is available" (p. 157). However, although both nationalization and the social democratic vote vary between countries at each point in time, the convergence and similarity between countries (see Figure 3.7) weaken the chances of success of a research strategy of the type "the earlier . . . the higher."

rian and peasant parties. In most countries, this type of party appeared roughly in the last two decades of the nineteenth century as a consequence of the rural–urban conflicts, produced by industrialization, between agricultural protectionist and free market positions. The origin of this party family is mostly defensive. Agriculture was confronted with the rapid decline as a sector of employment due to technological progress and acceleration of productivity. In a way very similar to that of the social democrats, therefore, these parties developed rapidly under the impact of both suffrage extension and social mobilization and – as evidence in Chapter 5 has shown – spread rapidly through territory. This means that, very soon, these parties stopped being a major source of territoriality in Europe.

Only in Scandinavia were agrarian interests channeled through large and electorally significant political parties. In the rest of Western Europe, if one excepts a peasant party that was established in some Protestant cantons of Switzerland in 1919, agrarian support was spread among several parties. Most of the research on the conditions for the emergence of large agrarian parties focuses on the organization of rural society and, in particular, on land ownership.[30] Agrarian political organizations were, in the first place, movements for the defense of small or medium-sized units of production, and their development depended on the market relationship between towns and countryside. This type of weak small farming occupation was much more exposed to the uncertainties of the rising free-market economy of urban environments. By contrast, where land ownership was organized in large estates – as in Britain, Spain, or large areas of Denmark, France, Prussia, and Italy[31] – the concentration of power and the social role of great landowners put the landed economy in a much stronger position. In

---

[30] See in particular Linz (1976) and Urwin (1980b: 160–205). The classical analysis of the role of the peasant world in the political revolutions is that of Moore (1966), who includes most of the vast existing literature on agrarian politics.

[31] Especially in Jutland (Denmark), in the territories in Prussia east of the Elbe, in southern Italy (*latifondo*), and in *Niederösterreich*. In Belgium, the Netherlands, and the Catholic cantons of Switzerland, by contrast, small farming was closely tied to the urban economy (Lipset and Rokkan 1967a: 45). The distribution of land appears from data presented by Russett (1964) and Taylor and Jodice (1983). From these data it appears that the largest inequalities can be observed in Italy, Spain, Greece, Austria, and the United Kingdom (Gini index between 80.3 and 71.0). By contrast, the Gini index indicates smaller farming structures for Denmark, Switzerland, Sweden, Belgium, Finland, and the Netherlands (Gini index between 45.8 and 60.5).

these cases, landed interests allied with, and were incorporated in, broader conservative fronts that saw an opportunity to gain support from the peasant world in exchange for enfranchisement of the peasants (as in Britain or Germany).

The opposition between rural and urban interests was further reinforced by cultural barriers. Autonomous organizations for the defense of agrarian parties developed in opposition to the moral and religious positions of the urban world (in alliance with nation-builders). This factor accounts for the differences with the Catholic countries and regions, where peasant parties and organizations outside the Catholic-conservative front rarely developed to a meaningful extent. Large agrarian parties formed not only in the Protestant countries of the North, where the religious dissident and nonconformist movements developed in the countryside in opposition to urban moral standards, but also in the Protestant cantons of Switzerland (mainly Berne), the more secularised *Länder* in Austria (Carinthia and Styria), and the regions of Bavaria on the remove from Oberbayern. In these three areas, furthermore, the development of agrarian parties was facilitated by the federal structure of the state.

The period after World War II witnessed both the decline and the transformation of agrarian parties. On the one hand, in most countries the small farmers' and peasant's parties described in Chapter 5 disappeared and were mainly absorbed by broader Catholic-conservative fronts. On the other hand, the large agrarian parties of the North – which, by World War I had already diffused through most national territories – started abandoning a strictly agrarian platform and began transforming into broader center parties. This created even more nationalized support. As with the social democratic parties and class politics, therefore, agrarian politics very soon became a source of nationalized electoral structures. The agrarian parties as a factor of territoriality in the case of both the small farmers' parties and the large agrarian formations have declined as a source of cross-country differentiation.

Enfranchisement and Equalization of Voting Rights

The temporal coincidence of nationalization processes and the rise of class parties on the one hand, and the development of mass politics through the extension of voting rights to the adult male population on the other, suggests that enfranchisement has played an important role in the formation of national party systems in Europe.[32] First, it has been argued that mass suffrage has been a crucial factor in the growth of nation-states and national identities. Political democratization – the extension of political rights and the incorporation of the masses into the political system – as well as the extension of citizenship rights, has been viewed as an attempt to strengthen national unity in decades of bitter class conflicts: "The development of the channels for mass politics was an important element in the growth and integration of territorially-defined nation-states" (Rokkan 1961: 133). For Bendix, as for Rokkan and Marshall, the process of democratization implies the shift from estate to national orientation and goes beyond the political sphere (political participation through the extension of voting rights) to include mass education and economic rights (individual contracts). The result is the unification of a national system of representation away from estates. Politics became nationwide when the lower classes had the opportunity to participate (Bendix 1977: 87–112, Bendix and Rokkan 1971). Second, it can be argued that enfranchisement has had an impact on the mobilization and electoral growth of class parties, which, in turn, have brought about the hegemony of a cross-local functional cleavage. This aspect will be discussed further on.

The general process of democratization consists of several dimensions, among which the most relevant historically have been the following:

- The process of *enfranchisement*: Abolition of restrictions to vote based on census (income, taxation, property, etc.) and capacity requirements (education, profession, etc.).[33]
- The process of *equalization of voting conditions*: Mainly from plural to equal vote and from indirect to direct elections. These elements must be distinguished from enfranchisement since an adult population may be fully enfranchised but de jure (plural and indirect voting) or de facto

[32] Rokkan's "second threshold of democratization" or Incorporation. Rokkan adopts Marshall's typology of civil, political, and social rights. See in particular Marshall (1964: 71–72). For Urwin, the democratizing reforms of the 1880s in Britain resulted in a more genuine national party system with both remarkably even turnout patterns, and uniform national swings (Urwin 1982a: 40–41).

[33] But also gender (exclusion of women) and age. The terms "enfranchisement" and "universal suffrage" do not entirely overlap. Voting age is not necessarily linked to universal suffrage, since the latter can coexist with different voting ages, which, historically, have continuously been reduced. Other requirements for the right to vote do not reduce in principle the scope of universal suffrage: citizenship, residence in the constituency over a given period of time, possession of civil rights, and mental health.

(influences and pressures allowed through open voting) may still suffer from unequal rights. This, however, does not influence the level of inclusiveness of participatory rights.[34]

As Table 6.1 shows, the introduction of (male) universal suffrage – although in many cases the process of enfranchisement was gradual, through the abolition of the main restrictions – occurred principally in the two decades between 1900 and 1918 (right after World War I).[35] In Austria and Belgium, universal suffrage was introduced in 1897 and 1894, respectively. However, in both cases the vote remained unequal. In the Austrian case, the Habsburg monarchy introduced a fifth general and universal curia in 1897. The suffrage for this curia was universal, but census and capacity requirements were maintained in the four other curiae. This system ended with the 1907 election. Belgium introduced the plural voting system together with universal male suffrage. One additional vote was given to those in the higher tax brackets, heads of households, and capitalists; a second additional vote was given to teachers and persons with higher education. The introduction of universal suffrage was therefore still accompanied by inequalities, and plural voting was discontinued only after World War I.

In the United Kingdom, all restrictions were lifted after World War I (the same applies to Ireland). Since 1918, therefore, the vote has not been considered plural even though university seats persisted (elected from the graduates from the universities of Oxford, Cambridge, Dublin, London, and the Scottish universities), as did the so-called business votes until 1948.

[34] The equality of voting conditions relates to the principle of "one voter, one vote." The term "plural voting" indicates the possibility for certain persons to cast more than one vote on the basis of census, capacity, race, religion, or social position (head of household). Historically, plural or unequal voting has taken two main forms: different numbers of votes or the privilege attributed to certain categories to elect more representatives (namely, in the curial systems). Furthermore, in many cases, indirect elections continued in several countries. In France in particular, this type of election was very common (see Caramani 2000: 57–58 for comparative tables). Elections were partly direct and partly indirect in Austria under the Habsburg monarchy from 1873 until 1900–01: direct in the first, second, and third curiae but indirect in the fourth and fifth curiae. The same is true of Finland in the estate of peasants from 1871 until 1905 (under Russian rule) and to Sweden from 1866 until 1908. In Portugal, direct elections were introduced with the constitution of 1822 but were replaced by indirect elections in 1826; direct elections were reintroduced in 1838. In Spain, direct elections were introduced in 1834 but then abolished when the 1812 constitution of Cadiz was reintroduced in 1836. Direct elections were reintroduced in 1837.

[35] For a full account of the national trajectories toward universal suffrage in 18 European countries, see Caramani (2000), both the comparative Chapter 2 in Part I and the different country chapters.

Table 6.1. *Steps in the Formation of National Mass Electorates in Europe After 1815*

Country	Abolition of: Census and Capacity Requirements	Abolition of: Plural Vote	Introduction of Universal Suffrage: Male	Introduction of Universal Suffrage: 50% Enfranchised	Abolition of Indirect Elections	Introduction of PR
Austria	1897 (5th curia)	1907 (curiae)	1897	1907	1907 (mostly)	1919 (d'H)
Belgium	1894	1919	1894	1894	1847	1900 (d'H)
Denmark	1849 (except servants)	–	1918	1849	–	1920 (d'H)
Finland	1907 (estate system)	1907	1907	1907	1907	1907 (d'H)
France	1848	1817	1871	1871	1831 (1793)	1945 (HB)
Germany	1848, 1867: *Reich* 1871	–	1871	1871	1849 (then 1871)	1919 (d'H)
Greece	1844	1844	1844	1844	1844	1926 (HB)
Iceland	1916 (except poor persons and servants)	1874	1916	1916	1874	1959 (d'H)
Ireland	1918 (under United Kingdom)	1918	1918	1886	–	1922 (STV)
Italy	1913	–	1919	1913	Piedmont: 1848	1919 (d'H)
Netherlands	1918	1849 (estates)	1918	1897	1848	1918 (LR–Hare)
Norway	1900	–	1900	1900	1906	1921 (d'H)
Portugal	1911: income for illiterates abolished	–	1911	1975	1838 (1822)	1975 (d'H)
Spain	1869	–	1869	1976	1837 (1834)	1976 (d'H)
Sweden	1911 (but taxes)	1866 (estates)	1911	1911	1911	1911 (d'H)
Switzerland	1848	–	1848	1848	1848	1919 (HB)
United Kingdom	1918 (university and business seats maintained)	1918	1918	1886	–	–

Notes: Dates refer to the first election in which abolition/introduction is applicable. Indirect elections: reversals shown in parentheses. In Iceland, PR was introduced in the October 1959 election. Year of 50% of the enfranchised population refers to the population above the legal voting age.
Legend: The symbol – stands for "never introduced."
Sources: *EWE-1815*, Flora et al. (1983), Rokkan and Meyriat (1969), Sternberger and Vogel (1969).

In Ireland, plural voting is regarded as having ended in 1923 even though university seats existed until the 1933 election. In Italy, suffrage granted in 1913 is usually considered almost universal: all men aged 30 were enfranchised, as were many other categories of citizens aged 21.[36]

In 1848 Denmark turned abruptly to general representation after a period of absolutism which had begun in 1660. However, the vote for the two houses of parliament (*Rigsdag*) was restricted until 1918, when universal suffrage for men and women was introduced. In Finland, plural voting as well as census and capacity requirements were abolished in 1907 together with the curial system. Plural voting from 1871 to 1904 refers to the estate of burgesses, for which voting was plural on the basis of local tax payment. Among the peasantry, suffrage was restricted to owners of real estate and leaseholders. Among the nobility, representation was secured through heads of families; in the clergy, through priests and, since 1869, university and school teachers as well as civil servants. In Iceland, universal suffrage was introduced in 1916, although persons receiving public assistance were not enfranchised (as in other Nordic countries) until 1934. In the Netherlands, elections remained indirect until 1848. In 1849 direct elections were introduced but suffrage remained restricted until 1918, when universal suffrage and PR were introduced. In Norway, indirect elections were held until 1903, with restricted suffrage. In 1906 elections became direct and universal male suffrage was introduced. In Sweden, the transition from estate to general representation occurred in 1866, but universal male suffrage was introduced with the 1911 election. In Portugal, all free male citizens were enfranchised in 1820 for the election of the constituent assembly, and under the constitution of 1822 only servants, persons under parental tutelage, and friars were excluded. Census requirements as such were introduced in 1826. In 1852 these were abolished for teachers and graduates, and in 1878 the franchise was extended to all male heads of households who could read and

---

[36] Women were partially enfranchised in Belgium in 1919 (widows of soldiers), and in the United Kingdom they were enfranchised in 1918 but with a higher voting age than men (30 instead of 21). In Ireland the United Kingdom figure applies for 1918. Equality between men and women was established after independence in 1923. Similarly, in Norway in 1909, women married to men paying taxes above a given minimum were enfranchised. The exclusion of persons under trial, bankrupts, the mentally ill, and criminals is of no major importance. By contrast, the exclusion of servants, farm workers not in possession of a household, and persons under public care has been considered a restriction of suffrage in Denmark.

write. In 1895 the qualification of being a head of household was abolished. In 1911, when universal suffrage was introduced, the literacy requirement was maintained.

The exceptions to this general shift to universal suffrage in the first two decades of the twentieth century are mainly France, Germany, Greece, and Switzerland. France introduced universal suffrage with the constitution of 1793. However, under the 1793 constitution, no election was held and servants were still excluded. After the empire period and the Restoration from 1820 to 1830, France introduced plural voting (the so-called *loi du double vote*). Restrictions based on capacity never existed; however, a franchise based on capacity qualification existed under the Monarchy of July (1830–46). Census requirements were abolished in 1848 with the introduction of universal male suffrage (the Second Republic), which was maintained in the subsequent periods including the Second Empire (Napoleon III) from 1852 to 1869. In Germany, estate parliaments were in force in the different states before unification. After the first attempt at unification in 1848–49 – the *Frankfurter Vorparlament* and the election to the *Nationalversammlung*, when all "independent" men were enfranchised – during the period of the reaction the 1815 constitutions were reintroduced with the exceptions of Baden and Bavaria, as well as Prussia, which introduced an unequal "three-class system." Universal male suffrage was definitively introduced in 1871 with unification. In Switzerland universal male suffrage was introduced in 1848 with the creation of the federal state.

For Greece and Spain too, early dates appear in Table 6.1. Greece could be considered the first country to introduce universal male suffrage in 1844 after regional assemblies had formed in 1821 after the revolution, and the constitution of 1822 introduced universal suffrage (which was, however, abolished with the restoration of the monarchy at the beginning of the 1830s). After 1844 universal male suffrage was never discontinued. In Spain, census requirements are considered to have existed under the parliament of Cadiz in 1810, since the right to vote was limited to heads of households. Also under the 1812 constitution of Cadiz the franchise was comparatively large, although the right to vote was granted only to financially independent men. Census and capacity requirements as such were introduced in 1834 with the *Estatuto Real*. All restrictions were lifted in 1869 with the First Republic, even though universal suffrage was again repealed in the 1876–88 period. As far as plural voting is concerned, in 1890 additional votes were granted to the members of given corporations (e.g., the chambers of commerce) that constituted special constituencies.

Greece and Switzerland are therefore the earliest cases of definite (with no reversals) introduction of male universal and equal suffrage in 1844–48, followed by France and Germany in 1871. In all other cases, male universal suffrage occurred from 1900 (Norway) on. For most countries, the dates of the introduction of universal suffrage are a reliable indicator of the enfranchisement of mass electorates. These dates – according to official census data and estimations from secondary sources (see notes in Table 6.1) – correspond roughly to the time when around 50 percent of the total adult population (above voting age) was enfranchised in the case of universal male suffrage or around 80–90 percent of the total adult population in cases where men and women were enfranchised at the same time. There are, however, cases in which the electorate reached 50 percent of the total adult population before universal suffrage occurred. The most important case is that of Denmark, where in 1849 almost 70 percent of the population above voting age was enfranchised. Furthermore, in Britain and Ireland, the 50 percent threshold was reached after the Third Reform Bill of 1885, and in the Netherlands this occurred in 1897. In all these cases, universal suffrage was introduced in 1918. A less striking case is that of Italy, where in 1913 almost universal suffrage was introduced; the male population was fully enfranchised in 1919.

The precocious transition to mass politics on its own, however, does not appear as a sufficient or necessary condition for the nationalization of electorates and party systems in these countries. Among the most nationalized party systems, only Denmark and France are cases of early massification (1849 and 1871, respectively) and, to some extent, Ireland (1885). The remaining systems that were nationalized by World War I are characterized by later enfranchisement of the masses: the Netherlands (1897), Norway (1900), Austria (1907), and Iceland (1916). These are all cases in which, when the masses were enfranchised, party systems were already nationalized. By contrast, Switzerland and Germany (and also Britain, with its more than 60 percent of the population enfranchised after 1885) are – in spite of their early democratization – up to the present among the less nationalized countries, which is also the case for two systems in which the masses were enfranchised later: Belgium and Finland (1894 and 1907, respectively).

Finally, figures concerning the rise of class parties and the increase in nationalization rates for entire party systems confirm that both processes had taken off independently of the extension of suffrage to all male adults. For the older party families – liberals and conservatives – enfranchisement did not cause a meaningful homogenization of their support. Furthermore, social democratic parties too grew, spread territorially, and homogenized in the last decade of the nineteenth century and at the beginning of the twentieth century (Figures 6.3–6.5). For most European class parties, the path toward nationalization begun already around 1890–1900 and displays a pattern of steep diffusion and homogenization up to World War I. For many of them, even, nationalization had started in the 1870s. Within a very short time, therefore, these parties nationalized and imposed a new nonterritorial functional alignment on the whole party system, both in the most industrialized countries and in the countries that maintained a predominantly agrarian structure for a longer period. The "external origin" of social democratic parties (Duverger 1951a: 3–20), implied a strong organizational structure and a mobilization of workers that had immediate effects with their enfranchisement in the first two decades of the twentieth century. The nationalization of social democrats too, therefore, occurred *before* the decisive steps toward mass electorates.

This finding is confirmed by evidence showing that left electorates are stronger in those countries in which enfranchisement occurred late and suddenly. Austria, Belgium, Denmark, Finland, Italy, Norway, and Sweden – where enfranchisement took place later and less gradually compared to Britain or Switzerland for example – are characterized by a relatively stronger left (Bartolini 2000b: 226). However, processes of nationalization can be observed earlier for all countries. Rather than being at the origin of the spread of social democrats and of their nationalization, therefore, enfranchisement processes *extended the process of nationalization to the masses*. The evolution toward nationalized electorates and party systems is a result of the supremacy of functional class politics – first through the two older party families and then through the clash of working parties resulting from industrial mobilization – rather than a result of mass politics through the extension of suffrage. If, on the one hand, center-building processes, state–church relationships, and industrialization were at the origin of the supremacy of the territorially homogeneous left–right opposition, enfranchisement, on the other hand, had the function of extending it to the masses once they were incorporated into the electoral channel of representation.

The Territorial Consequences of Electoral Laws

A further institutional factor – besides the extension of the franchise – to be considered in the development of nationwide political alignments is the change from majoritarian to PR formulas. Although Chapter 2 has shown that the larger size of territorial units for which data are available and the smaller number of constituencies under PR do not artificially influence levels of nationalization to a meaningful extent, the literature has argued that PR is a strong factor in the homogenization of party support.

First, PR lowers entry barriers and consequently favors the spread of social democrats, that is, homogeneous left–right alignments. PR is therefore an important institutional factor to be considered in regard to the conditions for the mobilization of working electorates and the development of mass labor parties. Second, the lowering of entry barriers caused by the electoral law is considered to be an important incentive for parties to spread in all constituencies – including those where they are weak. Majoritarian systems set very high thresholds for representation, making the entry of new and small parties problematic.[37] This concerns not only the new parties of the working class that mobilized the left electorate, but also established parties. Given the high thresholds typical of the majoritarian systems in force in all countries until the beginning of the twentieth century, these parties too were not encouraged to spread in constituencies in which they could not hope to reach the majority of the voters, which is indispensable in a "first-past-the-post" system. As a consequence, it has been argued that majoritarian systems inhibited the spread of parties in new areas by increasing the persistence of territorial and subcultural electoral strongholds.

According to Duverger (1950 and 1951b), majoritarian systems – in particular plurality systems based on single-member constituencies – do not foster the spread of parties in new constituencies. By contrast, plurality allows parties whose support is territorially concentrated to survive in spite of their national weakness: "minorities can secure representation on the national level only because they constitute the majority in certain constituencies. The effect is that the majority vote accentuates geographical divisions of opinion: it might even be said that it tends to convert a national current of opinion . . . into a regional opinion, as its only chance of representation is in those parts of the country where its strength is greatest"

---

[37] Rokkan's "third threshold of democratization" or Representation.

(Duverger 1951b: 331–32; see also Sartori 1986). In addition, parties have no incentive to increase their campaign efforts and to present candidates in those constituencies in which they do not have a chance of winning the seat. This is not the case with PR. PR creates a strong incentive for spreading in all constituencies and in adversaries' strongholds. Parties are encouraged to expand and to present candidates in all constituencies where, even with a small number of votes, it is possible to win seats: "in the countries which have adopted PR after having been used to the majority system, we can see a sort of gradual 'nationalization' of opinion" (Duverger 1951b: 332).[38]

This view of PR systems favoring the spread of competition is shared by other researchers. For Rose and Urwin, in "multi-member constituencies of proportional representation . . . there is much more incentive for parties to offer a full slate of candidates in all regions" (1975: 19). For example, Urwin notes about Germany that "[t]he particular variant of proportional representation introduced in the Weimar Republic encouraged parties to contest every electoral district" (1982b: 192). Also Rokkan notes that "proportional representation systems encourage a wider participation while majority systems discourage minorities" (1970a: 350).[39]

With list systems, the presence of several candidates of the same party prevents individual candidates from compaigning independently and favors a national standard partisan campaign that is carried out on ideological-programmatic lines. General issues therefore take precedence over particular local ones: "the list system . . . compels the elector to vote for a party rather than for personalities, that is to say, for a system of ideas and an organization of national scale rather than for the champions of local interests" (Duverger 1951b: 333; on the same point, see Rokkan 1970a: 21). In general, the fewer the seats returned in one constituency, the more small parties are penalized.[40] Therefore, parties have no incentive to present candidates in constituencies in which they are weak. This emphasizes the relationship between the disproportionality of the electoral formula (the

---

[38] A similar conclusion has been reached by Mair in his analysis of the nationalization of electoral strategies in Ireland under STV (Mair 1987: 128). As also noted by Hanham (1959) in the British case, elections were not always general in the sense that, for a long time, local and constituency-level factors prevailed over national competition.

[39] Furthermore, Rokkan notes that PR leads to the abandonment of local clienteles; with plurality systems, marginal votes are useless if the constituency is safe whether the party wins or loses the seat, while with PR each vote counts and therefore mobilization is encouraged in every single constituency (Rokkan 1970a: 333, 337).

[40] Among the many authors reaching this conclusion, see Taagepera and Shugart (1989) and Lijphart (1994).

difference in the share of votes and seats) and the spread of party support across constituencies. Historically, electoral formulas and magnitudes of constituencies largely overlapped: Plurality formulas and, more generally, majoritarian systems (repeated-ballot systems)[41] were usually based on single-member constituencies (although two- and three-member constituencies were frequent in Britain as well as in other countries); PR systems were always based on multimember constituencies.

These writings suggest, first, that the competitive behavior of political parties is at the origin of the spread and homogenization of political parties and, second, that this spread begins with the introduction of PR, when incentives for winning seats become high enough. The preceding evidence has shown that the process of territorial spread and homogenization of the main parties – including the social democrats since the 1870s – took place *long before* the introduction of PR and the lowering of entry barriers: generally after World War I or shortly before (see Table 6.1). Nevertheless, the hypothesis that nationalization processes were spurred by competitive factors, independent of social and institutional conditions, remains a very plausible hypothesis even under majoritarian systems.

The Development of Electoral Competition

Party Competition and Territorial Homogeneity

What follows is therefore concerned with the hypothesis that the spread of parties has been caused by *parties' competitive behavior*. Party competition is an important additional factor for understanding the spread of parties across constituencies affecting the territorial distribution of political forces. In particular, this factor allows us to fill in some voids: Processes of nationalization can be observed before the crucial steps of democratization and mass politics, as well as the predominance of the homogeneous left–right cleavage after the entry of social democratic parties. The remainder of this chapter therefore addresses the hypothesis that rather than being merely a product of socioeconomic development (industrialization) or institutional change (enfranchisement, PR), the increasing integration of national party

---

[41] The reasoning is the same with repeated-ballot formulas: Parties must have a strong chance to reach the second ballot to present a candidate, and this is possible only for larger parties in a given constituency. There is no incentive to present a candidate who has no chances to reach the second ballot since representation will not be secured.

systems is the result of political parties themselves and of their strategic-competitive action aiming at winning the highest number of seats.[42]

On the one hand, a competitive strategy implies the adaptation to changing social conditions that eroded territorial oppositions resulting from geographical mobility and peripheral integration through state formation and industrialization/urbanization, as well as through the growth of communication technologies. On the other hand, however, it is plausible that the loss of territoriality of political cleavages was not simply a by-product of the general integration of societies to which parties adapted, but was also the product of the action of parties themselves and of the competitive strategy that led them to break down territorial barriers. This competitive strategy of parties consists in expanding their support through territories. They increasingly tend to challenge other parties in their former strongholds and to "conquer" and "occupy" constituencies controlled by concurrent parties. Parties tend to expand in search of support all over the country and to cover as much space as possible. If parties faced and adapted to new social conditions, it is also true that they helped to create conditions that favored them, with the outcome of less clear-cut territorial oppositions.

Functional or ideological competition has been described after World War II by spatial analyses of electoral behavior and party systems. According to this model, political competition takes place in the "ideological space" in which political parties move in search of the optimal location for the maximization of votes (Downs 1957). This model was inspired by work on geographical localization of firms carried out by economists (Hotteling 1929; Smithies 1941) and is admittedly a functional *analogy* of what had been developed on the basis of originally geographical concepts – location, space, distance, and so on.[43] These models describe the competition of the second half of the twentieth century, when the geographical dimension of competition had already disappeared with the nationalization of electorates before World War I. Preceding evidence, however, suggests that the same competitive logic working in the ideological dimension might have worked on the territorial level at an earlier stage of electoral development – with parties being "catchallover parties" before becoming "catchall parties." This

---

[42] As Lipset and Rokkan wrote, "we consider the possibility that the *parties themselves* produce their own alignments independently from the geographical, social and cultural conditions of the movements" (1967a: 3).

[43] Or even "landscape," with a clearly spatial connotation. See Miller, Kollman, and Page (1997, 1998).

competition resulted in the spread of parties and the deterritorialization of political cleavages.

To mobilize the most remote and peripheral electorates, parties needed a capillary network of local organizations. They therefore developed centralized agencies at the national level for the control of local candidacies and relied upon more efficient campaigning techniques that became available with technological progress. Candidates in single-member constituencies during the period of majoritarian elections until World War I were increasingly "party candidates." They no longer represented merely their constituencies, but rather nationwide functional interests and values. Candidates became representatives chosen by national and central party organizations rather than the expression of the *notabilat local*. Parties also started intervening directly on questions and placed on the agenda issues that were not territorially delimited and that could be accepted in all areas of the country. They addressed issues and presented platforms that appealed to large sectors of the electorate. In much the same way as on the ideological level, positions of parties were "nationalized" to make them acceptable to a larger proportion of voters; on the territorial level, parties abandoned local claims and privileged national ones. This was done by emphasizing issues that were national in scope.

Indicators of Party Competition

In a historical perspective, an operative definition of electoral competition should start with its basic aspect. Competition is first a matter of *contestedness*: There is competition when there are at least two candidates for one seat.[44] By contrast, there is no competition in those constituencies in which the number of candidates equals the number of seats to be returned (e.g., one candidate for one seat). An indicator of the development of party competition is therefore the number of contested constituencies: The larger the number of contested constituencies, the higher the degree of competition. The majoritarian electoral formulas in force during the nineteenth and early twentieth centuries in all European countries were mostly based

---

[44] This concept refers to the first of four concepts introduced by Bartolini (1999, 2000a), "*contestability*" in regard to party competition. Contestability means the extent to which conditions for the electoral market to be open are met, that is, the thresholds for entry for candidates and parties. "*Contestedness*" is the degree to which elections are contested once the main barriers to entry have been removed. The former refers to whether or not it is possible to contest elections, the latter to how much elections are actually contested.

on single-member constituencies. A constituency is competitive insofar as the single seat is contested by at least two candidates.[45]

Because processes of nationalization took place before and up to World War I, the analysis of the impact of party competition on the reduction of the territoriality of the vote is carried out over a period starting with the first election available for each country until approximately World War I. However, given the large amount of missing information during this period, especially concerning the party affiliation of candidates, it is impossible to carry out a thorough exploration. Instead, what follows considers eight countries with majoritarian electoral systems:

- *Britain (1832–1935)*: plurality formula in single- and multimember constituencies; *Ireland (1832–1910)*, which is considered a separate case; *Denmark (1849–1913)*: plurality formula in single-member constituencies;
- *Belgium (1847–98)*, *Germany (1871–1912)*, the *Netherlands (1888–1913)*, and *Norway (1906–18)*: two-ballot formulas in mostly single-member constituencies. In *Switzerland (1848–1917)*, a three-ballot and then a two-ballot system (since 1900) was used.[46]

The use of such a simple indicator varies, depending upon the magnitude of constituencies. An important difference among majoritarian formulas is whether they are based on single-member or multimember constituencies.

---

[45] The contestedness of constituencies has been considered in a number of studies (Cornford 1970; Rose and Urwin 1975; Craig 1977; Urwin 1982a). As mentioned in Chapter 2, the link between territorially uniform electoral support for parties and the competitiveness of elections was first established by Schattschneider in his study on American politics, but was later made also by Urwin (1974, 1982a, 1982b). However, Claggett, Flanigan, and Zingale (1984: 81) have noted that "there appears to be some confusion between increasing nationalization in this sense of convergence in the levels of support and increasing competitiveness of the party system. These phenomena are not necessarily connected." As had already been noted by Stokes (1967) and by Sundquist (1973: 333–40), it is only if a 50-50 configuration is diffused in many constituencies that the rate of competition increases, both locally and nationally. Besides contestedness, therefore, a competitive situation arises with parties receiving evenly matched support and with equivalent chances to win the seat. By contrast, the greater the distance between the elected and nonelected candidate(s), the lower the competition in a constituency in terms of *marginality*, that is, when the shift from one party or candidate to the other of a reduced amount of votes is sufficient to modify the outcome.

[46] For Switzerland, data by party affiliation are available only at the level of 25 cantons rather than at the constituency level; for this reason, a systematic analysis of uncontested constituencies is not possible. There were between 47 and 52 (depending on the period) single- and multimember constituencies (*Bezirke*).

In electoral systems based on single-member constituencies, the number of constituencies equals the number of seats; therefore, the number of uncontested constituencies equals the number of unopposed seats. In most cases, however, single-member constituencies were combined with two-member or multimember constituencies (e.g., in Britain and Ireland). In systems based on multimember constituencies, the number of seats exceeds the number of constituencies. There is therefore a distinction to be made between uncontested *constituencies* and unopposed *seats*.[47] In several cases, two or more candidates of different parties were unopposed. Frequently in the United Kingdom, in two-member constituencies, one conservative and one liberal were unopposed. It can therefore be misleading to limit the count to uncontested constituencies in assessing the degree of competitiveness of a system.

An example of a pure single-member plurality system is Denmark from 1849 until 1915. When candidates were unopposed, voters could ask for a "yes" or "no" vote. Until 1898 secrecy was not provided, and the vote was carried out by a show of hands. The electoral committee decided, by looking at the crowd, whether or not a candidate could be declared elected on the basis of a show of hands, and only in cases of ambiguity was a count performed.[48] When there was more than one candidate, the electoral committee decided by looking at the crowd who had been elected (only in cases of uncertainty was a roll-call election carried out). Such cases have been counted as uncontested constituencies. The fact that no count was needed demonstrates that that constituency was uncontested (with only minor opposition candidates).

As the left-hand graph of Figure 6.7 shows, the number of uncontested constituencies decreases continuously from 1853 to 1905. This shows that fewer and fewer constituencies are dominated by one of the two main parties – *Højre* or *Venstre* – in which the other is absent, indicating a clear and progressive increase in the rate of competition in Danish electoral life.

---

[47] To stress terminologically the distinction between constituencies and seats, the terms "uncontested constituencies" and "unopposed seats" or "candidates" or "parties" will be used. For both single-member and multimember constituencies – because of the frequent redistricting and redistribution, and for the sake of cross-national comparison – figures presented below are mostly based on the number of uncontested constituencies as a percentage of the total number of constituencies. The total number of constituencies for which data are missing has been subtracted from the total number of constituencies.

[48] In Denmark, elections between 1849 and 1915 were held in 100–13 single-member *valgkredse*. After 1901 (when the secret ballot was introduced), if there was a single candidate, elections did not take place unless 50 voters asked for the "yes/no" vote.

234

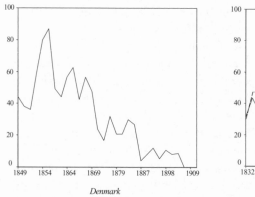

Denmark　　　　　　　　*Britain* ——　　*Ireland* ----

Figure 6.7　Percentage of uncontested constituencies in Denmark and the United Kingdom.

Uncontested constituencies displayed in the graph include mostly those won by *Højre* and *Venstre*, the two main Danish parties until World War I. Other parties won unopposed seats sporadically. These parties started to appear in 1872 (the Social Democrats contested one constituency). During the 1890s the United Liberals (*Forenede Venstre*), the Moderates (*Forhandlende Venstre*), the *Radikale Venstre*, and the Agrarians (since 1905) made their appearance.

A typical country with multimember plurality elections is the United Kingdom since 1832, including Ireland until 1918.[49] Constituencies returned up to four seats, although – through the mechanism of limited voting – a maximum of three votes could be cast. Variations occurred over time with "redistributions" of seats: The number of seats returned by constituencies was changed and, in some cases, constituencies were disenfranchised because of corrupt practices. As in Denmark, the party system was dominated by two main parties: Conservatives and Liberals. In the mid-nineteenth century, Chartist and, later, Liberal Unionist candidates started to challenge these parties, but the impact of third parties on the party system was limited until the appearance of Labour candidates toward the end of the century. In Ireland, Conservatives and Liberals were

---

[49] In Great Britain, the number of parliamentary constituencies varied between 333 in 1832 and 585 in 1935. For Ireland, considered separately for 1832–1910, the number of constituencies is 64–66 and 101 since 1885. Because figures for Britain do not include the number of Irish uncontested constituencies, they differ from those presented by Craig (1977: 624) and Urwin (1982a). For Britain, figures over the entire period include only Conservative/Liberal unopposed seats.

235

challenged since the 1870s by Nationalists and Unionists. Since the 1880s, conservative candidates ceased to contest Irish constituencies and the Liberals underwent a rapid decline (although they continued to contest Irish constituencies until 1918). As the right-hand graph of Figure 6.7 shows, Ireland and Great Britain present two different patterns. The number of uncontested constituencies declines in Great Britain, indicating a progressive increase in the rate of competition until the 1930s.[50]

What are the figures when we consider seats as well as constituencies? Table 6.2 gives the number of uncontested seats for the first, second, third, and fourth candidates for both Conservatives and Liberals in Britain. The first columns for both Conservatives and Liberals show that one candidate was declared elected because he was unopposed in his constituency. In 1832 this happened in 44 (out of 335) constituencies for the Conservatives and in 81 constituencies for the Liberals. Among the 44 constituencies in which a Conservative candidate was elected, in 6 of them a second Conservative candidate was also elected unopposed. Similarly, out of the 81 liberal uncontested constituencies, in 24 a second candidate was elected unopposed. The total number of uncontested *constituencies* in which candidates won an unopposed seat, therefore, appears in the first column for each party. The remaining columns provide information about the additional seats won by unopposed candidates in the same constituencies (e.g., in 1859 in one constituency, four Liberal candidates were elected unopposed). The sum of the columns, therefore, gives the total number of unopposed *seats* won in an election.

The table indicates, first, that constituencies in which more than two candidates of the same party were elected unopposed were rare (see the third and fourth candidate columns). Second, there is a sudden drop in

---

[50] In Ireland, the movement is more erratic and does not give rise to a clear trend. This difference is due to the persistent partisan structure in Britain and to the radical changes that occurred in the Irish party system. Whereas in Britain the Conservative and Liberal parties were never challenged until the growth of the Labour Party (see also Figure 6.4), in Ireland, by contrast, the decrease in the number of uncontested constituencies between 1874 and 1885 was caused by the appearance of two new antagonists: the Nationalists and the Unionists. Their presence in most constituencies made them competitive, and the overall number of uncontested constituencies declined rapidly. By 1885 nationalist candidates were mainly unopposed, increasing the overall number of uncontested constituencies for that particular election. In 1892, however, the Anti-Parnell Nationalists transformed Irish constituencies into competitive ones again by opposing the Parnell Nationalists. In 1895 the Anti-Parnell Nationalists were mainly uncontested. Since 1890 the (newly unified) Nationalists won the majority of the unopposed constituencies, making the system noncompetitive once again. Only a small number of uncontested constituencies was won by the Unionists.

Table 6.2. *Uncontested Constituencies and Unopposed Seats in the United Kingdom (without Ireland): 1832–1910*

Election Year	Conservatives				Liberals					Total		
	First Candidate	Second Candidate	Third Candidate	Total Conservative Seats	First Candidate	Second Candidate	Third Candidate	Fourth Candidate	Total Liberal Seats	Uncontested Constituencies	Sum of 1st Candidates	"Shared" Constituencies
1832	44	6	0	50	81	24	0	0	105	104	125	21
1835	80	20	0	100	100	26	0	0	126	146	180	34
1837	76	26	0	102	68	13	0	0	81	116	144	28
1841	123	56	4	183	70	13	0	0	83	166	193	27
1847	123	54	2	179	105	21	0	0	126	196	228	32
1852	99	42	2	143	65	13	0	0	78	147	164	17
1857	98	36	0	134	116	33	0	0	149	186	214	28
1859	115	41	0	156	127	30	1	1	159	197	242	45
1865	82	32	2	116	110	22	0	0	132	164	192	28
1868	43	22	0	65	69	11	0	0	80	100	112	12
1874	72	44	0	116	47	3	1	0	51	106	119	13
1880	29	23	0	52	36*	3	0	0	39	56	65	9
1885	4	2	0	6	12	1	0	0	13	17	16	0
1886	83	4	0	87	37	1	0	0	38	150	120	0
1892	22	2	0	24	10	1	0	0	11	42	32	0
1895	98	3	0	101	9	0	0	0	9	124	107	0
1900	121	4	0	125	22	0	0	0	22	165	143	0
1906	3	0	0	3	23	0	0	0	23	31	26	0
1910	5	1	0	6	0	0	0	0	0	10	5	0
1910	51	2	0	53	31	0	0	0	31	95	82	0

Notes: Irish constituencies (1832–1918) are not included. In 1910 there were two elections (January and December); (*) Among these candidates there was one Liberal/Labour candidate. These were nominees of Liberal associations, but they "campaigned mainly on trade union and labour issues" (Craig 1977: xv).

constituencies in which two candidates of the same party were elected unopposed after the Third Reform Bill (1884–85), which reduced the number of two-member constituencies in favor of single-member constituencies. Also constituencies in which two candidates of the same party were elected unopposed became rare. Third, the table gives the total number of constituencies in which candidates of *different* parties were elected unopposed. This more important information is obtained by subtracting the overall number of uncontested constituencies from the total number of constituencies in which either at least one Conservative or one Liberal candidate was elected unopposed. In 1832, for example, there were 125 constituencies in which either a Conservative or a Liberal was elected unopposed. However, in total there were 104 uncontested constituencies. Therefore, in 21 constituencies, both parties were present with unopposed candidates. These are "shared constituencies" in which both a Liberal and a Conservative candidate were elected unopposed.

Figure 6.8 shows the evolution of shared constituencies. Shared constituencies in which both a Conservative and a Liberal were unopposed disappeared in 1885 after the Third Reform Bill, which carried out a large redistribution of seats. Most multimember constituencies were replaced by single-member constituencies. For this reason, the overall number of constituencies increased from 352 to 542. As Figure 6.8 shows, the percentage of shared constituencies is quite limited, reaching a maximum of 45 in 1859 (12.8 percent of the total number of constituencies and 22.8 percent of the number of uncontested constituencies). The remainder of the uncontested constituencies were either single-member constituencies in which there was one unopposed candidate or two-member constituencies in which there were unopposed candidates of the same party. The fact that seats within the same constituency were rarely shared by the candidates of different parties reinforces previous indications of a low rate of competition. Most constituencies – either single- or multimember – indicate the presence of one party only.

Although the distinction between single-member and multimember constituencies also applies to repeated-ballot (two-ballot and three-ballot) formulas, with these formulas it is also possible to operationalize the level of competition by:

- counting the number of constituencies in which a second ballot was necessary to elect a representative (the larger the number of such constituencies, the higher the competition) or

238

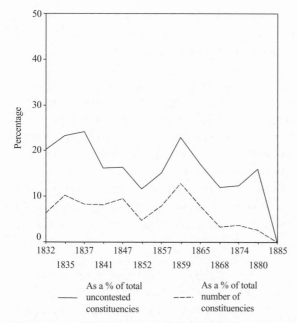

Figure 6.8 "Shared constituencies" in Britain, 1832–1910.

- counting the number of uncontested constituencies at second ballot (the larger the number of such constituencies, the lower the competition).[51]

Among the countries under scrutiny using a two-ballot formula, the number of uncontested constituencies at first ballots is very low.[52] At first sight, this indicates a higher rate of competition. However, if we also look at the second ballots, the picture changes. To assess the emergence of national competitive patterns in two-ballot formulas, the number of constituencies in which a second ballot was necessary to elect a representative is an important additional indicator in formulas in which seats are allocated on the second ballot: The more constituencies in which a second ballot was required, the higher the competition. For comparative purposes (through both space and time), the number of constituencies in which a second ballot was carried out as a percentage of the total number of constituencies is used.

---

[51] To do this, cases in which the exhaustive ballot is uncontested because of the withdrawal of candidates before election must be added.

[52] The number of uncontested constituencies in Belgium was one in 1848 and one in 1894 (both on the first ballot). In the Netherlands, the number of uncontested constituencies was also low: from a minimum of 5 in 1913 to a maximum of 11 in 1901–09.

239

Two-ballot formulas were used mostly in single-member constituencies.[53] As shown in Figure 6.9, the longest trend is that of Belgium, for which both partial and general elections have been considered. The two types of elections display a parallel trend: Elections held alternatively in 19 and 22 *arrondissements* and general renewals of the *Chambre des représentants* are characterized by a small number of second ballots until the early 1880s. This number then increases suddenly to a maximum of almost 60 percent of the constituencies, indicating an increase in competitiveness paralleling the introduction of male universal suffrage in 1893 (PR was introduced in 1898). The same trend characterizes the *Reich* period of two-ballot elections in single-member constituencies from 1871 until 1912, the last election before the Weimar constitution was introduced: The number of constituencies in which no candidate achieved an absolute majority on the first ballot increased from zero in 1871 and 1874 to almost 50 percent during the 1880s and 1890s.

For the Netherlands and Norway, the period of time is shorter. After the abolition of "double constituencies" in the Netherlands in 1888, elections were held in single-member *kiesdistricten*. Until World War I, the percentage of second ballots is similar to those of Belgium and Germany during the same period. In the Netherlands, it is interesting to consider the number of constituencies in which second ballots were uncontested. These are cases in which one of the two runoff candidates withdrew, which occurred often during the 1888–1917 period: from a minimum of 50 out of 100 constituencies in 1897 to a maximum of 63 in 1909. Therefore, although, in many constituencies no candidate could be declared elected on the first ballot, in most of them the difference in terms of votes between the two runoff candidates was high enough to cause one of the two candidates to withdraw.

From 1815 until 1903 Norway voted with an indirect system: *valgmandsvalgene* (election of great electors) and *storthingsvalgene* (election

---

[53] In Germany, the Netherlands, and Norway (1906–18), the two-ballot formula was combined with single-member constituencies, whereas in Belgium and Switzerland the two-ballot (or three-ballot) formula was based on both single-member and multimember constituencies. In Belgium, elections were held in 41 *arrondissements* during 1847–98 and were then grouped into 30 constituencies in 1900. In Germany, the 382 *Wahlkreise* of 1871 were increased to 397 in 1874 with the annexation of Alsace-Lorraine. In the Netherlands, the number of *kiesdistricten* was 100 over the entire 1888–1917 period. During 1906–18 elections in Norway were held in 123–26 *landdistrikter* and *kjøstaeder* (rural and urban districts).

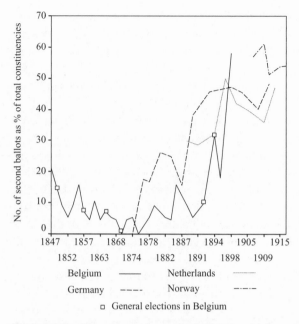

Figure 6.9 Percentage of constituencies in which a second ballot was held in Belgium, Germany, the Netherlands, and Norway, 1847–1918.

of representatives by great electors). Elections became direct in 1906 (two-ballot formula). Already since the 1880s, however, the two main parties had covered almost 100 percent of the constituencies (at least at the level of *valgmandsvalgene*). This competitive pattern therefore also appears in the number of second ballots needed to elect representatives in the 123–26 *valgkredsen* between 1906 and 1918, the last election before the introduction of PR. As Figure 6.9 shows, the percentage of second ballots as a percentage of the total number of constituencies is between 50 and 60 percent, a little higher than the percentages of Germany and the Netherlands.

The Impact of Party Competition

This empirical evidence confirms that competition between parties had been growing from the mid-nineteenth century until World War I. What was the impact of the increase in competition on the homogenization of the territorial configurations of the vote? The early timing of its takeoff compared to enlargement of suffrage (in the first two decades of the twentieth century), industrialization (with the entry of social democratic parties in the last two decades of the nineteenth century), and PR (mostly after World War I) supports the hypothesis that the competition between parties for votes in an increasing number of constituencies had a significant impact on the reduction of the territoriality of the vote.

First, in all countries under investigation, the different indicators used to measure the degree of contestedness of constituencies display a similar tendency toward increasing competition in the second half of the nineteenth century. For several countries, evidence shows that competition increases before the crucial extensions of voting rights, that is, before the introduction of male universal suffrage. Whereas in Belgium, Germany, and Switzerland male universal suffrage was introduced before or together with the development of competition and the homogenization of the vote in the second half of the nineteenth century, in Britain, Denmark, and the Netherlands during the same period, both competition and homogeneity increased in spite of a restricted franchise, which was not extended until after World War I.

Second, competition also seems to arise before – and independently of – the entry of social democratic parties. For Denmark and the United Kingdom, the number of seats won in uncontested constituencies by each party is also known, allowing us to verify whether the overall decline in the number of uncontested constituencies was caused by the appearance of new parties contesting an increasing number of seats that up to that point had been won by either the Conservatives or the Liberals or whether, alternatively, this decrease was determined by the spread of the support of the Conservatives and Liberals themselves – *Højre* or *Venstre* in Denmark – challenging the strongholds of the adversary party.

Figure 6.10 answers this question for Denmark. Social Democrats contested the first election in 1872. Apparently, however, by that time the overall number of uncontested constituencies had already drastically dropped. In Denmark, the entry of the Social Democrats affected the overall number of uncontested constituencies only marginally. As Figure 6.4 above shows, the spread of the Conservatives (*Højre*) and of the Liberals (*Venstre*) started long before 1872. Percentages of territorial coverage by these two parties increased continuously from 1849 until 1890, after which all three parties covered a similar proportion of territory (around 60–70 percent). Also the reduction in the number of uncontested constituencies started long before 1872 (Figure 6.10) through the "mutual challenge" of the

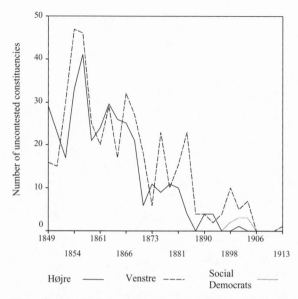

Figure 6.10 Number of uncontested constituencies for *Højre*, *Venstre*, and Social Democrats in Denmark, 1849–1913.

Conservatives and Liberals and the diffusion of these two parties through constituencies.[54]

According to Figure 6.11, the same pattern applies to Britain. Before the appearance of Labour toward the end of the nineteenth century, parties other than the Conservatives and the Liberals were weak and sporadic (the other main political formations were the Chartists, the Liberal Unionists, as well as independent candidates). The first Labour candidates did not enter the parliamentary arena before the end of the century. Their entry was then extremely sudden: by 1910, they covered around 80 percent of the constituencies. Since the 1850s, however, the Conservatives and Liberals had won a decreasing number of uncontested constituencies. Before 1900 the only antagonist that made these constituencies competitive was the "other" party, either the Conservative or the Liberal Party.

Unlike the situation in Denmark, however, Conservatives and Liberals were already present in almost all constituencies in 1832 (between 70 and 90 percent of territorial coverage). The reduction in the number of uncontested constituencies for both parties displayed in Figure 6.11, therefore,

---

[54] Unopposed seats won by *Radikale Venstre* and *Forhandlende Venstre* have not been included in the graph.

243

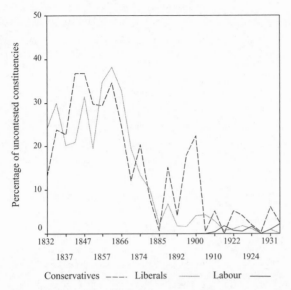

Figure 6.11 Percentage of uncontested constituencies for Conservatives, Liberals, and Labour in Britain, 1832–1935.

is caused less by the spread of these parties through constituencies than by the redistribution of seats. Part of the drop in the number of uncontested constituencies between 1866 and 1885 can be attributed to the roughly 20 percent of shared constituencies, which disappeared by 1885. These constituencies were uncontested, but both parties were present. If these are divided into single-member constituencies, the two parties contested the single seat.

In conclusion, therefore, whereas in Belgium the entry of new actors through the mobilization of the working-class electorate seems to have had a stronger impact, and in Britain it is also an effect of the redistricting and redistribution of seats, in all other countries by the time of the entry of new actors into the political arena, in general conservatives and liberals had already occupied the available political space and created competition *independently of new parties*. At their appearance, the new mass parties produced by the Industrial Revolution did not so much create a competitive configuration, but rather entered *already competitive party systems*. The fact that competition took off before the entry of new (social democratic) parties supports the hypothesis that the decrease in the number of uncontested constituencies resulted from the spread of conservatives and liberals themselves

244

who challenged the strongholds of the opposing party – the hypothesis of a "mutual challenge" between existing parties.

In addition, the hypothesis of a competitive logic at work independently of social and institutional conditions is strengthened by the fact that it took off before the introduction of PR and the lowering of entry barriers. What appears clearly in the different graphs is that the trend toward more competition in European party systems occurred before the introduction of PR. After World War I, PR increased the incentives for new and established parties to spread through constituencies and mobilized voters' turnout (all votes counted) by not hindering them from voting for the weakest parties in their constituencies. However, at the time PR was introduced, competition had already developed independently of changes in the rules of the game, with parties spreading in search of new votes in spite of the barriers set by disproportional representation systems.

PR did not so much increase electoral competition as change its nature. The single-member plurality formula is the ideal-typical case of winner-take-all competition, in which the candidate or party receiving the most votes takes 100 percent of the stakes in a constituency. With PR, by contrast, parties compete for the largest share of the cake in each constituency.[55] Instead of an "all-or-nothing" outcome, the rationale in multimember PR constituencies is to run for election even in those constituencies where support is supposed to be weak, since this will lead to some reward in terms of seats. Electoral formulas therefore had rather strong effects on the format of party competition (Caramani 2003a: 434–37). With the introduction of PR at the beginning of the twentieth century, new parties could be incorporated into a multiparty configuration.[56] In Britain, the process of *dépassement par la gauche* of the liberals as the second party of the system took place in the 1930s (see Figure 6.4), when the Liberal Party contested only about 30 percent of the constituencies. In other cases, social democrats – as well as agrarians and, later, communist parties – transformed competition from a

---

[55] More generally, this is true for all electoral systems – even majoritarian ones – based on multimember constituencies. Historically, however, majoritarian systems were based on small constituencies in terms of magnitude, whereas PR systems have always been based on much larger constituencies (if one excepts STV as a PR formula).

[56] This is Sartori's (1968) well-know hypothesis, sometimes referred to as the "strategy of the weak," about the introduction of PR in terms of survival of the old parties facing the challenge of new mass-mobilization parties and preferring the safety of their established positions of control in minority parties to the uncertainties of mergers (see also Rokkan 1970a: 88–90).

two-party into a multiparty competition. This difference is partly due to the electoral formula.

As the theoretical conclusions reached by previous investigators suggest, the introduction of PR certainly favored the nationalization of party support. It motivated parties to spread through constituencies, and it gave voters incentive to turn out (all votes counted). Nevertheless, at the time of introduction of PR, nationalization processes had already ended. The spread and homogenization of parties had already developed independently of a change in the rules of the game and in spite of the barriers set by disproportional representation systems. By the time of World War I, when PR was introduced in most cases, in most countries territorial configurations had reached their highest level of homogeneity, which did not increase further after the 1920s. The level of territorial diversity of voting behavior remained stable after World War I and could not be further compressed. Rather than having been a factor of homogenization of party support, therefore, PR appears to have been a factor of *stabilization* of territorial configurations in Europe.

Conclusion: Nationalization and Democratization

Figure 6.12 schematizes nationalization processes. There are two main sets of factors. The first is represented by the two dashed arrows pointing from the Industrial and National Revolutions to Nationalization. These arrows represent the general integration of society: (1) the social integration caused by industrialization and urbanization, and the consequent growth of mass communication, and (2) the cultural integration through processes of state formation and nation-building. Nationalization processes described in this book are part of the general integration of societies. What appears between the two dashed arrows schematizes the discussion in this chapter, that is, the *electoral* processes leading to nationalized party systems. The thick arrows represent the direct impact on national configurations, and the thin arrows indicate indirect effects on territorial structures.

The nationalization of European electorates and party systems was the result of two main factors: (1) the supremacy of functional left–right alignments and (2) electoral competition. Functional alignments emerged from the first parliamentary oppositions under restricted suffrage. The liberal and conservative party families were the two large families dominating politics during the nineteenth century, and both covered most national territories from the outset after the introduction of democratic

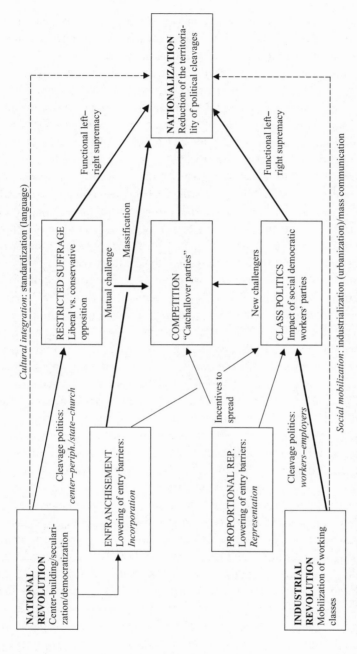

Figure 6.12   Schematic representation of nationalization processes.

parliaments and free elections. Both families resulted from the conflicts over transformations that occurred under the label of National Revolution: center-building, secularization, and democratization.

The functional left–right supremacy imposed itself definitely with the clash provoked by the entry of parties of the working class (class politics). Social democrats and labor parties abruptly entered the electoral arena under the impact of the mobilization of working populations caused by the Industrial Revolution and resulting in the workers–employers cleavage. Their entry constituted a further step toward the hegemony of the left–right functional cleavage. With the development of the nationwide opposition between secularized center-builders on the one hand, and religious-corporatist resistance on the other, the functional dimension progressively prevailed over territorial segmentations. However, it is through class politics opposing the rising wage-earning working population to propertied interests that the functional left–right opposition came to dominate the political space.

Evidence has shown that nationalization processes were also the result of electoral competition. Parties spread through territories in search of electoral support. The competition between the two main families of the nineteenth century – liberals and conservatives – led them to spread into new areas in a process of mutual challenge. Toward the end of the century, they were confronted with the challenge represented by mass parties of working electorates. However, competition between the two main political families of the nineteenth century had started before and independently of the entry of new challengers caused by the Industrial Revolution. When social democratic parties appeared, they entered already competitive arenas. Competition therefore appeared as a strong factor of territorial spread and homogenization prior to the appearance of new challengers.

The independence of party competition as a factor leading to nationalized party systems is also confirmed by its earlier development with respect to the two main institutional changes: (1) the lowering of entry barriers through the extension of suffrage (Incorporation) and (2) the introduction of PR (Representation). Competition took off both before the crucial steps toward full enfranchisement and before PR, that is, before the introduction of the strong incentives PR set for parties to spread in all regions – also in those where their support was weaker. The new electoral system introduced around the time of World War I in almost all European countries was therefore not the primary cause of the formation of national party systems but rather the cause of their stabilization after the 1920s. These configurations proved stable over the period since World War II, during which PR allowed the survival of minority politics in specific areas, namely, regions characterized by ethnolinguistic and religious peculiarities.

Also the functional left–right alignment appeared prior to, and independently of, these two institutional factors. First, the liberal–conservative opposition characterized the period of restricted suffrage and majoritarian electoral formulas (until World War I). Second, the nationwide spread of class politics – social democratic and labor parties – developed before the extension of voting rights to the entire adult male population and before the almost general switch to PR. The introduction of PR in most countries had rather strong effects on the format of party competition. New parties could be incorporated into a multiparty configuration, whereas under plurality systems the entry of new parties challenged the very existence of older parties.

As the preceding discussion shows, the different factors that appear in Figure 6.12 affecting nationalization processes occurred before the main waves of extension of voting rights. The enfranchisement of the male adult population in most countries took place in the first two decades of the twentieth century. At that time, competition had already started and class politics had entered politics. Social democratic parties developed in most cases prior to the crucial steps toward full enfranchisement. Although social democracy profited greatly from mass suffrage, candidates and party structures gave a strong impulse to the supremacy of a functional left–right alignment already under restricted suffrage. The incorporation of new working masses through the lowering of entry barriers, therefore, cannot be considered a central factor in the territorial diffusion of candidates and party structures or for the homogenization of electoral support.

How, therefore, can we explain the bold arrow in Figure 6.12 pointing from Enfranchisement to Nationalization? Processes of diffusion and homogenization of party support took place before full democratization through extension of the franchise to the lower classes. Electoral competition and the hegemony of functional nonterritorial alignments led to nationalized party systems before the main waves of enfranchisement. Nevertheless, the idea of the nationalization of politics is not merely that of the spread of parties and candidates and the supremacy of functional over territorial cleavages. This historical process includes the participation of *mass electorates*. Nationalization cannot therefore be dissociated from the inclusion and mobilization of mass electorates – an aspect that indices of homogeneity do not take into account. The most formidable change in political life that occurred during the nineteenth century, with the birth of mass democracies, implies that processes of nationalization involve more than mere territorial homogenization; these processes concern the formation of national electorates in the sense of *universal electorates*. There is therefore no nationalization without democratization, and European electorates became fully nationalized only when they also became fully democratic.

7

The Comparative Perspective

NATION-BUILDING AND
CULTURAL HETEROGENEITY

In spite of the general trend toward the nationalization of party systems described in the previous chapter differences between countries in regard to the levels of territoriality of voting behavior have not disappeared. In some countries, territorial politics plays an important role to this day. In other words, although there are common factors leading to the nationalization of all party systems (state formation and democratization processes leading to a predominantly functional dimension), there are also factors that differentiate them.

To explain cross-country differences this chapter uses factors that vary between countries, that is, differentiated pathways and types of nation-building. Chapter 5 has identified three main sources of deviation from the main nationalizing trend: (1) religious differentiation, (2) agrarian structures, and (3) ethnoregional defense. However, it has also been shown that agrarian politics declined after World War I both as a factor of territorialization within countries and differentiation between countries. The main agrarian parties have transformed into center parties and have not caused relevant differences in the levels of nationalization between countries since World War II. This chapter therefore focuses on the first and third sources of deviation. The different trajectories of formation of the nation-state that distinguish European countries caused the survival of preindustrial cleavages such as ethnolinguistic, religious, and regional cleavages in several systems.

Cultural heterogeneity has a direct impact on nationalization levels, as it translated into a number of highly territorialized cleavages. In addition, cultural fragmentation has an impact on the levels of nationalization, as it affects the nationwide spread of the class functional cross-local cleavage that emerged from the social mobilization of the new working class

251

through the processes of industrialization and urbanization. Processes of class mobilization faced many forms of resistance in the form of preindustrial cultural and territorial identity. Cultural cleavages created feelings of belonging and group identity before the emergence of class conflicts. Cleavages created by the Industrial Revolution entered already complex constellations of political alignments and consolidated systems of group identities, and where cultural and territorial identities were strongest, class mobilization proved more difficult.[1]

Accordingly, the first section of this chapter focuses on the timing and the type of formation of national states. The remaining sections investigate the relationship between a set of factors relating to cultural and socioeconomic fragmentation and degree of territoriality on the one hand, and the levels of nationalization on the other.

Patterns of Formation of National States

Timing of State Formation and Cultural Heterogeneity

At the time when some political systems had already started democratizing and rationalizing their institutions (e.g., Britain in 1832), other systems were not yet formed as unified or independent nations (Germany or Switzerland). In still other cases, some countries developed autonomous parliamentary institutions before national unification (Piedmont) or secession (Finland, Iceland, Norway). This has two consequences. First, methodologically, it makes a thorough and systematic comparison complex – a problem of historical "periodization" (which also concerns the timing of democratization, as the analysis starts with the first elections based on general representation after national unification and/or independence). Second, analytically, the timing of state formation and democratization should be regarded as discriminant factors between countries.

To make the picture clearer, Table 7.1 gives the *dates of unification and/or independence*, as well as dates of the *transition to general parliamentary representation* – the first and most fundamental step toward democratization[2] – either from (foreign) absolutism or from estate representation. The

---

[1] On this point, see Bartolini (2000b: 180–205).
[2] For an overview see Palmer (1959), Hintze (1970), and Koenigsberger (1971). For comparative tables see Caramani (2000: 47–65).

transition from estate representation to general parliamentary representation is also important, as the franchise in the former system is mediated by estates or curiae. The electoral franchise, as ruled by electoral laws, therefore has a different meaning. The franchise in the estate system is based on the size of the groups represented (nobility, clergy, etc.) and on the represented groups themselves, in particular whether the towns and the peasants are represented (as in the Nordic countries) or not. The franchise as such assumes a greater importance when estates are abolished and no longer mediate participation in the representation process. The transition from estate to general representation, therefore, must be considered before franchise levels as fixed by census and capacity qualifications.

In Table 7.1, Norway is considered as an independent case of electoral development despite its union with Sweden until 1905. The transition occurred as early as 1815 (although Sweden itself abolished estate representation only in 1866). In other cases, however, the timing of democratization was heavily conditioned by the country's relation to other countries; that is, the path toward democratization was determined by an "external" source. This is the case of Ireland with respect to Great Britain. In some cases of delayed national unification, dates refer to the prenational political units (e.g., Piedmont, whose institutions and constitution were extended to the Italian nation-state after unification). In Austria, although a general fifth curia was created in 1897, the estate system was abolished only in 1907. For this reason, the latter date is indicated as the year of transition. For Iceland, 1874 is the date when the *Alþingi* was granted its own powers under Danish rule. In Greece, regional assemblies were elected starting in 1822. The year 1822 also refers to the election to the First National Assembly. The struggle for independence started in 1821, and independence was formally achieved in 1830. Finland introduced a general parliament in 1907 while still under Russian rule (although it had estate institutions inherited from its previous union with Sweden). For Portugal, 1820 indicates the convocation of the parliament that adopted the constitution of 1822. In Germany, representation continued to be organized by estates in most states of the German Union until 1848, when the *Vorparlament* adopted the *Reichsverfassung* introducing general representation for the *Nationalversammlung*. This also occurred in most state parliaments. During the reactionary period that followed, however, most state parliaments were reorganized into curial systems (with the exceptions of Bavaria, Baden, and of Prussia, where the "three-class" electoral system was introduced).

For Britain and Ireland, the date given for the transition to general parliamentary representation is 1832. This date – as for Switzerland in 1848 – has been chosen even though the parliamentary evolution was rather different from that of the other countries. Whereas in most European continental countries since the thirteenth century representation had been by estates, in England representation had always been territorial. The House of Commons represented cities, boroughs, and counties – the English geographical-political units (*communitates*) that gave the name to the Commons. The transition to the representation of the English people proper took place only after 1832 with the adoption of the Representation of the People Act and the accompanying redistribution of seats.

The movements of unification and independence were often at the same time movements of democratization. This is shown in Table 7.1, where the transition to general parliamentary representation occurs (almost) simultaneously with the creation of *independent nation-states* in Belgium, Finland, and Greece through secession and in Germany and Switzerland through the transformation of the confederation into a federal state. The same applies to Italy, where however, the unifying center had already introduced constitutional and some parliamentary practices into political life before national unification. These cases of simultaneous democratization and unification or independence are indicated with dates in italics.

Besides the definite transition to general representation, Table 7.1 distinguishes "old" from "new" states. Among the states that formed before the Congress of Vienna – in other words, those established through the Peace of Westphalia (1648) – we find the landward and seaward monarchies that consolidated at the periphery of the core areas of the old German-Roman Empire (the so-called city-belt):[3] the two strong Scandinavian centers (Denmark and Sweden), the Iberian monarchies (Portugal and Spain), the Habsburg landward empire, the two commercial seaward monarchies (the Netherlands and Britain), and "amphibious" France.[4] The remaining countries formed in the course of the nineteenth century's revolutions and struggles for independence and national unification. These were mainly the two big "cultural territories" of Germany and Italy and the smaller plural systems of the city-belt (Belgium and Switzerland). Furthermore, to these

---

[3] This work does not give a full account of the conceptual map of Europe. See Rokkan (1999: 135–52), Rokkan and Urwin (1982, 1983), and Rokkan et al. (1987).

[4] The term is quoted in Skocpol (1979: 60) from Behrens's work (1967) concerning its military vocation, which is neither fully maritime nor fully continental.

Table 7.1. *Patterns of National Independence and Unification, and Transition to General Parliamentary Representation*

Year of Independence or Unification		Year of Transition to General Parliamentary Representation From:			
		(Foreign) Absolutism		Representation by Estates	
"Old" States (Before 1815)	*"New" States* (After 1815)	First, with Reversal	Definite	First, with Reversal	Definite
United Kingdom		Continuous since the Middle Ages: 1832			
	Ireland (1922)	In the United Kingdom since 1800: 1832			
	Switzerland	Continuous since the Middle Ages: *1848*			
	Norway (1905)	1815			
	Belgium				*1830*
Netherlands					1848
	Italy	(1848)^a	*1861*		
Denmark			1849		
Spain		(1812)^b	1869		
France		(1789)	1870		
	Germany			(1848)^c	*1871*
Sweden					1866
	Iceland (1944)				1874
Habsburg Empire	Austria (1918)				1907
	Finland (1917)				*1907*
Portugal		(1820)	1911		
	Greece (1830)	*(1822)*	1926		

Notes: Countries are listed by year of definite transition to general representation. Italics denote transitions simultaneous with independence/unification or the creation of an autonomous parliament. For details see *EWE-1815.*
^a Piedmont.
^b Cadiz.
^c *Nationalversammlung.*

newer states also belong the secession states of the North (Finland, Iceland, Ireland, Norway) and one of the Balkans (Greece), as well as Austria with the birth of the Republic in the former German-speaking core area of the Habsburg Empire (*Deutschösterreich*).

What is the impact of the "early" formation of unified and independent territories on the degree of territorial integration and cultural homogeneity? Did early processes lead to more integration than "delayed" processes? It is reasonable to hypothesize that the duration of the processes of state formation has an impact on the homogeneity of territorial structures independently of the timing of the introduction of general representation and the transition to democratic elections: The older the state, the more integrated its territory and the more homogeneous its culture.[5] In Table 7.2 cultural homogeneity has been operationalized as an ethnolinguistic and religious composition in which one language or religion predominates in at least 90 percent of the population.[6] There are 10 countries that are both religiously and linguistically homogeneous. Among the seven remaining fragmented countries, in four we find ethnolinguistic fragmentation: Belgium, Finland, Britain, and Spain. These countries, however, are characterized by religious homogeneity. By contrast, two countries are religiously heterogeneous but linguistically homogeneous: Germany and the Netherlands. Finally, Switzerland is heterogeneous in both dimensions: it is the only such case, although the linguistic divide is not politicized as seen in Chapter 4. All other religious and linguistic cleavages translate into the party system, giving rise to Catholic and ethnoregionalist parties with strong territorial concentration.

If we observe the differences in the levels of nationalization in relation to the timing of the processes of state formation, it appears that older states – those that were formed as stable territorial entities by the Peace of Westphalia – tend to be characterized by homogeneous cultures: Denmark, France, Portugal, and Sweden. However, there are two main exceptions: Britain and Spain. Furthermore, of the 10 new states that formed between 1830 and the aftermath of World War I, only 4 are characterized by cultural heterogeneity: Belgium and Switzerland above all, but also Finland and Germany. Austria, Greece, Iceland, Ireland, Norway, and to a lesser extent Italy, by contrast, are homogeneous countries (like old established states). These are all cases of secession of peripheries from larger multinational political entities. This suggests that, although early processes of state formation – and, consequently, of nation-building – led to the progressive incorporation of cultural and economic peripheries and to the reduction of cultural heterogeneity (with the two exceptions of Spain and, partly, of Britain), timing is only one factor in discriminating between countries, which suggests that the reduced heterogeneity in several new countries

---

[5] On the state formation and nation-building processes in France, the paradigmatic case of national integration from the center, see Finer (1974) and Weber (1976). These theories are often referred to as "diffusionism" (see Keating 1988: 1–24 and 1998: 16–38).

[6] The A-index indicates the probability that two individuals have two different native languages. The index ranges from 0 (all the same language) to 1 (all different languages). See Lieberson, Dalto, and Marsden (1981: 51–52).

Table 7.2. *Ethnolinguistic and Religious Fragmentation in Europe*

Level of Fragmentation	Country (with A-Index for Language)	Ethnolinguistic Composition			Religious Composition		
		Over 90%	50–90%	10–50%	Over 90%	50–90%	10–50%
Fragmented	Switzerland (.47)	–	German	French	–	Protestant	Catholic
	Belgium (.56)	–	Flemish	French	Catholic	–	–
	Finland (.14)	–	Finnish	Swedish	Protestant	–	–
	Germany (.00)	German	–	–	–	Protestant	Catholic
	The Netherlands (.05)	Dutch	–	–	–	Refor./Calvinist	Catholic[a]
	UK-Britain (.05)	–	English	Scottish[b]	Protestant	–	–
	Spain (.45)	–	Spanish	Catalan	Catholic	–	–
Homogeneous	Austria[c] (n.a.)	German	–	–	German	–	–
	Denmark (.05)	Danish	–	–	Protestant	–	–
	France (.25)	French	–	–	Catholic	–	–
	Greece (n.a.)	Greek	–	–	Orthodox	–	–
	Iceland (n.a.)	Icelandic	–	–	Protestant	–	–
	Ireland[d] (n.a.)	Irish	–	–	Catholic	–	–
	Italy (.02)	Italian	–	–	Catholic	–	–
	Norway (.01)	Norwegian	–	–	Protestant	–	–
	Portugal (.00)	Portuguese	–	–	Catholic	–	–
	Sweden (.04)	Swedish	–	–	Protestant	–	–

Notes: Minorities comprising less than 10 percent of the total population are not considered. Countries have been ordered according to the number of cleavages.

[a] Increase in Catholics and decrease in Reformed congregations and Calvinists over time.

[b] Ethnically rather than linguistically.

[c] Figures concern the Republic since 1918.

[d] Figures concern the territory of the Republic, and Irish homogeneity refers to ethnicity rather than language, for which there is a divide between the English only-speaking majority and the English- and Irish-speaking minority.

Sources: Flora et al. (1983: 55–71) and statistical yearbooks. For the A-index, see Lieberson, Dalto, and Marsden (1981: 50–52).

was caused not only by the duration of the processes of state formation, but also by the type of state formation.

Old Established States, Secessions, Unifications

To understand the variations among states in the survival of culturally diverse configurations, it is necessary to address more systematically the question of how the formation of independent territorial systems occurred. In particular, this process stresses the role of religious and ethnolinguistic (regionalist) distinctiveness in secession patterns. The type of state formation is one of the dimensions considered in Figure 7.1 below. According to this hypothesis, the variations among European territorial systems originated to a large extent from the incomplete process of "retrenchment" and the imperfect correspondence between political and membership boundaries or between "states" and "nations," which both witnessed a decisive thrust toward their consolidation in the nineteenth century after the Congress of Vienna and the rise of nationalist ideologies, as well as the disruptive changes due to the border modifications with the Treaties of Paris. Both the nineteenth and early twentieth centuries were characterized by processes of independence from older dominant states and of unification, with a strong impact on the territorial configuration of Europe today.

Among old established states we can distinguish two groups of countries. First, the "peripheral" states of France, Portugal, and Spain are characterized by minor border changes since general parliamentary representation was introduced. France acquired larger territories during the Napoleonic wars, and after the Congress of Vienna, the main modifications concerned Alsace (excluding the Territoire-de-Belfort) and Lorraine (excluding the department of Meurthe-et-Moselle). These two regions were annexed by Germany in 1871 and remained German until 1918. After World War I, Alsace-Lorraine returned to France. Furthermore, in 1860, Savoy and Nice were acquired from the Kingdom of Sardinia, then becoming the Kingdom of Italy. No border change took place in Portugal since 1250, when the original area of Portus Cale expanded southward to Algarve.[7] Similarly, no change took place in Spain after the unification of the kingdoms of Aragon and Castile in 1479 and the *Reconquista*, which ended in 1492.

---

[7] Colonies and border modifications outside the "metropoles" of Britain, France, Spain, and Portugal in particular have not been considered.

A second group of old established states is located in the North. Sweden controlled the Finnish territories from the twelfth to the nineteenth century.[8] In 1808 the entire province of Finland became part of the Tsarist empire of Alexander I (as a grand duchy) after the Swedish defeat in the war against Russia. On the other hand, Norway passed from Danish to Swedish control in 1813 as a consequence of the Danish defeat in the battle of Lipsia on the side of Napoleon. Norway had come under Danish control in 1380, when Denmark inherited the Norwegian crown. When in 1813 Norway came under Swedish control, Denmark was able to retain Greenland, Iceland, and the Faeroes.[9] The provinces of Schleswig, Holstein, and Lauenburg constitute more complex cases due to their proximity to the core European areas. After World War I, the issue was settled when the northern half of Schleswig voted for annexation to Denmark, while the other two provinces voted to remain within Germany. The present border is still drawn on the basis of that vote.[10]

Unlike the south, where secession states are absent, in this area there are three main secession states: Finland, Iceland, and Norway. Under Russian rule since 1808, the grand duchy of Finland was granted some autonomy with a four-estate Diet and the *Regeringsform* inherited from the union with Sweden. As a consequence of the 1905 Russian Revolution, the unicameral *Eduskunta* was created and elected by universal suffrage even though full independence was reached only in 1917 after the Soviet Revolution. Iceland established its own assembly (*Alþingi*) while still under Danish rule. In 1904 the Danish administration established home rule for the island, and in 1918 a Danish-Icelandic Act of Union was signed. However, it was only in 1944 that Iceland gained full independence. Norway finally reached independence in 1905 after almost a century of Swedish rule, during which,

---

[8] Although from 1397 until the mid-fifteenth century, Sweden was part of the Kalmar Union with Denmark and Norway under the Danish crown.

[9] As for Iceland, Greenland and the Faeroes became Danish when Denmark inherited the Norwegian crown in 1380, bringing Norway under Danish rule until 1814, when it was annexed to the Kingdom of Sweden. Denmark was, however, able to retain Greenland, Iceland, and the Faeroes. In the 1920s Norway claimed its rights to the territories of Greenland, but in 1933 the Court of Justice in The Hague decided in favor of Denmark. In 1953 a constitutional amendment changed the status of Greenland from colony to constitutive part of the kingdom. In 1979 Greenland was granted home rule after a referendum, and in 1985 it left the European Economic Community.

[10] On the German minority in North Schleswig see Elklit, Noack, and Tonsgaard (1981). For a more general overview of the emergence of territorial politics in Denmark after the war against Prussia and Austria, see Frandsen (1995).

however, Norway maintained all political rights established by the Norwegian national convention that met in 1814, as well as a unicameral parliament (*Storting*).

In the British Isles, the uniting of the kingdom began in the Middle Ages, when four main territorial units existed on the islands of Britain (England, Scotland, and Wales) and Ireland. The beginning of the integration is usually dated 802 with the rise of the Kingdom of Wessex, the most prominent of the Anglo-Saxon kingdoms. Wales lost independence in 1277, and in 1536 it was formally absorbed. Scotland remained independent until 1707, when the parliaments of the two kingdoms ratified the Act of Union.[11] The formal union with Ireland was concluded in 1800 (the United Kingdom of Great Britain and Ireland). Of these units, Ireland is the only that seceded. After centuries of oppression, in 1690 William of Orange deprived Ireland of all political rights, and in 1800 the disempowered parliament was dissolved. Only more than a century later (1922) did Ireland achieve incomplete independence, with Britain retaining the six wealthiest northeastern counties (composing Ulster, one of the four historical regions of Ireland).[12]

There are two further – though anomalous – cases of state formation through secession. The first is the creation of the Austrian Republic after the disintegration of the Habsburg Empire, a multinational political and military power that included territories of what today is Poland, Ukraine, the Czech Republic, Slovakia, Italy, Slovenia, Croatia, and Romania, besides Hungary and Austria proper. With the unification of Italy the empire lost several Italian territories, and with the *Ausgleich* of 1867 it was divided into two parts, with the Leitha River forming part of the border between the Austrian half (Cisleithania) and the Hungarian half (Transleithania). The empire dissolved at the end of World War I. In 1918 the German-speaking representatives of the former *Reichsrath* formed the Provisional National Assembly of the Autonomous German-Austrian State and declared the foundation of the new republic. The second case is that of Greece, which achieved independence from the Ottoman Empire

---

[11] Mackenzie (1981) describes the interconnections between home rule for one nation and the consequences for the other. However, Irish independence had little effect on autonomist movements in Scotland and Wales.

[12] During the years of highest national mobilization (1918–32) the polarization between Pro-Treaty and Anti-Treaty Republicans had a clear geographical dimension, with the former concentrating in the eastern half of the island (more urbanized) and the latter concentrating on the western coast (more rural). See Garvin (1974) and Manning (1972).

in 1830 with the establishment of the monarchy, although most territories of present-day Greece were acquired in later periods.

In the European city-belt we find no cases of old established states and only one case of secession (Belgium). The predominant type of state formation in this area in the course of the nineteenth century is unification. The most complex case is that of the Low Countries. In some respects, this can be considered an old established state. Located in the European city-belt and originating from the autonomous territories that emerged in the Middle Ages, the United Provinces of the Netherlands declared independence from Spain in 1581 – well before the Peace of Westphalia.[13] However, it remained a loose confederation that was eventually transformed into a centralized state during the Batavian Republic (1795–1806). With the end of the French occupation, the new constitution of 1815 retained the inherited centralized structure of the state. The Congress of Vienna annexed the Belgian Low Countries (belonging to Austria and ruled by the Habsburg since 1713, and occupied by France in 1795) to the United Kingdom of the Netherlands, including the province of Luxembourg, which became a grand duchy and the 18th province of the Netherlands. The Belgian revolution of 1830 and the following Conference of London in January 1831 established an independent territory of Belgium that included the province of Luxembourg (the Treaty of London of 1839 stated that the French-speaking part of Luxembourg would become Belgian and the German-speaking eastern half would be controlled by the *Deutsche Bund*).[14]

Unlike the Netherlands, after the centralization imposed by Napoleonic organization of the *République helvétique* in 1798, which deprived the cantons of their sovereignty, with the Restoration of 1814 Switzerland returned to the decentralized structure that had characterized the confederation since its beginnings in the thirteenth century. The current structure was formally set with the Constitution of 1848 when the loose *Staatenbund*, an alliance of independent sovereign units, became an increasingly centralized *Bundesstaat* (federal state).

As far as the two major cases of unification are concerned – Germany and Italy – both took place later. In 1815 the German territories were those

---

[13] After 1543 the Low Countries were ruled by Charles V.
[14] After World War I, Belgium acquired the mostly German-speaking territories of Moresnet, Eupen, Sankt Vith, and Malmédy from the German Empire. On the historical aspects of the cleavage structure in Belgium, see in particular Lorwin (1966) and Lijphart (1981).

of the different German states excluding Austria. These territories were united within the German Empire in 1871, which also incorporated Alsace-Lorraine, acquired from the war against France. After World War I, with the Treaties of Paris, Germany lost different border territories to France (Alsace-Lorraine), the reconstituted Polish state (Western Prussia, Posen, and Upper Silesia), Denmark (Schleswig), Belgium (Moresnet and Malmédy), Lithuania (Memel), and the newly created state of Czechoslovakia (Hultschin). Several other territories were put under the administration of the League of Nations. To some extent, the loss of a number of non-German-speaking territories represented a cultural retrenchment of Germany and a reduction of its internal fragmentation.[15]

The House of Savoy, with the support of Napoleon III, was able to unify most of the Italian peninsula in 1859–60 and proclaim the establishment of the Kingdom of Italy on March 14, 1861. Only Venetia remained part of the Habsburg Empire; Savoy and Nice were ceded to France to compensate for its support in the war against Austria. The second wave of unification occurred in 1866, when Venetia was acquired from Austria as a result of the alliance with Bismarck's Prussia. In 1870, finally, Rome was conquered (including the region of Latium). After World War I, Italy annexed the region of Trentino and South Tyrol, including German-speaking areas up to the highest point of the Alps. Furthermore, it acquired the Slovene and Croat territories of Tarvisio, Gorizia, and Istria. The new state of Yugoslavia acquired the Dalmatian coast. The main losses after World War II were the Istrian peninsula and the cities of Zara and Fiume.

These different patterns of state formation have a strong impact on national territorial structures. First, *secessions* generally result in culturally homogeneous populations. Secessions are carried out on the basis of homogeneous cultural distinctiveness – ethnolinguistic and religious – within more complex territorial systems. Secession states therefore tend to be culturally homogeneous. This is the case of ethnolinguistic distinctiveness for Norway (from Sweden) and Iceland (from Denmark), and of religious distinctiveness for Ireland (from the United Kingdom). Consequently, the states from which they seceded also lost elements of cultural diversity (Denmark and Sweden).[16] In two more cases, secession

---

[15] This is confirmed by the evolution over time of the A-index for language (not displayed in Table 7.2), from .15 in 1910 to .00 in 1960.

[16] The main exception is the Ulster region, which maintained Catholicism as a distinctive cultural feature in the British party system. This case, however, has been treated only marginally in this book.

led to homogeneous territorial systems – Austria and Greece – although it was a breakup of multinational empires rather than a secession proper. In all these cases, secessions produced homogeneous cultural patterns, as they curtailed the potential for diversity by dividing previously heterogeneous territorial systems through the very lines of conflict.

This is also the case for secessions that did not lead to homogeneous structures. Belgium, like Ireland, was a Catholic periphery within a larger territorial system. The secession of the Belgian provinces from the Low Countries in 1830 was mainly of a religious nature: Catholicism versus Protestantism of the Dutch elite. In this case, however, not only did the cross-cutting character of cleavages in these areas produce a religiously homogeneous but linguistically heterogeneous configuration in the seceding part (Belgium), but also in the Netherlands a hetero-geneous pattern survived due to a conspicuous Catholic population: a linguistically homogeneous but religiously heterogeneous configuration. The case of Finland too is one of a secession territory that incorporated a linguistic (Swedish-speaking) minority. In the cases of Belgium and Finland, cultural cleavages therefore survived state formation through secession.

Second, *unification processes* result in culturally heterogeneous popu-lations. With the exception of Belgium and Finland, the new countries characterized by divided territorial configurations are all the product of unification processes. Italy is the most homogeneous case with unification proper, rather than federalization, and with no politicization until recently of the socioeconomic territorial differences between north and south. In Germany and Switzerland, by contrast, we see processes of federalization of diverse territorial units. From the outset, the German *Reich* adopted a federal structure that was maintained in the Weimar Republic and in the *Bundesrepublik*.

Third, whereas for four *old established states* there is only marginal cul-tural heterogeneity (Denmark, France, Portugal, and Sweden), in other states (Britain and Spain) the level of fragmentation is higher. If, therefore, on the one hand unification and federalization processes are associated with culturally heterogeneous patterns, and secession states tend – if one excludes the two exceptions of Belgium and Finland – to be associated with homogeneous patterns, on the other hand, among the older states, there is no clear association. Whereas Denmark, France, Portugal, and Sweden are culturally homogeneous, Britain and Spain are much more heterogeneous. As mentioned, the Netherlands is an ambiguous case in that the United

Provinces were established long before the Peace of Westphalia but remained a loose confederation until 1815. To a certain extent, therefore, the Netherlands could almost be considered a case of "precocious unification" in the nineteenth century (as later were Switzerland, Germany, and Italy) rather than an old established state. Britain and Spain, on the other hand, resemble the landward multinational empires (the Habsburg monarchy)[17] that did not break up, but also that did not reach the level of integration of France (which was originally highly heterogeneous)[18] or have the level of ethnic and linguistic homogeneity of the German or Italian "cultural territories."

Cultural Fragmentation and Territorial Cleavages

The previous section has taken into account the relationship between the patterns of formation of political-territorial spaces on the one hand, and the levels of cultural heterogeneity on the other. The next step is to see how cultural heterogeneity translates into cleavages that survived the rise of class and mass politics, and to what extent this determined the persistence of territorial politics. The following discussion is therefore concerned with formed political-territorial systems rather than with their formation, and focuses on the relationship between national cleavage constellations and party systems' nationalization. To do this, Figure 7.1 combines patterns of state formation, on the one hand, and cultural heterogeneity, on the other – primarily religious and ethnolinguistic fragmentation.

---

[17] For this reason, some authors have used the oxymoron "internal colonialism" (Hechter 1975) in the case of Britain. Spain, more than Britain, came close to a breakup, for example during the Civil War of the 1930s, when Catalonia declared independence. The uniting of Britain, furthermore, took place later than that of France and Spain: 1707 for Scotland and 1800 for Ireland. For the United Kingdom as a "multinational state," see also Rose (1970a,1970b), Madgwick and Rose (1982), and Keating (1998: 93). On the role of the Gaelic language in Wales and Scotland, see Millar (1995). More generally on cultural identities in Britain, see Brockliss and Eastwood (1997).

[18] See Finer (1974) and Weber (1976). The strong heterogeneity of France and conflicts between peripheries and the center lastly appeared in the counterrevolutionary movement in the Vendée in March 1793 after four years of growing tension (since 1789). The protest was directed not only against the increasing attempts of penetration from the center, but also, and above all, against the anticlerical policy of revolutionary elites who ordered the sale of church property and, in 1792, issued a decree of immediate deportation of priests who refused to take the oath of submission (Tilly 1964).

Religious Fragmentation

The outcome of the Reformation and the Thirty Years' War created three distinct religious areas in Europe: (1) a homogeneous Protestant Nordic periphery, (2) homogeneous Catholic central and southern areas, and (3) religiously mixed territories in the European city-belt. As Figure 7.1 shows, the United Kingdom has been considered a religiously mixed territorial system, principally because of the (Northern) Irish question. The remaining religiously mixed countries are Germany, Switzerland, and the Netherlands.[19] In terms of the territorial structures of the vote, three factors in particular must be considered regarding the outcome of the Reformation:

- The nationalizing impact of the alliances between nation-builders and established national churches in the Protestant countries;
- The strength of Catholic minorities in religiously mixed countries (and the extent to which it led to secessions from older established states);
- The delaying effect of alliances between the Catholic Church and the *ancien régime* on the emergence of national party systems in the countries of the Counter-Reformation.

As far as the first point is concerned, there is a close interaction between the breakaway from Roman Catholicism on the one hand, and language on the other. The Reformation in the Nordic countries was a major step toward the emergence of national identities and the definition of "territorial nations" (Rokkan 1973). With the switch to Protestantism (in all Nordic countries the percentage of Lutherans is more than 95 percent), both religion and the written culture were territorialized and nationalized. The creation of national churches during the Reformation, therefore, facilitated early nation-building in the north of the European continent. On the other hand, alliances between nation-builders and established national churches prevented the state–church cleavage and the birth of strong Christian parties.[20] In the Nordic countries, the cultural (religiously dissident) barriers between countryside and town were expressed in agrarian

---

[19] The Low Countries have been considered mixed also before the secession of the Catholic Belgian provinces in 1830.

[20] As a basic principle, Protestantism stated that if the church is unable to enforce its rules, then secular agencies should. This principle led to the alliance between church and civil authorities in the Protestant countries. The need for support in the enforcement of religious rules meant a close link between church and state, with Protestantism becoming a state religion.

parties, which, as noted in Chapter 5, were formerly major causes of regionalism in these areas but declined as a factor of territoriality, with agrarian issues having lost relevance and agrarian parties having been transformed into ideologically broader center parties.

Religious territorial configurations look very different in the core areas of the city-belt of the European continent, where the outcome of the Reformation has been a mixed structure. The areas of the Old German Empire, the Swiss Confederation of cantons, and the Low Countries are characterized by the presence of Reformed, Calvinist, and Roman Catholic populations. During the Empire and Weimar periods, Protestants made up on average 63 percent of the population of Germany, whereas this proportion decreased to around 50 percent during the Federal Republic. Catholics, by contrast, rose from 34 to 44 percent from the time of the Empire to the Federal Republic.[21] Also in the Netherlands there has been a shift over time in the proportion of individuals belonging to the Reformed Church of the Netherlands: from 54 percent in 1849 to 23 percent in the 1970s. Calvinists rose from 2 to 10 percent, while Roman Catholics always constituted 35–40 percent of the Dutch population. In Switzerland, the two main religious groups – Protestants and Catholics – represent, respectively, 56 and 40 percent of the total population, with minor variations over time.[22]

The fragmented territorial state structure – loose unions or confederations of many small sovereign states – favored to some extent the territorial concentration of these populations. Processes of state formation in the nineteenth century in Germany, the Netherlands, and Switzerland were led by the more secularized Protestant nation-building centers, and the newly unified states incorporated the territorially concentrated Catholic minorities. In Switzerland, these populations today are concentrated in the Catholic cantons that in 1848 formed the *Sonderbund*. In Germany they are concentrated in the south (Baden-Württemberg and Bavaria) and west (Rhineland-Palatinate, Saar, and North Rhine Westphalia), as in the Netherlands (North Brabant and Limburg), the country where the territorial concentration of religious groups is weaker.

---

[21] For historical census data see Flora et al. (1983: 55–70).

[22] Only one religious census is available for Great Britain (1851). The percentage of Catholics is small (below 5 percent). The rest of the population is Reformed, with a predominance of Anglicans in England and Wales (roughly 50 percent of the population belonging to the Church of England), Methodists (20 percent), and Congregationalists (10 percent) and more than 80 percent Presbyterians in Scotland. The source of religious fragmentation in the United Kingdom is therefore mainly (Northern) Ireland.

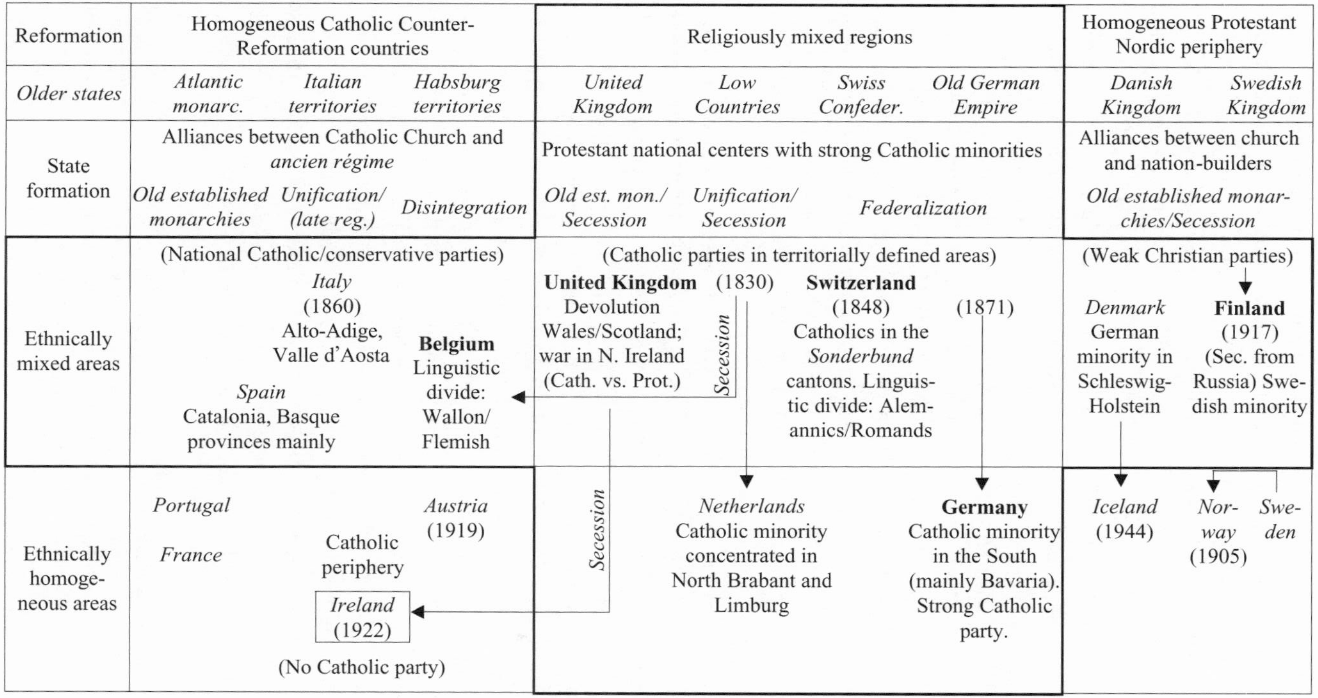

Reformation	Homogeneous Catholic Counter-Reformation countries			Religiously mixed regions				Homogeneous Protestant Nordic periphery	
Older states	*Atlantic monarc.*	*Italian territories*	*Habsburg territories*	*United Kingdom*	*Low Countries*	*Swiss Confeder.*	*Old German Empire*	*Danish Kingdom*	*Swedish Kingdom*
State formation	Alliances between Catholic Church and *ancien régime*			Protestant national centers with strong Catholic minorities				Alliances between church and nation-builders	
	Old established monarchies	*Unification/ (late reg.)*	*Disintegration*	*Old est. mon./ Secession*	*Unification/ Secession*		*Federalization*	*Old established monar-chies/Secession*	
Ethnically mixed areas	(National Catholic/conservative parties)			(Catholic parties in territorially defined areas)				(Weak Christian parties)	
		Italy (1860)	*Austria* (1919)	**United Kingdom** (1830)		**Switzerland** (1848) (1871)		**Finland** (1917) (Sec. from Russia) Swedish minority	
		Alto-Adige, Valle d'Aosta		Devolution Wales/Scotland; war in N. Ireland (Cath. vs. Prot.)	*Netherlands* Catholic minority concentrated in North Brabant and Limburg	Catholics in the *Sonderbund* cantons. Linguistic divide: Alemannics/Romands	**Germany** Catholic minority in the South (mainly Bavaria). Strong Catholic party.	*Denmark* German minority in Schleswig-Holstein	
	Belgium Linguistic divide: Wallon/ Flemish	*Spain* Catalonia, Basque provinces mainly		*Secession*	*Secession*				
Ethnically homogeneous areas	*Portugal*							*Iceland* (1944)	*Nor-way* (1905)
	France	Catholic periphery							
		Ireland (1922) (No Catholic party)							

Figure 7.1 Patterns of formation of national territorial systems according to linguistic and religious homogeneity.

267

Religious cleavages facilitated the formation of Catholic parties, often in the place of conservative formations. The support for these parties was territorially concentrated in given areas, producing a regionalized pattern of voting behavior. This was the case of the *Deutsche Zentrumspartei* during the Empire period in Germany, which included the clergy and ultramontans from 1884 until 1890 and was strongly concentrated in the south (during the Weimar Republic this party included the *Bayerische Volkspartei*), and today the mostly Catholic *Christlich-Soziale Union*. Similarly, in Switzerland – despite the severe crisis after the defeat in the *Sonderbund* war – the initially so-called *Katholische Konservative* or *Conservateurs catholiques* dominated the Catholic cantons of Luzern, Uri, Schwyz, Ob- and Nidwalden, Appenzell Inner-Rhoden, Zug, St. Gallen, Solothurn, and the bilingual Fribourg and Valais. In the Netherlands, what initially was only an electoral league (*Rooms-Katholieke Bond van Kiesverenigingen*), at the beginning of the twentieth century was supported by more than 80 percent of the votes in the provinces of Noordbrabant ('s-Hertogenbosh and Tilburg) and Limburg in the south of the country.

The arrow in Figure 7.1 moves two cases of secession of Catholic units from broader multireligious territorial systems – Belgium and Ireland[23] – to the category of homogeneous Catholic countries. As the arrows indicate, Ireland moves away from the "cross" in the figure, and the Low Countries move to religiously homogeneous (Belgium) and linguistically homogeneous (the Netherlands). The other homogeneous Catholic countries are the major Counter-Reformation states: Austria, France, Italy, Portugal, and Spain. In these countries the Catholic Church supported the conservative forces of the *ancien régime*, and the alliance resulted in the delay in the structuring of the party system in all these countries. The papal ban or – more generally – the clerical skepticism about Christian democracy delayed the formation of Catholic parties, leading to the electoral predominance of the liberal front, which – in contrast to Belgium, Denmark, or Britain, where conservatives accepted earlier electoral-parliamentary rule, as seen in Chapter 6[24] – remained unstructured and organizationally weak,

---

[23] In Ireland before secession, Catholics constituted about 75 percent of the population, with another 22–24 percent consisting of Protestants (Church of Ireland, Presbyterians, Methodists). In the Republic of Ireland since independence in 1922, the proportion of Catholics rose to more than 90 percent. In Northern Ireland since 1922, the percentage of Catholics has been around 33 percent and that of Protestants around 60 percent.

[24] To some extent, also Switzerland, where, however, the Catholic party was marginalized after the defeat in the *Sonderbundkrieg* against the Radical secularized center-builders and

with strong localized patronage influences. In some of these countries Catholic parties eventually formed (Austria, France to some extent with the *Movement républicain populaire*, Italy), whereas in others, the alliance was translated into broader conservative alliances (France in the Fifth Republic, Spain). In all cases, however, the local *notabilats* remained strong, leading to more fragmented patterns than in cases of early structuring and consolidation of parties.

Ethnolinguistic Fragmentation

The second element of cultural fragmentation is language and ethnic identity. In terms of the territorial structure of the vote, four factors in particular must be considered:

- The survival of peripheral ethnic identities in the old established nation-states;
- The emergence of national languages in politically fragmented areas of the city-belt (Germany, Italy, the Netherlands);
- The differentiated impact of language in multilingual structures;
- The interaction between language and the outcome of the Reformation on the one hand, and the patterns of state formation on the other.

The last point was mentioned earlier. The Reformation – especially in the old established states, where it had been possible to adopt Protestantism as a national religion – was a strong factor in the nationalization of language. In the Nordic countries, as well as in England, the Reformation resulted in the abandonment of Latin and in the territorialization and nationalization not only of religion but also of the written language (Rokkan 1975). Denmark and Sweden consolidated their state structures as early as the eleventh century but especially after the dissolution of the Kalmar Union, and the independent development of the two dialects – which were very similar to each other – was facilitated by the printing press and the Reformation.

In both Denmark and Sweden, however, a number of units were successful in carrying out a secession. In Norway, the printed language was Danish (although it was pronounced differently). The oral language replaced Danish and was used as a written language (*riksmål* or *bokmål*) in

therefore did not create a party organization until the end of the nineteenth century (see Gruner 1969).

269

the phases of diffusion of mass education and political mobilization toward the end of the nineteenth century – although it was long challenged (until World War II approximately) by the *nynorsk* or *landsmål* spoken in the rural areas. In Iceland, both the remote geographical location of the island and the long literary tradition of the Middle Ages made Icelandic automatically the national language when in 1874 Iceland was granted autonomy from Denmark. Furthermore, the role of religion was strong, with the translation of the Bible into Icelandic immediately after the Reformation.

In Finland – the major case of a multilingual structure in the north – Swedish was the language of the ruling elite as well as of the Swedish rural settlements in Ostrobothnia and in the southwestern islands. After a series of bitter conflicts toward the middle of the nineteenth century, Swedish minorities supported Finnish linguistic claims to counter Russian rule, under which Finland had come in 1808.[25] In 1883 Finnish and Swedish were given equal status and the 1922 Language Act determined the rights of each of the two communities.

In the north, the German-speaking population in Denmark (and of Faroese, for which, however, the political accommodation is different) is a case of survival of peripheral languages. Notwithstanding the vote after World War I and the definition of the border, small minorities survived on both sides, Danish in Germany and Germans in Denmark. Only the German-speaking minority in Denmark, however, developed a significant party (*Slesviske parti* or *Schleswigsche Partei*) – although its counterpart existed in Germany for a period of time (*Südschleswigscher Wählerverband* or *Sydslesvigsk vælgerforening*).

As for the first point, peripheral languages and ethnic identities survived in one old established state of early territorial consolidation. In Spain, the large number of regionalist parties confirms the combination of strong peripheral identities and Castilian centralization over the centuries (notwithstanding the medieval legacy of federalism). To a large extent, it remains true that Spain has to the present day remained a state and not a nation (Rokkan 1975). The Catalan and Basque peripheries in particular (but also the Galician periphery) never accepted Castilian domination. Distinctive languages and economic success have recently reawakened autonomist feelings.

---

[25] For a description of the "Russification" policies under Tsar Nicolas II see Allardt and Pesonen (1967). On the domination of the *Svenska folkspartiet* in the Swedish-speaking areas see Rantala (1967).

A similar case is that of the United Kingdom, another old established state combining strong peripheral identities and English centralization over the centuries. England achieved linguistic homogeneity early and was able to expand into the Scottish and Welsh Celtic fringes. In spite of the consciousness of a separate identity, in Scotland no protracted attempt was ever made to replace English. In Ireland, by contrast, nationalists tried hard but without success to reintroduce Gaelic, which had been suppressed by the English. Ireland represents a case of successful secession that maintained the external linguistic standard. It is a case of territorial sovereignty but not of linguistic distinctiveness, and Irish ethnic feelings were based not on language but rather on Catholicism.

Among the remaining old established states, in France and in Portugal no surviving peripheral identity (e.g., Corsica or Brittany) was translated into strong political parties. Whereas since the expansion of the early structure to the Algarve, Portugal remained a unified and linguistically homogeneous nation, in France cultural standardization took place later, especially after the thrust toward centralization of the French Revolution and during the Third Republic when the dialect of the Île de France was expanded throughout the country with the ideology of the nation-state.

Concerning the second point, in the territories of the Old German Empire and on the Italian peninsula national languages emerged in spite of political fragmentation and the absence of a military-administrative center of nation-builders. Whereas in Italy the national standard began with a single dialect (Tuscan), in Germany *Hochdeutsch* emerged as a combination of different dialects. In both cases, however, the result was that cultural unification was achieved many centuries before political unification (in Germany, the nationalization of the written culture was facilitated by the Reformation). German covers the entire national territory. It is, however, also a "supranational" language, as *Hochdeutsch* is also spoken in Austria (a linguistically homogeneous territorial system) and Switzerland (a multilingual system). Furthermore, through the loss of eastern territories, Germany became more homogeneous, as the arrow in Figure 7.1 indicates.

Italian is not spoken outside the borders of Italy with the exception of small parts of Istria and Dalmatia in the past, and Ticino in Switzerland today (which only recently has produced a regionalist party). It did not survive in Nice after its transfer to France. On the other hand, a number of non-Italian cultural identities survive south of the Alps, the two main ones being the French and German ones (both have produced regionalist political parties). Alto Adige or South Tyrol became Italian after World War I, when the border was moved along the Alpine peak line, disregarding cultural boundaries. During the Fascist regime in the 1920s–30s, unsuccessful efforts were made to "Italianize" the German-speaking populations, and after World War II the *Südtiroler Volkspartei* was continuously represented in parliament. Valle d'Aosta, by contrast, has long been part of the Savoy possessions, and the Duchy, later the Kingdom, of Sardinia could rightly be considered a multiethnic state. Its culture and language were well rooted and could therefore survive in the unified Italian state, and its interests were defended in parliament by the *Union valdotaîne*. Among the other ethnic minorities (Ladins, Fiulians, etc.), the Sardinians are the only other group that has formed a political party (*Partito sardo d'azione*). More recently, the *Lega Nord* attempted to artificially create a distinctive ethnic identity among the northern "Celtic" populations backed by Lombard dialects and ad hoc mythologies.

The Netherlands are a linguistically homogeneous country. As with Germany and Italy, cultural unification came before political unification. The Low Countries did not consolidate into a unified state in the Middle Ages but rather created a system of principalities, bishoprics, cities, and so on. The linguistic line divided Germanic and Romance speakers. The creation of the two states of the Netherlands and Belgium after the Napoleonic invasions and the Revolution of 1830 created a religiously mixed but linguistically homogeneous system in the Netherlands (in spite of the Friesian minority in the north of the country) and a religiously homogeneous and linguistically mixed system in Belgium. Dutch standardized in the course of the nineteenth century in the form of the *Algemeen Beschaafd Nederlands* and was also accepted in Flanders. As with Germany, through the loss of Belgium, the Netherlands became linguistically homogeneous.

Finally, whereas the Netherlands were able to create their own linguistic standard, Belgium and Switzerland adopted external languages – even though Dutch originated from the medieval literary tradition of the presently Belgian Flanders. Belgium and Switzerland are today the two major countries with multilingual structures in Europe, both located on the central city-belt. Both countries are characterized by two main languages, French and Dutch (Flemish) in Belgium and German and French in Switzerland, and the presence of minor languages, German in Belgium and Italian and – with a more recent recognition – Rhaeto-Romanic in Switzerland. Although the percentages of linguistic populations are more balanced in Belgium, in both countries one language is dominant. French in Belgium and German in Switzerland are the languages of the nation-building centers.

The impact on the party system, however, is very different in the two countries. In Belgium the linguistic cleavage is highly politicized. First, the French-speaking domination resulted in the reaction of the Flemish-speaking areas, which in turn produced a number of regionalist parties, mainly on the Flemish side (*Volksunie* and, more recently, *Vlaamse bloc*) but also on the Walloon side. Second, as noted earlier, all major parties split along the linguistic cleavage in the 1960s and 1970s, producing two party systems. By contrast, language did not have the same impact on the party system of Switzerland, with the exception of the vote on some referenda (especially those on the participation in European institutions). Ethnic peripherality does not seem to be important in such a decentralized country in which no center appears clearly. Regionalist parties do not exist if one excepts the *Lega dei ticinesi* and the movement for an independent Jura. Rather than language, it is religion that determines a regionalized pattern of voting behavior. This is confirmed by the fact that the Catholic party displays high levels of heterogeneity in Switzerland (see Table 4.2). Catholics are absent in cantons such as Glarus, Schaffausen, and Neuchâtel; they dominate in the main Catholic strongholds of Obwalden, Nidwalden, and Appenzell Inner-Rhoden, where Social Democrats and Radicals are practically absent. Furthermore, Agrarians are traditionally strong in a Protestant large canton such as Berne but also in Graubünden and Thurgau. Since 1979 they have dominated in Glarus, where they receive more than 80 percent of the vote.

As Rokkan and Urwin note, the acceptance in Switzerland of "an external standard equally remote from all the local dialects" was the "least likely to disturb the federation" (1983: 84). The high degree of independence of the units composing the federation led to a reciprocal "ignorance." The decentralized federal structure of the confederation hindered the creation of a national party system where 26 different party systems seem to exist (Girod 1964a, 1964b), defined by radical traditions versus Catholicism, the presence of agrarian movements, and a strong working-class organization in the larger cities such as Zurich, Basel, and Geneva, as well as a liberal tradition in several French-speaking cantons. On the contrary, in Belgium the centralized state created in 1830 and the domination of the Walloon French-speaking nation-building elite caused the politicization of the linguistic cleavage, particularly with the economic growth of Flanders after World War II.

Cultural Heterogeneity and the Class Cleavage

Conclusions about the role of cultural heterogeneity as a factor accounting for the survival of territoriality in some countries are strengthened by the impact of cultural heterogeneity on the homogeneity of the class cleavage. As mentioned earlier, processes of class mobilization faced many forms of resistances of preindustrial cultural identities that determined differentiated levels of class mobilization by geographical areas. Rather than being a factor of dishomogeneity itself, therefore, the homogeneity of the left–right dimension appears to have been "distorted" by the intersection with particularly strong cultural and territorial identities.

Cultural heterogeneity has been operationalized as reported in Table 7.2, whereas in measuring the homogeneity of the left–right dimension, the levels of territorial coverage and homogeneity of social democratic parties have again been used (see Table 5.3). What appears from Table 7.3 on the relationship between cultural fragmentation (language and religion) on the one hand, and the levels of territorial homogeneity of the class dimension on the other, is that the greater the cultural fragmentation, the higher the territorial disparities in the levels of support for socialist and social democratic parties. First, the levels of regionalization of the left vote increase regularly from countries where both language and religion are homogeneous (e.g., Scandinavian countries) to those where both are heterogeneous (Switzerland). Measures range from territorial coverage of 100 percent of the constituencies in the former case (with a homogeneous IPR of .26) to 78.32 percent in the latter (with an IPR of .54 indicating much higher regionalization).

Second, linguistic heterogeneity appears to have a stronger impact on the regionalization of class voting than religion. For countries with linguistic fragmentation territorial coverage is incomplete (94.81 percent), with an IPR of .38 indicating greater regionalization of electoral support for social democrats. These countries are Belgium, Britain, Finland, and Spain.[26] In countries with religious fragmentation, territorial coverage is complete and the IPR indicates greater homogeneity (.32), although the left vote is

---

[26] The Belgian Socialists have been considered as one national party also after the split along the linguistic divide. If they had been considered separately, the impact of the intersection of the linguistic cleavage would have been much stronger (also for Catholics and Liberals).

Table 7.3. *Relationship Between Cultural Heterogeneity and Territorial Homogeneity of Social Democratic Parties (Coverage and IPR)*

		Language	
Religion		Heterogeneous	Homogeneous
Heterogeneous	Coverage (%)	78.32	100.00
	IPR	.54	.32
Homogeneous	Coverage (%)	94.81	100.00
	IPR	.38	.26

Notes: For definitions of heterogeneous and homogeneous language and religion see Table 7.2.

still more regionalized than in homogeneous countries on both cultural dimensions. These countries are Germany and the Netherlands.[27] More generally, this confirms the stronger impact on territoriality of language as compared to religion, for which the only country with true territorial segmentation today is Switzerland.

The existence of a number of cleavages that cut across the left–right alignment reduces therefore the hegemonic and homogenizing effect of the functional class dimension. This is shown clearly by the data on linguistic and religious cleavages, that is, the major cleavages besides the left–right one after the decline of rural–urban alignments and agrarian parties. In Switzerland, the major case of cultural fragmentation, social democrats are particularly weak in Catholic strongholds such as St. Gallen, Appenzell Inner-Rhoden, Luzern, Wallis, the two half-cantons of Obwalden and Nidwalden, and so on, as well as in the cantons dominated by the Radicals such as Uri.[28]

However, cultural cleavages should not be considered the only ones able to distort the fundamental homogenizing tendency of the class cleavage. Table 5.3 showed that there are culturally homogeneous countries where the social democrats appear rather regionalized. The other case comparable to Switzerland in regard of the regionalization of the social democrats is – besides the mentioned case of Belgium – Ireland. The IPR of Ireland

---

[27] In the German case it has been noted that the social democratic vote is stronger in the north (Ritter and Niehuss 1991).

[28] This confirms that in Switzerland the impact of the religious cleavage is stronger than that of the linguistic one, which has never been expressed in party organizations and causes less variation in support for Social Democrats and Radicals. Exceptions are the Liberals and the Communists, which have strongholds in a number of French-speaking cantons.

for Labour support indicates a regionalization even higher than that of the Swiss Social Democrats. This is again a case where we do not find the left–right hegemony but rather a sui generis party system in which the Anglo-Irish Treaty cleavage is predominant. To a lesser extent, the same pattern can be observed in Iceland and Finland. The first case attests to the survival of the rural–urban cleavage cutting across left–right alignments. Social democrats are particularly strong in the urban area of Reykjavík and weak in the constituencies where the Agrarians are dominant.[29] Similarly, in Finland, the Social Democrats are weak in the areas where Agrarians are strong (Vaasan, Oulun) and in the strongholds of the Swedish People's Party (the Åland Islands particularly).

These data emphasize that not only does cultural fragmentation limit the nationalization of electoral behavior by maintaining a number of territorialized linguistic and religious cleavages that are expressed in regionalized support for political parties, but also that in a number of countries cultural fragmentation has an indirect impact on the territoriality of party systems by reducing the homogeneity of the functional class dimension. Where these cleavages are present, the left–right dimension is less homogeneous. Furthermore, if on the one hand cultural heterogeneity determines the survival of territorial politics both directly and indirectly, on the other hand it is an important factor of discrimination between countries. The hegemony of the left–right cleavage leads to the domination of a functional and nonterritorial dimension in Western party systems. However, the extent to which this occurs varies between countries due to the more or less strong resistance of preindustrial (mainly cultural) factors.

The Territoriality of Cleavages and Their Institutional Expression

Federal structures are the institutional "expression" of the territoriality of social cleavages. This section addresses the relationship between the territoriality of cleavages and decentralized institutions, especially in regard to the recent trend toward devolution in some countries, as well as the impact of federalism and economic regional growth on the territorialization of voting behavior.

Recent research (Lijphart 1999: 185–99) has demonstrated the relationship between plural societies and federalism. However, not in all plural

---

[29] These are the two constituencies of Norðurlandskjördæmi (vestra and eystra), Austurlandskjördæmi, and Sundurlandskjordæmi. In these areas also Communists are strong.

societies is cultural heterogeneity expressed in federal structures. In some cases, nonterritorial arrangements are adopted. A comparison between the Netherlands and Switzerland is useful to illustrate this general point.[30] Both countries are characterized by a high level of cultural heterogeneity. However, among the different features that contrast these two countries is the varying degree of territoriality of cultural cleavages, that is, a territorial character of cultural fragmentation in Switzerland in contrast to the functional character of cleavages in the Netherlands.[31] This led to different types of institutional organization: federalism in Switzerland and pillarization (*verzuiling*) in the Netherlands based on the three nonspatially delimited subcultures: general, Roman Catholic, and Reformed-Calvinist.

The distinction between "functional" and "territorial" institutional arrangements has been widely described, from Carl Friedrich on "functional federalism" in the Baltic states (1968) to Wandruska (1954) concerning Austria, and Lehmbruch (1967) in his comparison of Austria and Switzerland, in which the first country is characterized by the formation of *Lager*, a vertical and functional concept, and the second by "sectionalism," a horizontal and territorial concept.[32] The clearest institutional expression of the territoriality of cleavages is federal systems – in particular asymmetric (Tarlton 1965) or incongruent ones (Lijphart 1999) – meaning that constitutive state borders correspond to ethnolinguistic or religious boundaries.

It is possible to illustrate the territoriality of cleavages by considering the distinctiveness of regions according to social groups. As far as religion is concerned, cleavages can be considered highly territorial when most regions are either homogeneously Catholic or Protestant (more than 80 percent) and when only a few regions are mixed. As Table 7.4 shows, the territoriality of the religious cleavage in Switzerland was formerly very high: In the 1860s, for example, 19 cantons out of 25 had a religiously

[30] Concerning these two countries, Rokkan noted that "an analysis of the diversity between Switzerland and The Netherlands would tell us a great deal on the different conditions for the growth of cultural isolation" (1970a: 181). For a comparison of the two countries see Kriesi (1990, 1993), as well as Dahl and Tufte (1973: 98–109) and Daalder (1971a).

[31] To some extent, each group has its traditional geographical stronghold. The Catholics in the south are the most concentrated, but also for the Calvinists in the southwest and center and for the secularized populations in the northwest there is some degree of concentration. However, these groups are not isolated from each other, and all are well represented throughout the country (see Lijphart 1968: 18).

[32] In the same perspective, Dahl spoke of "sociological federalism" (quoted in Verba 1967: 126 and Lijphart 1999: 191). On federalism see also Riker (1975).

homogeneous population, that is, with at least 80 percent of the population belonging to the same confession. Of these cantons, 8 were Protestant and 11 Catholic. The Netherlands, by contrast, are characterized by low territoriality: Out of 11 provinces, only 3 have a religiously homogeneous configuration (the two Catholic provinces of North Brabant and Limburg and the Protestant province of Drenthe).

Also, the territoriality of the linguistic cleavage is high in Switzerland (see Table 7.5). According to the same operational definition, there are only four nonhomogeneous cantons: Uri (in the nineteenth century more than 20 percent of the population spoke Italian), Wallis-Valais and Freiburg-Fribourg (two French- and German-speaking cantons), and Graubünden-Grigioni (a German-speaking canton with an Italian-speaking minority beyond the Bernina Pass as well as the Rhaeto-Romanic community, the fourth Swiss national language). Another country in which the territoriality of the linguistic cleavage is high is Belgium, where there is only one mixed region (Brabant, where a large proportion of the population is both French- and Flemish-speaking) in spite of the German-speaking minority in the east of the country.[33]

In countries such as Switzerland the "territorial principle" has never been questioned (Rokkan and Urwin 1983: 85).[34] This principle bases political-institutional conflict resolution on spatial organization and division of power. More generally, the territorial principle dominates in countries with clear territorial sedimentations of social oppositions – federal countries such as Germany and Switzerland – whereas the functional principle

[33] See Dunn (1972) for a comparison of the linguistic cleavage between Belgium and Switzerland, and see Lijphart (1979) for a wider comparison. See also the two volumes by McRae (1983, 1986), the first on Switzerland and the second on Belgium.

[34] The territorial principle results from the historical legacies of premodern periods. Territorial separation has in many cases been the solution to religious conflicts. Depending on the territorial distribution of social groups, fundamental conflicts can be solved by "exit." This is the lesson of, for example, Appenzell in the course of religious wars – from 1529 until 1712. All Swiss cantons were heavily involved in religious conflicts between the Catholic Church and the Reformers. In some cantons, such as Glarus, nonterritorial solutions proved viable, but only after decades of bitter confrontation, when religious parity was established. In Appenzell, the territoriality of the conflict allowed for a different outcome, leading to the division of sovereignty. The solution in Appenzell was to divide into two parts: Inner-Rhoden (the Catholic communes) and Außer-Rhoden (the Reformed communes), a typical case of "settlement of conflict through territorial separation" (Rokkan et al. 1987: 244). The same applies to the secession of Jura from the largest canton, Berne (Deutsch 1976; Ganguillet 1985). The consolidation of nation-states, however, made solutions based on territorial exit rare.

dominates where the territorial dimension of oppositions is weaker. To the Netherlands one can add the previously mentioned case of Austria, although this country too adopted a formally federal structure. Since 1993 in Belgium, both principles have been combined with the institution of the Regions (territorial) and linguistic Communities (functional). The basic goal in both types of institutional arrangements is the respect of minority rights and the inclusion of minorities in the decision-making process, that is, an accommodation of the various subcultures through the "violation" of the majority principle.

The territorial principle in countries like Switzerland has been repeatedly reaffirmed in spite of a trend toward the deterritorialization of social oppositions during the twentieth century – in particular the deterritorialization of the religious cleavage. The 19 religiously homogeneous cantons of the 1860s were reduced to 10 by 1970. These 10 cantons are all homogeneously Catholic, meaning that it is the originally Protestant cantons that were mixed, but not the Catholic ones. This is an effect of the processes of social mobilization described in Chapter 6, involving the social and geographic mobility of population. In the Swiss case, the reduction of the territoriality of the religious cleavage is a consequence of the geographic mobility caused by processes of industrialization and urbanization that were mostly unidirectional, with people leaving given areas – the less developed Catholic cantons – and going to the industrial and urban centers of Zurich and Basel.[35]

However, in other cases of heterogeneity – Belgium, Italy, Spain, Britain – in which there is also a high degree of territoriality of social and cultural cleavages, the institutional framework of the state opposed the idea of the division of power between center and periphery. Social fragmentation was not expressed in federal institutional arrangements. Whereas Switzerland emerged as a defensive league against imperial powers (the Habsburg monarchy in particular), Belgium, Spain, and Britain were strong centralized monarchies. In both Spain and Belgium, Catholicism played an important role. In Spain the kingdom was built up through alliances of Christian kingdoms that consolidated during the *Reconquista*; in Belgium the Catholic monarchy seceded from the Protestant north of the Low

---

[35] By contrast, the Dutch data (Table 7.4) show that general secularization of the society took place. This occurred mainly in the Protestant population. The percentage of Protestant populations in each province declined drastically, whereas the percentage of Catholics remained stable. In this case too, a general deterritorialization of the cleavage appears in the table and only the two Catholic provinces remained religiously homogeneous.

Table 7.4. *Territoriality and Deterritorialization of the Religious Cleavage in Switzerland and the Netherlands: Percentage of Population by Religion in the Nineteenth and Twentieth Centuries*

Territorial Units	Protestants/Calvinists Reformed Church		Roman Catholics	
Swiss cantons	*1860*	*1970*	*1860*	*1970*
Appenzell Außer-Rhoden	95.4	69.8	4.5	27.6
Zürich	95.3	59.6	4.2	36.7
Vaud	93.6	60.7	6.0	36.2
Schaffausen	92.8	64.2	7.0	32.0
Neuchâtel	88.3	57.9	10.6	38.4
Bern	86.8	75.2	12.5	23.3
Glarus	82.7	55.6	17.2	43.8
Basel Land	80.7	57.7	18.9	39.1
Thurgau	75.2	55.0	24.4	43.5
Basel Stadt	75.0	52.7	24.0	40.7
Graubünden-Grigioni	56.0	45.9	44.0	52.9
Aargau	53.6	47.3	45.5	49.8
Genève	48.3	38.1	50.8	53.4
St. Gallen	38.5	34.8	61.4	63.6
Freiburg-Fribourg	14.7	13.4	85.3	85.8
Solothurn	13.8	37.3	86.1	59.1
Zug	3.1	17.4	96.8	80.6
Luzern	2.0	13.4	98.0	85.2
Schwyz	1.2	7.9	98.8	91.4
Appenzell Inner-Rhoden	1.0	4.7	99.0	94.9
Wallis-Valais	0.8	4.4	99.2	95.0
Obwalden	0.7	4.2	99.3	95.4
Uri	0.3	6.6	99.7	93.1
Nidwalden	0.4	8.9	99.6	90.2
Ticino	0.1	7.8	99.9	89.8
Dutch provinces	*1879*	*1971*	*1879*	*1971*
Drenthe	80.3	42.0	5.5	9.5
Friesland	77.7	30.0	7.9	8.0
Groningen	73.8	28.0	7.0	7.0
Zuid-Holland	68.0	30.0	24.1	24.0
Zeeland	65.9	37.5	25.7	26.5
Overijssel	63.4	30.5	28.3	31.5
Gelderland	59.6	34.5	36.6	38.0
Utrecht	59.1	29.0	35.6	30.5
Noord-Holland	53.2	15.0	27.3	30.0
Noordbrabant	10.4	6.1	87.8	84.5
Limburg	1.2	2.5	98.0	91.5

Note: Cantons and provinces are ordered by the percentage of the Protestant population in the nineteenth century.
Source: Flora et al. (1983: 61).

The Comparative Perspective

Table 7.5. *Territoriality and Deterritorialization of the Linguistic Cleavage in Switzerland and Belgium: Percentage of Population by Language in the Nineteenth and Twentieth Centuries*

Territorial Units	Alemannic German/ Flemish		French	
Swiss cantons	*1880*	*1970*	*1880*	*1970*
Appenzell Inner-Rhoden	99.9	92.7	0.0	0.1
Appenzell Außer-Rhoden	99.6	88.2	0.1	0.4
Aargau	99.6	84.0	0.2	0.9
Thurgau	99.5	85.5	0.2	0.5
Basel Land	99.5	82.9	0.4	2.5
Luzern	99.5	90.9	0.2	0.7
Glarus	99.4	84.5	0.1	0.3
Schaffausen	99.4	84.4	0.4	0.8
Obwalden	99.3	94.7	0.1	0.5
St. Gallen	99.2	88.4	0.2	0.4
Nidwalden	99.0	91.9	0.2	0.5
Solothurn	98.9	85.5	0.9	1.5
Zurich	98.8	83.0	0.5	1.7
Zug	98.3	86.7	0.5	1.0
Schwyz	96.9	90.1	0.3	0.3
Basel Stadt	96.2	82.7	2.9	3.7
Bern	84.9	77.6	14.8	13.6
Uri	76.1	92.5	1.2	0.3
Graubünden-Grigioni	46.0	57.6	0.1	0.5
Wallis-Valais	31.9	32.4	67.1	59.3
Freiburg-Fribourg	31.0	32.4	68.7	60.3
Neuchâtel	23.6	9.2	74.7	73.0
Genève	11.3	10.9	85.1	65.4
Vaud	9.1	8.9	88.9	73.6
Ticino	0.8	10.5	0.2	1.7
Belgian provinces	*1866*	*1947*	*1866*	*1947*
West Vlaanderen-Flandres occ.	92.4	78.1	1.0	1.0
Antwerpen-Anvers	92.4	76.5	0.8	0.8
Limburg-Limbourg	88.7	77.1	4.5	2.0
Oost Vlaanderen-Flandres or.	88.0	69.7	4.1	4.3
Brabant	56.1	30.9	26.6	29.3
Liège-Luik	3.9	1.2	89.6	77.7
Hainaut-Henegouwen	1.8	0.5	95.8	85.7
Luxembourg-Luxemburg	0.1	0.1	84.8	87.7
Namur-Namen	0.1	0.2	99.0	90.6

Notes: In Ticino 99.0 percent (1880) and 85.7 percent (1970) of the population speaks Italian. In Graubünden-Grigioni 53.9 percent (1880) and 41.9 (1970) percent of the population speaks Italian. Cantons and provinces are ordered by the percentage of the German/Flemish-speaking population in the nineteenth century.
Source: Flora et al. (1983: 68–69).

Countries.[36] Whereas Germany – the core territory of the Holy Roman Empire – was unified as a federation of territories, cities, and principalities, and both the Weimar and Federal Republics did not modify the decentralized framework of the state, in Italy, notwithstanding a northern tradition of communal independence and federation (e.g., the *Lega lombarda* against the emperors), the new state was founded as a unitary kingdom in which the dominating north could annex the backward southern periphery (the Kingdom of the Two Sicilies) without the need to federalize the union.[37] Similarly, the imbalance between Wales, Scotland, and Ireland and the English center did not require – until recently – federalizing solutions.

The weak correlation between federal structures and cultural heterogeneity therefore seems to indicate that rather than being an expression of fragmentation, federal structures are the result of power relationships – military or economic – between the territorial units. We find culturally heterogeneous countries with federal and decentralized structures (Switzerland), or with unitary and decentralized structures (Finland), or even with unitary and centralized structures (Italy, Spain, Belgium, and Britain before the 1980s).[38] Federal arrangements, as determined by power relationships between center and periphery, could also explain recent changes toward decentralization, federalization, and devolution that have been observed in Belgium, Britain, and Spain, as well as Italy. Changing center–periphery relationships have had different origins, in particular the recent economic growth of some regions but also the politicization of older socioeconomic cleavages (as in Italy). In Belgium, the cultural cleavage was reinforced after World War II by the economic growth of the Flanders – a formerly mostly agrarian territory opposed to the more industrialized Wallonia.[39] The Basque and Catalan regions also combine cultural distinctiveness and recent industrial strength.[40] In Italy, the strongest demands for decentralization come from the industrialized north. These recent

---

[36] Together with a few other factors, the monarchy is one of the strongest elements of national identity in Belgium (Lorwin 1966: 71).

[37] See Gourevitch (1978).

[38] An interpretation of federalism as a distribution of power between different centers can be found in Elazar (1997).

[39] The overlap between linguistic, socioeconomic (rural Flanders vs. industrialized Wallonia), and religious (Catholic Flanders vs. secularized Wallonia) cleavages has been described by Lorwin (1966: 158–59).

[40] Concerning the cleavage between the industrial metropolis (Barcelona) and the capital of the monarchy (Madrid), see the image of the "tale of the two cities" (Linz 1967a: 208). See also Linz (1973) and Linz and de Miguel (1966).

phenomena have been described by a wealth of literature.[41] It is worth noting, however, that in all cases, with perhaps the exception of the *Lega Nord* in Italy, these "new" regionalist phenomena mobilized along the lines of older cultural oppositions. That is to say, recent regional competition, economic growth, and institutional autonomy had the effect of *mobilizing previously constituted cultural identities rather than creating new oppositions between socioeconomic regions*. Recent economic changes, therefore, are strong agents of regional mobilization but of already existing and long-standing cultural identities. Economic growth revived Catalan and Basque identities that had maintained their cultural distinctiveness for centuries in spite of efforts of national integration. In Belgium, economic growth in Flanders deepened the cultural cleavage between Flanders and Wallonia. In a more homogeneous country such as Italy, the few "federal" institutional arrangements occurred in those areas where a cultural minority was territorially concentrated: Alto Adige, with the *Proporzpaket* ratified in 1972, and Valle d'Aosta (the other autonomous regions being Sicily, Sardinia, and Friuli Venezia Giulia). Even in the countries that achieved deeper cultural integration, it is in areas of territorial concentration of countercultures that federal institutional settings can be found (e.g., the Åland Islands in Finland, or in Britain, where devolution trends take place along cultural-historical lines).

The existence of long-standing cultural cleavages along which the recent regional mobilization has taken place also explains why these changes *did not lead* to fundamental modifications of territorial electoral alignments, as shown in Chapter 3. Only in a few cases – Belgium, Britain, and Italy – has there been some trend toward the reterritorialization of voting behavior. Furthermore, even though the new federalizing tendencies might have had an impact as federal structures created autonomous spaces of electoral competition within countries,[42] the opening up of new channels of

---

[41] For recent examples of literature on "new" regionalism see Keating (1997, 1998), Molle, van Holst, and Smit (1980), Rhodes (1995), and Scott and Storper (1992a). On competitive regionalism see Eskelinen and Snickers (1995).

[42] The classic literature on the nationalization theme stresses the impact of institutions on territorially homogeneous voting behavior. Besides federal institutions that have a negative impact on the level of vote homogeneity, this literature – ranging from the previously mentioned works of Schattschneider to those of Stokes and Katz – has identified presidential institutions as a factor that has a strong positive impact on the levels of party vote homogeneity. Speaking of Switzerland, Kerr writes that "it is difficult to speak of federal elections in terms of a national competitive arena; it is more correct to speak of political contexts inserted in segmented spheres of competition defined by the relative weight of the axes along which partisan conflicts are modelled" (Kerr 1974: 30; see also Girod 1964a,1964b and Katz 1984).

representation through territorial autonomy seems to have had the opposite effect of reducing the probability of regionalist voices expressed in the party system.[43] In systems in which the balance of power – in terms of autonomy of finance (income and expenditure), as well as decision making and implementation – favors decentralized territorial units, it is usually assumed that local issues, leaders, and alignments tend to take on greater relevance. By contrast, the visibility of national political leaders, issues, and parties would be higher in nonaccommodation systems with strong, centralized institutions.

Consequently, it has often been claimed that in most federal countries, the federated units are ruled by idiosyncratic party systems based on segmented cleavage systems that change across the territory. However, as evidence has shown, it is in the centralized states that strong regionalism has appeared – Belgium before the 1980s, Spain before the creation of regional autonomies (the Basque and Catalan minorities), Italy before and after regionalization in the 1970s, and Britain before devolution (Northern Ireland, Scotland, and Wales) – whereas in federal states such as Austria, Switzerland, and Germany, the only significant case of regionalism is the CSU, which, however, appears as such only if considered separately from the CDU and not as part of a broader interconfessional political formation. "Recent" changes are therefore perhaps not so recent, but rather reflect long-standing preindustrial cleavages that, in a few cases, have found new energy through economic growth in the last decades.[44] In all these cases, regionalism is a legacy of the past and of early organizations: the Catalan *Lliga* and *Esquerra* at the beginning of the twentieth century and the Basque *Partido nacionalista vasco* and *Solidaridad de obreros vascos*, the Bavarian *Bayerische Volkspartei* during the Weimar Republic or the Danish minority party *Dänen* of the Empire, the Swedish People's Party in Finland (continuously present since the transition to general representation in 1907), the early Scottish workers' and peasants' organizations of the late nineteenth century,[45] the Flemish *Frontspartij* since 1919, later *Vlaamsch nationaal verbond*, and then since 1954 *Volksunie*, and so on.

---

[43] In addition, in many cases federalism has had a reduced impact on territorial voting diversity, as there is a strong "isomorphism" between states and federation (in particular concerning electoral laws).

[44] For an interpretation of regionalism based on its social origins see and Coakley (1992).

[45] On Spain see Linz (1967a: 219–22). In contrast to most nationalist movements, the Basque and Catalan nationalists were not united but internally divided along the left–right

Cultural Cleavages and Their Impact on Territorial Voting Structures

This chapter has attempted to show the impact of cultural heterogeneity on nationalization levels. Although the supremacy of the left–right cleavage determined an evolution toward the nationalization of party systems all over Europe, the intersection of cultural cleavages hindered the process of full integration. Cultural cleavages survived the advent of class politics in opposition to the process of territorial homogenization and full compression of regional diversity. Ethnolinguistic and religious cleavages – the main surviving preindustrial alignments – are the main cause of territorial diversity today. Insofar as cultural cleavages survived in some countries more than in others, they are furthermore at the origin of differences between countries: Whereas in some cases the cultural dimension is absent, in other cases it remains an important dimension of the party system.

A number of factors have been introduced to account for the survival of territorial diversity in Europe and, consequently, for differences between countries. The first of these elements is the age of political systems. However, the hypothesis that the duration of the processes of state formation have an impact on the homogeneity of territorial structures is not supported by evidence. First, as can be seen in Figure 7.2, whereas older states such as Denmark, France, Portugal, and Sweden are culturally homogeneous and characterized by nationalized territorial structures (as defined in Figure 4.2), in a number of older systems there is persisting cultural diversity and territorial heterogeneity. The two main cases are Britain and Spain. Second, only 4 out of the 10 new states formed out of the national revolutions of the nineteenth century are "regionalized," "segmented," or "territorialized" systems (see Figure 4.2 for these types of territorial configurations): Belgium, Finland, Germany, and Switzerland. By contrast, Austria, Greece, Iceland, Ireland, and Norway (and Italy until recently) are characterized by nationalized configurations. These are mostly cases of secession from larger territorial systems, indicating that the type of state formation has an impact on both cultural homogeneity and the level of party system integration. Although for two cases of secession – Belgium and Finland – cultural heterogeneity has survived, the impact of the type of state formation is

---

dimension. Only in Scotland do we find a similar pattern. See Oberndörfer and Schmitt (1991) for an account of the regional traditions in Germany. In Scotland these organizations were the Scottish United Trades Councils Labour Party, the Scottish Land Restoration League, the Scottish Parliamentary Labour Party, and so on.

confirmed by unification cases: Germany and Switzerland – and to a lesser extent Italy – are culturally heterogeneous, with territorially divided party systems.

The duration of the parliamentary experience too seems to have had a very limited impact on the differences between countries in regard to the degree of national integration of party systems. Among the countries with the longer series of elections – under both restricted and universal (male) suffrage – are Belgium and Switzerland, as well as Britain, that is, all countries with persistent territorial fragmentation of the party system. By contrast, the other countries with long democratic experience include homogeneous ones such as Denmark, Ireland, the Netherlands, and Norway. Furthermore, among the countries for which the transition to free elections occurred in the 1860s–70s, there are some with marked territoriality due to the delayed structuring of party fronts (Germany and, partly, France and Italy), as well as some with geographical homogeneity (Iceland and Sweden). Finally, whereas Finland has a regionalized party system, Austria has a nationalized party system – and both are among the most recent transitions to parliamentary democracy (1907).[46]

In most old established states and in secession states, deep cultural cleavages are absent. As the upper-left-hand cell of Figure 7.2 shows, the countries in which left–right, urban–rural, and state–church cleavages are dominant in the party system – and in which there are no cultural or center–periphery cleavages – are all old established states (Denmark, France, Portugal, Sweden) or secession states (Austria, Greece, Iceland, Ireland, Norway). As mentioned, the two exceptions to this relationship are Britain and Spain, which, in spite of early formation and consolidation, are characterized by territorial tensions. As far as secession states are concerned, the two exceptions are Belgium and Finland, cases of secession without (linguistic) homogeneity. In the first case, the outcome of the secession from the Low Countries was a religiously homogeneous population but in which the linguistic divide remained. In the second case, Finnish nationalists and the Swedish elite found early agreement on the basis of the Russian-Soviet threat that led to a bilingual structure.

---

[46] Greece, Portugal, and Spain were characterized by the most frequent reversals of democratization processes until very recently. For this reason, they have not been considered in this paragraph on the impact of the parliamentary duration on nationalization levels.

If, on the one hand, the relationship between types of state formation and cultural heterogeneity is characterized by several exceptions,[47] on the other hand, the extent of the impact of ethnolinguistic, religious, and center–periphery cleavages (in which territorial areas oppose integration through national centers) on the regionalization of party systems appears clearly in Figure 7.2. Left–right, urban–rural, and state–church cleavages do not give rise to major territorial differentiations within party systems. These cleavages are characterized by a fundamental homogeneity expressed in the votes for the party families that arose from them: socialist and communists, liberals and conservatives, as well as Catholic people's and interconfessional parties. The countries in which the cultural dimension is absent are electorally highly homogeneous countries. By contrast, countries in which cultural and center-periphery cleavages are present are characterized by a higher level of territoriality in the party system and voting behavior. In Switzerland, both the linguistic and the religious dimensions are present, although only the second translated into a major political formation (the Catholic *Christlich-Demokratische Volkspartei*), and recently, small ethnolinguistic parties appeared (the *Lega dei ticinesi*). Similarly, in Germany, the religious cleavage is expressed in the party system in a major regionalist-confessional party (the *Christlich-Soziale Union*). In Belgium, the linguistic divide led the major parties to separate into two linguistic wings. Furthermore, a number of ethnolinguistic parties exist (Flemish and Walloon) and are at the origin of a highly regionalized vote. In Finland, the Swedish-speaking minority is represented by the large *Svenska folkspartiet*.

In Figure 7.2 the Netherlands constitute a problematic case. First, it is disputable whether it should be considered an old established state or a case of unification in the early nineteenth century, that is, a type of state formation associated with culturally divided patterns. Second, the Netherlands have deep religious cleavages that did give rise to a number of Protestant and Catholic parties but that, however, did not produce territorially differentiated voting behavior. As seen earlier, the religious cleavage is predominantly functional and did not produce clear territorial sedimentations. This is also the case in Germany, a religiously mixed country, for which, however, the mostly Catholic CSU has been considered separately from the interconfessional CDU.[48]

---

[47] "Among countries, cultural diversity depends heavily on unique historical factors" (Dahl and Tufte 1973: 35).

[48] Linz describes Germany as a party system in which there is "no deep religious cleavage" (Linz 1967b: 301).

Cultural diversity (cleavages)	Levels of nationalization (dichotomy based on Table 3.2)			
	Nationalized systems		Heterogeneous systems	
Homogeneous — Left–right dominant (presence of urban–rural and state–church)	Denmark France Portugal Sweden	*Austria Greece Iceland Ireland Norway*	Britain **Italy**	–
Fragmented — Presence of religious cleavage (religiously mixed countries)	The Netherlands		**Germany**	
			Switzerland	
Presence of ethnolin-guistic cleavage	–		*Belgium, Finland Spain*	

Figure 7.2   Relationship between timing and patterns of state formation, cultural fragmentation, and levels of nationalization of party systems.
Notes: Heterogeneous systems include regionalized, territorialized, segmented systems (see Figure 4.2).
Legend: Roman: = old established states (consolidated by 1648); Italics = new secession states (nineteenth and early twentieth centuries); Bold = new unification states (nineteenth century).

Finally, not only does cultural fragmentation (religion and language) limit the nationalization of electoral behavior by maintaining a number of highly territorialized cleavages that are expressed in regionalized support for political parties; in addition, cultural fragmentation has an indirect impact on the territoriality of party systems by reducing the homogeneity of the functional class dimension. Whereas, on the one hand cultural heterogeneity determines the survival of territorial politics, on the other hand the extent to which the hegemony of the left–right cleavage leads to the domination of a functional and nonterritorial dimension in Western European party systems varies between countries on the basis of the more or less strong resistance of preindustrial cultural factors (Belgium, Switzerland), but also rural–urban differences, as in Finland and Iceland, or the nationalist cleavage in Ireland. The existence of other cleavages causes the distortion of the homogenizing effect of the left–right dimension, adding another factor to the explanation of country differences.

Conclusion

FROM TERRITORIAL TO
FUNCTIONAL POLITICS

The territorial distribution of social groups is a crucial dimension of conflict, as well as of conflict resolution. The ideal of homogeneous territorial nation-states has haunted Europe for centuries up to the present day. The correspondence between territory and culture – state and nation – has not only been the goal of nation-builders, but was also seen by peacemakers as the only viable solution to protracted conflicts. After World War I and II, borders were moved repeatedly in the attempt to fit groups and territories. However, only in a few cases was this carried out through democratic referenda, and where borders could not be moved, populations were transferred.[1] In both cases, the solution was sought through territorial separation. Recently, this solution has proved viable in the former Czechoslovakia. Although territorial division was also adopted in some parts of the former Yugoslavia, in others it took the cruel form of "ethnic cleansing."

For a long time, political theory too has supported the argument that liberal democracy was workable only within culturally homogeneous contexts,[2] and only after the inclusion in international comparisons of multicultural cases – Belgium, the Netherlands, Switzerland[3] – was this view amended, with important consequences today for normative democratic theory in multi- and postnational backgrounds. In Western Europe the different degrees of territoriality of ethnic and religious cleavages have led to different institutional arrangements. Territorial federalism, on the one

---

[1] On the principle of self-representation see Anderson (1997). See Coakley (1983) and Tägil (1983) for a historical overview of border regions and the correspondence between ethnic and historical frontiers in Europe in the twentieth century.

[2] For a recent review and discussion of these theories see Abizadeh (2002).

[3] On the three cases see Lorwin (1966), Lijphart (1968), Steiner (1974). On consociational nation-building see Daalder (1973).

hand, characterizes systems with a high territoriality of social groups (e.g., Switzerland), and the survival of territorial politics has led to important institutional reforms toward regional autonomy in Belgium, Spain, Britain, and possibly Italy. On the other hand, however, the "territorial principle" could not be applied to all conflicts, in particular those of intermingled populations such as that of Northern Ireland, or where functional federalism in the form of *verzuiling* or regional communities proved a viable solution.

This book has analyzed the territoriality of political cleavages in a broad historical and comparative perspective. To what extent did politics nationalize over time? To what extent did regional diversity survive in given countries?

Over a century and a half, politics in Europe transformed toward deterritorialization or nationalization. Within the two-dimensional political space, the *functional* dimension came rapidly to predominate over the *territorial* one in the second half of the nineteenth century until World War I. What the previous analysis has therefore shown is that the process of nationalization and the formation of nationalized electorates and party systems in Europe took place *early*, meaning that it was a transformation that characterized *forming systems starting immediately after their (external) territorial consolidation and (internal) political democratization*. This implies that it was a process that took place before the social, political, and technological changes that previous literature has identified as the main causes of the process of nationalization: universal suffrage, PR, mass political communication, and nationwide issues that emerged from the two world wars and the Cold war, as well as the economic crisis in the 1930s and the growth of the welfare state. By contrast, the long-term historical approach of this work indicates that the crucial factors explaining nationalization processes in Europe must be sought before World War I, that is, during the early stages of *formation and structuring of cleavage constellations and party systems*.

Historical data presented earlier further demonstrate that the nationalization of voting behavior and the reduction of territorial differences of party support have been *continuous processes* since the first phases of competitive elections in all European countries, and that there have been no significant reversals up to the present. Yet, it was an evolution in *two phases*. Curves of territorial diversity of voting behavior fall steeply until World War I and then stabilize. The democratization or "massification" of politics around the time of World War I with the extension of voting rights, the introduction of PR, and the organization of mass parties for the mobilization

290

of enfranchised electorates therefore represents a crucial turn in the evolution of nationalization. This moment marked the *end of a macropolitical evolutionary process* that can be inserted in an even broader and longer process of national integration – economic, administrative, and cultural – through new communication possibilities, agencies of national socialization (state religion, compulsory education, the army), market integration, and social and spatial mobility.

By contrast, the period since World War II has witnessed a fundamental *stability* of the territorial configurations of the vote in Europe, with strong similarities with other long-term electoral analyses – namely, those of the "freezing hypothesis": Territorial structures crystallized after World War I and remained stable in the following decades. This suggests that levels of territorial homogeneity after World War II have reached their apex. It seems as if it was impossible to compress further the already reduced regional diversity attained at this stage. This has an important implication. It means that *no factor intervening after World War II was able to modify the existing territorial structures*: neither the further development of communication technologies (through electronic media in particular), nor the transformation of social structures from agrarian societies into industrial and service economies or the process of secularization, nor, finally, the transformation of political parties from mass parties with heavy organizations and strict ideologies into broader catchall parties deprived of solid socioelectoral bases, dense organizational networks, and constraining ideologies – all processes of dilution of social cleavages.

Not only do data not support the hypothesis of a further significant nationalization after World War II under the impact of these political and socioeconomic changes but, in addition, results presented above question the many conclusions reached in recent works about processes of reterritorialization and "new" regionalism. Only in a few cases, which have been documented in the previous chapters, can a pattern toward regionalization be detected, the most important being Belgium, with the division of the main Liberal, Catholic, and Socialist parties in the 1960s–70s along the linguistic cleavage; Britain, with the growth of Scottish and Welsh vote since the 1970s; and Italy, with the politicization of the north–south cleavage through the *Lega Nord*. Even though there has been a strong trend toward institutional decentralization in all countries, new federal structures did not lead to the regionalization of voting behavior in the past few decades. First, the comparison between countries has shown that, rather than being a cause of territorialization of voting behavior, federal structures reduce the expression of regional protest in the party system by opening up institutional channels of voice. Second, most of the so-called phenomena of new regionalism are in reality *legacies of the past*, namely, of cultural (religious and linguistic) and center–periphery preindustrial cleavages.

The survival of territoriality in politics today can therefore be explained principally through cultural cleavages that resisted the homogenizing impact of class politics – the most important cause of nationalization processes – in the early phases of political-electoral mobilization. The progressive and rapid formation of nationalized electorates and party systems must be explained through the *supremacy of the functional nonterritorial left–right alignment* that resulted from state–church conflicts and centralization processes first – that is, processes of state formation and nation-building – and, later, from the class cleavage that developed out of industrialization and urbanization. These fundamental oppositions that characterized the National and Industrial Revolutions – the "twin revolutions of the West" in R. Bendix's words[4] – expressed in the political parties that the analysis of party families has shown are the most *homogeneous* compared to the ethnoregionalist, linguistic, and confessional (Protestant and Catholic) party families. The left–right dimension is everywhere evenly distributed. It is a functional cleavage in which the territorial element is nearly absent.

First, liberals and conservatives (or Catholics in many countries) were the party families that dominated Western party systems until the advent of class parties. They had the monopoly of representation and appeared as nationalized parties from the beginning of competitive politics. Liberals and conservatives were opposed on the fundamental issues of political modernization – democratization and secularization – that is, nationwide and nonterritorial oppositions. Their trend toward nationalization was *continuous and progressive*, as they had the opportunity to carry out the first mobilization of restricted electorates. These two families have been present in large parts of national territories since the earliest democratic elections.

Second, socialist and agrarian parties appeared later under the double impact of the Industrial Revolution and the extension of suffrage. These are the parties that developed out of mass politics, and their evolution toward the nationalization of electoral support, in contrast to that of the liberals and conservatives, was *sudden and fast*. Social democrats relied initially upon uneven support mainly from the urban industrialized centers where they

---

[4] Similarly, the two master processes of the modern era are, according to Tilly (1981), the formation of states and the expansion of capitalism.

first presented candidates. However, after an increase of inequality in the early stages of industrialization, differences decreased rapidly. The rural–urban cleavage too was characterized by high territoriality in the nineteenth century. The process of industrialization, however, weakened the social basis of agricultural traditional societies, and by World War II many farmers' and peasants' parties had disappeared from most countries. The larger agrarian parties of the Nordic countries nationalized further after World War II, when they transformed into ideologically broader center parties (in the 1950s–60s). Small farmers' and peasants' parties, as well as the large agrarian parties of the North, are therefore no longer a significant element of territoriality in Western Europe.

Cleavages that resulted from processes of state formation (centralization, secularization, and democratization) and nation-building (cultural standardization), as well as the cleavages that resulted from the mobilization-incorporation of the working classes since the first phases of their mobilization, imposed the supremacy of the functional left–right dimension in the political space of Western party systems. In addition, through the process of geographical mobilization caused by parallel urbanization processes and the growth of communication possibilities, nonterritorial nationwide ideological identities soon eradicated and overwhelmed preindustrial territorial identities and ethnolinguistic or religious group affiliations.

The supremacy of a left–right alignment over cultural and center–periphery cleavages is one of the two factors that this analysis has identified as the motor of nationalization. Evidence presented here, however, has shown that the transformation of political cleavages has not only been a result of the general integration of societies, but also the product of the *action of parties themselves and of their competitive behavior*, which led them to spread across territorial barriers. Parties expanded in search of support all over national territories. At the territorial level – as later at the ideological level – they tended to cover as much space as possible and were "catchallover parties" before becoming "catchall parties." If, on the one hand, parties faced and adapted to new social conditions, on the other they contributed to create these conditions. Electoral competition resulted in the spread of parties across territories and in the deterritorialization of political cleavages.

To mobilize the most remote and peripheral electorates, parties developed capillary networks of local organizations controlled by centralized national agencies. Competition relied upon more efficient nationwide campaigning techniques that developed with technological progress. Independent and local powerful political personalities were replaced by candidates controlled by national parties, and no longer represented local interests but rather national ideologies and issues. Already during the period of restricted franchise, the two dominating party families increasingly competed nationwide in what has been described here in terms of a "mutual challenge." Liberals and conservatives spread into adversaries' strongholds in search of electoral support. This tells us that competition was inherent in the strategic behavior of political parties since the beginning of free elections, and not the result of either the entry of new competitors – namely, social democrats toward the end of the nineteenth century – or the institutional modification of the rules of the game.

On the one hand, although the entry of parties of the mobilized working masses represented a formidable challenge to established elites, the competition between liberals and conservatives had already started, and social democrats entered already competitive configurations. On the other hand, the impact of competitive and strategic factors is confirmed insofar as it started developing before the lowering of entry barriers through two main institutional changes (see Figure 6.12): first, before the incorporation of masses (enfranchisement) and, second, before the access to representation (PR). The latter factor in particular has often been identified as crucial for the development of competition. PR lowers the representation threshold and therefore provides a strong incentive for parties to spread in all constituencies, including those in which they are traditionally weaker. However, in most countries at the moment of introduction of PR – that is, around the time of World War I – the process of nationalization was already coming to a conclusion. Rather than being a factor of nationalization, therefore, PR was a factor of stabilization of the territorial configurations of party systems. Territorial configurations proved stable after World War II, when PR allowed the survival of a number of parties in given areas, namely, those characterized by ethnolinguistic and religious specificities.

The nationalization of voting behavior must therefore be interpreted in a double perspective. This double perspective not only involves considering the distributions of party support as an *expression* of the general integration of societies or the transforming of social structures and oppositions in given countries. Nor is it possible to consider that parties merely *adapted* to changing social conditions. In a competitive-strategic perspective, national electoral behavior and party systems were created by the *parties themselves* through their competitive strategies. Only a combined "bottom-up" and "top-down" perspective therefore allows us to comprehend fully this complex phenomenon.

The development of party competition and the predominance of functional left–right alignments are processes of the nineteenth century until World War I. These factors account for the parallel trend toward increasingly nationalized electorates and party systems in all European countries. They are therefore factors of *similarity and convergence* between countries. Nevertheless, territorial politics did not disappear. In a number of party systems, preindustrial cleavages survived the rise of class politics and reduced the scope of its homogenizing impact. Such cleavages are mainly cultural: ethnolinguistic and religious cleavages. These are "distorting cleavages" that modify the general evolution toward homogenization and cause the deviation of a number of countries. They are therefore factors of *difference and divergence* between countries. This means that in spite of a general trend toward the nationalization of party systems, differences between countries persist on the basis of cultural factors.

First, the comparison between cleavages and party families has shown that regionalist, ethnolinguistic, and religious party families (Protestant and Catholic) are those with the highest levels of territoriality. These are the party families that resisted the processes of centralization (state formation) and cultural standardization (nation-building). Second, language has a stronger impact than religion on the territoriality of the vote.[5] In the case of religious parties, these families opposed the construction of a secularized state. It is therefore the cleavages that emerged from the National Revolution that led to a territorial fragmentation that long survived. Denominational parties today seem to be characterized by a trend toward regionalization. However, this concerns above all Catholic and Protestant parties in religiously mixed countries that – following the general process of secularization and decline in electoral support – have retrenched in their traditional strongholds. This is not true of the larger Catholic parties in homogeneous Catholic countries (Austria, Italy) or Belgium, where the division of the Catholics occurred along the linguistic divide (as it did for

---

[5] The main exception is Switzerland, where the linguistic cleavage does not translate into the party system, whereas religious fragmentation is not only expressed in a large political party but also strongly affects the levels of territoriality of other major parties (Radicals and Socialists).

Liberals and Socialists). Nor is it true of the large interconfessional people's parties in religiously mixed countries (the *Christlich-Demokratische Union* in Germany and the *Christen democratisch appèl* in the Netherlands).

Where and why did such cleavages survive in given party systems more than in others? The answer to this question is the key to the interpretation of country differences. Different patterns of state formation (secession from old established states or unification) and nation-building (whether or not multicultural solutions were viable) have led in some cases to culturally homogeneous territorial systems and in other cases to culturally fragmented and diverse territorial systems.

However, the partisan "translation" or politicization of cultural cleavages differs in the various systems. The two countries with the highest territorial fragmentation are Switzerland and Belgium. The former is a religiously and linguistically heterogeneous country. This first type of territorial configuration has been described as "territorialized" insofar as there are no significant parties of regional defense. By contrast, all the major parties are unevenly distributed across cantons as a consequence of the religious cleavage between the Catholic and Protestant-secularized cultures. In contrast to the Netherlands – the other case together with Germany of religious heterogeneity – the territoriality of the religious cleavage is very high in Switzerland. In Belgium too since the 1960s–70s, the main parties are divided along the linguistic dimension. In addition, however, a number of large long-standing parties for regionalist defense exist in both the Flemish and Walloon (as well as German-speaking) areas. In the past few decades, therefore, this has been the main case of a "regionalized" territorial configuration in Europe. A third type of territorial configuration is represented by three "segmented" cases: In Finland, Germany, and Italy since the 1990s, we find homogeneous party systems with one main large, distinct area. In Finland, this is the Swedish-speaking minority represented by the *Svenska folkspartiet*, although there has been a decline in the Swedish-speaking population over the past few decades. In Germany – although the case could be interpreted as one large interconfessional party – this area is mainly Bavaria, with its strong *Christlich-Soziale Union*. In Italy, the *Lega Nord* in the past decade politicized for the first time the north–south cleavage and surpassed the two historical ethnolinguistic minorities of Valle d'Aosta and South Tyrol. Fourth, Spain is characterized by a large number of very small regionalist parties (the larger ones being the Basque and Catalan groups). These four different types of regionalized countries are those in which territorial politics is stronger today in Western Europe.

By contrast, the most nationalized countries are the culturally homogeneous ones, in particular those of the North, where Protestantism was an important factor in the nationalization of both religion and language. However, there are also cases of cultural fragmentation associated with homogeneous territories. The Netherlands is a country of deep cleavages that are not territorial. *Verzuiling* – the strict social division into Catholic, Reformed-Calvinist, and general subcultures – is, or better was, a functional cleavage without strong territorial sedimentation.

Finally, cultural heterogeneity further differentiates countries for it reduces the homogenizing impact of the functional class dimension. The extent to which the hegemony of the left–right cleavage leads to the domination of a functional and nonterritorial dimension in Western party systems varies between countries, depending on the more or less strong resistance of preindustrial cultural factors (Belgium, Switzerland), but also the intersection of rural–urban differences (Finland) or the nationalist cleavage (Ireland). In all these countries, the vote for the main left parties (social democrats and labor parties) is highly regionalized. The existence of other cleavages therefore distorts the homogenizing effect of the left–right dimension, which adds to the effect of cultural heterogeneity in the form of territorialized ethnolinguistic and religious parties.

The fact that nationalization processes took place "early," that is, from the first phases after the transition to competitive elections on, suggests that the transition from territorial to functional politics is typical of forming democratic institutional systems. This aspect cannot be ignored today when looking at European societies and politics. With the acceleration of the European integration process in the political sphere in the past decade – after an earlier integration in the economic and legal spheres – we are currently confronted with the formation of a new political space. One of the questions for the future is therefore whether what has been described in this book at the level of nation-states can be used to interpret the structuring of a European political space.[6]

Given the uniqueness of the process of European integration, theoretical models will have to be modified, adapted, and updated. In particular, with the breakdown of communist rule and European enlargement, Central and East European countries will increase the territorial and cultural diversity of Europe. On the one hand, these countries are ethnically still

---

[6] A number of efforts have already been made in this direction. See, for example, Bartolini (2000c) and Flora (2000).

much more diverse than West European ones (Flora 1999: 88–91). On the other hand, these territories had a totally different historical experience. Nation-states formed more laboriously because of the domination of the Habsburg, Ottoman, and Russian empires that collapsed after World War I. This means that they did not experience protracted phases of state formation and nation-building. They were also less exposed to political modernization, being more distant from the development of Atlantic capitalism and Napoleonic reforms. And, finally, they experienced socialist dominance after World War II.[7]

The territorial and cultural dimensions – which at the national level have been overwhelmed by the functional dimension – may therefore reappear at the European level. Nation-states, as much of the recent literature stresses, may well have lost their predominant sovereign position and decision-making capacity in a world system. But there are fewer signs that, after centuries of nation-building processes, they have lost their role and capacity in maintaining identities and in shaping beliefs and expectations. As this study demonstrates, nation-states remain powerful sources of group identity and political mobilization, in particular in Europe, where they first developed. Furthermore, European territories differ not only in regard to national cultures and ethnic, linguistic, and religious identities, but also in the types of state traditions and citizenship – with political nations based on a legalistic notion of citizenship and universalistic values opposed to ethnic nations – and in the relationship to the political system and styles of participation. Institutional diversity and historical experiences have strongly influenced citizens' attitudes toward state authority, either reinforcing or inhibiting traditions of self-government and political participation and influencing the "civicness" of political attitudes.[8] Today, with the integration

[7] On diversity in Central and Eastern Europe see the two recent works by Zielonka (2002) and Mair and Zielonka (2002). For an interpretation of the cultural contrasts between Central and Western Europe in a macrohistorical sociological perspective, see Caramani (2003b). On the political geography of Central and Eastern Europe see O'Loughlin and van der Wusten (1993).

[8] On these differences, see Chapter 1. On the diverse state and civic traditions and types of citizenships see Dyson (1980) and Brubaker (1992), as well as Putnam (1993) on a national scale. The classical literature on political culture in the 1950s and 1960s pointed to its basic function, namely, the survival and workability of democratic institutions after their breakdown in the interwar period (Almond and Verba 1963). For the role of political cultures in the functioning of political systems see Almond and Powell (1966). Although, after democratic consolidation in Europe, the concept of political culture has been dropped, today attitudes toward a new European political system have become a fundamental element of its formation and legitimacy. For examples of the role of cultural and identity factors in the European

of Europe in a common political system, these diversities acquire an entirely new weight and meaning, and may become a much stronger source of tension than the left–right dimension, on which there is an increasing convergence.

Nationalization – or, more generally, the integration of political structures and processes – is also a central element in processes of democratization. At the level of the nation-states, the nationalization of electoral alignments and political parties has meant the transition from a fragmented type of politics with strong and autonomous local political figures to national mechanisms of political accountability in which candidates are submitted to controls and sanctions from national electorates. National party organizations with strict vertical controls over local branches gave the masses the ability to directly influence national decision-making processes. This replaced the great fragmentation of political representation. Candidates no longer merely represented their constituencies, but rather nationwide functional interests and values. The building of nationwide electoral alignments and party organizations in control of the behavior of single personalities therefore increased their responsiveness in a political process that was no longer run by powerful personalities but was inserted in stable structures in which programs and policies were debated through a much larger mass participation at all levels.[9] Nationalization is therefore a central element of the formation of a *political and democratic citizenship* (Rokkan 1970a: 227). Also in Europe today, the construction of a political and democratic citizenship – similar to the development of an economic and legal citizenship – is at the center of the debates on the "democratic deficit" of the European Union.

Many other questions of this type could be asked. What will be the impact of distinctive cultures and identities on the European institutions under construction? Further questions address the European cleavage constellation and the balance between territorial and functional dimensions: whether the latter will predominate over the former or whether territorial resistances will survive and be expressed in the European party system. As this analysis has shown, center–periphery relationships – with the disclosing of federal channels of voice – determine the degree to which territorial interests and identities are expressed through institutional or partisan

Union see Schmitt and Thomassen (1999) and Van Deth (1999). On the reappearance of the territorial dimension see Kohler-Koch (1998).

[9] For a discussion of this theme, see Fox (1994).

channels. Nation-states did not all follow the same model but rather adopted different levels of centralization, and in federal Switzerland today the territorial tensions are lower than in many (formerly) centralized states such as Belgium, Britain, or Spain. Which model will prevail in Europe?

These several points raise more questions than answers. However, all of them seem to indicate that cultures and territories might once again play a major role in European developments and shall therefore deserve a careful look in the future.

Appendix 1

Party Codes

A series of standard codes have been given to parties to increase the comparability of the data *across countries* and *time*. Codes also allow us to compare European *party families*.

Names of parties have changed greatly over the past 150 years, and a detailed description is not a priority of this book. Shortcuts and simplified names are therefore used. For details on name changes, mergers, splits, and so on, readers are referred to the country-specific synopses in *EWE-1815*. Table A.1 on the classification of all parties includes parties for the entire period, although tables and figures in the chapters are often limited to the periods since World Wars I and II. For the general criteria used for selection of parties and attribution of codes, see Chapter 2. The following lists a series of specific problems for the classification into party families.

Confessional Parties

1. Confessional parties are divided into Catholic, Protestant, and interconfessional people's parties, but in some cases they are grouped together as religious parties.

2. In Chapter 5, in some cases confessional parties have been grouped as: Catholics in homogeneous Catholic countries (code CH); Catholics in religiously mixed countries (CM); Protestants in homogeneous Protestant countries (PH); Protestants in religiously mixed countries (PM); and interconfessional parties in religiously mixed countries (IC). In some cases, the label "people's parties" has been preferred for some religious parties.

3. The Bavarian *Christlich-Soziale Union* has been considered mainly as a distinct Catholic party, although this is disputable as (1) Bavaria is internally fragmented religiously and (2) the CDU and CSU are often considered a

Table A.1. *Party Families*

Value	Code	Cases Included in Categories
1 *Socialists,* *social* *democrats,* *labor parties*	S	Sozialistische Partei Österreich (AU), Parti socialiste-Socialistische partij (BE), Socialdemokratiet (DK), Suomen sosialdemokraattinen puolue (FI), Parti socialiste (FR), Sozialdemokratische Partei Deutschlands (GE), Pasok (GR), Alþýðuflokkur (IC), Irish Labour Party (IR), Partito socialista italiano (IT), Partij van der arbeid (NL), Det norske arbeiderparti (NO), Partido socialista português (PT), Partido socialista obrero español (SP), Sweriges socialdemokratistiska arbetareparti (SW), Sozialdemokratische Partei der Schweiz (SZ), Labour Party (GB).
2 *Conservative* *parties*	C	Højre-Konservative folkeparti (DK), (Old/Young) Finnish Party, Kansallinen kokoomuspuolue (FI), Conservateurs-Modérés, Gaullists (FR), Deutsch-Konservativ (GE), Sympraxi Syntiritikon, Ellinikos Synagermos (GR), Sjálfstæðisflokkur (IC), Fianna Fáil, Fine Gael (IR), Høire (NO), Partido do centro democrático social (PT), Alianza popular-Partido popular (SP), Moderata samlingspartiet (SW), Schweizerische Freisinnig-Demokratische Partei (SZ), Conservative Party (GB).
3 *Liberal* *parties*	L	Freiheitliche Partei Österreichs (AU), Parti de la liberté et du progrès-Partij voor vrijheid en vooruitgang (BE), Venstre (DK), Kansallinen edistypuolue (FI), Action libérale populaire-Union démocratique française (FR), Liberalen, Freiheitliche Partei Deutschlands (GE), Komma Fileleftheron-Enosi Kentrou (GR), Frjálsyndi flokkurinn (IC), Partito liberale italiano (IT), Volkspartij voor vrijheid en democratie (NL), Venstre (NO), Partido popular democrático (PT), Unión del centro democratico (SP), Folkpartiet (SW), Parti libéral suisse (SZ), Liberal Party (GB).
4 *Communist* *parties*	K	Kommunistische Partei Österreich (AU), Parti communiste de Belgique (BE), Denmarks kommunistiske parti (DK), Kommunistinen työväenpuolue (FI), Parti communiste français (FR), Kommunistische Partei Deutschlands (GE), Enomeni aristera-Ethniki Proodeftiki Enosis Kentrou (GR), Alþiðubandalag (IC), Partito comunista italiano (IT), Communistische partij Nederland (NL), Norske kommunistiske parti (NO), Partido comunista português (PT), Izquierda unida (SP), Sweriges kommunistiska parti (SW), Partei der Arbeit (SZ).
5 *Catholic* *parties*	CC	Österreichische Volkspartei (AU), Parti social chrétien-Christelijke volkspartij (BE), Zentrum, Christlich-Soziale Union (GE), Mouvement républicain populaire (FR), Partito cattolico, Democrazia cristiana (IT), Katholieke volkspartij (NL), Schweizerische Christlich-Demokratische Volkspartei (SZ).
6 *Interconfessional* *parties*	IC	Christlich-Demokratische Union (GE), Christen democratisch appèl (NL).

Party Codes

Table A.1 *(continued)*

Value	Code	Cases Included in Categories
7 *Protestant,* *calvinist,* *reformed* *parties*	PR	Kristeligt folkepartiet (DK), Suomen kristillinen työväen puolue, Suomen kristillinen litto (FI), Christlich-Sozialer Volkdienst- Evangelische Bewegung (GE), Gereformeerd politiek verbond, Anti-revolutionaire partij, Christelijk-historische unie, Christelijk democratische unie, Staatkundig gereformeerde partij (NL), Kristelig folkeparti (NO), Kristen demokratisk samling (SW), Evangelische Konservative, Schweizerische Evangelische Volkspartei (SZ).
8 *Regionalist,* *ethnic,* *linguistic* *parties*	REG	Deutschsprächige Belgier, Volksunie, Vlaamse blok, Rassemblement wallon, FDF (BE), Slesvigske parti (DK), Svenska folkspartiet (FI), Polen, Dänen, Welfen, Süddeutsche Volkspartei, Partikularisten (Elsaß-Lothringen), Bayerische Volkspartei, Bayernpartei, Südschleswigscher Wählerbund (GE), Union of Crete (GR), Suðurlandslistinn, Vestfjarðalistinn (IC), Concentrazione slava, Blocco partiti tedeschi, Lega Nord, Movimento Sicilia, Liga veneta, Partito sardo d'azione, Associazione per Trieste, Lega d'azione meridionale, Südtiroler Volkspartei, Union valdotaîne (IT), Framtid for Finnmark (NO), Partido andalucista, Partido socialista de Andalusía, Bloque gallego, Esquerra republicana de Catalunya, Convergencia y unió, Democracia cristiana de Catalunya, Pacte democratic Catalunya, Herri batasuna, Coalición esquerra Cataluña, Eusko Alkartasuna, Euskadiko ezkerra, Partido nacionalista vasco, Partido aragonés, Coalición canaria, Union del pueblo canario, Union valenciana, Agrupaciones ind. Canarias, Partido de Ceuta, Unión del pueblo navarro, Candidatura aragones, Coalición Baleares, Convergencia Navarra (SP), Bernische Volkspartei, Lega dei ticinesi, Partito socialista autonomo (SZ), Plaid Cymru, Scottish National Party, Scottish Prohibition Party (GB).
9 *Agrarians,* *peasants'* *parties* *(and center* *parties)*	A	Landbund für Österreich (AU), Bondepartiet (DK), Suomen keskusta, Peintalonpojat, Suomen maaseudun puolue-Suomen pienviljeliänin puolue (FI), Centre national des indépendants et des paysans (FR), Deutsches Landvolk, Landbund, Deutsche Bauernpartei, Bund der Landwirte (GE), Agrotikon-Ergatikon komma, Agrotikon komma, Synagermos agroton kai ergazomenon (GR), Ohádir bændur, Bændaflokkur, Framsóknarflokkur (IC), Farmers' Party (IR), Partito agrario, Partito dei contadini, Concentrazione di unità rurale (IT), Boerenpartij, Nationaal Boeren-, Tuin- en Middenstandspartij (NL), Landmandsforbundet-Senderpartiet (NO), Bondeförbundet-Centerpartiet, Jordbrukarnas riksförbund (SW), Landwirtschaft/ Gewerbevereins, Schweizerische Volkspartei (SZ), Agriculturists/ Farmers (GB).
10 *Green,* *ecological* *parties*	G	Die Grüne (AU), Agalev, Ecolo (BE), Enhedslisten-de Rød-Grønne (DK), Vihreä liitto (FI), Les verts-Parti écologiste (FR), Die Grüne-Bündnis '90 (GE), Ikologi Enallaktiki (GR), Comhaontás Glas (IR), Federazione nazionale per i verdi (IT), Partido ecologista os verdes (PT), Miljöpartiet de gröna (SW), Die Grüne Partei der Schweiz (SZ), Green Party (GB).

single party because the former does not contest Bavarian constituencies and because the two parties share a long history of electoral and governmental alliances.

Belgian Parties

The main Belgian parties – Catholics, Liberals, and Socialists, as well as the Greens – divided during the 1960s–70s along the linguistic cleavage. Catholics divided in 1968 into the *Parti social-chrétien* (Walloon) and the *Christelijke volkspartij* (Flemish). The *Parti de la liberté et du progrès-Partij voor vrijheid en vooruitgang* (PVV, Liberals) divided in 1974 into the *Parti réformateur* and the *PVV*. The *Parti socialiste belge-Belgische socialistische partij* divided in 1977. Greens were formed as two separate parties: *Ecolo* (1978) and *Agalev* (1982). Since these dates of division, these parties are dealt with separately. Each of the two linguistic wings of the Belgian parties has been considered as a party of the ideological family and not as a regionalist party (e.g., the two socialist parties *Parti socialiste belge* and *Belgische socialistische partij* have both been coded "s"; the same applies to Liberals, Catholics, and Greens).

Conservative Parties

The two main Irish parties, *Fianna Fáil* and *Fine Gael*, have both been included in the conservative family, as have the French Gaullists, the Greek Rally (*Ellenikos Synagermos*, reorganized as *Nea demokratia* in 1974), the Icelandic Independence Party, the Portuguese *Partido do centro democrático social*, and the Swiss Radicals (*Freisinnig-Demokratische Partei*); furthermore, from 1907 to 1916, the Finnish Party (or Old Finns or Compilers; *Suomalainen puolue*) and the Young Finnish Party (*Nuorsuomalainen puolue*) have been considered conservative parties (in 1917 the two parties merged); since 1919, the National Coalition Party has been classified as conservative.

Miscellaneous Parties

1. In Italy in 1948 and 1968, respectively, the *Fronte democratico popolare* (alliance between the Communists and Socialists) and the *Partito socialista unificato* (alliance between *Partito socialista* and *Partito social-democratico*) have been coded "s."
2. Divided or minor green parties have not been considered. These include *Die Grüne Alternative* and the *Vereinte Grüne Österreichs*, which were divided

in 1990, as well as the Swiss *Grün-Alternativ*, which has been excluded for 1987–90.

3. *Framtid for Finnmark*, a regional splinter of the Norwegian Social Democrats in the *fylke* (province) of Finnmark, has been considered a regionalist party; the same applies to the *Partito socialista autonomo* of the Italian-speaking canton Ticino in Switzerland.

Appendix 2

Territorial Units

Austria

1919–70. Elections by PR in 25 *Wahlkreise*. In 1923 the two constituencies of Tyrol are merged into a single *Land* constituency, and Burgenland is added. *Wahlkreise* can be aggregated into *Länder*. There are eight *Länder* in 1919–21 and nine since 1923 (addition of Burgenland).

1971–94. *Wahlkreise* reduced to nine, corresponding to the *Länder*.

1995–present. Nine *Landeswahlkreise* transformed into second-tier units, the first tier being 43 *Regionalwahlkreise*.

Belgium

1847–98. There are 41 *arrondissements administratifs*, which can be aggregated into nine *provinces*.

1900–91. *Arrondissements administratifs* are aggregated into 30 constituencies as follows: Fournes/Dixmude/Ostende; Roulers/Tielt; Tournai/Ath; Huy/Waremme; Gand/Eeklo; Tongres/Maaseik; Arlon/Marche/Bastogne; Neufchâteau/Virton; Dinant/Philippeville.

1995–present. There are 20 *circonscriptions* (or *kiesdistricte*) and provinces increase to 11 given the division of the former province of Brabant into three parts: Bruxelles, Brabant flamand (Louvain), and Brabant wallon (Nivelles).

Denmark

1848–1915. There are 100–13 *valgkredse*, which can be aggregated into 22 *amter* corresponding to the *amtskredse* and *storkredse* of 1918–68.

1918. There are 110 *valgkredse*. The majority of the country still votes in single-member plurality constituencies. Voting by PR occurs only in the former 15 constituencies of Copenhagen and the three of Frederiksberg (the 18 constituencies form one PR constituency).

1920–68. PR in 22 constituencies: *storkredse* (the 3 constituencies of Copenhagen) and *amtskredse*. After the September 1920 election, there are 23 units (with the addition of northern Schleswig).

1971–present. There are 17 units: 3 in Copenhagen (*storkredse*), 7 in mainland Jutland, and 7 in the islands (*amtskredse*).

Finland

1907–present. The overall number of electoral districts or "electoral areas" (*vaalipiirit*) is fixed by law between 12 and 18. Since 1907 their number has varied between 15 and 16. According to the peace treaty after World War II, Finland loses the Viipuri region (two constituencies) to the Soviet Union. Single-member constituencies with plurality elections are found in Lapland (1907–38) and in the Åland Islands (since 1948).

France

1910–present. Election results are available mostly at the level of *départements* instead of constituencies. Their number varies between 88 (until 1936) and 96 (since 1978).

Germany

1871–1912. At the first *Reichstag* election in 1871, there are 382 *Wahlkreise*, which can be aggregated into 25 federated states (*Staaten*). With the acquisition of Alsace-Lorraine in 1874, the number of constituencies becomes 397 (26 federated states).

1919. PR election (Constituent Assembly) occurs in 36 constituencies.

1920–33. There are 35 constituencies.

1949–present. In 1949 elections are held in 242 *Erststimmen* constituencies (even though double voting was introduced in 1953). *Länder* change and assume their present form in West Germany (*Zweitstimmen* constituencies). The three *Länder* of Württemberg-Baden, Baden, and Württemberg-Hohenzollern are combined to form the *Land* of Baden-Württemberg (10 *Länder* overall). In 1957 Saarland returns to Germany, increasing the number of *Länder* by one and the number of constituencies to 247. In 1965, after the Constitutional Court ruled malapportionment unconstitutional, the number of constituencies increases from 247 to 248. In 1976 new districting occurs but the number of constituencies is unchanged. In 1990 the six new eastern *Länder* are added. The number of constituencies becomes 328. For 1949–87 figures for West Berlin are never included. In 1998 new districting occurs but no major changes in the number and names of the constituencies (except for Berlin).

Greece

1926–56 (excluding 1928, 1933, and 1952). Electoral constituencies are mainly departments (*nomoí*), but also municipalities and ethnic districts for Jews and Muslims. There are 40 units in 1926, 43 in 1932, and 38 in 1936 and 1946. In 1950 the Dodecanese is added to the *nomós* of the Aegean (39 units). In 1951 two *nomoí* are created, Imathia and Pieria (41 units). The second electoral tier consists of the nine districts of the Courts of Appeal. The third tier is the national constituency. In 1956 (mixed formula) there was only one tier.

1928–33. Three plurality elections are held in 98 units (1928 and 1933) and 99 (1952).

1958–64. Until the military dictatorship of 1964, there are 55 *nomoí*.

1974–present. The *nomoí* increase to 56 (with the addition of Grevena). The second tier from 1958 until 1985 consists of nine regions and, since 1989, of 13 regions.

Iceland

1874–1959. The number of constituencies varies between 19 and 28 (single- and two-member). Since 1916 there is also nationwide (*Landskjör*) allocation of a number of seats. In 1934 *Landskjör* elections are abolished but there is nationwide allocation of supplementary seats (*Uppbótarngsæti*).

1959–present. Since the second 1959 election, constituencies have been reduced to eight.

Ireland

1922–present. (Ireland part of the United Kingdom during 1832–1918). Frequent district changes occur in the Republic. The number of *Dáil* constituencies (STV) varies between 30 and 42.

Italy

1861–1913. There are 508 *collegi*. For the three elections between 1882 and 1890 held with lists, the country is divided into 135 multimember constituencies. Party results are available since 1876 at the level of 14–16 *regioni*.

1919–21. In 1919 the country is divided into 54 multimember constituencies (*collegi*). In 1921 the number of multimember constituencies is reduced to 40. Two more regions are annexed before the 1921 election, making the total 18 (with the addition of Venezia Tridentina and Venezia Giulia-Zara). These regions differ from those created in the 1970s.

1946–92. In 1946–53, there are 31 constituencies (*circoscrizioni*) including the *Collegio Unico Valle d'Aosta*, in which elections are held by plurality. In 1958 the constituency of Trieste is added with the city's return to Italy. Two further levels of aggregation are available: 89–95 *province* (provinces) and 20 *regioni* (regions) are created as administrative units in the 1970s.

1994–present. There are 475 constituencies (*collegi uninominali*) for the election by plurality of 75 percent of the representatives. For the remaining 25 percent of the representatives, there is PR in 26 multimember constituencies (*circoscrizioni*). Data concerning this second PR vote are also available for the 475 smaller units. Both levels can be aggregated into 20 regions.

The Netherlands

1888–1917. There are 100 single-member *kiesdistricten*, which can be aggregated into 11 provinces.

1918–present. A single national constituency is divided into 18 *kamerkieskringen* (for the presentation of candidatures and establishment of lists), which can be aggregated into 11 provinces. In 1986 the new province and *kamerkieskring* of Flevoland is created, increasing the number of provinces to 12 and the number of *kamerkieskringen* to 19. The new unit of postal voters (*briefstemmer*) is also created.

Norway

1815–1903. Constituencies are subdivided into rural (*landdistrikterne*) and urban (*kjøbstæderne*) constituencies. Overall, there are between 38 and 58 districts.

1906–18. In 1906 there are 123 *valgkredsen*: 82 rural and 41 urban constituencies. In 1918 they increase to 126.

1921–49. A PR system is established with 29 *valgdistrikter*: 1 to 18 *landdistrikter* (rural districts) and 19 to 29 *bydistrikter* (city districts).

1953–present. Constituencies correspond to the 20 *fylker*, and the distinction between rural and urban districts is abolished. In 1973 the number of constituencies is reduced to 19 (the Bergen district is incorporated into Hordaland).

Portugal

1975–present. The *distritos administrativos* constitute the *círculos eleitorais*. There are 20 units (18 *distritos* and two autonomous regions, the *Região autónoma dos Açores* and the *Região autónoma da Madeira*). In 1975 and 1976 the two autonomous regions constitute four districts: Angra do Heroísmo, Horta, Ponta Delgada (Açores), and Funchal (Madeira). The two overseas constituencies, *Círculo da Europa* and *Círculo de fora da Europa* (Macao), are not included.

Spain

1977–present. Elections are held in 50 *provincias* and in Ceuta and Melilla (northern Africa), adding up to 52 *circunscripciones*.

Sweden

1866–1908. The number of constituencies varies between 173 (1866) and 201 (1908). *Valkretsar* change very frequently, at almost each election except those from 1896 to 1905.

1911–20. With PR, the country is divided into 56 *valkretsar*.

1921–94. There are 28 *valkretsar*, largely corresponding to the provinces (*län*). In 1994, Malmöhus län is divided into north and south (29 *valkretsar*).

1998. Modification of constituencies (the number remains 29).

Switzerland

1848–present. Until 1917 there are between 47 and 52 single- and multi-member constituencies, but results by parties are available for 25 cantons.

With the introduction of PR in 1919, cantons become the constituencies (25 until 1975, then 26 with the secession of Jura from Berne).

United Kingdom

The description of the territorial units is divided into (1) Britain, (2) Ireland (1832–1918), and (3) Northern Ireland (1922–present).

Britain

1832–80. There are between 333 and 352 constituencies in England, Wales and Monmouth, Scotland, and the universities. In 1866 several constituencies change from two-member to single-member or from single-member to two- or three-member.

1885–1910. There are 542 constituencies. No constituency changes take place.

1918–45. The number of constituencies is 585, returning one to two seats each. In 1945 the number of constituencies is slightly modified (609).

1950–70. There are 613 constituencies. Since 1950 the number of constituencies and the number of seats returned have been identical (with abolition of multimember constituencies). In 1955 the number of constituencies increases to 618.

1974–79. There are 623 constituencies.

1983–92. The number of constituencies increases to 633. In 1992 the districts are the same as for 1983 and 1987, with one minor change: The constituencies of Buckingham and Milton Keynes are redrawn to form three constituencies: Buckingham, Milton Keynes North-East, and Milton Keynes South-West. The overall number of constituencies is therefore 634.

1997. Parliamentary constituencies change radically. Only 165 constituencies are left unaltered. Seven additional seats are created. The overall number of constituencies is 641.

Ireland (1832–1918)

1832–80. Ireland returns 105 seats to Westminster. In 1870 the Cashel and Sligo constituencies are disenfranchised for corrupt practices. The number of constituencies is therefore reduced from 66 to 64 in the 1874 election.

1885–1910. There are 99 single-member constituencies and 2 two-member constituencies (Cork City and Dublin University).

1918. There are 103 single-member constituencies. The 1918 election is the last all-Ireland election.

Northern Ireland (1922–present)

1922–45. There are 10 constituencies.

1950–79. There are 12 single-member constituencies (university seats are abolished, as in the rest of the United Kingdom).

1983–92. There are 17 constituencies.

1997. The number of Northern Irish constituencies increases to 18.

Appendix 3

Computations

Based on Percentage Distribution of Votes by Parties

Mean absolute deviation: $\text{MAD} = \Sigma \mid X - \bar{X} \mid / n$
(also called "index of variation" [Rose and Urwin 1975: 24])
Mean squared deviation: $\text{MSD} = \Sigma (X - \bar{X})^2 / n$
Variance: $S^2 = \Sigma (X - \bar{X})^2 / n - 1$
Standard deviation: $S = \sqrt{S^2}$ or $S = \sqrt{\Sigma (X - \bar{X})^2 / n - 1}$
Lee index: $\text{LEE} = \Sigma \mid X - \bar{X} \mid / 2$
Variability coefficient: $\text{CV} = S / \bar{X}$
$\text{IPR} = \sqrt{n} \; \Sigma \mid X - \bar{X} \mid / (2 (n - 1) \Sigma X)$

Based on Percentages of Parties' Vote Distribution by Constituencies

Cumulative regional inequality index: $\text{CRII} = 1/2 \; \Sigma \mid \text{votes} - \text{voters} \mid$
(not applicable to turnout).

The formula is divided by 100 to vary between 0 and 1 (Rose and Urwin 1975). When voters' figures are not available, electorate figures are used.

All Constituencies versus Constituencies in Which the Party Is Present Only

For party support, all previous indices have been computed (1) on the *total number of constituencies* (party not present = 0) and (2) on the constituencies in which the party was *present* only (party not present = system missing). This distinction does not apply to the CRII or to turnout figures.

Territorial Coverage by Parties

The simplest measure used to assess the spread of parties across regions is the number of constituencies in which a party is present (nominator) as a percentage of the total number of constituencies (denominator). A constituency in which a party is unopposed (an uncontested constituency) is considered a constituency in which the party is present.

The computation of this percentage is complicated by *missing data* for some constituencies; that is, it is not known whether a party is present or not in a number of constituencies. This occurs especially in earlier periods. In such cases, *the territorial coverage by parties is underestimated.* To adjust for this, the number of missing constituencies has been subtracted from the total number of constituencies, which, like all estimations, is not perfect (since we still do not know what the missing constituencies looked like). This is obviously not applicable to turnout, which is always "present" in 100 percent of the constituencies.

Table A.3 lists the cases in which information on some or all constituencies is missing (for party votes).

Table A.3. *Main Missing Data*

Country	Election Years	Cases (Parties)	Total Number of Constituencies	Number of Missing Constituencies
Belgium	1848, 1859, 1888, and 1894	All parties	41	1
Denmark	1879, 1901, and 1915	All parties	101–13	1
Germany	1912	*Nationalliberale, Deutsche Konservative, Zentrum, Polen, Wirtschaftsvereinigung, Deutsche Reichspartei,* and *Deutsche Reform Partei*	397	3–329
Iceland	1916, 1922, and 1926	All parties	25–26	25–26
Netherlands	1888–94	All parties	100	16
Switzerland	1848–69	All parties	25 cantons	6 cantons

Notes: Countries with missing information at the constituency level for turnout (as well as persons entitled to vote) are not listed. The total number of constituencies varies according to districting in different years. The number of missing constituencies varies according to parties and to the first/second ballot. For Switzerland 1848–1917 constituency-level data not available (only cantonal data available).

Estimates

1. *Party support*: Unopposed parties or candidates in uncontested constituencies have been estimated receiving 100 percent of the votes. This applies to both single-member and multimember uncontested constituencies.
2. *Turnout*: Voting did not take place in such constituencies. Turnout has been estimated at 100 percent, although this is an overestimation, especially for earlier periods.

Appendix 4

Country Specificities

This appendix lists countries specificities, when applicable, broken down by periods according to electoral formulas. Data errors in original sources have not been listed here but are available by pressing the "help" buttons on the CD-ROM *EWE-1815*. Unless otherwise stated, data errors are considered missing cases when it was not possible to refer to estimates.

Belgium

1848–98. For the 1847–92 period, only the *first ballot* is considered. *Partial elections* were carried out every two years with two alternating groups of *arrondissements*: 19 and 22 districts from 1847 until 1898 and then two groups of 15 districts from 1900 until 1914 (the last partial election). In 1870 two elections were held, a partial and a general election. Only *general elections* have been considered for the computation of indices (see Chapter 6 for partial elections and second ballots). Because of multiple voting (1847–98), *1:1 estimates* have been used for the computation of indices.

1900–95. Between the 1960s and 1980s, the major Belgian parties split according to the linguistic cleavage (see Appendix 1). Results are presented for each of the *two linguistic parties*. Only since 1991, however, have official publications distinguished between the two wings of the socialist, liberal, Catholic, and green parties. Before this date, results for the two wings have been disaggregated according to the *arrondissements* in which each wing is present. In Brussels both wings are present, and before 1991 it is not possible to separate the results of the two wings. The aggregated results for the two wings of each of the four parties in Brussels have been added to the column of the Walloon party.

Denmark

1849–1915. *Estimates* have been used for open elections without counting (*valgt ved kåring*) until 1901. Computation of national totals is not possible, which affects a number of indices (e.g., CRII). *Unknown votes* are excluded from computations. Two elections in the same year occurred in 1853, 1864, and 1881. For computations of indices, party sums of candidate votes have been used.

1918–present. Missing values for persons entitled to vote and voters in several elections affect the computation of CRII and turnout figures. Three elections were held in 1920 and two in 1953.

France

1910–present. In alliances of the Socialist Party and the Ecologist Party, or of the Socialist Party and the Radical Socialist Party, votes have been ranged under "s" (*Parti socialiste*). Votes for dissident candidates of the *Union pour la démocratie française* and of the *Rassemblement pour la république* have not been added to these parties. Constituencies in Corsica: Votes for several candidates of the *Rassemblement pour la république* were added together at the first ballot. In 1946 two elections were held.

Germany

1871–1912. Only *first ballots* are considered (see Chapter 6 for second ballots). In the 1871 and 1874 elections there was no second ballot. In 1912 there were several missing values (see Appendix 3). The following parties have been excluded from analysis because many data were missing: *Polen, Wirtschaftsvereinigung, Deutsche Reichspartei*, and *Deutsche Reform Partei*.

1919–33. In 1924 and 1932 two elections were held in each year.

1949–present. Since 1953 *Zweitstimmen* have been used for the computation of indices but using the 242–328 *Erststimme Wahlkreise*. Until 1987 figures never include Berlin (see Appendix 2).

Greece

1974–present. In 1989 two elections were held.

Iceland

1874–1914. Information is limited to the number of voters and votes for elected candidates on one of the three ballots.

1916–present. From 1916 until 1933 two types of elections were held: *kjørdæmaksningar* (election by plurality in single- or two-member constituencies) and *landskosningar* (elections for supplementary seats with national lists). In two-member constituencies of *kjørdæmaksningar* (multiple voting) *1:1 estimates* and party sums of candidate votes were used. In 1916, 1926, 1942, and 1959, two elections were held in each year.

Ireland

1922–present. *First preferences* (STV) have been used for computations. From 1922 until 1965, the CRII was computed on the "number of persons entitled to vote" instead on the "number of voters" because of missing figures. In 1927 and 1982 two elections were held in each year.

Italy

1860–1913. Figures concern only *first ballots*.

1994–96. The PR vote (election of 25 percent of the representatives in multimember constituencies) has been used instead of the plurality vote in single-member constituencies because of results by parties instead of coalitions. PR results are available for the 475 plurality constituencies. However, since Valle d'Aosta does not participate in the PR vote, its values have been derived from the plurality vote.

The Netherlands

1888–1917. Only *first ballots* are considered (see Chapter 6 for second ballots). The 1917 election was not considered because an of agreement between the parties that the distribution of seats would remain unchanged. Half of the seats were returned unopposed after the first ballot.

1918–present. *Briefstemmers* (postal voting) exists since 1986 and constitutes a unit apart. These votes are not distributed across provinces or *kamerkieskringen* since the allocation of seats is national. Until 1982 figures of the *Centraal bevolkeningsregister* (or *personenregister*) were part of Zuidholland, that is, the four following *kamerkieskringen*: Rotterdam (no. 11), 's-Gravenhage (no. 12), Leiden (no. 13), and Dordrecht (no. 14).

Norway

1815–1903. Indirect elections took place. Since 1882 party results are available. Information includes votes in the primary elections for *Høire* and *Venstre*.

1906–18. Only first ballots are considered.

1921–present. *Fellelister* in 1949: when possible, votes were redistributed among the parties forming these alliances; otherwise, *Fellelister* have been excluded from computations.

Portugal

1975–present. Party (regional) alliances:

1. *Aliança democrática*, a coalition formed for the 1979 and 1980 elections including the *Partido social democráta*, the *Centro democrático social* (the former *Partido democrático popular*) and the *Partido popular-monárquico*. This coalition, however, did not exist in the two autonomous regions (Açores and Madeira). In these two constituencies, the *Centro democrático social* and *Partido social democráta* contested the elections of 1979 and 1980 as independent lists.

2. In the 1980 election, the *Partido socialista português* formed an electoral alliance with the *União de esquerda para a democracia socialista* and the *Associação social democráta independente* called the *Frente republicana e socialista*. As for (1), the coalition was not extended to the two autonomous regions. In this case, the votes for the *Partido socialista português* in the two autonomous regions were incorporated with the votes of the *Frente republicana e socialista*. Furthermore, the Socialist name was maintained.

3. The *Partido comunista português*, from 1979 to 1985, formed an alliance with the *Movimiento democrático português* called *Aliança povo unido*. Since 1987, the alliance has included the *Movimiento ecologista português/ Os verdes* (since 1991 the *Partido ecologista os verdes*) and is called the *Coligação democrática unitária*. The Communist label has been maintained for the sake of continuity.

Sweden

1866–1908. Indirect elections were not considered. No party figures were available. In 1887 two elections were held. 1911–20. In 1914 two elections were held.

Switzerland

1848–1917. Only first ballots are considered. Uncontested constituencies are not applicable because of the level of aggregation of the data (cantons instead of constituencies). Six cantons are missing until 1869 because of open voting (see Appendix 3). In subsequent elections, these small cantons were often characterized by uncontested elections. The party affiliation of the unopposed candidate is not known. During 1896–1917, the Democrats of Zürich have not been added to the Radicals (*Schweizerische Freisinnig-Demokratische Partei*). The Liberals of Zürich are ranged under Liberal-Conservatives rather than under Radicals. Because of multiple voting and *panachage*, figures based on "fictitious voter" estimates were devised by the *Bundesamt für Statistik* (votes obtained by a party multiplied by the ratio between the total valid ballots obtained in each canton and the total votes expressed in each canton).

United Kingdom (Britain)

1832–present. Analysis limited to Britain (for Ireland 1832–1918 see Chapter 6; Northern Ireland for 1922–present excluded). Sums of votes for candidates of the same party were considered instead of single candidates. Until 1945, the CRII could not be computed because of missing information on voters. Valid votes could not replace voters' figures because of multiple voting (as many votes as seats to be returned in a constituency). In 1910 and 1974 two elections were held in the same year.

Appendix 5

Sources

The election-by-election list of both *official* (periodical publications or series, statistical yearbooks, and retrospective volumes by ministries and national statistical offices) and *secondary sources* (mainly work by private scholars or academic research projects) of electoral results by constituencies is available for each country in *EWE-1815* (pp. 1017–53). A comment on the birth and development of election statistics is also available, as well as the list, addresses, and websites of the major national and international electronic archives and databases (see Appendix 2, "A Note on Election Statistics," in *EWE-1815*, pp. 1005–15).

References

Abizadeh, A., 2002. Does Liberal Democracy Presuppose a Cultural Nation? Four Arguments. *American Political Science Review* 96: 495–509.

Agnew, J., 1987. *Place and Politics: The Geographical Mediation of State and Society.* London: Allen and Unwin.

1988. "Better Thieves Than Reds"? The Nationalisation Thesis and the Possibility of a Geography of Italian Politics. *Political Geography Quarterly* 12: 307–21.

Alber, J., 1982. *Vom Armenhaus zum Wohlfahrtsstaat: Analysen zur Entwicklung der Sozialversicherung in Westeuropa.* Frankfurt-am-Main: Campus.

Alker, H., Jr., 1969. *A Typology of Ecological Fallacies.* In Dogan and Rokkan (1969b: 69–86).

Allardt, E. and Y. Littunen, eds., 1964. *Cleavages, Ideologies, and Party Systems: Contributions to Comparative Political Sociology* (Transactions of the Westermarck Society: Volume 10). Helsinki: Academic Bookstore.

Allardt, E. and P. Pesonen, 1967. *Cleavages in Finnish Politics.* In Lipset and Rokkan (1967b: 325–66).

Allardt, E. and S. Rokkan, eds., 1970. *Mass Politics: Studies in Political Sociology.* New York: The Free Press.

Alliès, P., 1980. *L'Invention du Territoire* (Critique du Droit, no. 6). Grenoble: Presses Universitaires.

Allison, P., 1978. Measures of Inequality. *American Sociological Review* 43: 865–80.

Almond, G. and J. Coleman, eds., 1960. *The Politics of Developing Areas.* Princeton, N.J.: Princeton University Press.

Almond, G. and B. Powell, 1966. *Comparative Politics: A Developmental Approach.* Boston: Little, Brown, and Co.

Almond, G. and S. Verba, 1963. *The Civic Culture: Political Attitudes and Democracy in Five Nations.* Princeton, N.J.: Princeton University Press.

Anderson, B., 1983. *Imagined Communities: Reflections on the Origin and Spread of Nationalism.* London: Verso.

Anderson, M., 1974. *Conservative Politics in France.* London: Allen and Unwin.

ed., 1983. *Frontier Regions in Western Europe.* London: Cass.

References

1997. *Frontiers: Territory and State Formation in the Modern World.* Malden, Mass.: Polity Press.

Apter, D., 1965. *The Politics of Modernization.* Chicago: University of Chicago Press.

Atkinson, A., 1970. On the Measurement of Inequality. *Journal of Economic Theory* 2: 244–63.

Bartolini, B., 1976. Insediamento Subculturale e Distribuzione dei Suffragi in Italia. *Rivista Italiana di Scienza Politica* 6: 481–514.

Bartolini, S., 1993. On Time and Comparative Research. *Journal of Theoretical Politics* 5: 131–67.

1999. Collusion, Competition, and Democracy. Part I. *Journal of Theoretical Politics* 11: 435–70.

2000a. Collusion, Competition, and Democracy: Part II. *Journal of Theoretical Politics* 12: 33–65.

2000b. *The Political Mobilization of the European Left, 1860–1980: The Class Cleavage.* Cambridge: Cambridge University Press.

2000c. *Old and New Peripheries in the European Process of Territorial Expansion* (Working Paper no. 153). Madrid: Instituto Juan March.

Bartolini, S., D. Caramani, and S. Hug, 1997. A Bibliography on Parties and Party Systems in Europe since 1945. *EURODATA Newsletters* 6: 18–21.

1998. *Parties and Party Systems: A Bibliographic Guide to the Literature on Parties and Party Systems in Europe since 1945 on CD-ROM.* London: Sage.

Bartolini, S. and P. Mair, 1990. *Identity, Competition, and Electoral Availability: The Stabilisation of European Electorates: 1885–1985.* Cambridge: Cambridge University Press.

Behrens, C., 1967. *The Ancien Régime.* London: Harcourt, Brace, and World.

Bendix, R., 1961. The Lower Classes and the Democratic Revolution. *Industrial Relations* 1: 91–116.

1977. *Nation-Building and Citizenship: Studies of Our Changing Social Order* (new enlarged edition). Berkeley: University of California Press.

Bendix, R. and S. Rokkan, 1971. *The Extension of Citizenship to the Lower Classes.* In Dogan and Rose (1971: 12–23).

Benedikt, H., ed., 1954. *Geschichte der Republik Österreich.* Vienna: Verlag für Geschichte und Politik.

Berglund, S., 1990. *Introduction.* In Berglund and Thomsen (1990: 1–11).

Berglund, S. and S. Thomsen, eds., 1990. *Modern Political Ecological Analysis.* Åbo, Sweden: Åbo Akademis Förlag.

Beyme, K. von, 1985. *Political Parties in Western Democracies.* Aldershot, U.K.: Gower.

Bialer, S. and S. Sluzar, eds., 1977. *Radicalism in the Contemporary Age* (Volume 1: *Sources of Contemporary Radicalism*). Boulder, Colo.: Westview Press.

Biorcio, R., 1991. *La Lega come Attore Politico: Dal Federalismo al Populismo Regionalista.* In Mannheimer (1991: 34–82).

Black, C., 1967. *The Dynamics of Modernization: A Study in Comparative History.* New York: Harper and Row.

Blalock, H., 1972. *Social Statistics* (second edition). Tokyo: McGraw-Hill.

References

Board, C., 1969. *Progress in Geography* (Volume 1). London: Edward Arnold.

Bogdanor, V., 1983. *Liberal Party Politics*. Oxford: Oxford University Press.

Bogdanor, V. and W. Field, 1993. Lessons of History: Core and Periphery in British Electoral Behaviour, 1910–92. *Electoral Studies* 12: 203–24.

Bomier-Landowski, A., 1951. *Les Groupes Parlementaires de l'Assemblée Nationale et de la Chambre des Députés de 1871 à 1940*. In Goguel and Dupeux (1951: 75–89).

Brockliss, L. and D. Eastwood, eds., 1997. *A Union of Multiple Identities: The British Isles, c.1750–c.1850*. Manchester: Manchester University Press.

Brubaker, R., 1991. Immigration, Citoyenneté et État-Nation en France et en Allemagne: Une Analyse Historique Comparative. *Les Temps Modernes* 46: 293–332.

1992. *Citizenship and Nationhood in France and Germany*. Cambridge: Cambridge University Press.

Brusa, C., 1984. *Geografia Elettorale nell'Italia del Dopoguerra: Edizione Aggiornata ai Risultati delle Elezioni Politiche 1983*. Milano: Edizioni Unicopli.

Budge, I. and D. Hearl, 1990. Scelte di Voto e Spazio Regionale: Un'Analisi Comparata dei Paesi della Comunità Europea (1968–88). *Quaderni dell'Osservatorio Elettorale* 24: 5–33.

Burnett, N., n.d. *Exit, Voice, and Ireland, 1936–58*. Unpublished manuscript.

1976. *Emigration in Modern Ireland* (doctoral dissertation). Baltimore: Johns Hopkins University.

Büsch, O., ed., 1980. *Wählerbewegung in der europäische Geschichte*. Berlin: Colloquium Verlag.

Butler, D. and D. Stokes, 1974. *Political Change in Britain: The Evolution of Electoral Choice* (second edition). London: Macmillan.

Caramani, D., 1994. La Nazionalizzazione del Voto. *Rivista Italiana di Scienza Politica* 24: 237–85.

1996a. The Nationalisation of Electoral Politics: A Conceptual Reconstruction and a Review of the Literature. *West European Politics* 19: 205–24.

1996b. La Partecipazione Elettorale: Gli Effetti della Competizione Maggioritaria. *Rivista Italiana di Scienza Politica* 26: 585–608.

2000. *Elections in Western Europe since 1815: Electoral Results by Constituencies* [supplemented with CD-ROM]. London and New York: Macmillan (abbreviated as *EWE-1815* in the present volume).

2003a. The End of Silent Elections: The Birth of Electoral Competition, 1832–1915. *Party Politics* 9: 411–43.

2003b. *State Administration and Regional Construction in Central Europe. A Historical Perspective*. In Keating and Hugues (2003: 21–50).

Caramani, D. and S. Hug, 1998. The Literature on European Parties and Party Systems since 1945: A Quantitative Analysis. *European Journal of Political Research* 33: 497–524.

Carrothers, R. and J. Stonecash, 1985. Communications: Comment on Claggett, Flanigan, and Zingale (Vol. 78, March, 1984, pp. 77–91). *American Political Science Review* 79: 1170–71.

References

Chambers, W. and W. Burnham, eds., 1967. *The American Party Systems: Stages of Political Development.* New York: Oxford University Press.

Chhibber, P. and K. Kollman, 1998. Party Aggregation and the Number of Parties in India and the United States. *American Political Science Review* 92: 329–42.

Cipolla, C.-M., 1969. *Literacy and Development in the West.* Harmondsworth, U.K.: Penguin.

ed., 1973. *The Emergence of Industrial Societies.* London: Fontana.

Claggett, W., 1987. The Nationalization of Congressional Turnout. *Western Political Quarterly* 40: 527–33.

Claggett, W., W. Flanigan, and N. Zingale, 1984. Nationalization of the American Electorate. *American Political Science Review* 78: 77–91.

1985. Communications: Reply [to Carrothers and Stonecash (1985)]. *American Political Science Review* 79: 1171–73.

Claunch, J., ed., 1965. *Mathematics Applications in Political Science.* Dallas: The Arnold Foundation.

Coakley, J., 1983. *National Territories and Cultural Frontiers: Conflicts of Principle in the Formation of States in Europe.* In Anderson (1983: 34–49).

ed., 1992. *The Social Origins of Nationalist Movements.* London: Sage.

Coleman, J., 1965. *Education and Political Development.* Princeton, N.J.: Princeton University Press.

Compagna, F., 1950. *La Lotta Politica in Italia nel Secondo Dopoguerra e il Mezzogiorno.* Bari-Roma: Laterza.

Compagna, F. and V. de Caprariis, 1954. *Geografia delle Elezioni Italiane dal 1946 al 1953.* Bologna: Il Mulino.

Connor, W., 1967. Self-Determination: The New Phase. *World Politics* 20: 30–53.

1972. Nation-Building or Nation-Destroying? *World Politics* 24: 319–55.

Converse, P., 1969. *Survey Research and the Decoding of Patterns in Ecological Data.* In Dogan and Rokkan (1969b: 459–485).

Cornford, J., 1970. *Aggregate Election Data and British Party Alignments, 1885–1910.* In Allardt and Rokkan (1970: 107–16).

Coulter, P., 1989. *Measuring Inequality: A Methodological Handbook.* Boulder, Colo.: Westview Press.

Cowell, F., 1977. *Measuring Inequality.* Oxford: Philip Allan.

Cox, K., 1969a. *The Voting Decision in a Spatial Context.* In Board et al. (1969: 81–117).

1969b. *The Spatial Structuring of Information Flow and Partisan Attitudes.* In Dogan and Rokkan (1969b: 157–85).

1969c. *The Spatial Evolution of National Voting Response Surfaces: Theory and Measurement* (Discussion Paper no. 9). Columbus: Department of Geography, Ohio State University.

1970. *Geography, Social Context, and Voting Behavior in Wales, 1861–1951.* In Allardt and Rokkan (1970: 117–59).

Craig, F., 1977. *British Parliamentary Election Results 1832–85.* London: Macmillan.

Daalder, H., 1966. *The Netherlands: Opposition in a Segmented Society.* In Dahl (1966: 188–236).

References

1971a. On Building Consociational Nations: The Cases of the Netherlands and Switzerland. *International Social Science Journal* 23: 355–70.

1971b. The Consociational Democracy Theme. *World Politics* 26: 604–21.

1973. *Building Consociational Nations*. In Eisenstadt and Rokkan (1973b: 14–31).

ed., 1987. *Party Systems in Denmark, Austria, Switzerland, the Netherlands, and Belgium*. London: Francis Pinter.

Daalder, H. and P. Mair, eds., 1983. *Western European Party Systems: Continuity and Change*. London: Sage.

Dahl, R., 1957. *A Preface to Democratic Theory*. Chicago: University of Chicago Press.

ed., 1966. *Political Oppositions in Western Democracies*. New Haven, Conn.: Yale University Press.

Dahl, R. and E. Tufte, 1973. *Size and Democracy*. Stanford, Calif.: Stanford University Press.

Denver, D. and H. Hands, 1974. Marginality and Turnout in British General Elections. *British Journal of Political Science* 4: 17–35.

Deutsch, K., 1953. *Nationalism and Social Communication: An Inquiry into the Foundations of Nationality*. Cambridge, Mass.: The MIT Press.

1961. Social Mobilization and Political Development. *American Political Science Review* 55: 493–514.

1966. *Nation-Building and National Development: Some Issues for Political Research*. In Deutsch and Foltz (1966: 1–16).

1969. *Nationalism and Its Alternatives*. New York: Knopf.

1976. *Die Schweiz als paradigmatischer Fall politischer Integration*. Bern: Haupt.

1981. *On Nationalism, World Regions, and the Nature of the West*. In Torsvik (1981: 51–93).

Deutsch, K. and W. Foltz, eds., 1966. *Nation-Building*. New York: Atherton Press.

De Winter, L. and H. Türsan, eds., 1998. *Regionalist Parties in Western Europe*. London and New York: Routledge.

Dogan, M. and S. Rokkan, 1969a. *Introduction*. In Dogan and Rokkan (1969b: 1–15).

eds., 1969b. *Quantitative Ecological Analysis in the Social Sciences*. Cambridge, Mass.: The MIT Press.

Dogan, M. and R. Rose, eds., 1971. *European Politics: A Reader*. Boston: Little, Brown, and Co.

Downs, A., 1957. *An Economic Theory of Democracy*. New York: Harper and Row.

Dumont, L., 1991. *Homo Æqualis II. L'Idéologie Allemande: France-Allemagne et Retour*. Paris: Gallimard.

Dunn, J., Jr., 1972. Consociational Democracy and Language Conflict: A Comparison of the Belgian and Swiss Experiences. *Comparative Political Studies* 5: 3–40.

Duverger, M., 1950. *L'Influence des Systèmes Électoraux sur la Vie Politique*. Paris: Presses de la Fondation Nationale des Sciences Politiques.

1951a. *Les Partis Politiques*. Paris: Armand Colin.

1951b. The Influence of the Electoral System on Political Life. *International Social Science Bulletin* 3: 314–52.

References

Dyson, K., 1980. *The State Tradition in Western Europe: A Study of an Idea and an Institution*. Oxford: Robertson.

Eisenstadt, S. and S. Rokkan, eds., 1973a. *Building States and Nations* (Volume 1). Beverly Hills, Calif.: Sage.

1973b. *Building States and Nations* (Volume 2). Beverly Hills, Calif.: Sage.

Elazar, D., 1997. Contrasting Unitary and Federal Systems. *International Political Science Review* 18: 237–51.

Elklit, J., J. Noack, and O. Tonsgaard, 1981. *A National Group as a Social System: The German Minority in North Schleswig*. In Torsvik (1981: 296–318).

Ersson, S., K. Janda, and J.-E. Lane, 1985. Ecology of Party Strength in Western Europe: A Regional Analysis. *Comparative Political Studies* 18: 170–205.

Eskelinen, H. and F. Snickers, eds., 1995. *Competitive European Peripheries*. Berlin: Springer.

Faul, E., ed., 1960. *Wahlen und Wähler in Westdeutschland*. Villingen: Ring Verlag.

Finer, S., 1974. State-Building, State Boundaries, and Border Control: An Essay on Certain Aspects of the First Phase of State-Building in Western Europe Considered in the Light of the Rokkan–Hirschman Model. *Social Science Information* 13: 79–126.

Flora, P., 1972. Historische Prozesse sozialer Mobilisierung: Urbanisierung und Alphabetisierung, 1850–1965. *Zeitschrift für Soziologie* 1: 85–117.

1977. *Quantitative Historical Sociology: A Trend Report and Bibliography* (Current Sociology no. 23). The Hague and Paris: Mouton.

1999. *Introduction and Interpretation*. In Rokkan (1999: 1–91).

2000. Externe Grenzbildung und interne Strukturierung – Europa und seine Nationen. Eine Rokkan'sche Forschungsperspektive. *Berliner Journal für Soziologie* 10: 151–65.

Flora, P. et al., 1983–87. *State, Economy, and Society in Western Europe 1815–1975: A Data Handbook in Two Volumes*. Volume 1: Flora, P., J. Alber, and F. Kraus, 1983. *The Growth of Mass Democracies and Welfare States*. Volume 2: Flora, P., F. Kraus, and W. Pfenning, 1987. *The Growth of Industrial Societies and Capitalist Economies*. Frankfurt-am-Main: Campus.

Foucher, M., 1986. *L'Invention des Frontières*. Paris: La Documentation Française.

Fox, J., 1994. The Difficult Transition from Clientelism to Citizenship: Lessons from Mexico. *World Politics* 46: 151–84.

1997. The Salience of Religious Issues in Ethnic Conflicts: A Large-*N* Study. *Nationalism and Ethnic Politics* 3: 1–19.

Frandsen, S., 1995. *The Discovery of Jutland: The Existence of a Regional Dimension in Denmark, 1814–64*. In Sørensen (1995: 111–25).

Franklin, M., T. Mackie, and H. Valen, 1992. *Electoral Change: Responses to Evolving Social and Attitudinal Structures in Western Countries*. Cambridge: Cambridge University Press.

Friedrich, C., 1968. *Trends of Federalism in Theory and Praxis*. New York: Praeger.

Fustel de Coulanges, N., 1957. *La Cité Antique*. Paris: Achette.

Ganguillet, G., 1985. *Die Jurafrage als peripherer Minderheitenkonflikt*. In Kriesi (1985: 81–126).

References

Garvin, T., 1974. Political Cleavage, Party Politics, and Urbanisation in Ireland: The Case of the Periphery-Dominated Centre. *European Journal of Political Research* 2: 307–27.

Gellner, E., 1983. *Nations and Nationalism*. Ithaca, N.Y.: Cornell University Press.

Gerlich, P., 1987. *Consociationalism to Competition: The Austrian Party System since 1945*. In Daalder (1987: 61–106).

Gini, C., 1933. *Trattato Elementare di Statistica*. Milano: Giuffrè.

Girod, R., 1964a. *Geography of the Swiss Party System*. In Allardt and Littunen (1964: 132–61).

1964b. Géographie des Partis en Suisse. *Revue Française de Science Politique* 14: 1114–33.

Goguel, F. and G. Dupeux, avec la collaboration de A. Bomier-Landowski, 1951. *Sociologie Électorale. Esquisse d'un Bilan: Guide des Recherches*. Paris: Armand Colin.

Gottmann, J., 1973. *The Significance of Territory*. Charlottesville: University Press of Virginia.

ed., 1980. *Centre and Periphery: Spatial Variations in Politics*. Beverly Hills, Calif.: Sage.

Gourevitch, P., 1978. *Reforming the Napoleonic State: The Creation of Regional Governments in France and Italy*. In Tarrow, Katzenstein, and Graziano (1978: 28–63).

Greenstein, F. and N. Polsby, eds., 1975. *Handbook of Political Science*. Volume 5: *Governmental Institutions and Processes*. Reading, Mass.: Addison-Wesley.

Grofman, B. and A. Lijphart, eds., 1986. *Electoral Laws and Their Political Consequences*. New York: Agathon Press.

Grofman, B. et al., eds., 1982. *Representation and Redistricting Issues*. Lexington, Ky.: Lexington Books.

Gruner, E., 1969. *Die Parteien der Schweiz*. Bern: Franke.

Gruner, E., Andrey, G., et al., 1978. *Die Wahlen in dem Schweizerischen Nationalrat – Les Élections au Conseil National Suisse, 1848–1919* (three volumes). Bern: Franke.

Hanham, H., 1959. *Elections and Party Management: Politics in the Time of Disraeli and Gladstone*. London: Longmans.

Harvie, C., 1994. *The Rise of Regional Europe*. London: Routledge.

Hearl, D., I. Budge, and B. Pearson, 1996. Distinctiveness of Regional Voting: A Comparative Analysis Across the European Community (1979–83). *Electoral Studies* 15: 167–82.

Hechter, M., 1975. *Internal Colonialism: The Celtic Fringe in British National Development, 1536–1966*. London: Routledge and Kegan Paul.

Hintze, O., 1970. *Gesammelte Abhandlungen*. Volume 1: *Soziologie und Geschichte* (edited by G. Oestreich). Göttingen: Vandenhoeck und Ruprecht.

Hirschman, A., 1970. *Exit, Voice, and Loyalty: Responses to Decline in Firms, Organizations, and States*. Cambridge, Mass.: Harvard University Press.

1974. "Exit, Voice, and Loyalty": Further Reflections and a Survey of Recent Contributions. *Social Science Information* 13: 7–26.

329

1978. Exit, Voice, and the State. *World Politics* 31: 90–107.

1993. Exit, Voice, and the Fate of the German Democratic Republic: An Essay in Conceptual History. *World Politics* 45: 173–202.

Hoggart, K. and E. Kofman, eds., 1986. *Politics, Geography, and Social Stratification.* London: Croom Helm.

Holler, M., ed., 1987. *The Logic of Multiparty Systems.* Dordrecht: Kluwer Academic Publications.

Hoschka, P. and H. Schunck, 1976. *Regional Stability of Voting Behaviour in Federal Elections: A Longitudinal Aggregate Data Analysis.* In Kaase and von Beyme (1976: 31–52).

Hotteling, H., 1929. Stability in Competition. *The Economic Journal* 39: 41–57.

Immerfall, S., 1992. Macrohistorical Models in Historical-Electoral Research: A Fresh Look at the Stein–Rokkan Tradition. *Historical Social Research-Historische Sozialforschung* 17: 103–16.

Janda, K., 1989. Regional and Religious Support of Political Parties and Effects on Their Issue Positions. *International Political Science Review* 10: 349–70.

Janowitz, M., ed., 1961. *Community Political Systems.* Westport, Conn.: Greenwood Press.

Johnston, R., 1976. Contagion in Neighbourhoods. *Environment and Planning A* 8: 581–86.

1981a. Testing the Butler–Stokes Model of a Polarization Effect Around the National Swing in Partisan Preferences: England, 1979. *British Journal of Political Science* 9: 113–17.

1981b. Regional Variations in British Voting Trends: 1966–79: Test of an Ecological Model. *Regional Studies* 15: 23–32.

1985. *The Geography of English Politics.* London: Croom Helm.

Johnston, R. and A. Hay, 1982. On the Parameters of Uniform Swing in Single-Member Constituency Electoral Systems. *Environment and Planning A* 14: 61–74.

Johnston, R., A. O'Neill, and P. Taylor, 1987. *The Geography of Party Support: Comparative Studies in Electoral Stability.* In Holler (1987: 265–79).

Kaase, M. and K. von Beyme, eds., 1976. *Elections and Parties.* Volume 3: *German Political Studies.* London: Sage.

Katz, R., 1973a. The Attribution of Variance in Electoral Returns: An Alternative Measurement Technique. *American Political Science Review* 67: 817–28.

1973b. Rejoinder to "Comment" by Donald E. Stokes. *American Political Science Review* 67: 832–33.

1984. Dimensions of Partisan Conflict in Swiss Cantons. *Comparative Political Studies* 16: 505–27.

Kautsky, J., 1972. *The Political Consequences of Modernization.* New York: Wiley.

Kawato, S., 1987. Nationalization and Partisan Realignment in Congressional Elections. *American Political Science Review* 81: 1235–50.

Keating, M., 1988. *State and Regional Nationalism: Territorial Politics and the European State.* New York: Harvester Wheatsheaf.

1997. *The Political Economy of Regionalism.* In Keating and Loughlin (1997: 17–40).

References

1998. *The New Regionalism in Western Europe: Territorial Restructuring and Political Change*. Cheltenham, U.K.: Edward Elgar.

Keating, M. and J. Hugues, eds., 2003. *The Regional Challenge in Central and Eastern Europe: Territorial Restructuring and European Integration*. Brussels: Presses Interuniversitaires Européennes.

Keating, M. and J. Loughlin, eds., 1997. *The Political Economy of Regionalism*. London: Frank Cass.

Kerr, H., 1974. *Switzerland: Social Cleavages and Partisan Conflict*. London and Beverly Hills, Calif.: Sage Professional Papers in Contemporary Political Sociology (no. 2).

Key, V., Jr., 1964. *Politics, Parties, and Pressure Groups* (fifth edition). New York: Crowell.

Kirchheimer, O., 1966. *The Transformation of the European Party Systems*. In La Palombara and Weiner (1966b: 177–200).

Kirchner, E., 1988a. *Introduction*. In Kirchner (1988b: 1–15).

  ed., 1988b. *Liberal Parties in Western Europe*. Cambridge: Cambridge University Press.

Koenigsberger, H., 1971. *Estates and Revolutions: Essays in Early Modern European History*. Ithaca, N.Y.: Cornell University Press.

Kohler-Koch, B., 1998. *La Renaissance de la Dimension Territoriale en Europe*. Florence: EUI Working Papers (Robert Schuman Centre 98/38).

Kriesi, H., 1990. Federalism and Pillarization: The Netherlands and Switzerland Compared. *Acta Politica* 25: 433–50.

  1993. *Political Mobilization and Social Change: The Dutch Case in Comparative Perspective*. Aldershot, U.K.: Avebury.

  ed., 1985. *Bewegung in der schweizer Politik: Fallstudien zu politischen Mobilisierungsprozessen in der Schweiz*. Frankfurt-am-Main: Campus.

Langbein, L. and A. Lichtman, 1978. *Ecological Inference*. London and Beverly Hills, Calif.: Sage University Papers (Quantitative Applications in the Social Sciences, no. 07–010).

La Palombara, J. and M. Weiner, 1966a. *The Origin and Development of Political Parties*. In La Palombara and Weiner (1966b: 3–42).

  eds., 1966b. *Political Parties and Political Development*. Princeton, N.J.: Princeton University Press.

Laski, H., 1936. *The Rise of European Liberalism*. London: Allen and Unwin.

Lasswell, H., 1951. *The World Revolution of Our Time: A Framework for Basic Policy Research*. Stanford, Calif.: Stanford University Press.

Layton-Henry, Z., ed., 1982. *Conservative Politics in Western Europe*. London: Macmillan.

Lee, A., 1988. *The Persistence of Difference: Electoral Change in Cornwall*. Plymouth: Paper delivered at the Political Studies Association Conference.

Lehmbruch, G., 1967. *Proporzdemokratie*. Tübingen: Mohr.

Lerner, D., 1958. *The Passing of Traditional Society: Modernizing the Middle East*. Glencoe, Ill.: The Free Press.

Lieberson, S., ed., 1981. *Language Diversity and Language Contact*. Stanford, Calif.: Stanford University Press.

References

Lieberson, S., G. Dalto, and M. Marsden, 1981. *The Course of Mother-Tongue Diversity in Nations*. In Lieberson (1981: 48–82).

Lijphart, A., 1968. *The Politics of Accommodation: Pluralism and Democracy in the Netherlands*. Berkeley: University of California Press.

1971. Comparative Politics and Comparative Method. *American Political Science Review* 65: 682–93.

1979. Religious vs. Linguistic vs. Class Voting: The "Crucial Experiment" of Comparing Belgium, Canada, South Africa, and Switzerland. *American Political Science Review* 73: 442–58.

ed., 1981. *Conflict and Coexistence in Belgium: The Dynamics of a Culturally Divided Society*. Berkeley, Calif.: Institute of International Studies.

1994. *Electoral Systems and Party Systems: A Study of Twenty-Seven Democracies 1945–90*. Oxford: Oxford University Press.

1999. *Patterns of Democracy: Government Forms and Performance in Thirty-Six Countries*. New Haven, Conn.: Yale University Press.

Linz, J., 1967a. *The Party System of Spain: Past and Future*. In Lipset and Rokkan (1967b: 197–282).

1967b. *Cleavage and Consensus in West German Politics: The Early Fifties*. In Lipset and Rokkan (1967b: 283–321).

1973. *Early State-Building and Late Peripheral Nationalisms Against the State: The Case of Spain*. In Eisenstadt and Rokkan (1973b: 32–116).

1976. Patterns of Land Tenure, Division of Labor, and Voting Behavior in Europe. *Comparative Politics* 8: 365–430.

Linz, J. and A. de Miguel, 1966. *Within-Nation Differences and Comparisons: The Eight Spains*. In Merritt and Rokkan (1966: 267–319).

Lipset, S., 1977. *Why No Socialism in the United States?* In Bialer and Sluzar (1977: 31–149).

Lipset, S. and R. Bendix, 1992. *Social Mobility in Industrial Society*. New Brunswick, N.J.: Transaction Publishers.

Lipset, S. and S. Rokkan, 1967a. *Cleavage Structures, Party Systems, and Voter Alignments: An Introduction*. In Lipset and Rokkan (1967b: 1–64).

eds., 1967b. *Party Systems and Voter Alignments: Cross-National Perspectives*. New York: The Free Press.

Lorwin, V., 1966. *Belgium: Religion, Class, and Language in National Politics*. In Dahl (1966: 147–87).

MacDonald, J., 1963–64. Agricultural Organization, Migration, and Labour Militancy in Rural Italy. *Economic History Review* 16: 61–75.

Mackenzie, W., 1981. *Peripheries and Nationbuilding: The Case of Scotland*. In Torsvik (1981: 153–80).

Madgwick, P. and R. Rose, eds., 1982. *The Territorial Dimension in United Kingdom Politics*. London: Macmillan.

Mair, P., 1987. *Party Organization, Vote Management, and Candidate Selection: Toward the Nationalization of Electoral Strategy in Ireland*. In Penniman and Farrell (1987: 104–30).

References

Mair, P. and J. Zielonka, eds., 2002. *The Enlarged European Union: Diversity and Adaptation*. London: Frank Cass.

Mannheim, K., 1940. *Man and Society in an Age of Reconstruction*. London: Routledge and Kegan Paul.

Mannheimer, R., ed., 1991. *La Lega Lombarda*. Milano: Feltrinelli.

Manning, D., 1976. *Liberalism*. London: Dent.

Manning, M., 1972. *Irish Political Parties: An Introduction*. Dublin: Gill and Macmillan.

Marshall, T., 1964. *Class, Citizenship, and Social Development* (including the 1950 original essay *Citizenship and Social Class*). Garden City, N.Y.: Doubleday.

Martin, J. and L. Gray, 1971. Measurement of Relative Variation: Sociological Examples. *American Sociological Review* 36: 496–502.

McKenzie, R. and A. Silver, 1967. *The Delicate Experiment: Industrialism, Conservatism, and Working-Class Tories in England*. In Lipset and Rokkan (1967b: 115–25).

McLean, I., 1973. The Problem of Proportionate Swing. *Political Studies* 21: 57–63.

McLean, I. and D. Butler, eds., 1996. *Fixing the Boundaries: Defining and Redefining Single-Member Electoral Districts*. Aldershot, U.K.: Dartmouth.

McRae, K., 1983. *Conflict and Compromise in Multilingual Societies: Switzerland*. Waterloo, Belgium: Wilfrid Laurier University Press.

1986. *Conflict and Compromise in Multilingual Societies: Belgium*. Waterloo, Belgium: Wilfrid Laurier University Press.

Merritt, R. and S. Rokkan, eds., 1966. *Comparing Nations*. New Haven, Conn.: Yale University Press.

Millar, S., 1995. *The Meaning of Language: Ethnolinguistic Identity in the United Kingdom*. In Sørensen (1995: 173–88).

Miller, J., K. Kollman, and S. Page, 1997. Landscape Formation in a Spatial Voting Model. *Economics Letters* 55: 121–30.

1998. Political Parties and Electoral Landscapes. *British Journal of Political Science* 28: 139–58.

Mintzel, A., 1990. *Political and Socio-Economic Developments in the Postwar Era: The Case of Bavaria, 1945–89*. In Rohe (1990: 145–78).

Molle, W., A. van Holst, and H. Smit, 1980. *Regional Disparity and Economic Development in the European Community*. Farnborough, U.K.: Saxon House.

Monroe, B., 1994. Disproportionality and Malapportionment: Measuring Electoral Inequity. *Electoral Studies* 13: 132–49.

Moore, B., Jr., 1966. *Social Origins of Dictatorship and Democracy: Lord and Peasant in the Making of the Modern World*. Boston: Beacon Press.

Morgan, K., 1980. *Rebirth of a Nation: Wales, 1880–1980*. Oxford: Oxford University Press.

Mosse, G., 1975. *The Nationalization of the Masses: Political Symbolism and Mass Movements in Germany from the Napoleonic Wars Through the Third Reich*. New York: Fertig.

References

Moulin, H., 1988. *Axioms of Cooperative Decision Making*. Cambridge: Cambridge University Press.

Nicolacopoulos, I., 1984. *Géographie Électorale de la Grèce depuis 1945: Vers la Nationalisation du Vote*. Paper delivered at the ECPR Joint Sessions of Workshops, Salzburg.

Niemi, R. and H. Weisberg, eds., 1976. *Controversies in American Voting Behavior*. San Francisco: Freeman.

Nordengård, J., 1949. *Valgene til Rigsdagen i 100 aar*. Roskilde, Denmark: Eget Forlag.

Oberndörfer, D. and K. Schmitt, 1991. *Parteien und Regionale Politische Traditionen in der BRD*. Berlin: Duncker und Humbolt.

O'Loughlin, J. and H. van der Wusten, eds., 1993. *The New Political Geography of Eastern Europe*. London and New York: Belhaven Press.

Orbell, J., 1970. An Information-Flow Theory of Community Influence. *Journal of Politics* 32: 322–38.

Palmer, R., 1959. *The Age of Democratic Revolutions: The Challenge*. Princeton, N.J.: Princeton University Press.

Pavsic, R., 1985. Esiste una Tendenza all'Omogeneizzazione Territoriale nei Partiti Italiani? *Rivista Italiana di Scienza Politica* 15: 69–97.

Pedersen, M., 1983. *Is There Still Persistence? Electoral Change in Western Europe, 1948–79*. In Daalder and Mair (1983: 67–94).

Pelling, H., 1967. *Social Geography of British Elections, 1885–1910*. London: Macmillan.

Penniman, H. and B. Farrell, eds., 1987. *Ireland at the Polls 1981, 1982, and 1987: A Study of Four General Elections*. Washington, D.C.: American Enterprise Institute.

Pesonen, P., 1974. *Finland: Party Support in a Fragmented System*. In Rose (1974: 271–314).

Putnam, R., 1993. *Making Democracy Work: Civic Traditions in Modern Italy*. Princeton, N.J.: Princeton University Press.

Rae, D. and M. Taylor, 1970. *The Analysis of Political Cleavages*. New Haven, Conn.: Yale University Press.

Rantala, O., 1967. The Political Regions of Finland. *Scandinavian Political Studies* 2: 117–40.

Rhodes, M., ed., 1995. *Regions and the New Europe*. Manchester: Manchester University Press.

Riker, W., 1975. *Federalism*. In Greenstein and Polsby (1975: 93–172).

Ritter, G. and M. Niehuss, 1991. *Wahlen in Deutschland, 1946–91: Ein Handbuch*. Munich: Beck.

Robinson, W., 1950. Ecological Correlations and the Behavior of Individuals. *American Sociological Review* 15: 351–57.

Rohe, K., ed., 1990. *Elections, Parties, and Political Traditions: Social Foundations of German Parties and Party Systems, 1867–1987*. New York: Berg.

Rokkan, S., 1961. Mass Suffrage, Secret Voting, and Political Participation. *European Journal of Sociology* 1: 132–52.

References

1966a. *Norway: Numerical Democracy and Corporate Pluralism.* In Dahl (1966: 70–115).

1966b. *Electoral Mobilization, Party Competition, and National Integration.* In La Palombara and Weiner (1966b: 241–65).

1970a. *Citizens, Elections, Parties.* Oslo and New York: Universitetsforlaget-McKay.

1970b. The Growth and Structuring of Mass Politics in Western Europe: Reflections of Possible Models of Explanation. *Scandinavian Political Studies* (Yearbook) 5: 65–83.

1973. *Cities, States, and Nations: A Dimensional Model for the Study of Contrasts in Development.* In Eisenstadt and Rokkan (1973a: 73–97).

1974a. Politics Between Economy and Culture: An International Seminar on Albert O. Hirschman's Exit, Voice, and Loyalty. *Social Science Information* 13: 27–38.

1974b. Entries, Voices, Exits: Towards a Possible Generalization of the Hirschman Model. *Social Science Information* 13: 39–53.

1975. *Dimensions of State Formation and Nation-Building: A Possible Paradigm for Research on Variations Within Europe.* In Tilly (1975: 562–600).

1977. Towards a Generalised Concept of Verzuiling. *Political Studies* 25: 563–70.

1999. *State Formation, Nation-Building, and Mass Politics in Europe: The Theory of Stein Rokkan* (edited by P. Flora, with S. Kuhnle and D. Urwin). Oxford: Oxford University Press.

Rokkan, S. and F. Aarebrot, 1969. The Norwegian Archive of Historical Ecological Data: Progress Report. *Social Sciences Information* 8: 77–84.

Rokkan, S. and S. Lipset, 1967. *Geography, Religion, and Social Class: Cross-Cutting Cleavages in Norwegian Politics.* In Lipset and Rokkan (1967b: 367–444).

Rokkan, S. and J. Meyriat, eds., 1969. *International Guide to Electoral Statistics.* Volume 1: *National Elections in Western Europe.* The Hague and Paris: Mouton.

Rokkan, S. and D. Urwin, eds., 1982. *The Politics of Territorial Identity: Studies in European Regionalism.* London: Sage.

1983. *Economy, Territory, Identity: Politics of West European Peripheries.* London: Sage.

Rokkan, S., D. Urwin, F. Aarebrot, P. Malaba, and T. Sande, 1987. *Centre–Periphery Structures in Europe: An ISSC Workbook in Comparative Analysis.* Frankfurt and New York: Campus.

Rokkan, S. and H. Valen, 1970. *Regional Contrasts in Norwegian Politics: A Review of Data from Official Statistics and from Sample Surveys.* In Allardt and Rokkan (1970: 190–247).

Rose, R., 1970a. *The United Kingdom as a Multi-National State.* In Rose (1970b: 115–50).

ed., 1970b. *Studies in British Politics: A Reader in Political Sociology.* London: Macmillan.

1974. *Electoral Behavior: A Comparative Handbook.* New York: The Free Press.

References

Rose, R. and D. Urwin, 1970. Persistence and Change in Western Party Systems since 1945. *Political Studies* 18: 287–319.

1975. *Regional Differentiation and Political Unity in Western Nations.* London and Beverly Hills, Calif.: Sage Professional Papers in Contemporary Political Sociology (no. 06–007).

Rossiter, C., 1968. *Conservatism.* In Sills (1968: 290–94).

Russett, B., 1964. Inequality and Instability: The Relation of Land Tenure to Politics. *World Politics* 16: 442–54.

Sahlins, P., 1989. *Boundaries: The Making of France and Spain in the Pyrenees.* Berkeley: University of California Press.

Salvadori, M., 1977. *The Liberal Heresy: Origins and Historical Development.* London: Macmillan.

Sartori, G., 1968. *The Sociology of Parties: A Critical Review.* In Stammer (1968: 1–25).

1986. *The Influence of Electoral Systems: Faulty Laws or Faulty Method?* In Grofman and Lijphart (1986: 43–68).

1991. Comparing and Miscomparing. *Journal of Theoretical Politics* 3: 243–57.

Schadee, H., 1987. *A Regression Model for the Disaggregation of Aggregate (Electoral) Data.* Paper delivered at the ECPR Joint Sessions of Workshops, Amsterdam.

Schattschneider, E., 1960. *The Semisovereign People: A Realist's View of Democracy in America.* New York: Holt, Rinehart, and Winston.

Schmitt, H. and J. Thomassen, 1999. *Political Representation and Legitimacy in the European Union.* Oxford: Oxford University Press.

Schmitter, P. and G. Lehmbruch, eds., 1979. *Trends Toward Corporatist Intermediation.* Beverly Hills, Calif.: Sage.

Schutz, R., 1951. On the Measurement of Income Inequality. *American Political Science Review* 41: 107–22.

Scott, A. and M. Storper, 1992a. *Industrialization and Regional Development.* In Scott and Storper (1992b: 3–17).

eds., 1992b. *Pathways to Industrialization and Regional Development.* London and New York: Routledge.

Sills, D., ed., 1968. *International Encyclopedia of the Social Sciences.* New York: Macmillan.

Simmel, G., 1955. *Conflict and the Web of Group Affiliations.* Glencoe, Ill.: The Free Press.

Skocpol, T., 1979. *States and Social Revolutions: A Comparative Analysis of France, Russia, and China.* Cambridge: Cambridge University Press.

Smith, A., 1986. *The Ethnic Origins of Nations.* Oxford: Blackwell.

Smith, G., 1988. *Between Left and Right: The Ambivalence of European Liberalism.* In Kirchner (1988b: 16–28).

Smithies, A., 1941. Optimum Location in Spatial Competition. *The Journal of Political Economy* 49: 423–39.

Smithson, M., 1982. On Relative Dispersion: A New Solution for Some Old Problems. *Quality and Quantity* 16: 261–71.

References

Sombart, W., 1906. *Warum gibt es in den Vereinigten Staten keinen Sozialismus?* Tübingen: Mohr. Reprinted in *Archiv für Sozialwissenschaft und Sozialpolitik* 21, 1992. English translation 1976. *Why Is There No Socialism in the United States?* London: Macmillan.

Sørensen, N., ed., 1995. *European Identities: Cultural Diversity and Integration in Europe since 1700*. Odense, Denmark: Odense University Press.

Stammer, O., ed., 1968. *Party Systems, Party Organizations, and the Politics of New Masses*. Berlin: Institut für Politische Wissenschaft an der Freien Universität Berlin.

Steinberg, J., 1996. *Why Switzerland?* (second edition). Cambridge: Cambridge University Press.

Steiner, J., 1974. *Amicable Agreement versus Majority Rule: Conflic Resolution in Switzerland*. Chapel Hill: University of North Carolina Press.

Sternberger, D. and B. Vogel, eds., in collaboration with D. Nohlen, 1969. *Die Wahl der Parlamente und anderer Staatsorgane: Ein Handbuch* (two half-volumes). Volume 1: *Europa*. Berlin: Walter de Gruyter.

Stokes, D., 1965. *A Variance Components Model of Political Effects*. In Claunch (1965: 61–85).

1967. *Parties and the Nationalization of Electoral Forces*. In Chambers and Burnham (1967: 182–202) (reprinted in Stokes [1976]).

1973. Comment: On the Measurement of Electoral Dynamics. *American Political Science Review* 67: 829–31.

1976. *Parties and the Nationalization of Electoral Forces*. In Niemi and Weisberg (1976: 514–49) (reprinted from Stokes [1967]).

Sundquist, J., 1973. *Dynamics of the Party System: Alignment and Realignment of Political Parties in the United States*. Washington, D.C.: The Brookings Institution.

Taagepera, R. and M. Shugart, 1989. *Seats and Votes: The Effects and Determinants of Electoral Systems*. New Haven, Conn.: Yale University Press.

Tägil, S., 1983. *The Question of Border Regions in Western Europe: An Historical Background*. In Anderson (1983: 18–33).

Tarlton, C., 1965. Symmetry and Asymmetry as Elements of Federalism: A Theoretical Speculation. *Journal of Politics* 27: 861–74.

Tarrow, S., P. Katzenstein, and L. Graziano, eds., 1978. *Territorial Politics in Industrial Nations*. London and New York: Praeger.

Taylor, C. and D. Jodice, 1983. *World Handbook of Social and Political Indicators* (third edition). New Haven, Conn.: Yale University Press.

Taylor, P., G. Gudgin, and R. Johnston, 1986. *The Geography of Representation: A Review of Recent Findings*. In Grofman and Lijphart (1986: 183–92).

Taylor, P. and R. Johnston, 1979. *Geography of Elections*. New York: Holmes and Meier.

Tilly, C., 1964. *The Vendée*. Cambridge, Mass.: Harvard University Press.

ed., 1975. *The Formation of National States in Western Europe*. Princeton, N.J.: Princeton University Press.

1981. *As Sociology Meets History*. New York: Academic Press.

References

1984. *Big Structures, Large Processes, Huge Comparisons*. New York: Russell Sage Foundation.

Tobia, B., 1996. *Urban Space and Monuments in the "Nationalization of the Masses": The Italian Case*. In Woolf (1996: 171–91).

Torsvik, P., ed., 1981. *Mobilization, Center–Periphery Structures, and Nation-Building: A Volume in Commemoration of Stein Rokkan*. Bergen: Universitetsforlaget.

Ulich, R., 1961. *The Education of Nations*. Cambridge, Mass.: Harvard University Press.

Urwin, D., 1974. *Germany: Continuity and Change in Electoral Politics*. In Rose (1974: 107–70).

1980a. *Towards the Nationalisation of British Politics? The Party System, 1885–1940*. In Büsch (1980: 225–58).

1980b. *From Ploughshare to Ballotbox: The Politics of Agrarian Defence in Europe*. Oslo: Universitetsforlaget.

1982a. *Territorial Structures and Political Development in the United Kingdom*. In Rokkan and Urwin (1982: 19–74).

1982b. *Germany: From Geopolitical Expression to Regional Accommodation*. In Rokkan and Urwin (1982: 165–250).

1983. *Harbinger, Fossil or Fleabite? "Regionalism" and the West European Party Mosaic*. In Daalder and Mair (1983: 221–56).

Valen, H., 1976. National Conflict Structure and Foreign Politics: The Impact of the EEC Issue on Perceived Cleavages in Norwegian Politics. *European Journal of Political Research* 4: 47–82.

Valen, H. and P. Converse, 1971. Dimensions of Cleavage and Perceived Party Distances in Norwegian Voting. *Scandinavian Political Studies* 6: 107–52.

Valen, H. and D. Katz, 1961. *An Electoral Contest in a Norwegian Province*. In Janowitz (1961: 207–36).

1964. *Political Parties in Norway*. Oslo: Universitetsforlaget.

Valen, H. and S. Rokkan, 1974. *Norway: Conflict Structure and Mass Politics in a European Periphery*. In Rose (1974: 315–70).

Van Deth, J., 1999. *Social Capital and European Democracy*. London: Routledge.

Verba, S., 1967. Some Dilemmas in Comparative Research. *World Politics* 20: 111–27.

Wandruska, A., 1954. *Österreichs politische Struktur: Die Entwicklung der Parteien und der politische Bewegungen*. In Benedikt (1954: 289–485).

Watkins, S., 1991. *From Provinces into Nations: Demographic Integration in Western Europe, 1870–1960*. Princeton, N.J.: Princeton University Press.

Weber, E., 1976. *Peasants into Frenchmen: The Modernization of Rural France, 1870–1914*. Stanford, Calif.: Stanford University Press.

Weber, M., 1978. *Economy and Society: An Outline of Interpretative Sociology* (two volumes). Berkeley: University of California Press.

Williamson, J., 1965. Regional Inequality and the Process of National Development: A Description of the Patterns. *Economic Development and Cultural Change* 13: 3–84.

Wilson, E., 1975. *Sociobiology*. Cambridge, Mass.: Belknap.

References

Woolf, S., ed., 1996. *Nationalism in Europe: 1815 to the Present*. London and New York: Routledge.

Zielonka, J., ed., 2002. *Europe Unbound: Enlarging and Reshaping the Boundaries of the European Union*. London: Routledge.

Zuckerman, A., 1975. Political Cleavage: A Conceptual and Theoretical Analysis. *British Journal of Political Science* 5: 231–48.

Index

The index is subdivided into four parts: (1) concepts, (2) countries and regions, (3) parties and party families, and (4) historical events (periods). Industrial Revolution and National Revolution have been considered as concepts rather than historical events. For countries and regions only proper names have been considered, and not adjectives or languages (for example, Germany but not German). Parties are considered mainly as families.

Concepts

absolutism (-ist), 1, 27, 45, 214, 224, 252
aristocracy (*or* nobility), 26, 27, 198, 200, 202, 204, 224, 253

city-belt (*or* central belt), 25, 254, 261, 265, 266, 269, 272
centralization (-ed), center-building, 7, 31, 195, 196, 198–202, 227, 248, 261, 268, 270, 271, 292, 293, 295, 300
church, 17, 29, 32, 184, 199, 200, 201, 203, 206, 265
   Catholic, 142, 198, 201, 203, 264, 265, 268, 278
class, *see* cleavage, class (*see also* mobilization; industrialization)
cleavage(s)
   center–periphery, 4, 5, 7, 9, 28, 29–31, 73, 120, 145, 177, 185, 195, 198–202, 204, 205, 212, 279, 282, 286, 287, 292, 293, 299

church–state, 29, 172–177, 198–202, 203, 265, 286, 287, 292
class (*or* worker–employers/owner, left–right), 3, 4, 5, 7, 9, 29, 73, 78, 172–177, 196, 198, 205, 210, 211, 212–218, 221, 230, 248, 252, 274–276, 282, 286, 287, 288, 292, 297
cultural *or* preindustrial (ethnolinguistic, religious), 4, 5, 6, 7, 9, 29, 61, 73, 81, 90, 101, 121, 122, 150, 152, 153, 154, 160, 168, 172, 176, 177–189, 196, 197, 198, 199, 205, 211, 212, 251, 252, 256, 263, 268, 273, 274, 275, 276, 277, 278, 279, 282, 283, 284, 285–288, 289, 291, 292, 295, 296
   functional, 28, 31–32, 211, 212, 221, 248, 249, 251, 279, 287, 292, 293, 297
   structure *or* constellation, 7, 78, 116, 261, 264, 284, 290, 299

Index

343

Countries and Regions

Index

Parties and Party Families

Historical Events (Periods)

Index